Temperamental Journeys

Temperamental Journeys

➤ ➤ ➤ ➤ ESSAYS ON

➤ ➤ ➤ ➤ THE MODERN

➤ ➤ ➤ ➤ LITERATURE

➤ ➤ ➤ ➤ OF TRAVEL

Edited by Michael Kowalewski

THE UNIVERSITY OF GEORGIA PRESS
ATHENS AND LONDON

© 1992 by the University of Georgia Press
Athens, Georgia 30602
All rights reserved
Designed by Louise OFarrell
Set in 10/13 Sabon by Tseng Information Systems, Inc.
Printed and bound by Thomson-Shore, Inc.
The paper in this book meets the guidelines for
permanence and durability of the Committee on
Production Guidelines for Book Longevity of the
Council on Library Resources.

Printed in the United States of America

96 95 94 93 92   C   5 4 3 2 1

Library of Congress Cataloging in Publication Data
Temperamental journeys : essays on the modern
literature of travel / edited by Michael Kowalewski.
p. cm.
Includes bibliographical references.
ISBN 0-8203-1416-1 (alk. paper)
ISBN 0-8203-1431-5 (pbk. : alk. paper)
1. American prose literature—20th century—History
and criticism.   2. English prose literature—20th
century—History and criticism.   3. Travel in
literature.   4. Voyages and travels—History.
I. Kowalewski, Michael.
PS366.T73T4   1992
810.9'355—dc20   91-26602
                                                    CIP

British Library Cataloging in Publication Data
available

⮞ ⮞ ⮞ ⮞ ⮞ ⮞ Contents

> > > > > > **Acknowledgments**

The contributors to this volume deserve my gratitude first, as they have been both patient and supportive of this project since its inception in a 1987 MLA special session on contemporary American travel writing. I also wish to thank Brian Bremen and Tracy Brown, both of whom helped compile information for the bibliography in its initial stages. The reference and interlibrary staffs at Firestone Library, Princeton University, were invaluable in providing useful information as the bibliography took form. John Logan at Firestone deserves my special thanks for his good humor and his continuing interest in this project.

Karen Orchard, at the University of Georgia Press, is more responsible than anyone else for helping bring this collection into print, and I am grateful for her generous assistance, advice, and continuing interest. Madelaine Cooke guided the manuscript through editing, and David Nelson Blair's thoroughness and care in copyediting kept me honest: they both have my thanks for their aid and their patience.

I am indebted to the American Council of Learned Societies, as much of the initial work on this project was completed while I was supported by one of their Fellowships for Recent Recipients of the Ph.D. Princeton University provided the other half of the financial support for that sabbatical year, for which I am, as well, extremely grateful.

Much of the pleasure in compiling this book arose from conversations with and letters from various people—besides the contributors—interested in travel and travel writing. William Howarth (who also helped with the initial bibliography), James D. Houston, Shannon Applegate, Daniel Robertson, Gary Snyder, Marc Chénetier, Pete Petersen, John Witte, and William Stowe all have my thanks for stimulating company or for pulling books off the shelf when the topic was travel writing.

My last and greatest debt is to my wife and best editor, Catherine Kowalewski. Not only did she help with the time-consuming task of fine-tuning the bibliography, she has been a constant, steadying companion on most of the journeys in the last decade—to the Olympic Peninsula, to Longton, Kansas, to the Bay of Fundy—that lie behind my interest in travel writing. I owe her more than I can adequately express.

> > > > > > **Introduction: The Modern Literature of Travel**

MICHAEL KOWALEWSKI

In the last ten years there has been a resurgence of interest in travel writing unequaled since the twenties and thirties. This revival is evident not only in the recent reprinting of travel classics but in the remarkable number of new travel writers and otherwise established authors who try their hand at the genre, both commanding sizable popular audiences. Despite this fact, however, criticism of modern (by which I mean twentieth-century) travel writing has been scanty, especially in regard to American travel narratives. There has been very little critical effort to incorporate this burgeoning body of work into the literary canon or even to investigate why it resists incorporation.

Surely part of the reason this genre has been slighted is that many simply refuse to take it seriously, and in one way it is hard to blame them. Skepticism, or at least a knowing grin or a wince, seems the proper response to certain current forms of upwardly mobile pastoral like Condé Nast's *Traveler*. Adventure and risk-taking have been transformed by stores like the Banana Republic into commodities that have more to do with status anxieties and utopian longings than a genuine interest in other cultures. The illusion created by Banana Republic marketing, as Stephen Tatum notes, is that wearing uncombed cotton and wool products imported from independent artisans "itself qualifies as an adventurous feat" analogous to global adventures. If we are to undertake adventures that will redeem our devitalized lives, the consumer logic goes, we'd best do it in "authentic" clothing: Expedition Shirts, Populist Pants and African Mud-Cloth Jerseys.

Skepticism about this merchandising of adventure often seems to extend almost naturally to include travel writing as well. In a recently published interview, for instance, Wallace Stegner (whose work I both enjoy and re-

A version of this introduction appeared first in *Northwest Review* 28, no. 2 (1990): 111–27.

spect) spells out the kind of experience he thinks successful young writers need to have: "The way to gain experience is to live, but that does not mean one must go slumming for the exotic or outrageous or adventurous or sordid or, even, unusual." "Experience sought for the sake of writing about it may produce reporting, or travel books," he says, "but it is not likely to produce literature." Stegner is hardly alone in his distaste for manufactured "experience" and the kind of writing it inspires, and neither is the distaste particularly new. There is a venerable tradition of condescending to travel books as a second-rate literary form. Ernest Hemingway once remembered showing a first draft of *The Sun Also Rises* to the novelist Nathan Asch, only to receive the ultimate put-down. "Hem," Asch fulminated, "vaht do you mean saying you wrote a novel? . . . you are riding a travhel büch."

Travel writing can, at its worst, form the verbal equivalent of the "scenic" collages found in travel brochures. For his part, Kingsley Amis in 1955 found travel books too often "barnacled" with "rhetoric, generalisation and rhapsody" and organized as "a string of failed poems—failed not-very-good poems." The trouble, as Amis saw it, was not simply that travel writing degenerates "briskly into an empty and indecent poeticism, apparently based on a desire to get into the next edition of *The Oxford Book of English Prose*." "The escape-motive" behind the writing, he felt, remains closely allied to an untutored "feeling that the other fellow's grass is greener, that the really good time, or good life, is going on somewhere else." Going to Texas, William Faulkner once quipped in echoing such sentiments, is just an excuse for poor invention.

Yet those who, like myself, *do* in fact consider many travel narratives "literature," a form of what John McPhee and others have carefully called "the literature of fact," may be more curious than exasperated by dismissals of their worth. Stegner, for instance, goes on to quote Robert Frost in defining what good fiction seeks to accomplish: "Frost used to say that a fiction writer should be able to tell what happened to himself as if it has happened to someone else, and what happened to someone else as if it had happened to himself." This, it seems to me, is precisely what good travel writing attempts to do: whether in the guise of a Freya Stark celebrating the ruddy health of those who live "in some mountain land like the Dolomites, where the harvests are sufficient to feed the villages, and the families go in summer to cut their hay and live in their wooden chalets high up amid their pastures in the sun" or in the reports of passport restrictions, dysentery, and Thai gun smugglers we get from, say, Stuart Stevens or Christina Dodwell.

The peculiar challenges of travel writing—of "one civilisation reporting on another," as Colin Thubron puts it—have attracted an impressive roster of writers in this century. Many may associate Lawrence Durrell, Graham Greene, D. H. Lawrence, or John Steinbeck with the genre. Far fewer people know that Edith Wharton, William Carlos Williams, Mary McCarthy, William Dean Howells, Aldous Huxley, John G. Neihardt, John Dos Passos, Vachel Lindsay, Ford Madox Ford, Saul Bellow, Wyndham Lewis, W. H. Auden, Erskine Caldwell, and William Golding have all written travel narratives in the last ninety years. Word, we might say, needs to get out: not only as a testament to the rich diversity of voices and vantages this writing offers but because an informed sense of the full range of this genre will alter and complicate the kinds of questions we ask of it.

The essays in this collection focus upon the literature of travel rather than upon travel per se. Yet the two phenomena are so intimately interfused that any proper survey of the literary achievements of travel reportage in this century must begin with the predictions of its demise at mid-century or earlier.

"I do not expect to see many travel books in the near future," Evelyn Waugh lamented in 1946, in the wake of the destructive horrors of the Second World War and the production of the jet aircraft engine. "When I was a reviewer," Waugh says, travel books "used . . . to appear in batches of four or five a week, cram-full of charm and wit and enlarged Leica snapshots." But now, "in a world of 'displaced persons,' " true travel to Waugh seems impossible. This expression of cultural attenuation is hardly unique, and not everyone who has voiced it blames the situation on the dislocations of history. Writing nine years before Waugh, the Canadian writer Stephen Leacock saw the conventions of travel writing themselves as having superceded their own usefulness. "All travel writing and travel pictures in books are worn out and belong to a past age," he wearily asserted. "It is no longer possible to tell anyone anything new about anywhere."

A fear of diminishing cultural alternatives has not disappeared among travelers or travel writers and it seems partly attributable to contemporary forms of mass travel. As Wolfgang Shivelbusch has shown in his remarkable study of nineteenth-century railroads, *The Railway Journey* (1986), new modes of transport effect changes not only in conveyance and communication but in thought, feeling, behavior and human consciousness. Railroads, automobiles and airplanes have all placed new demands on travelers' eyes, nerves, and viscera. The motor car, E. M. Forster claimed in *Howards End*, was quickly turning landscape into "porridge."

The speed and perceptual disorientation attendant upon new modes of modern travel gradually become familiar and unthreatening, but so too do the kinds of experience for which these new forms of travel allow. "The easier it becomes to travel," John Julius Norwich notes, "the harder it is to be a traveller":

> Half a century ago, any young Englishman prepared to venture beyond the shores of Western Europe could lay claim to the title; patience, resourcefulness and robustness of digestion were the only qualities he needed. A year or two later he could return, the pride of his family, the envy of his friends: a trail-blazer, a hero. Alas, those days are over. Everybody goes everywhere—or nearly everywhere—buying their air tickets with their credit cards and being met by airport buses, secure in the knowledge that their hotel reservations have been confirmed, that the rent-a-car firm is expecting them, and that it will be perfectly safe to drink the Coca-Cola.

For many, all that seems left after World War II is what Bill Buford calls "the extraordinary imperialism of the American hamburger" and postmodern photo opportunities like those in Don DeLillo's novel *White Noise,* where visitors take pictures of people taking pictures of "the most photographed barn in America." "We're not here to capture an image," one character says, "we're here to maintain one."

Tourist agencies offer prepackaged, even (in travel videos and television cruise commercials) *pre-lived* experience. The imaginative impoverishment of contemporary conditions of travel can be accurately gauged by the complete lack of a literature of air travel. (What engaging nonfiction there is about air travel, such as that by Antoine de Saint-Exupéry, predates modern jet aircraft. Michael Parfit's remarkable book *Chasing the Glory* [1988] remains, unfortunately, the exception that proves the rule.) Travel today is done in the face of landscapes where there are already too many guidebooks. Travelers who do venture out find that oceans and wilderness areas are often already polluted, that jungles and rain forests have been wantonly destroyed and that an exported polystyrene culture of what Ihab Hassan calls "future shock [and] current shlock" proliferates on a worldwide scale. The lovely Syrian voice Jonathan Raban hears chanting the Koran on a May evening on the Euphrates in 1976 originates not, it turns out, from a hilltop shepherd but from his "Sanyo portable tape-recorder."

Yet Norwich is too discerning a thinker to take laments about the premature death of travel and travel writing as authoritative obituaries rather than as expressions of historical belatedness and a fear of diminishing cultural returns. "It is the first secret conceit of every voyager to imagine that he alone has found the world's last paradise," Pico Iyer says. "It is the second to believe that the door has slammed shut right behind him." Norwich reminds us first that tourism (the birth of the agency-arranged "protective cocoon of block bookings, meal vouchers and—most dangerous of all—

temperance") which supposedly helped destroy "real" travel began not in this century but in the preceding one: on Monday, July 5, 1841, to be precise, the day Thomas Cook's first organized tour of 570 people ventured the ten miles from Leicester to Loughborough and back by train. More importantly, Norwich qualifies his sense of what might otherwise be a false nostalgia for a Golden Age of Travel by rightly asserting that most of us have a highly ambivalent attitude about that era in the first place.

We want it both ways, Norwich contends. We "love to look on travel as an adventure, just as our grandfathers did," but we also crucially depend upon the very conveniences (airplanes, for instance) that have supposedly killed off this adventure. Our contemporary ambivalence about travel, like so much else in modern life, seems abiding and irreconcilable. It seems, in other words, a germinal ground for literature.

Paul Theroux, a seminal figure in anyone's account of contemporary travel writing, acknowledges the legitimacy of Waugh's complaints about postwar travel, but he finds in those conditions not the death of but the incentive for good travel reportage. There has been a resurgence in travel writing, Theroux argues, precisely because new methods of travel have defeated the more arduous traditional ones. There are two types of travelers in his opinion, real and mock travelers. Real travelers are the enterprising loners who put up with often hazardous, comfortless conditions and "endure a kind of alienation and panic in foreign parts for the after-taste of having sampled new scenes." Opposed to them are mock-travelers (not "tourists" because Theroux includes businessmen in this category). These are people who aspire, like Anne Tyler's "accidental tourist," to make a journey without seeming to have left home. Deeply opposed to exertion and dislocation, mock-travelers are afflicted by what I would call the Winnebago Syndrome. Like so many self-contained turtles or snails, these travelers take their homes with them, not just in cavernous RV's on America's backroads but abroad as well.

Mock-travelers arrange for their peregrinations to be, as Theroux puts it, "familiar, unshocking, homely and even [paradoxically] immobile." (Paul Fussell refers to such travelers as "stationary tourists.") But Theroux is sensible enough to realize the inevitability of this situation ("it is not possible for people to travel in large numbers and have it any other way"). And he is perceptive enough to highlight its cultural significance:

> It is very important to understand what is happening to travel and tourism . . . because only by examining them can one see why people get on donkeys and ride across Ethiopia, or hitchhike to India, or go slowly down the Ganges, or simply disappear in Brazil. The interest in travel today,

which is passionate, arises out of the fact that there is a form of travel prevalent that is now very easy—people want to find an antidote for the immobility that mass tourism has produced; people want to believe that somewhere, somehow, it is still very dangerous, bizarre, anxiety-making and exotic to travel. . . . Mock travel has produced a huge interest in clumsy, old-fashioned travel, with its disgusting food and miseries and long nights. It has also given rise to a lively interest in travel literature, and the affirmation that the world is still large and strange and, thank God, full of empty places that are nothing like home.

Theroux was writing in 1976 and if anything, the intervening decade and a half have proven the truth of his remarks far beyond what even he could have predicted. The signs of an invigorated contemporary interest in travel are everywhere to be seen in bookstores, mail-order catalogues, Sunday supplements and new "adventure travel" expeditionary agencies. Travel books of all stripes have been selling briskly for the past decade, and these include not simply pragmatic guides to snorkeling the Great Barrier Reef but the *literature* of travel as well. (Even travel guides themselves are moving away from promotional fluff to what David Walker, editorial director for travel books at Prentice Hall, calls guides with a "savvy, funny, politically sensitive viewpoint." Some of the proceeds for a recent guide to Peru, for instance, will go to a Peruvian relief organization.)

In 1981 the handsome and editorially savvy British journal *Granta* devoted its winter issue entirely to new travel writing (most of it excerpts from upcoming books). It was an instant best-seller in England, going into thirteen reprintings—an achievement unheard of for a journal this size. Interest in travel writing was so piqued that *Granta* repeated its success five years later with "In Trouble Again: A Special Issue of Travel Writing," and then with yet another issue (entitled simply "Travel") in the spring of 1989. Other journals soon followed suit.

Further indications of the revival of interest in this genre are not far to seek. William Least Heat-Moon's *Blue Highways* has sold more than 1.25 million copies since it first appeared in 1982. Five major anthologies of travel writing in the last five years (by houses such as Penguin, Norton, and Knopf) have helped solidify the genre's academic legitimacy (and marketability). The biannual *New York Times* supplement, *The Sophisticated Traveler*, showcases a variety of new and established writers, all recounting personal journeys and roamings and encounters with the exotic.

Large numbers of travel writers have been emerging in the last decade, and there is a rich choice of publishing venues for the dozens of new books that continue to appear.* Yet the critical response to this creative ferment has been woefully inadequate. There is presently no accessible general bibliography of travel writing in either England or the United States—this volume includes the most extensive bibliography of modern travel writing yet compiled. Further, no definitive study of twentieth-century travel writing has yet appeared, though Paul Fussell's exemplary study of British travelers between the wars, *Abroad* (1980), which is excerpted in this collection, sets a high standard for subsequent criticism.

Temperamental Journeys is the first collection of essays to focus exclusively on twentieth-century travel writing. There have been two previous collections of essays on travel writing in general. The first, *Literature As a Mode of Travel* (edited by Warner G. Rice), was a chapbook put out by the New York Public Library in 1963. It contained six essays, none of which dealt with any twentieth-century works. The second volume was *The Art of Travel: Essays on Travel Writing* (edited by Philip Dodd), which came out in 1982. Four of the eight essays in this fine collection dealt with twentieth-century writers, but none of them treated any American works. Though a glance through the appropriate critical bibliographies will reveal, say, a score of essays in the last twenty years on modern travel writing, they are scattered and of varying quality. In a time of severely overworked academic terrains, twentieth-century travel writing is virtually *terra incognita*.

This might not be worth noting except that it bears upon the nature of travel writing itself. Part of the reason this genre has been insufficiently recognized or studied piecemeal may have to do with its dauntingly heterogeneous character. Travel writing involves border crossings both literal and figurative. The first-person nonfictional narratives that form the heart of the genre usually display what Bill Buford terms a "generic androgyny," which is not easily categorized. Travel writing borrows freely from the memoir, journalism, letters, guidebooks, confessional narrative, and, most important, fiction. "Its omnivorous appetite for writing of all kinds," Raban asserts in "The Journey and the Book," testifies to "the resilience of the form":

---

*Besides publishers who have in the past consistently published travel books—Houghton Mifflin, William Morrow, Knopf, Jonathan Cape, William Heinemann, Macmillan, and Little, Brown, for example—several houses have established new imprints specifically dedicated to travel writing. These include Atlantic Monthly Press's "Atlantic Traveler" series, Vintage Departures, Century Hutchinson's Century Travellers, and Warner's Traveler's Bookshelf. Add to these new series of travel works from Viking-Penguin, Overlook, Paladin, Hogarth Press, Weidenfeld & Nicolson, and the Sierra Club—as well as reprint series of classic travel narratives by Beacon-Virago, the University of Oklahoma, and Paragon House—and the scope of this generic renewal starts to become apparent.

> As a literary form, travel writing is a notoriously raffish open house. . . . It
> accommodates the private diary, the essay, the short story, the prose poem,
> the rough note and polished table talk with indiscriminate hospitality. It
> freely mixes narrative and discursive writing. Much of its "factual" ma-
> terial, in the way of bills, menus, ticket-stubs, names and addresses, dates
> and destinations, is there to authenticate what is really fiction; while its
> wildest fictions have the status of possible facts.

The hybrid, "androgynous" qualities of travel writing that place it in an
unusual critical position are precisely those which deserve to be studied,
for the questions of form raised by this genre bear directly on its attempts
to intermix a sense of freedom with social awareness, an itch to escape
with a candid respect for unfamiliar landscapes and cultures.

Propelled in large part by a salutary curiosity about the habits and
customs and dimensions of other peoples' lives and surroundings, travel
writers have traditionally included vivid descriptions of flora, topography,
climate, animal and insect life, foodstuffs, and local sexual customs. This
preponderance of factual material helps explain why the genre has traditionally attracted the attention of historians and geographers rather than
literary critics. (Travel narratives are still typically shelved, in bookstores
and libraries, in sections devoted to the geographical areas included in
a book's itinerary. Some anthologies of travel writing still organize their
selections by nonliterary categories such as geography, thereby perpetuat-
ing this habit of classification.)

But while the best travel writing usually consists of part sociology and
part natural history, it has also traditionally gone beyond "mere" ethnography by being insistently autobiographical. The amalgamations of the
lyrical and the pragmatic in travel writing serve both to sustain and to
counter impulses toward personal intimacy on the one hand, and sociological abstraction on the other. "Travel has less to do with distance,"
Theroux asserts, "than with insight." Successful travel narratives have to
do with both. At the heart of this literary form, as Fussell notes in *Abroad*,
is a self-revealing figure whose passion is to make sense of new experience
and whose very attempts to do so are often as compelling as the material
with which a writer works.

The reliance upon narrative voice in this genre remains crucial because
more than its episodic "plot" or momentary characterizations, what shapes
a travel book's imaginative texture is its narrative intelligence. Modern
travel classics like Henry James's *The American Scene* (1907), Rebecca
West's *Black Lamb and Grey Falcon* (1941), Jonathan Raban's *Old Glory*

(1981), Henry Miller's *Air-Conditioned Nightmare* (1945), and Robert Byron's *The Road to Oxiana* (1937), which Fussell calls the *Ulysses* of travel books, are worth studying less for the facts they may contain than for their elegant, inventive, sometimes cranky styles of personal witness. One of the primary pleasures (and, at times, irritations) of reading travel writing consists of following the contours of a writer-narrator's varying responses—now marveling and appreciative, now caustic or perversely unresponsive—to the landscapes and people he or she encounters.

The title for this volume comes from Norman Douglas's suggestion that "the reader of a good travel-book is entitled not only to an exterior voyage, to descriptions of scenery and so forth, but to an interior, a sentimental or temperamental voyage, which takes place side by side with the outer one." The most successful travel narratives generally blend outward, spatial aspects of travel (social observation and evocations of alien settings and sensibilities) with the inward, temporal forms of memory and recollection. No matter how much "inside" description a traveler employs in evoking another culture and its people, a crucial element of all travel writing remains the author's "visitor" status. He or she remains, as the reader's surrogate, a cultural outsider who moves into, through and finally beyond the places and events encountered. A traveler's mobility, as Janet Giltrow says, "is essential to his vision and his art, for once he lingers for a profounder view, he begins to be assimilated by the foreign environment and to adopt its ways, and . . . qualify his judgments. He ceases to be a traveller and becomes an expatriate."

That said, it must be stressed that several dangers constantly dog this particular literary form, and not all authors rise above them. There is, for instance, the solipsistic attraction of turning a travel account into merely a personal diary, a kind of therapist's couch. Too exclusive a journey into self represents a risk because the main adventure in such private voyages often consists of, as John Krich says, "uncovering the motives for having departed": "the sites visited pale before the place left behind, and there is no destination but distance."

Self-therapy is not the only literary hazard that imperils a fully realized travel book. Surely part of the reason that some see this genre (at least in its traditional manifestations) as having been killed off has less to do with a poisoned, culturally homogenized world than with the fact that we are now more accustomed to narrow our eyes at signs of cultural chauvinism. A postcolonial legacy of cultural ignorance or willful distortion has simply made it more difficult to indulge in the sort of breezy generalities (or even outright bigotry) that characterizes much nineteenth- and early-twentieth-century travel narratives. Insofar as travel writing involves cultural description (especially of non-Western cultures), it has to be healthily aware of the problems encountered in interpretive ethnography. "The old traveller's delight . . . has waned a little," Colin Thubron contends in a foreword to a new anthology, "and a new unease has surfaced." It is hard to know, he concedes, which has deepened more, "the malaise in the spectacle or the sensitivity in the spectator." For the best travel writers, the problems of perception, knowledge, and communication initiate a humbling but not paralyzing self-examination.

Of course European travelers and explorers, as Wayne Franklin has demonstrated in *Discoverers, Explorers, Settlers* (1979), have confronted the representational inadequacies and the inhibiting cultural predispositions of language in describing alien cultures at least since Hernando Cortés. The reportable has to be imaginable, and the latter is always to some extent predetermined by a visitor's social and perceptual biases (at least, that is, until a great writer manages to loosen them). As Malcolm Andrews points out in his expert study *The Search for the Picturesque* (1989), such biases in English Picturesque tourists of the eighteenth century assumed an intriguingly palpable form. In addition to memorandum books, watercolors, barometers, telescopes, and pocket editions of William Cowper's poems, Picturesque tourists frequently toted a Claude glass. This device—a pocket mirror that a traveler could point over his or her shoulder to miniaturize a reflected landscape—helped tourists to tame and aesthetically control their "new and often intimidating visual experiences" abroad. To view a landscape properly, that is, a Picturesque tourist turned his back on it to gain an appropriately "framed" vantage. Perhaps no knickknack in the history of travel more suggestively exemplifies the cultural values and perceptual distortions attendant upon "sight-seeing" in strange places.

Modern travel writers continue to modify, alter, and recreate the countries and people about which they write; their Claude glasses have simply been internalized. Yet for a variety of reasons these writers also seem more aware of their own perceptual restrictions. An enriched sense of the diversity and complexity of other cultures has heightened their awareness of the pitfalls that stand in the way of more expressive and convincing travel accounts. Writers have been alerted, by way of a much-touted "crisis of confidence" in our collective ability to represent foreign peoples, to the limitations of the interpretive grids through which they view life at home or abroad. They are forewarned about the projections of desire that often constitute our images of the "primitive" or the "exotic." A travel writer today seems warier about the dangers of becoming what Arnold Rampersad (echoing W. E. B. Du Bois) calls "a car window sociologist, a car window psychologist, and a car window writer."

An impatience with celebrations of the merely "exotic" or "picturesque" is, of course, scarcely a recent phenomenon. Mark Twain, in *The Innocents Abroad* (1869), ends a grandiose description of a Mediterranean vista with the wry tag, "[Copyright secured according to law]." Nevertheless, postwar writers have become more acutely aware of the complexities of intercultural communication. James Clifford's remarks about contemporary ethnography bear pertinently upon the study of travel writing:

> Anthropology no longer speaks with automatic authority for others defined as unable to speak for themselves ("primitive," "pre-literate," "without history"). Other groups can less easily be . . . represented as if they were not involved in the present world systems that implicate ethnographers along with the peoples they study. "Cultures" do not hold still for their portraits. . . . An interest in the discursive aspects of cultural representation draws attention [to] . . . a *specification of discourses* in ethnography: who speaks? who writes? when and where? with or to whom? under what institutional and historical constraints?

"Writing up" a country or evoking a different culture has become a more tentative and ambiguous activity—one that often replaces confident encapsulations of cultures with more provisional, contingent or self-consciously "partial" descriptions. Studies such as Edward Said's *Orientalism* (1978), Peter Bishop's *The Myth of Shangri-La* (1989), Eric Cheyfitz's *The Poetics of Imperialism* (1991), and Stephen Greenblatt's *Marvelous Possessions* (1991) have all deepened our understanding of persevering tropes by which Westerners have imagined oriental, Arab, African, and Native American cultures. These and other works have sharpened our awareness of the ideological properties of writing and helped show how the vestiges of imperialism continue to linger: less in the narrow sense of militant jingoism or explicit advocacy for annexing new territory than in a more ingrained and nebulous confidence about being culturally and racially superior.

Yet this new sensitivity to cultural bias has not arrived without a price. In fact, the very acknowledgment that all cultural portrayals are limited and historically specific is often brandished as a triumphal indictment rather than offered as a salutary call for representational tact. In such a light, every journey might seem like just another "power trip." "No one reads from a neutral or final position," Clifford asserts. But "this rather obvious caution," he adds, "is often violated in new accounts that purport to set the record straight or to fill a gap in 'our' knowledge." Again the parallel of travel writing with anthropology seems germane:

> In popular imagery the ethnographer has shifted from a sympathetic, authoritative observer (best incarnated, perhaps, by Margaret Mead) to the unflattering figure portrayed by Vine Deloria in *Custer Died for Your Sins* (1969). Indeed, the negative portrait has sometimes hardened into caricature—the ambitious social scientist making off with tribal lore and giving nothing in return, imposing crude portraits on subtle peoples, or (most recently) serving as dupe for sophisticated informants. Such portraits are about as realistic as the earlier heroic versions of participant-observation.

In place of unapologetic cultural chauvinism, some have substituted cultural relativism and "the banal claim" (Clifford's words) "that all truths are constructed." In place of imperialistic domination and pillage some invoke a false ennoblement of others that allows for no criticism. Credulity is now sometimes proposed as an appropriate replacement for cultural superiority. The best travel writers continue to avoid reducing their options to either extreme. They acknowledge, as Ihab Hassan puts it, that "differences are preserved, ignored, or transacted in accordance with interests on *both* sides." "Encroaching on primal societies, the explorer finds, indeed *brings*, a serpent in every 'paradise'—which, always ready, has other serpents waiting there." Travel writers today often feel less culturally sure-footed than their predecessors; correspondingly, the criticism that seeks to appraise the modern literature of travel must be both judicious and intellectually generous. It must be socially responsible without becoming solemn and prohibitive.

The essays in this collection reflect a wide range of opinion about how best to consider travel writing, and it would be inappropriate for me to impose a false thematic unity on what are, in fact, disparate concerns. What all of the contributors do share is a fascination with the flourishing prodigality of travel writing in this century. As Michel Butor and Rockwell Gray's essays remind us, the *kinds* of journey a traveler can take comprise a complicated typology of motion with rich metaphorical extensions. The literature of seeking primitive "undiscovered" frontiers abroad, for example, differs markedly from that about encounters with long-established cultural realms (exemplified in the nineteenth century—especially in regard to Americans visiting Europe—in the theme of the Innocent or Ingenue Abroad). Moreover, literary encounters with foreign cultures (either modernized or "primitive") often differ markedly from the writing that emerges from journeys within one's own country. This remains true whether the author is celebrating the local and unfamiliar or—in a long tradition of social exploration—exposing and investigating conditions at home that most would prefer to ignore. Even the route and the means of conveyance a traveler utilizes (kayak? zebra? Land-Rover?) can crucially predetermine the kind of trip he or she might have.

Because it involves, in large measure, the gathering and organization of factual information, travel writing's affiliations with other kinds of factual writing are both complex and abiding. Several of the essays collected here (by William Least Heat-Moon, Nancy Cook, and Elton Glaser) investigate the identifiable structural and thematic features, the rhetorical ploys and generic conventions of travel narratives. Robert von Hallberg explores the subgenre of "tourist poetry" as it reflects American cultural and literary concerns in the postwar period, while Mark Z. Muggli examines the ways in which contemporary travel writing has been intimately shaped by the conventions of journalism. Robert Foulke and Terry Caesar both investigate the relations between travel books and one of their closest literary relatives—guidebooks.

Factual narratives are not alone, of course, in shaping the nature of the travel book. As Percy Adams makes abundantly clear in *Travel Literature and the Evolution of the Novel* (1983), travel accounts have historically formed one of the main sources for the novel and travel writers continue to utilize fictional devices such as an episodic structure, picaresque motifs, and (most significantly) the foregrounding of a narrator. As a consequence, questions about the narrator's role—as essays by Roger George and Charisse Gendron investigate in differing ways—remain central to this genre. Who speaks in a travel book and why should we listen to him? How does a narrator gain his knowledge of other countries and peoples? How does he establish a compelling authority over a subject other than by simply referring to the bibliographies, glossaries, and notes on pronunciation that so often accompany travel books? Likewise (as Heather Henderson and Jacinta Matos ask in their essays), to what degree are a writer's journeys mediated and shadowed by the observations and the "plottings" of those who have preceded them? What relationship does a traveler establish with his fellow travelers? (Tourists or mock-travelers are not only a theoretical category by means of which to distinguish "real" travel; they are also frequently characters who populate travel accounts, often as foils to the narrator's own sophistication or, at least, his own self-consciousness.)

All of these questions help animate our sense of the unique literary position travel books occupy, as can the questions pertaining to gender, which Mary Morris's essay raises. The unique difficulties women face in the act of traveling independently, without a chaperon, relate directly to issues of freedom and fulfillment that still confront women, whether they are writers or not. Renewed attention to women's travel writing may also help unhinge some prevailing assumptions about its range and accomplishment. Only three of the fifty-six authors anthologized in the *Norton Book of Travel* (1987), for instance, are women. A quick glance at Jane Robinson's invaluable annotated bibliography of women's travel writing, *Wayward Women* (1990), reveals the unjustly exclusionary nature of this oversight.

Finally, several of the essays in this volume (including David Espey's) examine how travelogues keep ambivalently calling up their implied opposite: home. Home is where a traveler has a history and a sense of connectedness with familiar landscapes and cultural mores. The constraints of such a condition often prompt individual journeys, while the absent comforts of home frequently hasten their conclusions. Not everyone rejoices upon returning home. "I admit that my first night home I woke up in a sudden sweat of fear," F. O. Matthiessen writes after returning from a six-month sojourn in Europe. "I was no longer in the favored position of an observer in a foreign country. I was back in a very uncertain battle."

Yet for every traveler who wants to light out for the territory ("All I wanted was to go somewheres," Huck Finn says, "all I wanted was a change, I warn't particular"), there's another who feels the craving en route, as Tom Disch puts it, "for all / That can be known without examination, / For the drab, assuring twilights of home." At least since Henry David Thoreau's exploration and mapping of his own backyard, travel reportage has been intimately tied to the literature of place. Travel usually remains meaningful precisely because its exhilarations are thrown into relief by some notion of home. Travel writing promises both adventure and return, escape and homecoming and it does so by tapping into what Percy Adams calls "the oldest and largest cluster of metaphors in any language . . . what Joseph Addison calls 'those beautiful metaphors in Scripture, where Life is termed a Pilgrimage, and those who pass through it are called Strangers and Sojourners on Earth.'"

The peculiar challenges, satisfactions, and even disappointments of reading modern travel narratives are more than simply belletristic. The search for adventure and genial escape evident in the "tramps," "jaunts," "rambles," and "scampers" in the early part of this century has been chastened and tempered by the force of subsequent historical disasters, environmental depredations, and the technology of accelerated transport.

"Chastened" but not extinguished. The "one essential condition" of travel writing, Jonathan Raban says in "The Journey and the Book," "isn't a private income, rough terrain, English imperial hauteur, tramp steamers, Baedeckers [or] the cheap franc. . . . It is the experience of living among strangers, away from home." The writing that continues to spring from that "condition" deserves a more agile investigation than it has thus far received. *Temperamental Journeys* seeks to spark that study with a clear-eyed view of the opportunities and the limitations of this particular genre. Readers habituated to other forms of literature might well be attracted by the spirit of oxygenated curiosity that enlivens so many travel books, some of which has rubbed off on the essays in this collection. It seems an auspicious time to be thinking—thinking hard—about travel and about those who find the act of recounting it a temperamental necessity.

WORKS CITED

Adams, Percy. *Travel Literature and the Evolution of the Novel.* Lexington: U of Kentucky P, 1982.

Amis, Kingsley. "Is the Travel-Book Dead?" *The Spectator,* 17 June 1955. Rpt. in *Views from Abroad: The Spectator Book of Travel Writing.* Eds. Philip Marsden-Smedley and Jeffrey Klinke. London: Grafton, 1988, 13, 12.

Andrews, Malcolm. *The Search for the Picturesque: Landscape Aesthetics and Tourism in Britain, 1760–1800.* Stanford: Stanford UP, 1989.

Buford, Bill. "Editorial." *Granta* 10 (1984): 5–7.

Clifford, James. "Introduction: Partial Truths." *Writing Culture: The Poetics and Politics of Ethnography.* Eds. James Clifford and George E. Marcus. Berkeley: U of California P, 1986, 1–26.

DeLillo, Don. *White Noise.* New York: Viking-Penguin, 1985.

Disch, Tom. "Nether: A Traveller's Notes." *Times Literary Supplement,* 5–11 January 1990, 4.

Douglas, Norman. "Arabia Deserta." In *Experiments.* New York: Robert M. McBride, 1925, 1–22.

Forster, E. M. *Howards End.* 1910. Rpt. New York: Vintage, 1921.

Fussell, Paul. *Abroad: British Literary Traveling Between the Wars.* New York: Oxford UP, 1980.

———. "The Stationary Tourist." *Harper's,* April 1979, 31–38.

Giltrow, Janet. "North American Travel Writing." Dissertation, Simon Fraser U, 1979.

Hassan, Ihab. *Selves at Risk: Patterns of Quest in Contemporary American Letters.* Madison: U of Wisconsin P, 1990.

Hemingway, Ernest. "Interview: The Art of Fiction XXI." *Paris Review* 18 (Spring 1958), 61–89.

Iyer, Pico. "How Paradise Is Lost—and Found." *Time*, 9 June 1986, 82.

Krich, John. "Lament for the Merrying of England." Review of *Coasting* by Jonathan Raban, *New York Times Book Review*, 1 February 1987, 14.

Leacock, Stephen. *My Discovery of the West.* Toronto: Thomas Allen, 1937.

Matthiessen, Francis Otto. *From the Heart of Europe.* New York: Oxford UP, 1948.

Norwich, John Julius. *A Taste for Travel.* London: Macmillan, 1985.

Raban, Jonathan. "Freya Stark on the Euphrates." In *For Love and Money: Writing, Reading, Travelling 1969–1987.* London: Collins Harvill, 1987, 233–38,

———. "The Journey and the Book." In *For Love and Money*, 253–60.

Rampersad, Arnold. "V. S. Naipaul: Turning in the South." *Raritan* 10, no. 1 (Summer 1990): 24–47.

Stark, Freya. "The Philosophy of Travel." *The Spectator*, 24 March 1950. Rpt. in *Views from Abroad*, 3–6.

Stegner, Wallace. *On the Teaching of Creative Writing.* Ed. Edward Connery Lathem. Hanover, N.H.: UP of New England, 1988.

Tatum, Stephen. "Adventure in the Fashion System." *Western Humanities Review* 43, no. 1 (Spring 1989): 5–26.

Theroux, Paul. "Stranger on a Train: The Pleasure of Railways." In *Sunrise with Seamonsters: Travels and Discoveries, 1964–1984.* Boston: Houghton Mifflin, 1985, 126–35.

Thubron, Colin. "Foreword." In *Views from Abroad*, x-xi.

———. "Travel Writing Today: It's Rise and Its Dilemma." In *Essays by Divers Hands: Being the Transactions of the Royal Society of Literature.* New Series: vol. XLIV. Ed. A. N. Wilson. London: Boydell, 167–81.

Twain, Mark. *Adventures of Huckleberry Finn.* In *Mark Twain: Mississippi Writings.* Ed. Guy Cardwell. New York: Library of America, 1982.

———. *The Innocents Abroad, or the New Pilgrims' Progress.* 1869. Rpt. New York: New American Library, 1966.

Walker, David. Quoted in Jean Crichton. "The Crowded World of Travel Books." *Publisher's Weekly*, 20 January 1989, 36–60.

Waugh, Evelyn. *When the Going Was Good.* London: Duckworth, 1946.

Styles of Witness

≻ ≻ ≻ ≻ ≻ ≻ Journeys into Kansas

WILLIAM LEAST HEAT-MOON

Writing about America—if not American writing—begins with the writings of the European travelers: the journals of Christopher Columbus, the account of Alvar Núñez Cabeza de Vaca, the narratives of Pedro Castañeda (Coronado's lieutenant), Thomas Harriot, and John Smith. Things may have changed now, but my university education managed to keep those men (as writers anyway) hidden from me. American literature, according to my textbooks and professors of the late fifties and early sixties, begins with *native* literature: works written by Americans. While I understand this approach, I find it a needlessly chauvinistic angle that misdirects students. After all, America was a literary subject almost before it was a known entity. Were I teaching American literature today, I'd rather take my chances of catching an inert sophomore's interest with the work of John Smith or Thomas Harriot or Cabeza de Vaca than with something from Michael Wigglesworth or Increase Mather or Charles Brockden Brown.

I attribute the slights to early American travel writing not to Anglo prejudice so much as to the huge and overwhelming and strangely American literary bias in favor of so-called imaginative literature (fiction, novels, poetry, and drama) as though the clear and evocative recording of fact requires no imagination. (Try to think of Thoreau or John McPhee as unimaginative writers.)

The *Harvard Guide to American History* gives a selective list of about five hundred accounts written by travelers in the United States. These are books selected for their historical importance as well as their capable expression. To that list I can add an almost equal number. A genre containing a thousand significant books, a genre that has come to shape—even more than the novel—our notions of who we are, where we are, and what we can accomplish, deserves the eye not just of American teachers but of young American writers who are seeking new forms in which to repre-

Delivered before a session on contemporary American travel writing, at the Modern Language Association Convention, San Francisco, December 1987.

sent their times. It's absolutely unhealthy for so many American travel writers to work in ignorance of this long list of evocatively recorded journeys. (Let me add here that American male travel writers on the Harvard list outnumber females by more than fifty to one. Our literature of travel desperately needs women's voices.)

I am attracted to the literature of travel and its relative, "the literature of place," because they have been for so long academic pariahs—and that seems odd since no genre of our literature is so typically American. After all, every American is a descendant of travelers from the eastern hemisphere. And surely no nation has ever believed quite so completely in the curative power of moving hither and yon. From the time of the first crossings over the Bering land bridge, mobility has been one of the elemental qualities of the American experience. No wonder we have produced in just four hundred years a literature of travel the equal of nations twice our age. I'm also attracted to the writing of nonfiction—especially travel writing—because of the opportunities it presents to me as a writer always hunting for new shapes and forms.

I am now in the last year—I assume, I hope—of a four-year project. In this new book, I am writing about a well-defined square of tallgrass prairie in our mid-latitudes. It's a report on a small place, a single county in east-central Kansas. After I began work on the book, it became apparent that almost all of the lively writing about the Kansas prairie occurred in the nineteenth century: Washington Irving, Josiah Gregg, Victor Tixier, Miriam Davis Colt, John Gihon, George Brewerton. These writers worked in a time when Kansas was a topic frequently talked about in the eastern press either as an unknown place of marvelous possibilities or a region for settlement or a land ripe for social experiments. (It was during the social-experiment stage, of course, that the slavery question gave the state its epithet, Bleeding Kansas.) The territory was *then* a hot topic. It is otherwise now.

Kansas today is a place seemingly not much suited to a travel writer in his right mind, because the rest of America assumes it knows all it wants to know about the state. But a region unknown because it is covered over by presumed knowledge is just as ready for a travel reporter as one not yet explored. So, my work in Kansas is still a response to the thrall of the unknown, the lure of ignorance—those classic motivations for a traveler. Viewed in that light, I am following one of the calls that pulled nineteenth-century travel writers into the region.

However, Josiah Gregg or Victor Tixier or Randolph Marcy did not

have to face the question, "So who *cares* about Kansas?" "Who cares?"—
always the writer's most fearsome question. But a reader may be made to
care if the writer looks closely and precisely, and, if after his travels, he
can show the reader that all maps today could still be accurately labeled
with that traditional Renaissance inscription: "Here be strange beasts." A
traveler's careful examination of any detail should reveal how little we see
of a thing, how poorly we have understood it, how ineffectually we have
let it touch our lives. It is this close examination that creates the traveler's
ultimate excitement: the realization that if he but has the perception, he is
a *perpetual* stranger in a strange land.

After my fieldwork, my task is always then to find for the topic the right
voice. (By "voice" I mean a public persona with a distinct point of view
who takes a certain tone in his telling.) With the job of finding an evocative
voice comes the need for an appropriate framework for it. The writer's
search for voice and structure can yield an excitement like that which the
traveler finds when his close observation reveals the *extra*-ordinary in the
ordinary.

In the instance of my current project, I have tried to let my traveler's
searches in the geographic territory lead me to a solution of the problem
of voice and form. It took two years for a workable concept to occur to
me, but once it did, almost all of my structural problems with the book
were, in a stroke, solved. Before I explain it, let me say that I wanted this
new book to avoid a kind of writing that I see as the major threat to good
travel reporting today: the journey that exists primarily to explore the soul
of the traveler.

Of recent books, you might think of *Zen and the Art of Motorcycle
Maintenance* (1974) or *The Snow Leopard* (1978). Both are fine books, but
they follow a dangerous course that can lead travel writing into memoirs
or fiction. I used this descent into self in *Blue Highways* (1982), wherein
the traveler-narrator leaves family and the familiar, and sets off heading
more into the country of his own interior than into the interior of the country. In *Blue Highways*, the narrator descends into the topography of self
for half the journey before he realizes the futility of that course. He then
begins to move from an inward-turning spiral of his own self-absorption
toward a spiral of discovery that opens outward to other lives and new
places. The figure or pattern for this route in *Blue Highways* is the Hopi
Indian maze of emergence—a glyph that has served for unknown millenia
to remind the Hopis of the necessity to move away from self into other
things in order to become fully human. (The Hopi maze is a sign I would

like to see cut into the turf of every collegiate quadrangle in this country.)

The journey in *Blue Highways*, then, is initially centripetal—an ever-closing spiral that leads inward to a finite point, a dead end. But as the traveler nears that central still point, he seeks to pass through it to another side, so to speak, where it progresses once again outward, if not upward. (It may help to visualize the pattern by imagining the point of a cone held against a mirror; the traveler moves toward his own reflection only to follow it outward again.) Centripetal motion, of course, pulls an object toward the center while centrifugal movement throws it toward the outside. So, the movement proceeds centripetally into the image of self and then from that still point, it proceeds centrifugally away from the center.

In my new book, I wanted a course that would lead outward from my own small observations of a small place into something larger. I have tried to go into the territory, into the tallgrass prairie, and move outward. It is just that urge to move from self into nonself (for want of a better word) that has made for difficulties. Whatever I have found in the prairie in the last few years will interest a reader not because it has lain undiscovered over the years, but rather because I—the traveler-writer—have been able to perceive it anew and present it so. (In your mind hear the Plato-Pound conflict: "There is nothing new under the sun" versus "Make it new!") My question in writing the book has been, "How do I steer away from self while depending on it almost absolutely for the discovery and formulation and presentation of the material?"

My physical course as a traveler led—after two years—to a structural solution for the writer. My book covers a single Kansas county of 774 square miles. To guide my searches and *re*-searches there by car, horse, and foot, I used twelve U.S. Geological Survey 7.5′ Series topographical maps that cover the county almost perfectly. One day while I was staring at those dozen maps laid out on the floor of my office, I saw that they looked like the grid an archaeologist lays over a site before he excavates. It came to me: wasn't I a kind of digger of shards, shards that would help me see and present this place?

That twelve-section grid, I realized, could continually hold me in a pattern that would not ever match up with the pattern of my own perception of the place. I would, in other words, have to leave my interior to travel, as a writer, a course laid out by an arbitrary geometric pattern. Because this shape would never match my own interior pattern, it would keep me locked away from the temptation of circling lines of self-exploration. Those grids were continual reminders—invitations, actually—to excavate the territory outside my own interior topography.

But after having found a possible course that would allow a strict controlling of self, I had to watch that the pattern did not then annihilate the self. Were I to write as a mere digger of test trenches, I would end up with a piece of archaeology perhaps, but I would not have the kind of literate evocation of the place after which I had started. So the struggle was to let the grid shape structures that the writer's voice could form and color. I hope the grid has prevented me from falling into some solipsistic hole, which, surely, is always the death of good travel writing.

As I see things, it is this very peril of the writer's self destroying the world he wants to present that the greatest book of twentieth-century American travel so brilliantly overcomes. The book I speak of is *Let Us Now Praise Famous Men* (1941). (If you haven't considered it a work of travel, you might reconsider.) *Let Us Now Praise Famous Men* is a splendid piece of our literature precisely because it resolves so originally and richly the centrifugal-centripetal problem of one writer's explorations. James Agee employs the framework of a scientist in his purely factual descriptions of three sharecropping families. (For an illustration of this, see his descriptions of the Gudgers' beds or the Ricketts's fireplace.) With an objectivity quite the match of Walker Evans's documentary photographs, Agee presents the details as precisely and fully as is readably possible, and *then* he blends in his own vision, his unique voice, and turns a sociological report into literature. The book moves between the hard and flat side of sharecropper life in Hale County, Alabama, and the sharp edge of his passionate intelligence and lambent prose. "Sprawling and overwritten!" you say? So is *Moby-Dick*.

Although we recognize Agee's book today as a classic—perhaps the most unread of American classics—writers of nonfiction, it seems to me, have not much built upon his method or been much inspired by his solution to the perpetual problem of the writer's self in its surroundings. Yet his achievement stands right at that critical juncture between factual writing and fiction. Agee's balance between self and surroundings, like a highwire act, always poises on the edge of falling to its death in the sawdust of fiction below—a plunge that Truman Capote did not survive in his *In Cold Blood*. To my mind, this balance between writing (and traveling) centrifugally or centripetally is the central problem to which the so-called New Journalism tried to address itself. Its solutions were full of energy but quite dangerous to the survival of nonfiction, where existence depends always on the primacy of fact.

My book about the prairie will neither look nor sound anything like *Let Us Now Praise Famous Men*, but it was James Agee's recognition and solution to the centrifugal-centripetal journey that started me on that course where I stumbled across a pattern in the traveler's USGS 7.5′ series topographic maps. He was the carpenter of the doorway, a structure that I, without reservation, recommend to contemporary travel writers.

Inner and Outer

MARY MORRIS

The late John Gardner once said that there are only two plots in all of literature: you go on a journey or the stranger comes to town. Since women have for so many years been denied the journey, we were left with only one plot to our lives—to await the coming of the stranger to town. Indeed, there is no picaresque tradition among women novelists. Women's literature from Jane Austen to Virginia Woolf is mostly a literature about waiting, and usually waiting for love. Denied the freedom to roam outside themselves, women turned inward, into their emotions. As the feminist critic Elaine Showalter puts it: "Denied participation in public life, women were forced to cultivate their feelings and to overvalue romance. Emotions rushed in to fill the vacuum of experience."

For centuries it was frowned upon for women to travel without escort, chaperone, or husband. To journey was to put one at risk not only physically but morally. A little freedom could be a dangerous thing. Erica Jong chose well when she picked the metaphor of fear of flying to depict the tremulous outset of a woman's sexual liberation. The language of sexual initiation is oddly similar to the language of travel. We speak of sexual "exploits" or "adventurers." Both body and globe are objects for exploration and the great "explorers," whether Marco Polo or Don Juan, have traditionally been men.

By contrast, I find it revealing that the bindings in women's corsets were called *stays*. Someone who wore stays wouldn't be going very far. The binding of feet in the Orient or the corseting of the body in the West were ways of restricting women's movement. There is an interesting reference to stays in the letters of Lady Mary Wortley Montagu, who went to Turkey with her husband in 1716. Upon visiting a Turkish bath where the women

Portions of this essay appeared first in *Nothing to Declare: Memoirs of a Woman Traveling Alone* (New York: Houghton Mifflin, 1988) 21–25. © 1988 by Mary Morris.

25

implored her to undress, Lady Mary wrote, "I was forced at last to open my shirt and shew them my stays; which satisfied them very well for, I saw, they believed I was so locked up in that machine that it was not in my own power to open it, which contrivance they attributed to my husband."

It was my mother who made a traveler out of me, not so much because of the places where she went as because of her yearning to go. She used to buy globes and maps and plan dream journeys she'd never take while her "real life" was ensconced in the PTA, the Girl Scouts, suburban lawn parties, and barbecues. She had many reasons—and sometimes, I think, excuses—for not going anywhere, but her main reason was that my father would not go.

Once, when I was a child, my parents were invited to a Suppressed Desire Ball. You were to come in a costume that depicted your secret wish, your heart's desire, that which you'd always yearned to do or be. My mother went into a kind of trance, then came home one day with blue taffeta, white fishnet gauze, travel posters and brochures, and began to construct the most remarkable costume I've ever seen.

She spent weeks on it. I would go down to the workroom, where she sewed, and she'd say to me, "Where should I put the Taj Mahal? Where should the pyramids go?" On and on, into the night, she pasted and sewed and cursed my father, who it seemed would have no costume at all (though in the end my bald father would win first prize with a toupee his barber lent him).

But it is my mother I remember. The night of the ball, she descended the stairs. On her head sat a tiny, silver rotating globe. Her skirts were the oceans, her body the land, and interlaced between all the layers of taffeta and fishnet were Paris, Tokyo, Istanbul, Tashkent. Instead of seeing the world, my mother became it.

How do you know if you are a traveler? What are the telltale signs? As with most compulsions—such as being a gambler, a kleptomaniac, or a writer—the obvious proof is that you can't stop. If you are hooked, you are hooked. One sure sign of travelers is their relationship to maps. I cannot say how much of my life I have spent looking at maps, but there is no map I won't stare at and study. I love to measure each detail with my thumb, to see how far I have come, how far I've yet to go. I love maps the way stamp collectors love stamps. Not for their usefulness but rather for the sheer beauty of the object itself. I love to look at a map, even if it is a map of Mars, and figure out where I am going and how I am going to get there, which route I will take. I imagine what adventures might await me even though I know that the journey is never what we plan for; it's what happens between the lines.

I come from the Midwest, from the bluffs along the shores of Lake Michigan. It is not an exotic place, though it is very beautiful. You might stumble on an arrowhead, and there are a few trees, bent and tied to the ground a century before by Indians, which mark trails. But other than that, there is nothing remarkable about the part of the world I come from. Nothing extraordinary ever happened to me in the years that I was growing up—except once.

One day as I was coming home from school, I spotted a bird, larger than myself, sitting in the lower branches of a tree in a wooded area I passed through every day. It was huge and peered down with dark, curious eyes. It appeared weary and a bit confused, surprised to find itself in a tree in the Chicago suburbs, yet it stretched its wings and fluttered them with tremendous dignity. I spent the better part of an afternoon watching until my mother, half crazed, came searching and found me entranced by a bald eagle.

The eagle, off course from its home in the wilderness, had somehow landed in my neighborhood. Though lost, it seemed sure of itself. I wondered then as I wonder now what led it to suburbia, so far away from where its nest should be. At times I have thought it just wanted to get away, to go somewhere else. I knew it would find its way.

It was the first traveler I ever encountered and it made me thirsty to take a trip. Whenever I find myself somewhere I don't think I belong, I remember the confidence of that lost wanderer. I have tried to imitate it.

As a child I had a great capacity for staring into space, and I liked doing this best from the backseat of cars, from the dome car of the Union Pacific Railroad when my family went west in the summer, and later from the windows of buses and trains. And what I liked to do best while in a moving vehicle, staring into a vast expanse of scrub desert or a suburban Chicago landscape was to daydream.

I dreamed I was a pioneer girl, an adventurer, a woman hero. I saw myself as an Indian maiden named White Eagle or Running Deer. I rode a pinto horse with bow and arrow at full gallop and my arrows always went straight to the heart. I was faithkeeper, peacemaker, diviner, matchmaker, sister, interpreter of magical signs. I envisioned myself in wagon trains and tepees, in jungles and exotic desert lands, discovering the flight of owls, blazing trails across virgin land.

Travelers, like writers—and, I suppose I must add, women—are dreamers. Our lives are filled with endless possibility. Like readers of romances, we think that anything can happen to us at any time. We forget that this is not our real life—our life of domestic details, work pressures, attempts and failures at human relations. We keep moving. From anecdote to anecdote, from hope to hope. Our motion is forward, whether by train or daydream. Our sights are always set on the horizon, across moonscapes, vast deserts, unfordable rivers, impenetrable ice peaks.

I never intended to be a travel writer, and it is possible that I'll never write another travel book. I went to Latin America to live in 1978 because I was tired of life in New York and I was weary of my own life as a single woman in America. I felt as if I lived in a foreign land, so I decided to actually live in a foreign land and see if I could figure out what home meant to me.

Though I have always kept journals and made notes, I never set out on the open road thinking I'd write about travel. The only time I did do this— a year and a half ago, when I went around the world, through China, Tibet, and the Soviet Union in search of my ancestral land—it was the kiss of death for me. This trip was hampered by bureaucratic restrictions, the lack of language, Chernobyl, and the fact that I was pregnant at the time, but mainly I think by the fact that I was on assignment for a magazine. Traveling on a magazine assignment I have learned is a little like going to a party intending to fall in love. The moment you go with intent, the chances of true, spontaneous discovery are nil.

My year and a half in Latin America was an entirely different matter from my travels through the Soviet Union. What began as an experience, an adventure, turned into a love affair with a culture, a language, a people, which has continued to the present day. For me the only way to really experience a place is to live there, to go for a long time without the props of everyday life. In Mexico I lived without telephone, radio, television, or people who knew me. I lived without resume, biography, personal history.

As I said, I did not go away intending to write about it, but a time came when I knew I would. Still, writing about Latin America must have been in the back of my head. When I began to write about it some eight years after going there for the first time, I read through my travel journals and found this passage: "What is happening to me here is very strong and I will not leave as I came. Perhaps someday, when I am far away, I will write about it."

I have always kept journals—the essential tool of the dreamer—since I was twelve years old and felt the need to record my secret life. That was the year an important event happened in my town and in my adolescence.

It was the year when Gary Niblock, a surfer from the beaches of Southern California, returned to live with his father in the landlocked Midwest. He was the first person I ever met from the fringes of the Empire, and he told me stories of high waves and stretches of white sand, of sea creatures that could devour you with one gulp and tall, blond girls.

He looked down at our surfless great lake and stared with disdain across the Illinois prairie. How could I not love this boy who longed to be elsewhere, who told stories of places I'd never seen. It was that winter of my eighth-grade year, while Gary shivered in misery, snowbound away from his surfboard and wet suit, that I went to Larsen's Stationery Store and purchased a small volume with a key, entitled "My Day and How I Shot It" and recorded my thoughts on the surfer boy I had grown to love.

Since then, I have put everything in my journals that I can. Scenes, strange happenings, conversations, ideas, descriptions, lists of things to do. I've often recorded these entries in a chaotic way I'm sure no one could ever make sense out of. But I cross-reference them and somehow when I go back I manage to recall what I need to recall. For instance, I might write "alfalfa field—Victoria—the psychic of lost dogs" and know immediately, even years later, what I want to say about Victoria who lived in a trailer in an alfalfa field along with her one-eyed, grey and white mutt who runs away, and so on.

I have never been successful trying to write about something soon after it happens to me, which is perhaps another reason why I don't do very well when I am sent away on assignment. It took me eight years to write about Latin America. I understand that Joan Didion wrote her book on El Salvador almost immediately upon returning from there, but that is not how I work. As I tell my students, if you want fuel, you don't throw a live dinosaur into a fire. Instead you let it die its natural death, pile on leaves and soil, let the centuries of memory pile upon it, let experience turn to sediment, and eventually it will be useful fuel for the imaginative fires.

I write in my journals as I travel not because I think that some day something may come of it, but rather because I have always carried on this continuing dialogue with myself. Whenever I actually turn back to my journals and find that my writing draws from the journal entries, I am surprised. I am always surprised when what began as raw experience somehow turns itself into memory, which turns itself into stories or, in the case of my travel memoir, *Nothing to Declare* (1988), into *memoire*.

In 1985 the *New York Times Book Review* listed the best new travel writing for the summer. I was struck by the fact that in the twenty or so best travel books mentioned, not one had been written by a woman. Though never intending to write a travel book, I now began to think seriously about women and travel and how the two relate to questions of self-realization and fulfillment. The great and sudden upsurge in travel writing probably has its roots in a complex restlessness in our culture that has to do with the breakdown of the family, a certain spiritual emptiness in our lives, and a thirst for the unusual. Whatever its sources, the recent interest in travel writing has inspired the recovery of lost travel narratives by women. Isak Dinesen's *Out of Africa* (1937) and Beryl Markham's elegant *West with the Night* (1942) have made it to the best-seller list. Beacon Press, in conjunction with Virago, has launched a reprint series of classic women travel writers, which includes Isabella Bird's remarkable writing about China and Japan, Kate O'Brien on Spain, and Mary Kingsley's *Travels in West Africa* (1897).

Still, many women who traveled and wrote about their adventures did so because of circumstances, not because they went off seeking excitement and intending to write about it. And they wrote about their experiences in a very different way than their male counterparts did. Isak Dinesen went to Africa to marry. Beryl Markham was raised in Africa and taught to fly by her father. As an editorial assistant just out of college, I recall being moved by the journals of a pioneer woman, Mary McClane, who wrote of life in the prairies where she grew up and who speaks of her deep longing that grew out of her loneliness in a way that was plainly sexual. It was, in fact, in reading the journals of Mary McClane that I began to see how women who wrote about their adventures experienced their lives differently than men. Or at least they were able to express what they experienced in a different way—one that, for better or worse, reflected their own inner workings.

Henry Miller says, in his wonderful travel narrative *The Colossus of Maroussi* (1941), that all voyages are accomplished inwardly and that the most difficult are made without moving from the spot. In saying this, he sums up the kind of inner dialogue that women who travel feel. Because of the way women have cultivated their inner lives, a journey often becomes a dialogue between the inner and the outer, between our emotional necessity and the reality of the external world. For me, writing and travel have always fed one another. As a writer I have found that what I experience externally I must process internally and what I feel inside I must test on the outside world.

I think something has always held women back, and I'm not sure this is necessarily bad. Women need and want to be connected, to be joined to other human beings. We don't easily go off alone into the wild, to the North Pole or in search of elusive beasts. Most women travel writers until the last fifty years went accompanied. Rebecca West begins *Black Lamb and Grey Falcon* (1941), her enormous tome on Yugoslavia, with a call to her husband who is asleep on a train: "My dear, I know I have inconvenienced you terribly by making you take a holiday now." A few single women like Mary Kingsley, who braved west Africa in the late nineteenth century, had plots for insuring their safety. Wherever Miss Kingsley arrived, the Africans asked where her husband was. She replied, "He is waiting for me, over there," pointing in the direction in which she was traveling. This insured her safe passage.

I have traveled wearing a wedding ring in such places as the Middle East. I am not proud of this fact but in some parts of the world, it helps to appear as if one belongs to a man. For many women, such as my mother, it helps to belong—period. It is not such a bad thing to be connected, but women have paid for their dependency. As a woman, I travel differently than a man. I believe most women do. When I read the classic travel memoirs, I am amazed at how many times women traveled in difficult parts of the world disguised as men. I am also amazed at how often there are sudden gaps in the writing of women travel writers of the previous century where they will say something like "the sailors won't leave me alone" and then leave no journal entry for two weeks. You must read between the lines.

Rape and abduction are realities for women traveling that make us wander differently than men. I have never walked down an unlit street or on a desolate strip of mountain road without some fear in my heart. Anything can happen at any time. It is like a whisper in the back of our brains, but it is there. I don't know if I'll ever just jump in my car and drive across America or walk across north Africa without recalling some of the terrible stories of women traveling that have been told to me. On the other hand, it will not stop me. I seem to have no choice.

From Penelope to the present, women have waited—for a phone call, a date, a proposal, the return of the intrepid man from the sea or war or a business trip. And Penelope, the archetypal waiter, is awaiting the return of the traveler. To wait is to be powerless. Like patients and prisoners women have waited for the freedom to enter the world. Now if we grow weary of waiting, we can walk out the door. The other half of the plots of all literature are now open to us: we can go on a journey, though perhaps a bit warier, more self-conscious than the other half of our species. We can be the stranger who comes to town.

WORKS CITED

Kingsley, Mary. *Travels in West Africa; Congo Français, Corisco and Cameroons.* 1897. Rpt. Boston: Beacon, 1988.

Montagu, Lady Mary Wortley. "The Turkish Bath at Sophia." In *A Book of Travellers' Tales.* Ed. Eric Newby. New York: Viking-Penguin, 1985, 117–18.

Showalter, Elaine. *A Literature of Their Own: British Women Novelists from Brontë to Lessing.* Princeton: Princeton UP, 1977.

West, Rebecca. *Black Lamb and Grey Falcon: A Journey Through Yugoslavia.* New York: Viking, 1941.

ROCKWELL GRAY

The experience of travel, in all its diverse forms, arises from some of the most basic features of our human condition. It is rooted, for example, in the interrelated facts of animal embodiment and motility. As animals— animated (ensouled) beings—we must move in order to live. We must be- take ourselves from one spot to another in search of shelter, nourishment, and the satisfaction of more complex needs like that of companionship. But, having bodies, we occupy space and are always, at any given mo- ment, in a concrete, bounded place with very particular circumstances. The latter term must be understood in the existential sense given it by Ortega y Gasset and other like-minded thinkers—as all that which "stands around" one (*circum-stantia*). This means much more than the assemblage of man-made and natural objects I find at hand or on my horizon: my circumstances also include the climate, the weather, the particular locale and its bordering territories, the foodstuffs available, the political system that obtains, and the prevailing patterns of social, educational, and com- munity organization. Obviously, there are many invisible dimensions to my circumstances, involving prevailing conceptual biases, traditions, and all manner of perceptual, cognitive, and interpretive frameworks. All this quickly becomes bewilderingly complex. If, for the moment, we consider only the most immediate physical settings through which we move, it is clear that one's entire life is an *ad-venture*, a venturing forth from one spot and situation to another. On the simplest level, this movement always involves the travail and the stimulus of change. Restless in our chairs or over a book, we take a little stroll. Refreshment comes in the spectacle of shifting sky and breeze, but we must carry our bodies across at least mildly resistant terrain to traverse our course. In this walking about lie several of the central metaphors for life—the course, road, or stream of experience undergone by man the wayfarer.

Experience is, in one sense, all that happens to us as we move through

This essay appeared first in *North Dakota Quarterly* 54, no. 4 (Fall 1986): 1–17.

the world. To the receptive soul upon whom nothing is lost, in Henry James's phrase, the slightest facet of his shifting circumstances will be instructive and formative:

> Humanity is immense, and reality has a myriad forms. . . . Experience is never limited, and it is never complete; it is an immense sensibility, a kind of huge spiderweb of the finest silken threads suspended in the chamber of consciousness, and catching every airborne particle in its tissue. It is the very atmosphere of the mind; and when the mind is imaginative— much more when it happens to be that of a man of genius—it takes to itself the faintest hints of life, it converts the very pulses of the air into revelations. . . . The power to guess the unseen from the seen, to trace the implication of things, to judge the whole piece by the pattern, the condition of feeling life so completely that you are well on your way to knowing any particular corner of it—this cluster of gifts may almost be said to consti-tute experience, and they occur in country and in town, and in the most differing stages of education. If experience consists of impressions, it may be said that impressions *are* experience, just as . . . they are the very air we breathe.

The etymology of the word points to the Latin *experīrī* (to try, to put to the test). From the same basic root we derive also "experiment," "peril," and "pirate," all suggesting risk and danger. To experience life is, in other words, to circulate about in the world, undergoing things, getting the lay of the land, surveying and reacting to the conditions under which we live. One of these is the vulnerability entailed by our embodiment. Given the conditions of our physical evolution, we are complexly needy, dependent, and interdependent creatures, prone not only to all the ills of the flesh, but requiring too an open, changing sense of territoriality and a great di-versity of sensory stimuli. In some sense, we are like the bear or the dog in our need to establish a home ground and return to it; but our superior mentality means that we are also endlessly curious about the vast outlying world beyond our familiar domain. In this regard, we are born travelers, always ready in mind and body to go visiting.

All physical travel has a mental dimension, just as mental travel takes place in a particular physical environment, generally one comfortable and secure enough to permit us imaginary voyaging. Yet even when physically constricted or under great stress, we travel in our minds, for thought, like actual movement through space, seems to follow a path or course. When an idea "comes" to us or "takes place" in our heads, we feel it to be in motion, on the way to provisional fulfillment and successive permutations.

Indeed, all our living and thinking is so much a matter of the onward way, that Gabriel Marcel's term *Homo viator* seems as essentially definitive of our race as the classic *Homo sapiens* and *Homo faber*. It is in our human nature never to be entirely in the present moment or place.

Our enormous capacity for vicarious experience is part of this essential and often salutary restlessness, as is our need to "get away" during vacations and see something new. Travel is the counter-rhythm to our boundedness in a web of local circumstances. I shoot off on occasion to New York or Chicago because my immediate environs are a rural locale halfway between them in the hills of western Pennsylvania. Thereby, also, West Virginia, Ohio, and western Maryland are on the horizon of my geographical imagination as they would not be if I lived, say, in Boston; and they are part of my larger bordering circumstances in a way the former two great cities are not. My personalized map of the region where I dwell is partly a question of physical distances, but our compass points and horizons are always largely symbolic. We convert landscape into story and legend, lending it much of what we wish to find there. Man the inveterate explorer brings with him the capacity to endow a place with wonder and romance. Our projections of desire define for us the map and the meaning of discovery: places we deem beyond the pale constitute what, differently for each of us, is "exotic."

Although Chicago and New York, for example, entail about the same traveling time from my current home, as a New Englander born I see the City on the Lake as the distant, fabled capital of the Great Hinterland. New York is emotionally closer to home, though its dense urban topography bears little comparison to the ecology of my childhood spent on the eastern shore of Narragansett Bay. In broad symbolic terms, New York and Chicago are my "East" and "West," somewhat as they were for Nick Carraway in *The Great Gatsby*, though for him the points of the compass were reversed: to go west was to head home, from prep school and college, back through Chicago's "old dim Union station at six o'clock of a December evening. . . . When we pulled out in the winter night and the real snow, our snow, began to stretch out beside us and twinkle against the windows, and the dim lights of small Wisconsin stations moved by, a sharp wild brace came suddenly into the air. . . . That's my Middle West—not the wheat or the prairies or the lost Swede towns, but the thrilling returning trains of my youth, and the street lamps and sleigh bells in the frosty dark and the shadows of holly wreaths thrown by lighted windows on the snow." The East, he adds, "had always for me a quality of distortion."

Our sense of place is a personalized yet broadly cultural creation. "My"

Chicago, different in many ways from Nick's or anyone else's, is a rich composite of what I have made from encounters with the actual city, together with what I have drawn from the storied one of lore and history—the great port and crossroads of mid-American development recreated a thousand times in American literature over the past century and more. I have written my own version of Chicago upon the palimpsest traced over by Jane Addams, Upton Sinclair, Theodore Dreiser, Sherwood Anderson, Carl Sandburg, Nelson Algren, Saul Bellow, and countless others. My vision of the city depends on its context in my personal history—from whence and at what age I first arrived there, the purpose of my journey, the urban circles in which I moved and the neighborhoods of my residence. Nothing could reveal better than close analysis of my "local knowledge" of Chicago the manner in which perspective and context determine the true import of our travels. To say accurately where one has been means to recreate the personal touch-points and the affective map of the journey. Literal geography is of less concern than what Guy Davenport calls "the geography of the imagination," shaped by the powerful stimuli of strange streets and coasts and neighborhoods.

The experience of crossing cultural frontiers is also germane. To travel from southern Texas to northern Mexico entails relatively little change of flora and fauna, but one's first hours in Nuevo Laredo or Matamoros convey unmistakably the sense of a distinctly different world. (Even there, of course, the cultural frontier can be located only approximately, for various features of cuisine, clothing, speech, and occupation are broadly shared on both sides of the border. The case of Canada, incidentally, is far more subtle; excepting parts of francophone Quebec, the presence of cultural patterns continuous with those of the northern United States seems obvious in much of Ontario and in the plains provinces as well.) To fly, as I recently did, from Moscow to Copenhagen is to know immediately many of the specific cultural differences suggested by those tyrannical abstractions *Soviet bloc* and *Western Europe*. The contrasting political systems of Russia and Denmark are invisible to the casual traveler, but one can hardly miss the startling contrast in facial expressions, product design, clothing, architecture, and food. Where Moscow is massive and somber, Copenhagen, intricate and lively, is built on a more "human" scale. Not for nothing is the Russian capital's subway system renowned, for to walk about that city during much of the year is both unpleasant and, given its sprawling growth, unfeasible. By contrast, the Danish city, easily known in a few pleasant hours of strolling, positively invites pedestrian traffic.

To travel is to move through differing geographical and cultural realms of multidetermined meaning. Such movement is at once engaging and stressful. Wherever I am to begin with, the project of getting somewhere else requires work, or travail. No significant travel—with its harvest of new insights, surprises, and difficulties—is ever altogether easy. An uneventful journey is, for our purposes, oxymoronic. To log the miles and complete the itinerary too smoothly is merely to go through the motions. Herein lies the disturbing feature of jet travel, which cancels out the sensation of space traversed. One can, of course, travel after rapid transfer to the distant locale, but the experience of getting there has been rendered almost unassimilable by the senses. Modern air transport abstracts one from the feeling of travel far more radically than the automobile, the train, or the trans-oceanic liner. These too involve a considerable degree of removal from the experience of the passage, but the literary evidence produced by passionate train travelers, for example, suggests that the very going provided much of the pleasure and the occasion for reflection. The traveler who boards a jet in New York at nine in the morning and steps off in San Francisco at noon, local time, has leapt blindly over vast stretches of geographical and social context. To a lesser degree, the motorist who speeds on interstate highways through the appalling spaces of corn, desert, and prairie also ignores the surrounding reality; but it is air travel above all that reduces our sense of the intervening space between departure and arrival. (This process of abstraction is echoed in the world-picture built for us by the modern communications media, particularly televised newscasting, which blots out or stereotypes as much as it reveals in whisking us nightly to those "hot spots" that editorial decisions and camera crews define as significant.)

The rapidly developing facilities for travel characteristic of the entire period since the Industrial Revolution prompt us to reflection. As it becomes easier to move about the world, and as mass tourism becomes the characteristic form for the modern traveler, one needs to redefine the essence of voyaging and exploring. In a longer perspective, Western man has been wandering the world ever since the great voyages of discovery beginning in the fifteenth century. Man, originally a roving hunter and gatherer, has always been a vagrant of sorts, but modern history as never before provides the spectacle of extensive and large-scale intraplanetary movement. To speak only of one portion of the globe, the earlier European voyages of conquest and colonization were followed by the dislocations caused by the Age of Revolutions, the growth of nationalism, the famines and land reforms of the nineteenth century, the great exodus of European emigrants to America, and, finally, the scattering of untold numbers of refugees and expatriates during and after the two world wars. Certainly in Europe (including Russia) and North America, the chances one will mature and die in the place of one's birth are surely much less today than they were, say, a few hundred years ago. Such a condition increases the difficulty of saying where, if anywhere, one is truly at home.

In modern terms, it is never easy to say where one actually is or belongs. Despite spending most of my year on a few hundred rural acres of a boys' boarding school, I am much more mentally absent than most of my colleagues. Through my library, in my correspondence, and in the rhythms of daydreaming, I engage constantly in imaginative travel. Actual physical trips projected and taken away from a spot I cannot quite call home seem, as much as for refreshment, attempts to enlarge my sense of place. For the educated man or woman, this process entails an extension of the sense of self. All authentic journeying means tracing new contours on our cognitive and affective maps. To explore and delineate them more fully becomes a lifelong pursuit. Though the physical globe, to be sure, seems overtraveled and even prepackaged for the tourist, there is no end to the symbolic dimension of travel as shaped in individual experience. Though the literal discovery of a virgin landscape is virtually impossible today, the evolving symbolic import of old places and well-worn routes is incalculably diverse and expansive. As Paul Theroux remarks, "It is a ridiculous conceit to think that this enormous world has been exhausted of interest." The horizon remains open, he adds, because "travel has less to do with distance than with insight; it is, very often, a way of seeing." By contrast, the modern mass tourist prefers to minimize the risks associated with genuinely new experience:

> Many people travel in order to feel at home, or to have an idealized experience of home: Spain is Home-plus-Sunshine; India is Home-plus-Servants; Africa is Home-plus-Elephants-and-Lions; Ecuador is Home-plus-Volcanoes. It is not possible for people to travel in large numbers and have it any other way. . . . This system, in an orderly way, defeats the traditional methods of travel and has made true travel almost obsolete. In order for large numbers of Americans to visit Bangkok, Bangkok must become somewhat like America.

In reaction against this growing condition, he notes, many travelers have begun to seek out the riskier and more difficult forms of travel in order to recapture, through that travail, the exhilaration and refreshment it brings. "The interest in travel today, which is passionate, arises out of the fact that there is a form of travel prevalent that is now very easy. . . . Mock-travel has produced a huge interest in clumsy, old-fashioned travel, with its disgusting food and miseries and long nights."

But if true travel is measured by insight, then one may often find it rather close to home, as Thoreau meant in saying he had traveled a good deal in Concord. He did so by tramping the woods and shores of Walden, but he also ventured abroad in the pages of his journals, demonstrating, in his capacity for concentrated experience, that we may travel far in hardly turning the corner. For him, the entire world was implicit in the little patch right under his nose. Each point *is* always a shore of the whole, a point of access to the enveloping cosmos. The modern world's distracted itch for the superficially exotic blurs this fact by promoting the need to get away from it all to the other end of the world. That prospect, of course, is not entirely bogus, for a trip to the Yucatán or the high Sierra may indeed renew us. But genuine refreshment must be achieved largely in the spirit, whether the setting be in the Himalayas or the neighboring wood. Without the inner search along the edges of one's known life, nothing is accomplished. The discovery of such novelty befalls us when we least expect it, as the Japanese Zen masters have known for centuries. Recently, my wife began to harvest a patch of wild raspberries at the edge of a wooded hillside behind our house. Developing a warren of paths into the thicket, she happily lost herself in the tranquil task, appearing an hour later refreshed from her sojourn. She had been away to a dark green place in mottled light under the trees, and her hands were stained with wild juices.

Each summer vacation, the prospect of suddenly "open" time threatens me with multiple possibilities of novelty. These often seem so diverse and unfocused as to cancel out any real sense of manageable choice. The ensuing bewilderment often produces the counter-impulse to return to my desk. This urge grows proportionately with the anticipated fatigue of being on the road. Sooner or later I actually strike out somewhere, for the inner roads of mental travel are not only enriched by but doubtless dependent for their very metaphorical form upon travels along the real roads of the world. Yet I wonder, for example, as I pack my bags, what will come of a colleague's summer bicycle trip from Pittsburgh to California and back. What will be the harvest for him of the hot, tedious hours along the shoulders of asphalt ribbons across the continent? What kernel of meditated experience will be his after he has eaten the dust of thousands of passing cars and trucks? If the work of insight does not keep pace with his turning pedals, he may simply get a good workout and become "the man who biked to California."

However it be done, true travel must both unsettle and delight us. The lesson of such journeying is that even in the ground of our existence, nothing is fixed. We know now not only that our globe orbits a sun which is a minuscule dot in an explosively expanding universe but that we walk on sliding plates ever adrift in the shuffle of continents. Man is *Homo viator* indeed, and the journey itself matters more than the arrival. Upon setting out on the road, we invoke a blessing before the risk of physical danger, but also do so because traveling has in it something sacred. One's mind and soul are tried and tempered by it in a manner reminiscent of the pilgrimage. In the quest for new places and sensations, even the neatly prepackaged trip may allow one a break from the ordinary round of profane experience, a taste of the sacred. Landscapes and buildings that are workaday settings for the native become, for the expectant visitor, functions of his need for mental and spiritual renewal.

The pilgrimage of travel is also a kind of rite of passage. Seeing all things afresh with eager eyes, the open-spirited journeyer steps outside of ordinary time. His senses spring awake. The food is pungently exotic, the coins feel different in his palm, the very air and light of new places become worthy of note. In his classic *The Rites of Passage* (1908), Arnold van Gennep speaks of the "magico-religious aspect of crossing frontiers," which harks back to the very early demarcation of sacred and forbidden zones. Countless social rituals involving passage from one physical territory or state of life to another call for what he designates as "pre-liminal," "liminal," and "post-liminal" ceremonies (from the Latin *limen*, threshold). Found at such crucial points as birth, the onset of puberty, marriage, founding a home, and funerals, these may also be called "rites of separation," "transition rites," and rites of "incorporation." As applied to passage from home territory to the wider world, or from one cultural zone to another, such ritualization of experience helps explain the traveler's sense of awe upon leaving behind his native ground and approaching his goal, be it Paris, Rome, Moscow, or Jerusalem, the Grand Canyon, the Hawaiian Islands, or the Antarctic. In modern civilized society, where the sense of the holy is weakened and less easily located than in primitive societies, any place may be made the sacred ground or mecca of a personalized pilgrimage. Even in earlier time, as van Gennep notes, "the presence of the sacred (and the performance of appropriate rites) is variable. Sacredness as an attribute is not absolute; it is brought into play by the nature of particular situations." Thus Nick Carraway in the Chicago station stood thrilled on the threshold of reincorporation into the magic of "his" Midwest.

The rare native, perhaps the poet or the painter, may sometimes achieve a refreshing distance from his own ground and make it strange. James

Joyce's Stephen Dedalus did it in his "epiphanic" Dublin moments, and the narrator of Marcel Proust's *Swann's Way* rediscovers in memory, out of his famous cup of lime-blossom tea, the deep wonder of childhood summers in "Combray." But the native can never entirely see with the eye of the sojourner for whom the place is a fresh stage on the road. Novelty of location is central to the latter's experience, but his rite of passage also involves an equally important shift in the order of time. He leaves behind the conventionally structured secular time of his own locale and culture to enter a zone of enhanced experience. There his subjective experience of time alters, as does also its collective measurement in the new culture around him. To his eager senses, a scant two or three days spent in the city of his dreams—Florence, Athens, Dublin, Copenhagen, Leningrad, Istanbul, Alexandria—may seem a little lifetime in itself. He can spend his strangely enlarged hours with a lavish freedom impossible at home, dining at unusual hours, lounging in cafés, or strolling idly to contemplate buildings, parks, and neighborhoods. Similar conditions held for the "liminal" period passed on the great transatlantic liners that previously offered a leisurely, gourmandizing transition from one world to another— New York to Southampton or Le Havre. Now that ocean-crossing is virtually puddle-jumping, and "Europe" has lost the exotic ring it had for the American pilgrim, best exemplified by Henry James's Lambert Strether in *The Ambassadors*, we have traded comfort in the journey for speed of passage, robbing ourselves of the tranquility needed to enjoy things once we arrive. Nor is the adventure after deplaning quite the same, as Daniel Boorstin observes: "Now, when one risks so little and experiences so little on the voyage, the experience of being there somehow becomes emptier and more trivial." For all the reduction of risk represented by the modern ocean liner, its passengers could at least anticipate the surprise encounters (often erotic) of shipboard society and the stimulus of shifting weather—rain and wind in one's face, or a view of moon sheen on still waters before bed.

Travel, when not made utterly routine by the efficiency of jet flights and tour itineraries, offers an antidote to the boredom of our familiar grooves. Such refreshment was formerly the privilege of only a very small percentage of mankind, generally the aristocracy; but it is now readily available, particularly in America and Western Europe, to huge numbers of people. As it becomes increasingly a mass phenomenon, the prospect grows that it too will become boring. When 35 million tourists annually visit Spain, one can no longer find there the piquant, exotic experiences of old. Frequent and ever easier travel back and forth between a strange place and one's home reduces cultural differences and homogenizes the world. Adventurous travel depends on maintaining a tension between the familiar and the strange. One mark that such tension is in effect is the experience of culture shock. Both going and coming back, we should be able to feel the stress of entry and reentry. The sense of a shifting, moving perspective is crucial. At times this experience may be had very close at hand. As Thoreau (once again) groped through the dark woods back to Walden from the lighted village, he remarked that a man needs to be turned around only once in this world to be lost. Indeed, we travel, in part, precisely to lose our bearings. As we proceed to make the world one broad paved highway, erasing or cushioning the salutary jolts provided by truly different environments, we rob our journeys of savor.

To grasp what today has become of most travel (and of reflection upon it), it is instructive to consider a modern classic of travel writing like D. H. Lawrence's *Sea and Sardinia* (1921). Moving about that island with uncanny alertness and dispatch, Lawrence (admittedly an exceptional observer) steeped himself in its still pristine otherness, finding in Sardinian peasant faces a "medieval" self-containedness. He *dwelt* in the place, absorbing it through his pores. Every turn in the road, every village and hillside, yielded bounty to his senses. The reader is astonished to discover that the time elapsed is a single week! The felicitous combination in the book of delicacy and force stems from the author's ability to render what he called the "quickness" of experience in rapid emotional turns and passionate ventings of attraction and distaste. Even the earth under his feet merits note:

> Wonderful to go out on a frozen road, to see the grass in shadow bluish with hoar-frost, to see the grass in the yellow winter sunrise beams melting and going cold-twinkly. Wonderful the bluish cold air, and things standing up in cold distance. . . . it is all so familiar to my *feet*, my very feet in contact, that I am wild as if I had made a discovery. And I realise that I hate limestone. . . . But granite! Granite is my favourite. It is so live under the feet, it has a deep sparkle of its own. I like its roundedness—and I hate the jaggy dryness of limestone, that burns in the sun, and withers.

Paul Fussell quotes H. M. Tomlinson calling Lawrence "a delicate sensorium, quivering and vociferating to every physical fact," and adds, "what Lawrence really saw in things and places was the Infinite. Like all literary travelers worth reading, he played a spume of imagination upon empirical phenomena, generating subtle emotional states and devising unique psychological forms and structures to contain them."

Travel reminds us that we live in a vast surrounding world. The boundaries between us and this world are loosely drawn. We venture forth constantly into it, while images and representations of it continually enter our thoughts and dreams. When we are not literally journeying, we are often recalling former trips and projecting future ones. While daydreaming in my study, I often attempt to make the whole world simultaneously present to mind, invoking its quite literally unimaginable (un-image-able) diversity and extent. Language in its highest reaches—in the hands of a supreme novelist or poet—can only begin to suggest what I am after.

Waking from a nap recently, I found myself thinking of southern Chile, where I last lived over twenty years ago. Lying in my bedroom, I realized someone was at that moment flying over the forested southern valleys near Temuco, Valdivia, or Puerto Montt, watching lights wink on below where folk were cooking their supper at twilight. In Pennsylvania it was raw February, but there summer was in full sway. My imagination reached toward the scene, but without a coherent story, it quickly blurred and shifted in the flow of half-formed images. What Clifford Geertz calls "thick description" could bring one closer to the settling summer evening six thousand miles away. But to grasp it well, one must become localized, immersed in the dense context of that other place. Each such immersion requires renunciation of the open possibilities we cultivate in the receptive, dreamy stasis of study chair or bed. Behind and within each concrete place lie the palimpsest-like layers of histories and traditions. To map it culturally and topographically, in time as well as space, requires the labor of years. By definition, the world is only sketchily drawn for each person, no matter how great the accumulated cartographic record of mankind. In my mind is a simulacrum of the totality, but its outer edges are diffuse, quickly fading into *terra incognita*. In bed in the gathering dark, I invoked huge stretches of territory at all points of the compass: Scandinavia, where the vivacious, glamorous Danish women dine together before a fireplace in an oak-beamed restaurant of the old section of Copenhagen; Latin America, stretching away from the desert of northern Mexico to the rain-lashed Chilean archipelago; our own West Coast, with fog-muffled cliffs rising from the Pacific; and Canada, all unknown above the familiar little belt that skirts the Great Lakes. These are the points of my personal compass. Flying out to them in imagination, I follow Whitman's lead in "Song of Myself":

> My voice goes after what my ears cannot reach,
> With the twirl of my tongue I encompass worlds and volumes of
> worlds. . . .
> My ties and ballasts leave me, my elbows rest in sea-gaps,

I skirt sierras, my palms cover continents,
I am afoot with my vision . . .

To invoke the arcane stretches of the earth is a form of psychic travel, a resistance to the rooted confinement of my bodily life and my social roles. Though my immediate sense of place is strictly circumscribed by the priorities of attention it demands, I can counter this limitation by allowing my mind to range among the regions of the earth that capture my imagination. Close to the source of such an urge, pursued either literally or figuratively, is Robert Louis Stevenson's remark in *Travels with a Donkey* (1879): "For my part, I travel not to go anywhere, but to go. I travel for travel's sake. The great affair is to move." Deep in our animal motility, responsive to the specifically human need for fresh sensory stimuli, lies the true source of all our journeys. Indeed, the very growth and maintenance of mind itself depends on exploratory behavior, the constant search for novelty. As one scientist, José M. R. Delgado, observes: "The literature on sensory deprivation is voluminous and shows conclusively that the cerebral cortex requires a stream of stimulation for the preservation of behavioral and mental normality. We should realize, therefore, that our cerebral and mental functions rely on the umbilical cord of sensory inputs and become disrupted if isolated from the environment." Even on the relatively local scale of our immediate surroundings, our entire cognitive apparatus is vitally fed by the little strolls we take, as by the shifting rhythms of weather and the circadian and seasonal cycles. Without this constant variety and our acutely sensitive response to it, we would be entirely different—and probably far less interesting—creatures.

That the small compass of a familiar place provides continuing uplift, heightening our powers and drawing us beyond solipsism, is beautifully evident in A. R. Ammons's poem "Corsons Inlet" (1965), one of the finest products of the poetic tradition coming down out of Ezra Pound, William Carlos Williams, and the Black Mountain School (especially Charles Olson). In sinuous yet dramatically broken lines, the poet reenacts the rhythm of his day's walk by the seashore, his perceptions dependent simultaneously on his own movement and on the undulations of nature. Educated originally in biology and chemistry, Ammons has an acute kinetic sense of his place in the total scheme. He invokes the constant interplay between the complementary rhythms of mind and environment:

I went for a walk over the dunes again this morning
to the sea,
then turned right along
    the surf

rounded a naked headland
and returned
along the inlet shore. . . .
the walk liberating, I was released from forms,
from the perpendiculars
straight lines, blocks, boxes, binds
of thought
into the hues, shadings, rises, flowing bends and blends
of sight. . . .
in nature there are few sharp lines: there are areas of
primrose
more or less dispersed;
disorderly orders of bayberry; between the rows
of dunes,
irregular swamps of reeds,
though not reeds alone, but grass, bayberry, yarrow, all . . .
predominantly reeds . . .

The poem fulfills the traveler's fondest hope for fresh insight. Within the routine of Ammons's daily constitutional, the world opens up again, as we do so with it. No event and no act is entirely repetitive. This is the wayfarer's article of faith, an assertion mounted against the threat of sameness. It is not strange that the modern bureaucratized and rationalized West should have spawned, in recent decades, a renewed poetry of "place" and a great outpouring of travel literature. Deeply critical of the technological transformation of our environment, it nonetheless shares with many practitioners of modern science a sense of wonder in the workings of "planet earth." In a spirit akin to Ammons's, many geologists, geographers, ecologists, climatologists, and astrophysicists are among our most acute modern travelers. They remind us, as does the earlier record of the voyages of discovery to North and South America, that journeys driven by the task of opening new territory—by the impetus of material need, territorial conquest, or scientific investigation—often constitute the most meaningful travel.

The scientific explorer, like the idle saunterer who discovers the purpose of his trip as he goes, may well find something he never dreamed of seeking. In both task-oriented and less purposeful travel, the key ingredient is observant openness, what the French call *disponibilité*. Sometimes the import of the journey remains unclear until years afterward, when one has surrendered to the fruitful working of time on the original experience. Proust, again, is the preeminent master of such experience. In *Remem-*

brance of Things Past, his narrator is fated to understand the import of his search for lost time only after the vast course of the entire seven-volume work. Yet even when the magic madeleine dipped in tea causes his childhood to unfold more fully than when he first lived it, he cannot divine the full import of that mnemonic flood. Similarly, Claude Lévi-Strauss in *Tristes Tropiques* (1955), the story of his travels and research among primitive Brazilian Indians, remarks on the difficulty of gaining the perspective with which to launch his story:

> Evanescent forms are becoming clearer, and confusion is being slowly dispelled. What has happened is that time has passed. Forgetfulness, by rolling my memories along in its tide, has done more than merely wear them down or consign them to oblivion. The profound structure it has created out of the fragments allows me to achieve a more stable equilibrium, and to see a clearer pattern. One order has been replaced by another. . . . Sharp edges have been blunted and whole sections have collapsed: periods and places collide, are juxtaposed or are inverted, like strata displaced by the tremors on the crust of an ageing planet. Some insignificant detail belonging to the distant past may now stand out like a peak, while whole layers of my past have disappeared without trace. Events without any apparent connection, and originating from incongruous periods and places, slide one over the other and suddenly crystallize into a sort of edifice which seems to have been conceived by an architect wiser than my personal history.

Lévi-Strauss is one of those modern writer-explorers who have taught us that reflection on travel can produce a prose equal in subtlety and imaginative power to the finest novel. Contemporary with *Tristes Tropiques*, works like Isak Dinesen's *Out of Africa* (1937), Lawrence's *Mornings in Mexico* (1927), Graham Greene's *Journey Without Maps* (1936) (about a trip to the interior of Libya in 1935), and Robert Byron's *The Road to Oxiana* (1937) all dramatized, in travels outside the borders of the civilized West, the absence of something vital at home. They remind us that the metaphor of going beyond the pale is central to much of the best literature of travel. Part of the larger history of Western primitivism, these quest journeys reveal civilized man's need for spiritual renewal through contact with non-Western cultures and relatively unknown regions of the world. Like earlier voyagers (e.g., Herman Melville, Robert Louis Stevenson, Paul Gauguin, Joseph Conrad) who sought spiritual and sensory refreshment in far-flung corners of the South Pacific, many more recent European travelers have turned away, often in disgust, from a civilization they deemed bent on self-destruction. (Ironically, during the same period, sensitive American travelers were finding their meccas in places like London, Paris, Rome, and Berlin.) Although the ordinary twentieth-century traveler seeks something simpler, and generally confines himself to less obviously exotic settings, he may still find immensely stirring the mere experience of crossing cultural frontiers within the civilized world, as when the overnight train from Paris to Madrid crosses from Hendaye to the lush valleys of the Spanish Basque country and then traverses the arid, electric meseta of northern Castile. The very taste of foreign food and drink is, like the sound of another tongue or the sight of a different architectural style or landscape, one of the chief pleasures of travel. Even the interstate American tourist, his Winnebago camper on his back, feels a frisson when crossing a state line that promises a change in topography, cuisine, or the lilt of the common tongue.

Altogether, the matter of crossing visible or invisible borders and frontiers is essential to meaningful travel. But one need not literally be "on a trip," for the simple transition from day into twilight and evening carries us daily from one zone of experience into another; and one may cook a Cajun dinner graced with excellent French wines without leaving his own home in, say, Boston or Buffalo. While physical travel dramatically engages our need for change, the tourist who commands all the conveniences of home on the road does not go very far, for there is no frontier or exotic zone that in and by itself guarantees the jolt of novelty. The thoroughly prosaic soul makes the whole world ordinary.

These reflections tend to assume a condition peculiar to modern travel as pursued by the relatively affluent tourist, namely, that the world unfolds before him like a supermarket display. Barring certain restrictions on the validity of his passport, or conditions of political unrest in certain countries, he may, any fine morning, board a plane for the most remote destination; and though he may choose to rough it, he generally smooths his path by arrangements designed to guarantee creature comforts along with a daily dose of novel sights and sensations. But it is wise to remember how recent is such elective travel, with its educational and recreational purposes, and how small a portion of mankind ever previously enjoyed it. Modern tourism dates only from the middle of the nineteenth century, and apart from Western Europe, parts of the Americas, and the exceptional industrialized non-Western nation like Japan, it is still relatively rare. Tragically more common over the ages, however, has been enforced travel, the wandering of people driven abroad by war, starvation, or persecution. Such transmigrations, many of which have left no written record, contrast sharply with travel undertaken as diversion or as the source for artistic and literary creation. Here and there, surely, emigration and diaspora produced a crafted cry of anguish—Dante's is the most famous case—to remind the world of the trauma of homelessness, but most of humanity's sufferings on the road have remained mute. Although modern history since the French Revolution has been marked by the experience of the refugee and the exile, retrospective studies of such sufferings have been far more common than testimony by the victims themselves.

There is, of course, a thickly textured literature of exile in the modernist canon, as George Steiner reminds us in *Extraterritorial* (1971), where he argues that a key trope of twentieth-century writing derives from the vantage point of the outsider living in alien territory. But the testimony of Joyce in Trieste and Paris, Pound in Italy, or Vladimir Nabokov immured in the snows of Ithaca hardly accounts for the travail endured by the millions of refugees and homeless persons produced by twentieth-century history alone. A pioneering work like W. I. Thomas and Florian Znaniecki's *The Polish Peasant in Europe and America* (1918) hinted at the wealth of stories entailed by the vast drama of European emigration to America around the turn of the century, but only the very occasional immigrant autobiography has managed to flesh out the story in individualized terms. For the most part, it remains an uncharted psychic territory kept in memory by word of mouth until the tale wanes in the minds of second- and third-generation descendants. Yet, in the total human record, journeys undertaken in desperation for sheer survival bulk indescribably larger than those recorded in the lively, polished accounts of modern travelers in search of adventure and refreshment. For the homeless wanderer, the semantic value of "home" differed profoundly from its connotations for those of us who have the choice to depart and return, enriching our sense of native realm by seeing it from afar.

At the same time, comfortable middle-class Americans, for example, undeniably feel a nagging sense of geographical and cultural placelessness, caused by our unprecedented mobility as well as by the homogenization of our environment. Perhaps mass tourism is a way of escaping this pervasive sense of rootlessness: taking to the road allows us, paradoxically, to forget how little we belong anywhere. Pessimistic observers suggest that the restless, casual travel of modern times has destroyed the earlier freshness of discovery to be found, for example, in the works of American expatriates in Paris during the twenties or in the superb English travel essays studied by Paul Fussell, who remarks of the subject: "The going was good for only twenty years, and after the [Second World] war all that remained was jet tourism among the ruins. . . . Claude Lévi-Strauss observes in 1974 that so full is the world now of its own garbage that 'journeys, those magic

caskets full of dreamlike promises, will never again yield up their treasures untarnished. . . .' What we have now is . . . 'mono-culture.' The
acute sense of place that attended travel between the wars has atrophied."
Such a judgment is persuasive. The modern tourist's hunger for new experiences becomes a kind of gnawing abstraction. Seeking the dynamic
image of one always on the go, he flies off to well-worn pleasure spots
like Jamaica, Acapulco, or the Spanish Costa del Sol. Ever since Thomas
Cook's first tours in the 1840s, large numbers of people have been traveling ever more efficiently and quickly through a panoramically exotic yet
disturbingly "flattened" world.

In the face of this fact, we need somehow to remind ourselves that the
earth remains, in many of its byways, more wondrous than we imagine.
There exists in the apparently tamed and charted globe a deep reservoir of
wildness and strangeness. Recent scientific advances in the study of continental drift and the mapping of the undersea ridges sharpen the profile
of our ignorance even as they dramatically increase our knowledge; and
the more we understand of the planet's systematic relation to the cosmos,
the more great stretches of dimly known phenomena unfold before us.
In the laboratories, computer centers, and telescope domes of the world,
the spirit of awed exploration is very much alive. On the simpler scale of
personal adventure, feats of mountaineering, river-rafting, hang-gliding,
and small-craft navigation engage growing numbers of people in the re-
discovery of the natural world. Such quests are of course different from
the wanderings of Lawrence in Oaxaca and Taos, or of Greene in the interior of Africa, but the spirit that drove the literary travelers is essentially
one with that of the poetically aware naturalist (e.g., Loren Eiseley, Henry
Beston, Aldo Leopold), the sensitive field geologist or ecologist, the far-
voyaging anthropologist, and the backpacker in the American West. The
aim, whether rendered in monograph or metaphor, is to chart the world
afresh. Often too, increased self-awareness is an additional fruit of the
journey, reminding us that the road or pathway is perhaps the most central metaphor for human life. "Man," Ortega y Gasset once wrote, "is a
substantial emigrant on a pilgrimage of being." From the personal pilgrimage of soul-making to the entire collective record of mankind's search to
understand the world, the essence of human life has been wayfaring.

WORKS CITED

Ammons, A. R. *The Selected Poems, 1951–1977.* New York: W. W. Norton, 1977.

Boorstin, Daniel. *The Image: A Guide to Pseudo-Events in America.* New York: Atheneum, 1975.

Delgado, José M. R. "Neurophysiology." In *Interdisciplinary Approaches to Human Communication.* Eds. Richard W. Budd and Brent D. Ruben. Rochelle Park, N.J.: Hayden, 1972, 119–34.

Fitzgerald, F. Scott. *The Great Gatsby.* New York: Charles Scribner's Sons, 1925.

Fussell, Paul. *Abroad: British Literary Traveling Between the Wars.* New York: Oxford UP, 1980.

Gennep, Arnold van. *The Rites of Passage.* Trans. Monica B. Vizedom and Gabrielle L. Caffee. 1908. Rpt. Chicago: U of Chicago P, 1960.

James, Henry. "The Art of Fiction." In *Henry James: Essays on Literature, American Writers, English Writers.* Ed. Leon Edel. New York: Library of America, 1984, 44–65.

Lawrence, D. H. *Sea and Sardinia.* 1921. Rpt. New York: Viking, 1963.

Lévi-Strauss, Claude. *Tristes Tropiques.* Trans. John and Doreen Weightman. 1955. Rpt. New York: Atheneum, 1973.

Ortega y Gasset, José. *History as a System.* Trans. William C. Atkinson. New York: W. W. Norton, 1961.

Stevenson, Robert Louis. *Travels with a Donkey: In the Cévennes.* 1879. Rpt. London: Chatto & Windus, 1986.

Theroux, Paul. "Stranger on a Train: The Pleasures of Railways." In *Sunrise with Seamonsters: Travels and Discoveries 1964–1984.* Boston: Houghton Mifflin, 1985, 126–39.

Whitman, Walt. "Song of Myself." In *Walt Whitman: Complete Poetry and Collected Prose.* Ed. Justin Kaplan. New York: Library of America, 1982, 27–88.

≺ ≺ ≺ ≺ ≺ ≺

Critical Itineraries

➤ ➤ ➤ ➤ ➤ ➤ Travel and Writing

MICHEL BUTOR

I have traveled a lot, it is said, yet certainly not enough to satisfy me; I need merely glance at a globe and see those innumerable regions where I have never been to be seized once again by a violent desire, the opposite of nostalgia, for which French has no name (there must be a reason for this lack), and to which I myself cannot give a name at the moment. Recently I have traveled less; I am growing wiser, it seems to me, and more settled; and I have problems of all sorts, it is true: I need to feel my surroundings secure (children grow up, objects accumulate and need to be ordered). But above all, I need to digest my previous travels, which I haven't yet quite finished, which I never shall feel completely finished; for me, it is a question of finding a modus vivendi with them through writing before being able to truly set forth again; so, in order to travel better, I actually travel less.

And I write. I have always felt the intense bond that exists between my travels and my writing; I travel in order to write—not only to find subject matter, topics or events, like those who go to Peru or China to return with lecture notes and newspaper articles (I also do this, although, unfortunately, not yet in those two particular countries; that will come in time)—but because to travel, at least in a certain manner, is to write (first of all because to travel is to read), and to write is to travel. It is this relationship that I would like to explore somewhat in this text.

If this kinship between travel and writing has always been (more or less) sensed (one need only think of the Roman journeys of François Rabelais and Michel Montaigne), it is certain that this feeling was the most evident in the Romantic era, notably in Germany and France. All our writers set out on the road. They made their journey to Italy or the Orient, published their accounts of it, and furnished us, in consequence, with an inestimable collection of documents and reflections upon this question.

This essay first appeared in English in *Mosaic* 8, no. 1 (1974): 1–16. It was translated by John Powers and K. Lisker.

Reading as Travel

ESCAPE

Let us enter the *métro parisien* (that of Moscow, Tokyo, or New York would serve equally well) at the end of a workday, during the evening rush hour. Examine the harassed, closed faces, exhaustion and boredom graying their skin. They wish to see nothing around them; they pay no attention to one another. Their eyes constantly avoid resting on anything or fix themselves on an insignificant detail, a raincoat button or a door handle; it is as if they were clinging to a buoy. They close from time to time, thinking of their overcrowded apartment, often hiding behind newspapers from which they glean a tidbit of news or some other distraction. But, among them, here is one who is reading a book. His eyes never leave the volume he fingers slowly, running along line after line, penetrating page after page. He smiles, beams in expectation. He has found an outlet, he is elsewhere: in the London fog, on the mesas of the Wild West, searching medieval forests, or even in the soundproofed room, the laboratory of the "writer."

There is travel, therefore, even if the work is not (at least outwardly) a *récit de voyage*; this is for two reasons:

First, because there is (at least) the path of the eye from sign to sign, like all sorts of itineraries that can often, but not always, be grossly simplified as the progression along a line from a point of departure to a point of arrival (a path that can become that of the head turning to decipher the inscription wound around the cupolas of *Saint-Marc*; or that of the entire body: such is the line read in a guidebook or a railway timetable: Fontaine-bleau, Sens, Dijon, Lyons—I can reread it from station to station while taking the train from Paris to Lyons, each word separated by kilometers).

And then because there is this outlet, this flight, this retreat; because through the skylight of the page I find myself elsewhere, whether it be in the writer's study or on his page (but wretched magician who leaves us on the page, poor master who cannot lead us elsewhere).

Notice immediately how often the stages of this last journey, perpendicular to the other one, obscure the others. Impatient, we wish to be immediately in Chicago, in Mexico, in Brocéliande; we scarcely consider all the intermediaries that permit our transportation: the creation of the work, the efforts of the author, his "ins and outs." We jump ahead to the point of arrival.

THE MYTHOLOGY OF WHITENESS

The escape that it provides from the wounding, pressing, hateful, obscure daily world makes reading a ceremony of purification, a ceremony often reinforced by a complete ritual. To discern this ritualized behavior is to clarify the role played, in our society, by that which might be called the vestment of whiteness. It is not happenstance that the paper in our books is white, always as white as possible, or that one of the most disturbing innovations of the Surrealists was their experimentation with printing on colored paper, experimentation that was, unfortunately, too rare and too disorganized. The "elsewhere" the book gives us appears, as we cross the page, to be penetrated with whiteness, baptized. Sometimes the refusal of the world as it is, the discouragement before the difficulties of transforming it, become so powerful that the reader prefers to remain suspended in the whiteness, calm at last. The "elsewhere" that appears thanks to textual signs may now be considered only as an inundation of white light; the signs themselves—a stain, the imprint of the real on this ingenuousness like a finger soiled with grease or ink—must deny themselves, efface themselves insofar as we read them. Just as in a detective story a second murder, that of the criminal by the detective, must erase the first, so in the mythology of the "pure-white writing"—so verbose, constantly lapping back upon itself like water in a washing machine—the second line must efface the first to leave us in this ocean of no-where, frontispiece of the *Snark Hunt*.

But just as the text can only create itself by creating something else, similarly it can only destroy itself by destroying something else.

Travel as Reading

TRAVELER-READERS

The *récit de voyage* effects and demonstrates this double journey that is all reading; it can carry the perpendicular path along with it to effect a displacement of the reader, to change his mental location, and finally, it can change his physical location.

This explains why a trip is, for our contemporaries, a privileged place for reading; how many read only in the subway, the train, the plane? These moving locations furnish the necessary retreat from the enchainments of daily life, the motion I see through the portholes and windows reinforces the movement of the *récit*, of the reading itself.

Beyond these two fundamental types of travel, reading may also super-impose at least three others:

That of the reader in the vehicle which permits him this leisure; this, in turn, can be doubly reflected: within the moving train, I can change cars between two chapters; furthermore, all the immobility upon the earth's surface is always only an illusion: we need enlarge only slightly our frame of reference to perceive that we are always moving in relation to other celestial bodies; we need merely apply time to space (travel is an illustra-tion of this) to arrive at that traditional, and inexhaustible, metaphor of the individual life, or even all of history, as a journey from birth to death.

That of the author—independent of the path of the writing on the paper—an author who can transport himself by writing (for example, if he keeps a diary of his journey).

That of the *récit* itself—which may or may not have characters (it may only have a succession of views or a montage of sequences)—with all the reflections that can intervene between the author or authors (a traveling critic speaking to us about a traveling writer) and the character or char-acters, with the superimposition of narrators or pseudonyms more or less fluid with respect to one another, who themselves can be reading *récits de voyages*, and so forth.

If there is a solidarity between perpendicular journeys (that is, if the path from the place "read about" to the place of reading sweeps along— or is swept along by—the movement of reading, in an effective oblique line that moves the reader himself, refreshing the world for him), it follows that the very form of the described trip cannot be completely separated from the form of its description or the effect it produces: its transforming power. An analysis of different types of travel will give us, in consequence, a new key for distinguishing between the literary genres in action, this emerging above all in the very "physics" of the book or writing.

ELEMENTARY CONSIDERATIONS OF A PORTABLE ITEROLOGY

I propose, therefore, a new science (they are springing up like mushrooms these days; they can be gathered in the shade of all Sorbonnes; some among the crop will even end by bearing fruit), strictly tied to literature, con-cerned with human travel; I amuse myself by naming this science *Iterology*. Naturally, I cannot actually found this science, but for those who will be employed therein, here are some preliminary ideas, packaged loosely.

Travel: a word repeated a thousand times in the streets, in advertising; it is seduction itself. It draws us to travel agencies. But, by this very fact, its popular meaning has become considerably restricted. We have the impression that there is only one type of travel, the "round trip." Given the fundamental metaphorical function of travel in all reading (and, correlatively, writing) and, in consequence, in our knowledge of the real and our action upon it, it is certain that the above-mentioned reduction will develop mythological powers all the more deceitful the less we notice it. It is easy to see that many human movements are one-way trips. But, in our charted regions, the railroad notion of a one-way trip itself implies a point of departure and a point of arrival (terms or termini), necessary because our society obliges us to have a fixed residence, the address inscribed on our identification cards. This rootage has not always existed, and in many places is, even today, not the case.

TRAVEL WITHOUT SPECIFIC LIMITS: WANDERING, NOMADISM

We come from nowhere in particular, we go nowhere in particular; carrying along all our belongings, we set up a tent or shelter of branches and leave no trace behind on departing.

A space so visited—even if it is not opposed to any forbidden exterior, to any domain possessed by another that can only be entered under certain conditions (like the Roman Empire behind its fixed borders, as opposed to limitless barbaric wandering)—can, nevertheless, be perfectly defined, and it is easy to show that it is already a reading space. Hunter tribes: animals are "tracked," a matter of reading their marks and the signs that betray them. Shepherd tribes: a matter of following the signs of vegetation and the seasons, in order to pass from one location to another at the proper time. There is quickly an (at least) provisional marking of the domains of these herds; it is necessary to read the signs of the defiant presence of some other herd or tribe. Points of reference become increasingly important. At the time of the transhumance, from one year to the next, we wish to enjoy once again the good trees, the pastures, the points of shade or water (Jean-Jacques Rousseau has already noted the importance of water sources in his *Essai sur l'origine des langues*). From this time on, a few recognizable sites, a few natural landmarks, are isolated, then named and consecrated; they are retained, preserved, in *récits*; the surface of the earth becomes a page and an imprint is left upon it. Wandering, then, is staked out with signs, with characters.

Death halts wandering abruptly. The individual journey has a limit.

Birth, on the other hand, is produced in movement itself; the child moves in his mother's womb even as she herself moves; the child can be born anywhere. On the other hand, he who dies is abandoned on the spot; even if he is burned and his ashes (or some relics) are carried along, his path stops there. The tomb is the mark par excellence for this very reason. Even today we see an equivalence between the sepulcher and the monument. In burial, the wanderer becomes a tree, a signifying sprout. This liaison between writing and death comes to us from the subsoil of history; cities will be founded upon such sacrifices.

So, for the Australian aborigine to move in what appears to us a desert is, in fact, to move within his own history.

TRAVEL WITH A SPECIFIC GOAL: SETTLEMENT, EXODUS

This millennial writing transforms the desert, bit by bit, into a text, a thick tissue of traces and marks. Different factors may drive these wanderers from one such marked-out area to another, almost virgin (at least for them) region, may provoke a migration that itself may be stopped by natural or political obstacles: the seashore, the boundary of an empire; or, perhaps, the cultural tissue becomes so strong, so powerful, that it becomes necessary to protect the borders, to maintain the tombs; a settlement, then, is established. The path of indefinite wandering "arrives" at some spot. This is particularly the case when a wandering civilization encounters another, long-settled, whose especially imposing and unavoidable monuments are automatically adopted as landmarks by the newly arrived.

This settling may be only partially complete. We find, then, an opposition between the "strong places"—cities, monuments—and a far less established countryside. It was not long ago that in many European countries a journey to a city was like passing from a mode of wandering to a settled state; this is true in many regions of Africa to this day.

If, in the wandering civilization, the end of an individual's journey is equivalent to his death, the settling of an entire people—even if it permits the enjoyment of an economic affluence immeasurably greater than that to which it was accustomed or the attainment of an incomparably more solid and efficient language—is always lived (in a certain fashion) rather like a death, an overcome death, ostentatious; a sort of life beyond death. We each keep, more or less hidden within us, a nostalgia for wandering. To travel is to live once again.

Inversely, a settled population can be driven from its habitation by an invasion or natural catastrophe. It carries off all the possessions possible, no longer having hopes of returning one day to its ravaged, destroyed "home." This is exodus. The previous language and the minute acquaintance with the terrain are no longer of any use; an immense nostalgia develops. There is a search for another place for settlement, a promised land.

As long as all possibility of return is not eliminated, as long as the lost language is still felt to be partially functional, it is exile, one of the conditions for the predilection toward poetic inventions: to preserve the ancient language, to re-actualize it, to refresh it.

TRAVEL BETWEEN TWO DEFINITE TERMS: CHANGING HOUSES, EMIGRATION

Although settled, we abandon one specific place in order to go to another specific place, carrying all our possessions, abandoning all rights to the former place. There will be no return. Someone else will live in the former home, without (in general) the previous occupant resenting any contact with the newcomer. This is changing houses, or "moving." In this case, the precise point of arrival is well known in advance: it has been visited, chosen. But such a term can also be quite vague: there is emigration. We know that we are going to America or Australia. We are resigned—having applied for and received our traveling papers—but we have, in reality, few pieces of specific information about these promised lands; we carry our few possessions, we know that we will settle ourselves, but we don't know quite where.

When the point of arrival is settled in advance, it exercises a general attraction, we desire it, it emits signs. Thus, in the countryside, the city glows, even if the population is settled to the point of serfdom, bound to a soil lined with the furrows of labor or terraces like long lines of writing. In similar fashion, the horizon gleams for the emigrant with the lights of an El Dorado.

TRAVEL WITH A DOUBLE TERM: ROUND-TRIPS

In this case, the final point of arrival coincides with the point of departure. We are truly settled. We depart, but leave behind our possessions, our roots; we keep our rights. It is well understood from the beginning that we will return.

If we suppose momentarily that this place of rootage (of attachment) is simple, we can distinguish a linear and a circular form, regardless of how they may appear when we follow them on a map. I call "linear" those trips in which the return trip is the exact reverse of the original outward journey; a "circular" trip is one in which we desire to see more countries and choose a different return route. The latter, generally, is filled with stopping-places, while the former is impatient, stretching as much toward the intermediate destination as to the home to which we return.

BUSINESS, VACATIONS

The linear journey, in its pure state, is the business trip. We do not leave our preoccupations; we pay no attention to the traveling itself. The sooner we can arrive the better, for the sooner we will be back again. But, the linear trip is mongrelized by "vacation," a trip in which time opens up, a perfect equivalent to that refuge offered by reading in the *métro* car. We need merely study vacation publicity to find once again the mythological whiteness of the page: it's to the beach, then, or the ski resort. Leave your worries! Escape!

In this vacation, travel can become theater. We mimic another trip, change houses for a while, settle elsewhere briefly, seek a new region to live, play at emigrating, at wandering; thus, we go camping and return to a tent or the open, starry skies; for a short time we have no fixed residence. We generally have a second point of departure (we take the train to such and such a station, it usually being too difficult to set out camping from our very house), a second point of arrival (our "forwarding address"); we wander between the two, taking advantage of the landmarks, trying to recapture the reading of natural signs. Bathing ourselves in original wandering, we exorcise the terror of exodus.

THE ALIEN

Upon arriving in a new place—and this is particularly true for the trip abroad, where another language is spoken—with the freedom of vacationing, I will need to begin learning to read once more. The gestures will not be the same: other manners, other laws, other traffic rules. I will decipher the billboards, the newspaper headlines, the street signs (sometimes in another alphabet, which, in China or Japan for example, can offer enormous resistance). My temporary lodging, my adaptation, my rest, my interest all depend in large part upon my ability to read. My own tongue will find itself refreshed, I will discover unsuspected aspects of it and my behavior as well; my departed home and country will soon become as seductive as the finally visited country of my dreams. I used to desire Venice; Venice made me desire Paris, Nevers, Maubeuge; it illuminates them.

Not all places have the same power, certainly; they are more or less difficult to read, more or less fascinating, more or less efficacious; above all, they form systems with respect to each other and to the original spot where we will return. Vacations are, then, organized in tours, in tourism.

RETURN TO THE NATIVE LAND

This is an essential Romantic theme; the notion expressed in this subtitle does not refer to a definitive return, but quite the reverse. It is well understood that the young man who left his village for Paris has adopted this village as his home. He wants to return to it. It is there he has left his possessions, his rights. He swears that he belongs to Paris. But one day he leaves in search of himself, of that former face abandoned, travestied, hidden, betrayed; moreover, this return to the native land is often involuntary: through a chance occurrence during a business trip or ordinary vacation he stumbles upon his past (in some manner); and that is the shock. A wall crumbles within him. He bursts into tears and returns to the capital another man.

The native land may be so thoroughly repressed at the time of emigration that the emigrant himself cannot return, nor even his children or grandchildren, who will do everything possible to conceal their origin in Italy, Poland or Ireland; they will even change their name. This is the phenomenon so well studied in the United States: the "third generation." Only when the family finally feels that it belongs, that it is well adopted by the new country, that it is first and foremost "American," will the descendants wish to visit their country of origin, to renew those ties so painfully cut. This, then, is travel in the history of one's family.

PILGRIMAGES

The word designates, first of all, the journey to the tomb of a saint, next to the spot of a vision, an oracular site; one carries his question there and expects a response, a curing of the body or soul. The sanctified spot detaches itself from the midst of profane regions; it is the skylight onto paradise. Later, the pilgrimage becomes a journey to those places that speak, that tell us of our history and ourselves. Such are the Roman pilgrimages in the Renaissance. Just as the town diffuses its semantic power onto the countryside, so certain sites carry, to this very day, the speech of a fundamental historical moment that detaches itself from the more vague epochs that it clarifies.

All the great Romantic tours are round-trip and are pilgrimages of the latter type. It seems to me that Chateaubriand's *L'Itinéraire de Paris à Jérusalem* (1811) is a particularly clear illustration of this beyond the fact that the trip itself was part of a design that was clearly conscious of writing (and, even then, not the design of that book but another: *Les Martyrs* [1809]), beyond the fact that it gives nineteenth-century French literature a prototype that numerous later writers will strive to imitate:

> I had stopped the plan of *Les Martyrs*: most of the books of this work were outlined; I did not believe that I had to write the last word in it before having seen the scene of the countries where my scene was set; others have their resources in themselves; for myself, I need to compensate for such a lack with all types of work. Also, when one does not find the description of such and such famous place in this *Itinéraire*, it is necessary to look for it in *Les Martyrs*.
>
> This principal motive which caused me to leave France again after so many years was joined by other considerations: a trip to the Orient completed the circle of studies that I had promised myself to finish. I had contemplated in the American deserts the monuments of nature; among the monuments of man I knew only two kinds of antiquities: Celtic and Roman; I still had to travel through the ruins of Athens, of Memphis, and of Carthage. I also wished to accomplish the pilgrimage to Jerusalem:
>
> *Il gran sepolcro adora, e cioglie il voto*
> . . . . *Qui devoto*
> [He adores the great sepulcher, and
>   fulfills the vow . . . Here made]
>
> It may seem strange to speak of vows and pilgrimages today, but on this point I am unashamed, and I set myself long ago in the class of superstitious and weak people. I will be perhaps the last Frenchman to set out from my country to the Holy Land with the ideas, the goal, and the sentiments of an ancient pilgrim.

In each of these places a great tomb. The whole *Itinéraire* is a "long pilgrimage to the tombs of great men." What reading of inscriptions!

Three fundamental stations, three ideogrammatic cities mark the way for the ideal Romantic journey, a journey never completely realized: Rome, Athens, Jerusalem, each accompanied by such and such a satellite, such and such a complement. Just as the emigrant's descendant breaks his parents' repression in his return to the native land, Chateaubriand, in his reading of ancestral cities, shatters the false antiquity and Christianity inherited from the Eighteenth Century. The horizon which separates Paris from Greece or Jerusalem is also a mental horizon.

EXPLORATION

To those travels in our history that are the Romantic pilgrimages—which allow us to reread (in another fashion) those messages historically transmitted to us—we must oppose others, equally "round trip" in their nature: voyages of exploration.

In this case, we set off for an unknown region (rather: a poorly known, or foreshadowed, one); only rarely can we trust *récits* or our own plans; by going to the other side of the physical or mental horizon we stretch this horizon. Such a miracle was Ferdinand Magellan's voyage when, without retracing his path, he returned to the point of departure.

The exploratory voyage allows us to rediscover primitive wandering in the parentheses of fixed residence; we must know how to read natural signs. The *récits* of the great navigators or explorers show that this reading generally requires a teacher. Usually, it is a (more or less) settled native who teaches the explorer to recognize the trails, to identify landmarks, to perceive the dangers. The unknown land is already elaborated like a text, even if the native translator is often eliminated in the end by his dangerous pupil.

Truly uninhabited lands always take the longest to penetrate; the most recent scientific instruments are necessary to aid us in our surveying. Even on our planet, uninhabited lands (Antarctica, for example) often remain unexplored to this day.

The voyage of discovery demonstrates most strikingly the phenomena of marking and writing. Crosses, monuments, tombs are erected and inscribed. The first thing that Americans do upon walking on the moon is to raise a flag, and no one even dreams of being surprised.

Where the textual fabric of the new land is already quite dense, the explorer will bring home the names taught him by native instructors, but even more often, he, the new Adam, will untiringly name each identifiable site; so, world maps will become covered with names, the tracing of the coastlines will be practically outlined by this throng of vocables. Even before the conqueror, the explorer seizes with his language the land he crosses.

THE ANIMATION OF TERMS

Our society has affixed us, it wishes to know us only with a single address; this organizes, still more, our representation of space—except in the vacation intervals that are (more or less) studious or laborious; but a more rigorous examination shows us that this prevalent notion of domicile (or rootage) is, today, more and more complex. In fact, these terms of which we speak are themselves constantly enlivened by movement. At the beginning of this text, I evoked the image of the *métro parisien*. When the traveler departs for the *club Méditerranée*, he not only leaves behind his apartment on the *boulevard Barbès*, but an entire ensemble of terms: the factory where he is foreman or the bank where he is employed, the path he treads (at least) every morning and evening. Similarly, the towns he is going to visit are not merely single hotel rooms, but a number of museums, churches, restaurants, landmarks, streets, and squares he will tour, a number of trams, taxis, and buses he will ride. Travel makes us pass from a first ensemble of pathways to a second.

MULTIPLICATION OF RESIDENCES

There are degrees of residency as of settlement. If I have my address in Paris, I can go to Rome so habitually that I find myself perfectly at home there; I may have an established room at a friend's house. We are seeing the multiplication of secondary residences. With a certain amount of fortune (at once monetary affluence and luck), it becomes impossible to distinguish the principal one among them. This is a higher form of nomadism, the union of residency and wandering.

This truly was the case with the kings and great lords of the Middle Ages. The knights were wanderers in comparison with the serfs bound to their fields. Kings promenaded from château to château. The monarchy's settlement at Versailles was the triumph of the Parisian bourgeoisie, which succeeded in mimicking, in its town, the semantic absolutism of the Rome of yesteryear.

VEHICLES

This becomes even more important as the diverse fixed residences are able to be connected by mobile ones. Kings between two châteaux simply set up tents. We are evoking here, in the distance, the portable palaces of Kubla Khan in Marco Polo.

And, at this point it becomes absolutely necessary to let the consideration of different vehicles intervene in our typology of travels. Some vehicles, in fact, are themselves domiciles; this was formerly the case with boats (microcosms of the world) or gypsy caravans, which the sedentary folk watched pass with a fright mingled with no little envy. Today, the domicile of each town dweller is augmented by that rolling room that is his car, in which he feels at home, and where he transports, at his pleasure, a number of objects by no means insignificant in comparison with those a knight of old might have carried.

And if we succeed in loosening somewhat this notion of personal possession, we can imagine the extent to which the notion of a fixed residence—with all the legislation attached to it—can become outdated.

SUGGESTIONS

To these first distinctions, we must add many others. Here are some examples. To study travels according to

Their scansion: Is the journey composed of stopping-places, and how far apart? Within these stages is there a change of vehicle or method of movement? We notice that almost all of our trips mix vehicles or modes of travel and that their scansion is (in general form) strictly tied to these in intention.

Their speed.

Their equipage.

Their company: solitary journeys (that of the knight errant in the romances of the Middle Ages), family trips, group trips, societal exoduses, hitch-hiking, family reunions, travels whose stages are marked by "acquaintances," "relatives," or "hosts."

VERTICALS

But even from the point of view of the geometry of the route, another dimension must be introduced. So far we have considered motion only on a single plane, on a surface. Let's occupy ourselves a bit with thicknesses:

Travels of ascent: to climb a mountain (Dante's *Purgatorio*), to be lifted in a balloon, an airplane, a rocket; they are characterized by a progressive enlargement of the horizon or system of reference: we situate the point of departure from the point of arrival: the path of reading is accomplished naturally in the discovery of this ascensional vector, which needs to be completed, equilibrated by its opposite.

Travels of descent (Dante's *Inferno*, so many pages of Victor Hugo's

Le Voyage au centre de la Terre), in which a provisional shrinking of the horizon leads to the opening up of immense caverns, makes us climb to the surface of the other side of the normal horizon and denounce this surface as a lie. It is a matter of reversed—and reversing—ascent, where the point of arrival situates the point of departure by making it undergo a reorientation (this is why this point of arrival is so often conceived of as a center), by forcing it to an avowal.

NERVAL AND CHATEAUBRIAND

Let's examine, for example, *Le Voyage en Orient* (1851) by Gérard de Nerval in comparison with *L'Itinéraire de Paris à Jérusalem*. The author of *Aurélia* (1855) carefully avoids the three essential stopping-places, the three key words, of the author of *Les Martyrs*: Rome, Athens, Jerusalem. He chooses, instead, three intermediary towns on his route as principal stations, and he takes them in reverse order: Cairo, Beirut, Constantinople.

Constantinople, the capital of an empire, will take the place of Rome; Cairo, with its Egyptian science, that of Athens; Beirut, with its proximity to the Druses and Hakem their messiah, that of Jerusalem. It is not that Nerval feels that these three towns can (in any sense) replace the three traditional ones of the West, but that traveling there permits him to test the elements of untruth in the "statement" offered us by the traditional towns.

Whereas Chateaubriand leaves France to allow his book to be veracious (this does not only concern the scenery, since the speech of these three places was deformed by eighteenth-century French), believing that in re-finding a place one becomes capable of understanding it in all its glory, Nerval estimates that it is not sufficient to go to Rome to eliminate the deformations of the Roman text, that this alteration is not only situated *between* Rome and Paris, but is already *in* the imperial and papal city. It is necessary, therefore, to post oneself in an exterior monitoring position in order to reveal the fissures of the Roman surface, to seize the text from below. . . . Wandering the streets or environs of Cairo, Beirut, or Constantinople, Nerval is always lying in wait for anything that will allow him to sense a cavern extending beneath Rome, Athens, and Jerusalem.

This is always achieved through the roundabout way of a *récit*, a fiction; the only true descent—prelude, in fact, to a *récit*, serving as a metaphor or sacrament to all the others—is that of the pyramid.

The science of the pyramid, masonic wisdom, is presented as the foundation for Athens's wisdom and science. The passion of Hakem, his sojourn in the *maristan*, the insane asylum, is the equivalent of an underground trip; it opposes another incarnation to that of the dead Christ at Jerusalem. And finally, in the nights of Ramadan, the storyteller leads us with Adoniram through the subterranean world where, not only the emperor Solomon, but also the same Jehovah from whom he draws his so clumsily apparent power, reveal themselves as usurpers.

Just as the three cities of Chateaubriand are in communication—Rome, with its emperors and popes, reassembling the heritage, the testament, of Athens and Jerusalem—the caverns of Nerval, by scrambling them slightly, become engaged in intercourse: the Drusian messiah lived his passion in Cairo; because it extends below Jerusalem, the underground world of Adoniram ends by mining the very soil of Rome.

There is, certainly, a subterranean presence in *L'Itinéraire*, due to the fundamental theme of the tombs, but Chateaubriand finds it sufficient to raise once again the monuments and inscriptions, to accept what has been retained of the dead person at the moment of his burial, his transformation in character; Nerval, in contrast, wishes to wrest from the dead the secret of what we have justly wished not to retain. For this reason, he is obliged to discover those oblique paths that allow him to sneak under the cobblestones.

Chateaubriand's pilgrimage is a journey in history; Nerval's is the falseness of history.

Travel as Writing

THE LIBRARY OF TRAVELS

Since our overall purpose is to place in evidence the ties between travel and the book, we must study different journeys according to their degree of "literariness."

All the Romantic voyages are bookish. Alphonse Marie Louis Lamartine, Théophile Gautier, Nerval, Gustave Flaubert, and others correct, complete, vary the theme set by Chateaubriand.

In all cases, books are at the origin of the trip; books read (in particular, *L'Itinéraire*), projected books (starting with *Les Martyrs*):

The travelers read books during their journeys.

They write them, usually keeping a journal.

And they always produce a book upon their return, otherwise we would not talk about them.

They travel in order to write, they travel while writing, because, for them, travel *is* writing.

SIGNATURES

It has been like this primeval wandering. While traveling, the horde clears a path, isolates landmarks, stakes out its territory and inscribes its tombs therein. The explorer marks the earth on which he lands. Our travelers will leave their traces in the towns of their pilgrimage: so many registers signed, checks cashed, mementos inscribed. And, in these books, what emotion is created when the traveler discovers the trace of a previous traveler!

To leave a trace of our passing is to belong to a spot, to become ourselves a Roman, Athenian, Cairote; therefore, we do it not only to return home with the light of these place-ideograms within us, but also to make our very existence a hopefully indelible "stroke" on a visited spot. For later travelers, it is certain that going to Athens is also—in a very slim measure by comparison with other reasons, but nonetheless surely—to go see the city visited by Chateaubriand, his visit being tied to certain other acts and illuminating them in a particular way.

Although we may understand perfectly well that the soldiers of the Napoleonic army wished absolutely to mark their passage by signing, with vigorous slashes, the upper casements of the first pylon of the grand temple of Karnak, and although it truly moves us to find them there, from the moment an exceptionally dense textual tissue re-covers the soil or the landscape, the modern traveler develops scruples about leaving a disturbing mark that he judges too uninteresting by comparison with what he would destroy in the process.

Thus, the early tourist is succeeded by one who, conscious of the troubles he brings to the refreshing and educational place, dreams of leaving it intact, who wishes not simply to be the only outsider, but also to be a kind of invisible intruder, without weight, without tainting effect: a sort of phantom who leaves no trace, like the man who wants to walk in snow without leaving footprints. Under another guise, we find once again our mythology of the white page.

THE BOOK AS MARK

Instead of the direct mark that risks destroying the previous signs (or even their absence), we often prefer a more respectful and elegant one (which often proves ultimately more conclusive): the creation of representative objects, an eminent example being the book. We have already mentioned the essential role of nomination in exploratory travel, an act whose product frequently is inscribed upon the place itself, first of all on maps and in *récits*; sometimes, this occurs after a long time: thus, the names the first Portuguese navigators gave to their moorings up and down the coast of Brazil are today inscribed on train stations, intersections, street signs.

It is travel itself that names places, but once these places are named successive voyages will repeat them in some order. The very complex "words" that are the great sites will be linked by the travelers in a sentence. Because he travels there by way of Venice, Athens, or Constantinople, Chateaubriand approaches the "term" Jerusalem in a certain way. One stopping-place produces the effect of a parenthesis or a digression, while another is, on the contrary, an essential stage of an argument. The grammar of the book will strive to restore the "grammar" of the path of travel.

Writing as Travel

It is not necessary, however, that there be a book; it suffices that there is a trace (whatever it may be), a recording of the travel; this is precisely what is difficult to avoid today. The mere fact that I create an itinerary, that I set towns or spots in a certain order, marks a stable sign on the surface, or even the thickness, of the world. Since I have already proposed a science, I can also propose an art: it would consist, quite simply, in traveling, and perhaps in leaving a few traces here and there; but, these would be purely subordinate to the general effect: such and such an innovation in the itinerary, such and such a change of vehicle, such and such a prolongation of stay being able to arouse as much admiration, or commentary, as a beautiful image in a great poem.

But, note those resources possessed by the book, all the guises in which it may dress itself these days (and let us dream for a moment about all the intermediaries between this travel of pure execution, prepared improvisation, and its bookish division); from the moment the book becomes the principal means of marking his passage, the writer is allowed, in working on his book, to work considerably upon this mark.

If Romantic travel leads to the composition of a book, this is because in writing a book one is engaged in the act of traveling. If reading is a crossing—even if it often pretends to be only an erased passage through the cloud of whiteness—writing, always the transformation of reading, is necessarily even more so.

The terms *Rome, Athens, Jerusalem* are arranged in a particular order by the sentence that is my journey, and they can be varied at the instruction of my traveling-writing; in the *récit* I propose, how many undergrounds and oblique views it becomes possible for me to discover.

Envoi

I seldom write "on the spot." I do not keep a travel diary. I speak of one place in another place, for another place. I need to make my travels travel. Between two terms of one of my sentences, between the verbal sites that I detach and mark, the earth turns.

I have created for myself an entire system of nations that I improve little by little.

Or rather:

I have created for myself a system of nations that improves itself little by little.

Or rather:

An entire system of countries that improves itself in creating me little by little.

And I send this text, all the way from the Maritime Alps, simultaneously to Paris, to Australia, and to California, that it may be diffused in many other places.

WORKS CITED

Chateaubriand, François René. *Travels to Jerusalem and the Holy Land Through Egypt.* 2 vols. Trans. Frederic Shoberl. 1811. Rpt. London: Henry Colburn, 1835.

> > > > > > Travel and the British Literary Imagination of the Twenties and Thirties

PAUL FUSSELL

A part of the "cultural archeology" of the twentieth century: that's what John Pearson has called the Eiffel Tower Restaurant in London, once a haunt of the Sitwells and their retinue. Pieces of the same cultural archeology are the ships and trains of the twenties and thirties together with their accessories and associations. What school child of the period can forget the hours wasted with colored paper and paste and poster paint on projects like "Transportation" or "Travel"? The ostentatiously "modern" mural devised in 1928 for the Bullock's Wilshire department store, in Los Angeles, conveys excitement in the form of an art-deco liner and train, and the artist has made the wave undulations resemble the smoke billows from the locomotive stack as if to suggest that the two means of "transportation" are romantic and wonderful in the same way. Two years later the decorators of the Chrysler Building in New York followed suit, making "travel" the theme of the painted ceiling in the lobby. Heady stuff. To travelers of the twenties like H. M. Tomlinson, the idea of travel is practically equivalent to the idea of ships, and the familiar spectacle of ships nearby—now, as we have seen, all but vanished—induced curious, subtle psychological ripples incident only to that time and place. "In New York, in the twenties and thirties," Alec Waugh remembers in *The Early Years of Alec Waugh*, "you were always conscious of the liners that you saw from your office and apartment windows. There was a feeling, in consequence, that you had very little time, that you had to make the most of every contact quickly."

Images of *sailing* and *sailing away* will assume a weight more than cliché-metaphoric when projected and received in a context in which real

From Paul Fussell, *Abroad: British Literary Traveling Between the Wars* (New York: Oxford UP, 1980), 50–60, 202–15. © 1980 by Paul Fussell. Reprinted by permission of Oxford University Press, Inc.

passenger vessels, "sailing days," "sailing parties," and even "sailing baskets" are a part. Once we look at the intercourse between literature and actuality this way, we sense that Hart Crane's "Voyages" (1926) is as rigorously of the period as things like Sutton Vane's popular play of 1923, *Outward Bound*, with its shipboard setting, or Osbert and Sacheverell Sitwell's play of the same year, *All at Sea: A Social Tragedy in Three Acts for First Class Passengers Only*. An American publishing enterprise of the twenties was called The Four Seas. Its now being defunct seems suggestive. Conrad Aiken published his novel *Blue Voyage* in 1927, the same year Yeats chose to title his poem not "Going" or "Proceeding to Byzantium" (one could get there overland, even in the early Middle Ages) but "Sailing to Byzantium." Noël Coward, not to mention Cole Porter, would have been virtually silent without ships, P & O as well as transatlantic, as devices and props and sets and occasions. Someday, and perhaps rather soon, Auden's lines

> You were a great Cunarder, I
> Was only a fishing smack,

are going to need annotation.

If a port like Dover was a magnet for homosexuals, ports attracted others as well. Harold Acton notices that in the twenties "the life of seaports held a fresh fascination for artists, poets and composers," composers like Erik Satie, a native of Honfleur, or Jacques Ibert, whose composition *Escales* (1924) is described by Nicolas Slonimsky in visual, indeed travelbook terms as a "triptych of geographic impressions." As Acton recalls, "Half the canvases at exhibitions were arrangements of ships and sailors. Poetry and fiction were pervaded by a tang of tar. Not the sea itself . . . , it was the port of call that excited creative artists—the bar half open on the jetty, the sailors and their molls." Acton's observation may do more than myth criticism can to suggest why those sailors and fishermen and even fish vendors are in *The Waste Land*, why we hear there

> Beside a public bar in Lower Thames Street,
> The pleasant whining of a mandoline
> And a clatter and a chatter from within
> Where fishmen lounge at noon. . . .

Indeed, to read such modern masterpieces as *The Waste Land*, *Ulysses*, and *A Draft of XVI Cantos*, all from the early or mid-twenties, with a renewed awareness of their "period" travel dimension is perhaps to reattach some meaning to them which has been largely adrift since their time. I am thinking not only of things so obvious as the presence of the *Odyssey* in both *Ulysses* and the *Cantos*, and the guide-book obsession in *Ulysses*. I am thinking also of what a geographical work *The Waste Land* is, and how concerned with topography it is, how it is the work of an imagination stimulated by great presiding motifs of movements between Germany, Russia, Greece, India, Switzerland, Smyrna, Carthage, Phoenicia, Jerusalem, Egypt, and Austria, as well as by shifts of perceived landscape and setting—sand, rock, water, mountains, plains, snow, sea, city, river, ship, even hotels. Eliot weaves into his poem 31 different place-names or precise geographical locations. The poem, like the works of Oswald Spengler and Leo Viktor Frobenius, both registers and stimulates the "travel" imagination. It is wonderful that a poem so central to the age should be so geographical. And we can observe a similar sensitivity to the topographical in another monument of the twenties, E. M. Forster's *Aspects of the Novel*, which originated as the Clark Lectures at Cambridge in 1927. In his first lecture, Forster pays homage to William George Clark, the Victorian Shakespearean scholar, and observes that he also wrote two travel books, one on Spain, one on Greece. And a couple of hundred words later we find Forster imagining the novel in terms of *mountains, rills, swamps, and tumps of grass,* the whole *spongy tract* "bounded by two chains of mountains neither of which rises very abruptly—the opposing ranges of Poetry and of History—and bounded on the third side by a sea—a sea that we shall encounter when we come to *Moby Dick*." Novelists as well as novels can be conceived topographically, as Lawrence does with himself when he tells a correspondent: "I am very conceited, but not lofty. . . . I am like a bit of hummocky ground, with many little amusing eminences— but Alpine—Oh dear No!"

To canvass merely the titles of works between the wars is to sense their permeation by the "travel" spirit, from Conrad's *The Rover* of 1923 to Isherwood's *Goodbye to Berlin* and Anthony Powell's *What's Become of Waring* of 1939. (Powell is alluding to Robert Browning's poem of 1842, which begins,

What's become of Waring
Since he gave us all the slip,
Chose land-travel or seafaring,
Boots and chest or staff and scrip,
Rather than pace up and down
Any longer London-town?

Like Matthew Arnold "explaining" Arthur Hugh Clough's departure from England, Browning, here, at least, conceives that voluntary flight from London requires some justification.) In 1919 there is Somerset Maugham's

The Moon and Sixpence; in 1920, Pound's "Mauberley"; in 1922, Lawrence's *Aaron's Rod*; and in 1923, *Kangaroo*. The year 1924 brings forth such "spatial" works as Sacheverell Sitwell's *Southern Baroque Art*, Hemingway's *In Our Time*, and Forster's *Passage to India*. In 1926 Lawrence is in Mexico with *The Plumed Serpent* and Hemingway has gone to Paris and Pamplona in *The Sun Also Rises*. In 1927 C. E. Montague's novel takes the reader *Right Off the Map*, Eliot invites him to join the "Journey of the Magi," and Elizabeth Bowen allows him to live in *The Hotel*. (Hotel-consciousness is a largely unexamined feature of the imaginative life of the period. Between 1927 and 1932 the Dorchester, Park Lane, Mayfair, Grosvenor House, and Strand Palace were all built in London, and everyone seems to have been remarkably hotel-minded. When young Anthony Carson arrived at his private school in America, the first thing it reminded him of was a hotel: it had "lifts, a ballroom, cinema and tiled swimming pool where you could buy sundaes and sodas." A very popular easy read in the early thirties was Vicki Baum's *Grand Hotel*, which, if written today, would have to be re-conceived as *Grand Motel*. The equivalent popular novel of the seventies is, typically, *Airport*.)

In 1928 Siegfried Sassoon gives the reader glimpses of *The Heart's Journey*, and William Carlos Williams takes him along on a *Voyage to Pagany* (that is, Europe). R. C. Sherriff's play about trench warfare, produced in 1929, is called *Journey's End*, a title so familiar now that it's hard to get the original context back. To 1929 belongs Sinclair Lewis's *Dodsworth*, which resembles not merely a travel book but, when it's treating Venice, a guide book. Aldous Huxley's well-known essay "Wordsworth in the Tropics" (1929) could hardly have been written without the travel atmosphere of its moment. For Huxley, William Wordsworth is defective because "he never traveled beyond the boundaries of Europe," never "spent a few weeks in Malaya or Borneo," never took "a voyage." The result is an ultimate inhibition of imagination. The year 1929 is notable too for a very different sort of performance. One of the sensations that year was a book by one Joan Lowell, *The Cradle of the Deep*, widely bought and enthusiastically received: the first printing was seventy-five thousand copies. It purported to record, with coy lubriciousness, the author's adventures on sailing ships in the South Seas. It was full of implausible situations and unbelievably gooey dialogue. In fact, it was a fraud, as Lawrence perceived—"The girl at sea is a feeble fake," he wrote a friend—but it indicates the avid market for anything approximating a narrative of travel or adventure personally attested.

In 1930 Sassoon is *In Sicily* while John Dos Passos is surveying *The 42nd Parallel*. More hotel comedy surfaces in Rose Macaulay's best-seller of

1931, *Going Abroad*, while the same year Pearl Buck is getting off hundreds of thousands of copies of her "China" novel, *The Good Earth*. Hemingway is doing guide-book Spain again in 1932 with *Death in the Afternoon*, J. R. Ackerley is wondering at the attractively anomalous Indian scene in *Hindoo Holiday*, and Graham Greene is exploiting the Orient Express railway fad in *Stamboul Train*. (J. B. Priestley angrily saw himself satirized in the character of Greene's complacent plebeian novelist Quin Savory, traveling to the Orient in search of material not for a travel book but for a novel, to be titled *Going Abroad*, "An Adventure of the Cockney Spirit.") The year 1933 brings Powell's comic novel *Venusberg*, which opens with Lushington being told by his editor, "Seeing the world broadens the outlook. You can learn a lot abroad"; the same year gives us George Orwell's *Down and Out in Paris and London*, Michael Roberts's anthology of largely left-wing poetry titled *New Country*, and a stern warning by the now-reactionary Sassoon, *The Road to Ruin*. In 1934 Orwell publishes *Burmese Days*, Waugh *A Handful of Dust* (where we say farewell to Tony Last, trapped in a quasi-Brazilian jungle), and H. V. Morton *In the Steps of the Master*. This last is forgotten today—just as well: it is gravely naïve—but in its day it was an important bourgeois devotional classic and sold 210,000 copies the first two years. The book assumes the precise history of Jesus and locates topographically all the events depicted in the Gospels. "I have attempted," says Morton, "to put down in this book the thoughts that come to a man as he travels through Palestine with the New Testament in his hands." The book is interesting here because it suggests the readiness of the thirties audience to receive essayistic views and improving exposition so long as they were attended by the décor of travel—the palm trees of the Holy Land can't have hurt—or seemed to issue harmlessly as an adjunct to geography. (In 1936 Morton repeated the performance, traveling to Greece and Turkey and delivering his homilies under the title *In the Steps of St. Paul*.)

A very different kind of book, but still an "abroad" book belongs to 1935, Connolly's *The Rock Pool*. The same year Hemingway published his *Green Hills of Africa* and Isherwood *Mr. Norris Changes Trains*. The later thirties will attach the conventional British sense of abroad to the war in Spain: 1937 is the year of Arthur Koestler's *Spanish Testament* and Elliot Paul's *The Life and Death of a Spanish Town*, 1938 of Orwell's *Homage to Catalonia* and MacNeice's *I Crossed the Minch*. At the same time it was being generally agreed that sympathizers with the USSR's external political policies in Spain and elsewhere should be named not *friends* or *approvers* or *supporters* but *fellow-travelers*. And then in 1939 the atmosphere begins to dissipate: Henry Green's *Party Going* enacts the abortion

of travel just as Isherwood's *Goodbye to Berlin* notates the end of "resid-
ing abroad." Auden and Isherwood's *Journey to a War* (the Sino-Japanese
one) plays out the sad if necessary action by which the travel book finally
mutates into the book of war reporting.

Steinbeck's *The Grapes of Wrath*, of 1939, seems identifiably a work
conceived within the travel atmosphere, with its "documentary" registra-
tion of what things are like in unfamiliar places. I find suggestive of the
prevailing atmosphere even Eliot's titling the *Four Quartets* after places,
as well as declaring, in "Burnt Norton," that "the detail of the pattern is
movement" and resuming that theme in "The Dry Salvages" while transforming the sense data of "travel" into metaphysics:

> When the train starts, and the passengers are settled
> To fruit, periodicals and business letters
> (And those who saw them off have left the platform)
> Their faces relax from grief into relief,
> To the sleepy rhythm of a hundred hours.
> Fare forward, travelers! not escaping from the past
> Into different lives, or into any future;
> You are not the same people who left that station
> Or who will arrive at any terminus,
> While the narrowing rails slide together behind you;
> And on the deck of the drumming liner
> Watching the furrow that widens behind you,
> You shall not think "the past is finished"
> Or the "future is before us."
> At nightfall, in the rigging and the aerial,
> Is a voice descanting (though not to the ear,
> The murmuring shell of time, and not in any language)
> "Fare forward, you who think that you are voyaging;
> You are not those who saw the harbor
> Receding, or those who will disembark. . . ."

And these paradoxes of travel as metaphysical perception of eternity return
at the end of "Little Gidding":

> We shall not cease from exploration
> And the end of all our exploring
> Will be to arrive where we started
> And know the place for the first time.

But one can infer more about the spirit of the age from a pack-rat like
Archibald MacLeish than from a master like Eliot. "Nimble at other men's

arts how I picked up the trick of it," Edmund Wilson has him say, designating a talent that makes him both "A clean and clever lad / who is doing / his best / to get on" and a performer indispensable to the subsequent student of period themes. MacLeish's poems of the twenties and thirties encapsulate the public interests of the moment, and in nothing so much as their devotion to the travel—or perhaps even tourist—motif. Hear some lines from "Cinema of a Man" (1930):

> He sits in the rue St. Jacques at the iron table
>
> . . .
>
> Now he sits on the porch of the Villa Serbelloni
>
> . . .
>
> Above Bordeaux by the canal
> His shadow passes on the evening wall
>
> . . .
>
> He wakes in the Grand Hotel Vierjahrzeiten
>
> . . .
>
> Now he is by the sea at St.-Tropez,

et cetera. (Impossible to keep from thinking of the late-sixties film satirizing catch-all tourism, *If It's Tuesday, This Must be Belgium*.) Even MacLeish's well-known poem "You, Andrew Marvell," which seems to be about Marvell's ability to imagine the whole planet at once, proves to be as well an exhibition of its author's familiarity with place-names and topographical features. And perhaps no poem of MacLeish's is more representative of its age than "Tourist Death," dedicated, if not addressed, to Sylvia Beach, where life itself is equated with travel-and-tourist actions until finally the addressee is presented with the question: "Do you ask to travel forever?" (It was a favorite conceit of the period: witness not merely Eliot's performance but Sassoon's "The Traveler to His Soul," a poem assuming that "traveler" will be understood specifically as "living person, moving from birth to death.") Regardless of his poetic merits, MacLeish superbly represents that between-the-wars generation that shared, as Robert Wohl has observed, "a mentality, a collective state of mind, that left its imprint on the language and literature of the 1920s." Sacred to this generation is the image not just of the traveler but of the wanderer, the vagabond, or even Chaplin's cinema tramp, all skilled in the techniques of shrewd evasion and makeshift appropriate to the age's open road.

The figure of the open road had of course been a staple of Romanticism at least since Whitman, but between the wars it takes on renewed vigor. The American Schuyler Jackson, intimate of Robert Graves and Laura Riding, conceived the idea of a publishing enterprise called the Open Road Press, devoted largely to issuing I Hate It Here materials. J. B. Priestley's cheerful novel *The Good Companions* (1929) appropriates the open road theme for purposes of optimistic propaganda, while as Charles Loch Mowat points out, "A. P. Herbert's *Water Gypsies* (1930) sent everyone vagabonding in imagination of the canals." Walter Starkie's *Raggle-Taggle: Adventures with a Fiddle in Hungary and Roumania* (1933) had much the same effect, although here the images were of roughing it around campfires. The image of the neo-medieval wandering minstrel or clerk, as in Villon, enticed more young people than Ezra Pound to Provence and environs. Looking back from 1977, Patrick Leigh Fermor locates the literary influences that impelled him to walk over Europe in the thirties: "Set on my way by my Villon craze, I had discovered and devoured Helen Waddell's . . . *The Wandering Scholars* [1927] . . . and I wasn't slow . . . to identify myself with one of those itinerant medieval clerks." We should notice the way the titles even of scholarly works like Waddell's seize on the prevailing imagery. Thus, if we have Richard Halliburton's *The Royal Road to Romance* and Huxley's *Along the Road* in 1925, and Orwell's *The Road to Wigan Pier* and Robert Byron's *The Road to Oxiana* in 1937, between them we find John Livingston Lowes's source study of the preeminently geographical "Kubla Khan," *The Road to Xanadu* (1927). In 1928 Van Wyck Brooks seems to recognize the travel atmosphere by choosing the title *The Pilgrimage of Henry James*, just as A. J. Symons does in 1934 with *The Quest for Corvo*. It seems appropriate that looking back from the fifties on his experiences in the twenties with Lawrence at Taos, Witter Bynner should title his malicious memoirs *Journey with Genius* (1951), just as it seems fitting for Jeffrey Amherst to title his memoirs of the twenties and thirties *Wandering Abroad* (1976). Indeed, there seems no literary place too high or too low for the travel obsession to show itself. Thus Emily Post's *Etiquette* (1922). The book illustrates its principles with playlets involving characters (usually depicted at table) like the Worldlys, Lucy Gilding (*née* Wellborn), Mr. and Mrs. Kindheart, and the distinguished Mrs. Oldname: she is a model of the "tactful hostess who never forgets to say to a lady guest, 'Mr. Traveler, who is sitting next to you . . . , has just come back from two years alone with the cannibals.'"

Perhaps the most pleasant relics of this lost age of travel to hold and handle are the little volumes of the Travelers' Library, which seem quite ordinary artifacts until we realize how unlikely it would be that any other age would produce them. Jonathan Cape began publishing the series in 1926, and by 1932 it included 180 titles with over a million copies in print. The volumes, smaller than 5 by 7 inches, bound in a fine light-blue, gold-stamped cloth and selling for 3s. 6d. each (about a dollar), were "designed for the pocket"—of travelers, that is—and, the ad continues, "A semi-flexible form of binding has been adopted, as a safeguard against the damage inevitably associated with hasty packing." (*Hasty packing*: what excitement that phrase can still engender, even if those who hastily pack now are corporate persons sent to hurriedly called sales meetings or correspondents sent abroad in a crisis not to travel but to remit official copy.) By 1929 the Travelers' Library list included so many travel books that we must suppose that reading about someone else's travel while traveling oneself was an action widely practiced. It was assumed, indeed, to constitute a large part of what traveling was, which is to say that traveling was considered to be, ipso facto, literary traveling.

Abroad, one traveled literally, but by reading, figuratively as well, making an exciting metaphoric relation between one's current travel and someone else's travel in the past. Stuck at home, one "traveled" too by reading about it; there, the act of reading easily became a substitute if not a trope for the act of traveling. Even for stay-at-homes a pinch of exoticism could be had for ⅜ to convey some romance, freedom, desire, and warmth into the chill Midlands evening well before the invention of television. Both travelers and nontravelers could regale themselves with such Travelers' Library titles as Henry Festing Jones's *Diversions in Sicily* (1909), Constant Sitwell's *Flowers and Elephants* (travels in India, 1927; introduction by E. M. Forster), Edith Wharton's *Italian Backgrounds* (1905) and *In Morocco* (1919), Marmaduke Pickthall's *Oriental Encounters* (1918), D. H. Lawrence's *Twilight in Italy* (1916), John Dos Passos's *Orient Express* (1927), Max Murray's *The World's Back Doors* (a journey around the world, 1927), *The Travels of Marco Polo*, Maugham's *On a Chinese Screen* (1922), Henry James Forman's *Grecian Italy* (1924), Percy Lubbock's *Roman Pictures* (1923), and even something nice to read specifically in a deckchair, Eugene O'Neill's *The Moon of the Caribees, and Other Plays of the Sea* (1923). Of course W. H. Davies' *Autobiography of a Super-Tramp* is on the list: although published in 1908, it remained popular and influential throughout the twenties and thirties. We can be fairly sure that the author of *Down and Out in Paris and London* and *The Road to Wigan Pier* knew it well. As Michael S. Howard has indicated in his account of Jonathan Cape as a publisher, that house was acute in sensing the postwar demand for travel books of all kinds—Lady Warren's *Through Algeria and*

Tunisia on a Motor Cycle was on the 1922 list—and signing up some of the brightest stars, like Robert Byron, Peter Fleming, and Beverley Nichols.

If as a reading nontraveler of the thirties you wanted a more direct experience of literary traveling, there was the "Things Seen" series of pocket-sized guides, "so well written," says the *Bristol Times*, "that one may follow the writer in his lively description without the fatigue of the actual journey." The list of titles (*Things Seen In . . .*) suggests the places the between-the-wars British traveler took as his province: *Kashmir, Japan, China, Egypt, Northern India, Palestine, Constantinople, Bay of Naples, Sicily, Ceylon.* A pleasant feature, on the back endpaper, is a "Calendar for Readers Who Intend To Go Abroad," which suggests the best months for traveling in different places. . . .

After encountering a number of these books, it's time to inquire what they are. Perhaps it is when we cannot satisfactorily designate a kind of work with a single word (*epic, novel, romance, story, novella, memoir, sonnet, sermon, essay*) but must invoke two (*war memoir, Black autobiography, first novel, picture book, travel book*) that we sense we're entering complicated territory, where description, let alone definition, is hazardous, an act closer to exploration than to travel. Criticism has never quite known what to call books like these. Some commentators, perhaps recalling the illustrated travel lectures of their youth or the travel films that used to be shown as "short subjects," call them *travelogues.* Others, more literary, render that term *travel logs*, apparently thinking of literal, responsible daily diaries, like ships' logs. This latter usage is the one preferred by David Lodge, who says of thirties writing that "it tended to model itself on historical kinds of discourse—the autobiography, the eye-witness account, the travel log: *Journey to a War, Letters from Iceland, The Road to Wigan Pier, Journey without Maps, Autumn Journal,* 'Berlin Diary,' are some characteristic titles." Even Forster is uncertain what to call these things. In 1941 he calls them *travelogues*, in 1949 *travel books.*

Let's call them travel books, and distinguish them initially from guide books, which are not autobiographical and are not sustained by a narrative exploiting the devices of fiction. A guide book is addressed to those who plan to follow the traveler, doing what he has done, but more selectively. A travel book, at its purest, is addressed to those who do not plan to follow the traveler at all, but who require the exotic or comic anomalies, wonders, and scandals of the literary form *romance*, which their own place or time cannot entirely supply. Travel books are a subspecies of memoir in which the autobiographical narrative arises from the speaker's encounter with distant or unfamiliar data, and in which the narrative—unlike that in a novel or a romance—claims literal validity by constant reference to actuality. The speaker in any travel book exhibits himself as physically more free than the reader, and thus every such book, even when it depicts its speaker trapped in Boa Vista, is an implicit celebration of freedom. It resembles a poetic ode, an Ode to Freedom. The illusion of freedom is a precious thing in the twenties and thirties, when the shades of the modern prison-house are closing in, when the passports and queues and guided tours and social security numbers and customs regulations and currency controls are beginning gradually to constrict life. What makes travel books seem so necessary between the wars is what Fleming pointed to in *One's Company*, "that lamb-like subservience to red tape which is perhaps the most striking characteristic of modern man." Intellectual and moral pusillanimity is another characteristic of modern man. Hence Norman Douglas's emphasis on the exemplary function of the travel writer's internal freedom and philosophic courage: "It seems to me that the reader of a good travel-book is entitled not only to an exterior voyage, to descriptions of scenery and so forth, but to an interior, a sentimental or temperamental voyage, which takes place side by side with the outer one." Thus "the ideal book of this kind" invites the reader to undertake three tours simultaneously: "abroad, into the author's brain, and into his own." It follows that "the writer should . . . possess a brain worth exploring; some philosophy of life—not necessarily, though by preference, of his own forging—and the courage to proclaim it and put it to the test; he must be naif and profound, both child and sage." And if the enterprise succeeds, the reader's "brain" will instinctively adjust itself to accord in some degree with the pattern established by the author's travel, both external and internal: that is, it will experience an access of moral freedom. It is thus possible to consider the between-the-wars travel books as a subtle instrument of ethics, replacing such former vehicles as sermons and essays.

A fact of modern publishing history is the virtual disappearance of the essay as a salable commodity (I mean the essay, not the "article"). If you want to raise a laugh in a publisher's office, enter with a manuscript collection of essays on all sorts of subjects. And if you want to raise an even louder laugh, contrive that your essays have a moral tendency, even if they stop short of aspiring to promulgate wisdom. The more we attend to what's going on in the travel book between the wars, the more we perceive that the genre is a device for getting published essays which, without the travel "menstruum" (as Samuel Taylor Coleridge would say), would appear too old-fashioned for generic credit, too reminiscent of Charles Lamb and Robert Louis Stevenson, and G. K. Chesterton. Thus the travel books of Aldous Huxley, a way of presenting learned essays that without exotic narrative support would find no audience. Thus also the performances of Douglas and of Osbert Sitwell, who, for all his defects, has thought long and hard about the essayistic element in the travel book and has coined for it the eccentric term *discursion*, as in his titles *Discursions on Travel, Art and Life* (1925) and *Winters of Content and Other Discursions on Mediterranean Art and Travel* (1950). "Discursions," he says in the former, is "a word of my own minting, coined from *discourse* and *discursive*, and designed to epitomize the manner in which a traveler formulates his loose impressions, as, for example, he sits in a train, looking out [the] window, and allows the sights he so rapidly glimpses, one after another, to break in upon the thread of his . . . thoughts." *Discursions*, he goes on, "is an attempt . . . to find a new name for a particular kind of essay, that unites in the stream of travel . . . many very personal random reflections and sentiments."

Thus in Sitwell's "travel books" we find a general essay on cabs, prompted by the cabs of Lecce, and one on the theory of bourgeois domestic architecture triggered by the sights of southern Germany. Neither essay could achieve a wide audience if detached from the sense data of the place abroad which has justified it. Alan Pryce-Jones's *The Spring Journey* (1931) is a good example of a travel book that functions as a mere framework for essays. The travel is to Egypt, Palestine, Syria, and Greece, but it is only a medium for inset Carlylean essays and discursive flourishes on the follies of modern education, the difference between Imagination and Fancy, the decay of contemporary civilization, and the superiority of music to "the other arts." An American counterpart is Hemingway's *Green Hills of Africa* (1935). Because of the public persona he has chosen, Hemingway can't plausibly write "essays" in the old schoolmasterly sense. He can get away with essays on bullfighting if he connects his learned comments with memories of toreros he has known and thus validates his remarks as memoir. But for him to discourse professorially about history and literature would seem unnatural—stuffy, pompous, very un-outdoors. He thus lodges his major essay on the character and history of American literature, his version of Lawrence's *Studies in Classic American Literature*, in a travel book, and presents it there as a conversation with a person encountered by chance, the character Kandinsky, an Austrian who is made to ask who the great writers are. "Tell me. Please tell me," he says, not very credibly. Hemingway responds with an essay of twelve hundred words, presented as dialogue, considering the merits of Poe, Melville, Emerson,

Hawthorne, Whittier, James, Crane, and Twain. We easily remember his brilliant remark, one of the most acute critical perceptions any scholar or critic has uttered, that "all modern American literature comes from one book by Mark Twain called *Huckleberry Finn*," but we may forget that it gets uttered at all because on the African veldt "under the dining tent fly" an Austrian has asked him about American writers. It is an open-air remark, a travel, not a library, remark.

Similarly, if one approached a publisher in 1940 with a collection of assorted ethical and historical essays one would have less chance of success than if one arranged them as "A Journey Through Yugoslavia" and titled the whole immense work *Black Lamb and Grey Falcon* (1941), as Rebecca West did. We recognize Lawrence's *Aaron's Rod* as akin to a travel book less, perhaps, because it goes to some lengths to describe abroad than because it provides a medium for promulgating essays. Lawrence will suddenly cast away his narrative pretenses entirely, face his audience directly, and issue what we perceive is the "topic sentence" of an old-fashioned moral essay. On some of these occasions he sounds like a sort of Hilaire Belloc turned inside out: "The *idée fixe* of today," he will proclaim, "is that every individual shall not only give himself, but shall achieve the last glory of giving himself away." Or: "The David in the Piazza della Signoria, there under the dark great Palace, in the position Michelangelo chose for him, there, standing forward stripped and exposed and eternally half-shrinking, half-wishing to expose himself, he is the genius of Florence."

But to emphasize the presence of the essay element in the travel book is to risk not noticing sufficiently this genre's complex relation to adjacent forms that also require two words to designate them: *war memoir, comic novel, quest romance, picaresque romance, pastoral romance*. The memorable war memoirs of the late twenties and early thirties, by Graves and Edmund Blunden and Sassoon, are very like travel books and would doubtless show different characteristics if they'd not been written in the travel context of the period between the wars. They are ironic or parodic or nightmare travels, to France and Belgium, with the Channel ferries and the forty-and-eights replacing the liners and chic trains of real travel, with dugouts standing for hotel rooms and lobbies, and with Other Ranks serving the travel-book function of "native" porters and servants. Curiously, at the end of the Second World War the war book has something of the same "travel" element attached to it, the same obsession with topography and the mystery of place, with even something like Lawrence's adhesions to the prepositional, like *into*. Recalling his first idea for *The Naked and the Dead*, Mailer says: "I wanted to write a short novel about a long patrol. . . .

Probably [the idea] was stimulated by a few war books I had read: John Hersey's *Into the Valley*, Harry Brown's *A Walk in the Sun*."

The element of the comic novel is visible not merely in the travel books of Byron and Waugh; it is visible as well in Lawrence's *Sea and Sardinia* (1921), in much of Douglas, and even, if we can conceive the "seedy" as inherently comic, as a pathetic parody of a civilization not worth imitating, in much of Graham Greene. Anomaly is what unites comic novel and travel experience. A baron "traveling in cosmetics" and shaving in beer because the water in the wagons-lits has run out is an anomaly Anthony Powell met in Yugoslavia once. It fitted perfectly into his comic novel *Venusberg*, where the baron is presented as Count Bobel. The comic novel between the wars would be an impoverished thing without its multitude of anomalous strangers—like Mr. Norris—encountered on actual trains and ships.

If as a form of prose fiction a "romance" is more likely than a novel to be set abroad or in an exotic place, then *romance*, whether "quest," picaresque, or pastoral, will suggest itself as a term to designate an indispensable element of the travel book. One could ask: aren't travel books really romances in the old sense, with the difference that the adventures are located within an actual, often famous, topography to satisfy an audience that demands it both ways—that wants to go adventuring vicariously, as it always has, but that at the same time wants to feel itself within a world declared real by such up-to-date studies as political science, sociology, anthropology, economics, and contemporary history? The proximity of the travel book to the thoroughly empirical picaresque romance, contrived from a multitude of adventures in noncausal series, can perhaps be inferred from Freya Stark's disappointment with Gertrude Bell's *Syria* (1907). She felt the book let her down: "[Bell] did not have enough adventures." (On one of her Persian explorations in 1932 Stark took along *Pilgrim's Progress*, and in Brazil an item in Fleming's travel kit was "1 copy of *Tom Jones*.") As in a romance, the modern traveler leaves the familiar and predictable to wander, episodically, into the unfamiliar or unknown, encountering strange adventures, and finally, after travail and ordeals, returns safely. Somehow, we feel a travel book isn't wholly satisfying unless the traveler returns to his starting point: the action, as in a quest romance, must be completed. We are gratified—indeed, comforted—by the "sense of an ending," the completion of the circuit, as we are at the end of Waugh's *Labels: A Mediterranean Journal* (1930) or Byron's *The Road to Oxiana* or Greene's *Journey Without Maps* (1936), where the "hero" invites us to enjoy his success in returning home.

All this is to suggest that the modern travel book is what Northrup Frye would call a myth that has been "displaced"—that is, lowered, brought

down to earth, rendered credible "scientifically"—and that the myth resembles the archetypal monomyth of heroic adventure defined by Joseph
Campbell. The myth of the hero, Campbell explains, is tripartite: first, the
setting out, the disjunction from the familiar; second, the trials of initiation and adventure; and third, the return and the hero's reintegration into
society. Even if there is no return, the monomyth still assumes tripartite
form, as in *Pilgrim's Progress*, whose title page declares that the hero's
"progress, from this world, to that which is to come" will be conceived
in three stages: "The manner of his setting out; His Dangerous Journey;
and Safe Arrival at the Desired Country." The first and last stages of the
tripartite experience tend to be moments of heightened ritual or magic,
even in entirely "secular" travel writings. Eliot understands this, and so
does Auden. Witness stanza four of Auden's "Dover" (1937):

> The eyes of departing migrants are fixed on the sea,
> Conjuring destinies out of impersonal water:
> "I see an important decision made on a lake,
> An illness, a beard, Arabia found in a bed,
>   Nanny defeated. Money."

Listening to the ship's engine as he sets out from Southampton for Spain,
V. S. Pritchett writes in *Marching Spain* (1928), "Every man who heard
those sounds must have seemed to himself as great a hero as Ulysses and
pitted against as mysterious a destiny, the strange destiny of the outward
bound." Starting on his Brazilian adventure, Peter Fleming notices something odd, which he can describe only thus: "We were through the looking-
glass." And returning is equally full of portent and mystery. Waugh threw
his champagne glass overboard in *Labels*, a gesture which, he says, "has
become oddly important to me," somehow "bound up with the turgid, indefinite feelings of homecoming." Fleming would suggest that the magical
feeling upon returning arises from moving from a form of nonexistence
back to existence, or recovering one's normal self-consciousness before
one's accustomed audience. The traveler "who has for weeks or months
seen himself only as a puny and irrelevant alien crawling laboriously over a
country in which he has no roots and no background, suddenly [on return-
ing] encounters his other self, a relatively solid and considerable figure,
with . . . a place in the minds of certain people." Or, as Auden registers
the magical act of reintegration in stanza five of "Dover,"

> Red after years of failure or bright with fame,
> The eyes of homecomers thank these historical cliffs:
> "The mirror can no longer lie nor the clock reproach;

> In the shadow under the yew, at the children's party,
>   Everything must be explained."

Indeed, the stages of the classic monomyth of the adventuring hero cannot avoid sketching an allegory of human life itself. As Campbell notes, the "call to adventure" is a figure for the onset of adolescence; adult life is "the travel"; old age, the "return." For the literary imagination, says Auden, "It is impossible to take a train or an airplane without having a fantasy of oneself as a Quest Hero setting off in search of an enchanted princess or the Waters of Life." That's why we enjoy reading travel books, even if we imagine we're enjoying only the curiosities of Liberia, British Guiana, Persia, or Patagonia. Even the souvenirs brought back so religiously by tourists are brought back "religiously." According to the anthropologist Nelson Graburn, tourists bring back souvenirs in unwitting imitation of the Grail Knight returning with his inestimable prize. Even for mass tourists, "the Holy Grail is . . . sought on the journey, and the success of a holiday is proportionate to the degree that the myth is realized."

But travel books are not merely displaced quest romances. They are also displaced pastoral romances. If William Empson is right to define traditional pastoral as a mode of presentation implying "a beautiful relation between rich and poor," then pastoral is a powerful element in most travel books, for, unless he is a *Wandervogel* or similar kind of layabout (few of whom write books), the traveler is almost always richer and freer than those he's among. He is both a plutocrat pro tem and the sort of plutocrat the natives don't mind having around. Byron and Waugh and Greene hire drivers and porters and bearers and pay outrageous prices for decrepit horses and cars; Lawrence pays bus and steamer fares; Norman Douglas keeps employed numerous waiters and *sommeliers*. If the cash nexus can be considered "a beautiful relation," the behavior of these characters is like the behavior of the court class in Renaissance pastoral, and there's a closer resemblance between Sir Philip Sidney's *Arcadia* and a modern travel book than is obvious on the surface. Consider the Lawrence of *Twilight in Italy* (1916), attended by his aristocratic consort. Consider the affectionate patronizing of the Persian peasants in Byron's dialogue involving "The Caliph of Rum." And it is with the pastoral strain in travel books that we can associate the implicit elegiac tendency of these works. Pastoral has built into it a natural retrograde emotion. It is instinct with elegy. To the degree that literary travel between the wars constitutes an implicit rejection of industrialism and everything implied by the concept "modern northern Europe," it is a celebration of a Golden Age, and recalling the

Ideal Places of Waugh, Auden, and Priestley, we can locate that Golden Age in the middle of the preceding century. One travels to experience the past, and travel is thus an adventure in time as well as distance.

"The King's life is moving peacefully to its close," the BBC announced in January 1936, invoking for this most solemn, magical moment the root metaphor of human imaginative experience, the figure of time rendered as space. If, as this essential trope persuades us, life is a journey (to the Eliot of the *Quartets*, a never-ending one), then literary accounts of journeys take us very deeply into the center of instinctive imaginative life. Like no other kinds of writing, travel books exercise and exploit the fundamental intellectual and emotional figure of thought, by which the past is conceived as back and the future as forward. They manipulate the whole alliance between temporal and spatial that we use to orient ourselves in time by invoking the dimension of space. That is, travel books make more or less conscious an activity usually unconscious. Travel books are special because the metaphor they imply is so essential. Works we recognize as somehow "classical" derive much of their status and authority from their open exploitation of this metaphor. A. E. Housman is an example:

> Into my heart an air that kills
> From yon far country blows:
> What are those blue remembered hills,
> What spires, what farms are those?
>
> That is the land of lost content,
> I see it shining plain,
> The happy highways where I went
> And cannot come again.

"When I was a young man," says Borges, "I was always hunting for new metaphors. Then I found out that good metaphors are always the same. I mean you compare time to a road, death to sleeping, life to dreaming, and those are the great metaphors in literature because they correspond to something essential." An Italian friend of Norman Douglas, indicating that his fifteen-year-old son has died of tuberculosis, says, "He has gone into that other country."

And if living and dying are like traveling, so are reading and writing. As Michel Butor points out, the eyes of the reader "travel" along the lines of print as the reader is "guided" by the writer, as his imagination "escapes" his own I Hate It Here world. Thus in reading, of all books, a travel book, the reader becomes doubly a traveler, moving from beginning to end of the book while touring along with the literary traveler. " 'O where are you going?' said the reader to rider," writes Auden in the Epilogue to *The Orators* (1932). His near rhyme implies the parallelism between reading and riding, a parallelism as suggestive as the one Connolly instinctively falls into when designating the three things his Oxford crowd in the early twenties "had a passion for": "literature, travel, and the visual arts." And writing, as Butor perceives, is like traveling. Figures of travel occupy any writer's imagination as he starts out, makes transitions, digresses, returns, goes forward, divagates, pauses, approaches the subject from a slightly different direction, and observes things from various points of view (like Norman Douglas on his eminences). Thus, as Osbert Sitwell says in *The Four Continents* (1954), "To begin a book is . . . to embark on a long and perilous voyage," but to begin a travel book "doubles the sense of starting on a journey."

Thus to speak of "literary traveling" is almost a tautology, so intimately are literature and travel implicated with each other. Any child senses this, and any adult recalling his childhood remembers moments when reading was revealed to be traveling. Peter Quennell's first awareness that he had actually learned to read occurred at the age of four or five when he was looking through bound volumes of *The Boy's Own Paper* at home. "The story I scrutinized was . . . the work of some unknown author who described an African caravan, journeying to the sound of camel-bells from oasis to oasis. Suddenly, the printed words I painfully spelt out melted into a continuous narrative, whence a procession of fascinating images emerged and wound its way across my mental landscape." Gerald Brenan's mental landscape was formed, he reports, not just by the romances of William Morris, with their "descriptions of imaginary travel," but also by Elisée Reclus's *Universal Geography* in nineteen volumes, which he discovered at school. From Reclus he gathered that "foreign countries alone offered something to the imagination," and he filled notebooks with a plan for a tour of the world "which would last, with continuous traveling, some thirty years." As a boy Robin Maugham read all his uncle's short stories set in the Far East, "and then determined," he says, "that one day I would visit the strange, exotic places about which he wrote. This I have done." A reading of Maugham also set Alec Waugh on his traveling career. "Were the South Seas really like that?" he wondered in the summer of 1926 after reading *The Moon and Sixpence* and *The Trembling of a Leaf*. "I had to find out for myself. I bought a round the world ticket that included Tahiti," and "I have been on the move ever since."

Names like Brenan, Quennell, and the Maughams suggest the next question: how serious artistically and intellectually can a travel book be? Is there not perhaps something in the genre that attracts second-rate talents? Certainly the travel book will have little generic prestige in today's atmosphere, where if you identify yourself as a "writer," everyone will instantly assume you're a novelist. The genres with current prestige are the novel and the lyric poem, although it doesn't seem to matter that very few memorable examples of either ever appear. The status of those two kinds is largely an unearned and unexamined snob increment from late-Romantic theories of imaginative art as religion-cum-metaphysics. Other kinds of works— those relegated to simple-minded categories like "the literature of fact" or "the literature of argument"—are in lower esteem artistically because the term *creative* has been widely misunderstood, enabling its votaries to vest it with magical powers. Before that word had been promoted to the highest esteem, that is, before the Romantic movement, a masterpiece was conceivable in a "non-fictional" genre like historiography or memoir or the long essay or biography or the travel book.

As recently as 1918 things were different. Fiction had not yet attained its current high status. *Ulysses* was waiting in the wings, not to appear until 1922. *À la Recherche du Temps Perdu* had not been translated. *The Magic Mountain* hadn't been written, not to mention *Les Faux-Monnayeurs, The Sound and the Fury,* and *The Sun Also Rises.* In the *Century Magazine* for February, 1918, Henry Seidel Canby felt obliged to plead for the dignity and importance of fiction, which, as an editorial in the *New York Times Review of Books* commented, the reading public was accustomed to treat with "a certain condescension." But now a similar condescension is visited on forms thought to be nonfictional. Martin Green is one who doesn't think travel books are serious. They seem to him the natural métier of the dandy. "In *Work Suspended*," he says, "Waugh portrayed himself as a writer of detective novels; in *Brideshead Revisited,* as a painter of English country houses; these occupations, and writing travel books, were the métiers of the dandies. Notably lacking in anything large-scale, even in the dandy line—not to mention anything really serious, whether political or literary-critical." Yet between the wars writing travel books was not at all considered incompatible with a serious literary career. And who would not find *Sea and Sardinia* a better book than *The Plumed Serpent,* Forster's *Alexandria* (1922) a better book than *Maurice,* Ackerley's *Hindoo Holiday* better than the collected novels of Hugh Walpole? We can hardly condescend to the travel book when it is in that genre that Robert Byron wrote a masterpiece that (in England, at least) has outlived all but a half-dozen novels of its decade.

The problem for the critic is to resist the drowsy habit of laying aside his sharpest tools when he's dealing with things that don't seem to be fiction. It takes someone more like a common reader than a critic, someone like H. M. Tomlinson, to remind us of what's going on in these "non-fictional" genres. "We know that in the literature of travel our language is very rich," he writes; "yet as a rule we are satisfied with our certainty that these books exist. . . . We surmise vaguely that a book of travel must be nearly . . . all background. . . . We shrink from the threat of the vigilance it will exact; we shall have to keep all our wits about us." In short, "We have the idle way of allowing books of travel to pass without the test to which poetry must submit." That "test," we can assume, is the test both of a complicated coherence and of a subtle mediation between texture and form, data and significant shape. Like poems—and like any successful kind of literary performance—successful travel books effect a triumphant mediation between two different dimensions: the dimension of individual physical things, on the one hand, and the dimension of universal significance, on the other. The one is Coleridge's "particular"; the other, his "general." The travel book authenticates itself by the sanction of actualities—ships, trains, hotels, bizarre customs, odd people, crazy weather, startling architecture, curious food. At the same time it reaches in the opposite direction, most often to the generic convention that the traveling must be represented as something more than traveling, that it shall assume a meaning either metaphysical, psychological, artistic, religious, or political, but always ethical. A travel book is like a poem in giving universal significance to a local texture.

The gross physicality of a travel book's texture should not lead us to patronize it, for the constant recourse to the locatable is its convention. Within that convention, as we have seen, there is ample room for the activities of the "fictionalizing" imagination. And an active, organic, and, if you will, "creative" mediation between fact and fiction is exactly the activity of the mind exhibited in the travel book, which Samuel Hynes has accurately perceived to be "a dual-plane work with a strong realistic surface, which is yet a parable." In the thirties, he understands correctly, two apparently separated modes of perception, reportage and fable, literal record and parable, tend to coalesce, and nowhere more interestingly than in the travel book. What distinguished the travel books of the thirties from earlier classics like *Eothen* (1844) or even *Travels in Arabia Deserta* (1888) is the way, Hynes says, these writers between the wars "turned their travels into interior journeys and parables of their times, making landscape and incident [and, we must add, in Byron, architecture]—the factual materials of *reportage*—do the work of symbol and myth—the materials of fable."

And since the journey is "the most insistent of 'thirties metaphors, . . . one might say that the travel books simply act out, in the real world, the basic trope of the generation." Acting out a trope, like perceiving the metaphor lodging always in the literal, is the essential act of poetry. It is also the essential act of both traveling and writing about it.

WORKS CITED

Acton, Harold. *Memoirs of an Aesthete*. London: Methuen, 1948.

Auden, W. H. *The English Auden: Poems, Essays, and Dramatic Writings*. Ed. Edward Mendelson. New York: Random House, 1977.

Borges, Jorge Luis. Interview with Ronald Christ. *Writers at Work: Fourth Series*. Ed. George Plimpton. New York: Viking, 1976, 109–46.

Brenan, Gerald. *A Life of One's Own: Childhood & Youth*. London: Hamish Hamilton, 1962.

Butor, Michel. "Travel and Writing." *Mosaic* 8, no. 1 (Fall 1974): 1–16. Reprinted in this collection.

Campbell, Joseph. *The Hero with a Thousand Faces*. 2nd ed. Princeton: Princeton UP, 1968.

Carson, Anthony. *Travels: Near and Far Out*. New York: Pantheon, 1962.

Connolly, Cyril. "Oxford in Our Twenties." In *The Evening Colonnade*. New York: Harcourt Brace Jovanovich, 1975, 8–11.

Douglas, Norman. "Arabia Deserta." In *Experiments*. New York: Robert M. McBride, 1925, 1–22.

Eliot, T. S. *Collected Poems, 1909–1935*. New York: Harcourt, Brace, 1936.

Empson, William. *Some Versions of Pastoral*. London: Chatto & Windus, 1935.

Fermor, Patrick Leigh. *A Time of Gifts: On Foot to Constantinople: From the Hook of Holland to the Middle Danube*. London: John Murray, 1977.

Fleming, Peter. *Brazilian Adventure*. London: Jonathan Cape, 1933.

———. *One's Company: A Journey to China*. London: Jonathan Cape, 1934.

Forster, E. M. *Aspects of the Novel*. London: E. Arnold, 1927.

Frye, Northrup. *Anatomy of Criticism: Four Essays*. Princeton: Princeton UP, 1957.

Graburn, Nelson H. H. "Tourism: The Sacred Journey." In *Hosts and Guests: The Anthropology of Tourism*. Ed. Valene L. Smith. Philadelphia: U of Pennsylvania P, 1977, 21–36.

Green, Martin. *Children of the Sun: A Narrative of "Decadence" in England After 1918*. New York: Basic, 1976.

Hemingway, Ernest. *Green Hills of Africa*. New York: Charles Scribner's Sons, 1935.

Housman, A. E. *The Collected Poems of A. E. Housman*. New York: Holt, Rinehart & Winston, 1940.

Howard, Michael S. *Jonathan Cape, Publisher*. London: Jonathan Cape, 1971.

Huxley, Aldous. "Wordsworth in the Tropics." In *Collected Essays*. New York: Harper & Bros., 1959, 1–10.

Hynes, Samuel. *The Auden Generation: Literature and Politics in England in the 1930's*. London: Bodley Head, 1976.

Lawrence, D. H. *The Collected Letters of D. H. Lawrence*. 2 vols. Ed. Harry T. Moore. New York: Viking, 1962.

Lodge, David. "Modernism, Antimodernism, and Postmodernism." *New Review* 4, no. 38 (May 1977): 39–44.

MacLeish, Archibald. *Collected Poems*. Boston: Houghton Mifflin, 1952.

Mailer, Norman. Interview with Steven Marcus. In *Writers at Work: Third Series*. Ed. Alfred Kazin. New York: Viking, 1967, 253–78.

Maugham, Robin. *Escape from the Shadows*. London: Hodder & Stoughton, 1972.

Mowat, Charles Loch. *Britain Between the Wars, 1918–1940*. London: Methuen, 1955.

Pearson, John. *The Sitwells: A Family's Biography*. New York: Harcourt Brace Jovanovich, 1978.

Post, Emily. *Etiquette*. 1922. Rpt. New York: Funk & Wagnalls, 1928.

Pritchett, V. S. *Marching Spain*. London: E. Benn, 1928.

Quennell, Peter. *The Marble Foot: An Autobiography*. New York: Viking, 1977

Sitwell, Osbert. *Discursions on Travel, Art and Life*. London: G. Richards, 1925.

———. *The Four Continents: Being More Discursions on Travel, Art, and Life*. London: Macmillan, 1954.

Slonimsky, Nicolas. *Music Since 1900*. 3rd ed. New York: Coleman-Ross, 1949.

Tomlinson, H. M. *Norman Douglas*. London: Chatto & Windus, 1931.

Waugh, Alec. *The Early Years of Alec Waugh*. London: Cassell, 1962.

———. *A Year to Remember: A Reminiscence of 1931*. London: W. H. Allen, 1975.

Waugh, Evelyn. *Labels: A Mediterranean Journal*. London: Duckworth, 1930.

West, Rebecca. *Black Lamb and Grey Falcon*. London: Macmillan, 1941.

Wilson, Edmund. "The Omelet of A. MacLeish." In *Night Thoughts*. 1953. Rpt. New York: Farrar, Straus & Cudahy, 1961, 84–88.

Wohl, Robert. *The Generation of 1914*. Cambridge: Harvard UP, 1979.

> > > > > > The Guidebook Industry

ROBERT FOULKE

A working definition of travel literature will circumscribe the remnant of good writing about journeys and places that survives its moment in the marketplace. What we might value in travel guidebooks cannot be so easily separated from the booming industry that sustains their proliferation, marketing, and increasingly diverse uses. As more and more guidebooks are manufactured rather than written, compiled rather than edited, designed and packaged for mass distribution rather than reviewed and evaluated, they seem to represent a triumph of consumerism in the publishing world. If the successful travel book has always achieved some balance between inner voice and outer world, the guidebook is in danger of losing voice altogether in a mass of assembled information. To get tentative bearings on some of the ephemeral works in this genre, which have seldom been subject to analysis beyond the marketing staffs of publishers, I shall very briefly survey their audiences, purposes, assumptions, structures, contents, and styles, as well as speculate about their collective future.

Those of us who care about literature are often tempted to dismiss the genre out of hand. Working with a paradigm that makes an absolute distinction between travel and tourism, Paul Fussell in *Abroad* (1980) bewails the demise of true travel, which involves discovery and misadventure, and castigates the ascendancy of tourism, a mass-produced, protected movement through "pseudo-places." Attributing part of this shift to guidebooks produced by Fielding and Fodor, Fussell, in *The Norton Book of Travel* (1987), distinguishes the nineteenth-century handbook designed for "inner-directed" travelers from the twentieth-century guidebook, "largely a celebratory adjunct to the publicity operations of hotels, resorts, and even countries."

Casting mass tourism in the image of mass transit is easy enough when we watch busloads of bored tourists unload outside the British Museum or enter the vast dining rooms of specially built hotels along the Dalmatian coast. In a recent piece in the London *Guardian* called "The Quest for Reality," Fussell observes that "the tourist is at all times attended by his guides, couriers, and tour directors, lecturing at him, telling him things, and assiduously insulating him from abroad, its surprises, mysteries, and threats." It is easy to confirm such observations in almost any Sunday travel section, particularly in Britain, where the original Cooks tours spawned the glut of packages now dominating most segments of the travel industry. A recent ski preview in the *Sunday Times* entitled "Snowflake Survey," for example, evaluated the major tour operators in minute detail, discussed the adequacy of their "snow guarantees," and printed reader reports. When the destination airport of a return trip was made less convenient for one reader, she asserted that "it was the worst experience of travelling I have ever had," and another judged his tour to be "expensive and miserable" because of "booking problems, burnt porridge, and dinner not served until 9.30 p.m." Such complaints encourage us to accept one of Fussell's central observations—"the tourist is wholly protected from contingency, which might be taken to mean protected from life"—though the passengers who were on board the *Achille Lauro* might not agree.

Tourist bashing, like the object of its scorn, is a cliché among literate travel writers, as Fussell and other commentators acknowledge, and he is very careful to survey some common ground shared by tourism and genuine travel. But the distinction between travel books by and for the elect and guidebooks for the mass of the damned is still flawed, and the analogies built on it will not hold. In C. K. Ogden's terms, perhaps the distinction should be expressed as a scale rather than an either/or cut. The English language provides us with a wide spectrum of terms for those who wander about the world: heroes, pilgrims, and explorers, whom we admire and sometimes emulate; voyagers, travelers, tourists, wanderers, or wayfarers, whom we might join; vagabonds, tramps, and fugitives, whom we usually avoid or hunt down. The modernist bias of many commentators compresses that range of purposes and attitudes into the confines of a world-spread wasteland, where the only appropriate response is irony. After quoting E. M. Forster on the end of the age of independent travel, Fussell observes, in his *Guardian* article, that "the mass production inevitable in the late-industrial age had generated its own travel-spawn, tourism, which is to travel as plastic is to wood."

Yet group travel for purposes other than warfare, diplomacy, or trade is not exclusively a modern phenomenon. Lionel Casson, in *Travel in the Ancient World* (1974), notes that "from about 1500 B.C. on, we can discern in Egypt sure signs of tourism" in groups of scribes visiting the tombs and temples then a millennium old, and that there is evidence of collecting souvenirs and bargain shopping abroad from the same period. Travelers in the ancient world often banded together for mutual protection, and pilgrimages became the grand tours of the medieval world, complete with sociability and trinkets to take home. Conversely, modern touring is only partly prepackaged "tourism," and many guidebooks are aimed quite precisely at those who travel alone, pursuing their own interests. These tourists are not herds who need the constant solace of friendly guides and fixed arrangements: they buy guidebooks for information to direct themselves, much as their nineteenth-century predecessors did. Relegating what we don't like to tourism and salvaging the remnant for travel can become a reflex verbal putdown, and a rather patrician one at that.

The various kinds of books travelers might want to read before setting out on a journey all spin around some axis of information about place, so there is still a point in distinguishing the purposes of guidebooks from those of travel narratives. Much of what is valuable in the latter—a marked personal voice, melding of past and present, originality of perception, vividness in character sketches, economy in anecdote and dialogue, and an unobtrusive but compelling narrative flow—is either unobtainable or irrelevant in guidebooks. Most of these features argue for the permanent literary value of the travel narrative, a replacement for the experience of travel itself. Guidebooks are denied permanence and fluidity of form, and they experiment with idiosyncratic personal voice at great risk. Good ones must be up to date, accurate in detail, responsible in using sources, authenticated by the writer's direct experience, selective yet reasonably comprehensive, clearly focused, analytic in structure, organized for quick reference, and easy to read. The best also have a style that sharpens seeing and encourages imaginative reflection. Like many things needed in practical living, they are designed to be used and discarded when obsolete.

In the most elementary sense, the guidebook has always been a cheap, portable, and convenient substitute for a living guide, who may be more or less competent, reliable, avaricious, or lazy. (Thus the mass tourist, who is supplied with a surfeit of guides, lecturers, and arrangers, has no need of one.) The guidebook has been around for a long time. In a chapter entitled "Baedeker of the Ancient World" in *Travel in the Ancient World*, Lionel Casson reminds us that Pausanius, who spent twenty years in the second century A.D. writing a *Guidebook of Greece*, had many precedents in the fourth and third centuries B.C., including Diodorus, Heliodorus, and Polemo of Ilium. The guidebook has a long history because it serves fundamental needs: it provides a means of orientation, bringing readers to the top of a cathedral dome or campanile for a panoramic survey of an unfamiliar city. In this sense the guidebook is a verbal map comparable to the sailor's *periplus*, originally an oral compendium of navigation. The periplus redacted to text in the fourth century B.C. may have been the first guidebook of the Mediterranean; it told sailors what landmarks to watch for and what difficulties to expect in unfamiliar places. Within the nautical context, that tradition remains continuous for more than two millennia through routiers, mirrors of the sea, pilots, and charts, an evolution perhaps best represented as a passion for accuracy and perspective, information articulated for seeing. Nineteenth-century British Admiralty charts are still the best guide to some Greek waters because their margins are illuminated with meticulous steel engravings showing what landfalls will look like from various approaches.

Ashore, the work of British land surveyors provides climbers with the most graphic orientation to Aetna's many volcanic mouths, just as superbly shaded Swiss and German maps make us see the configuration of the Alps in new ways. Like nautical pilots and representations of mountain topography, which have similar purposes, guidebooks map in words, constrained always by the need to position us in space. They also have a temporal dimension that connects places with events and persons. Even the crassest examples are instructive: no visit to the Tower of London could be fully articulated without knowledge of who had been imprisoned or butchered there. That need for orientation to the human record is not dependent upon the traveler's openness to new experience, alertness, lack of distraction, or imagination. Visitors cannot invent associations of place or simply will to see them; lacking a Beefeater, they must turn to a guidebook. Reductive definitions of guidebooks as mere collections of boilerplate prose about places or substitutes for genuine experience miss precisely this point: without a core of information, there is no seeing.

If the guidebook spins on an axis of information and is in fact ephemeral and consumable—it is a common practice to rip out the relevant sections of fat European annuals and discard the rest as a husk—why do people collect old Baedekers, put Blue Guides on reference shelves, or read Jan Morris on cities they have no intention of visiting? Part of the motive may lie in the fascination of place itself, as the history of landscape painting attests, and part in the renewed interest in social and cultural history. The controlling assumptions of guidebooks offer an index to why people travel as well as where they want to go. In 1954, a passage by Norman D. Ford, which might have been written by Ford Madox Ford's John Dowell, provides an unwitting parody of early postwar assumptions: "Simply stated, the purpose of this book is to help you see the best sights in Europe via the best itineraries while staying at the best hotels, eating at the best restaurants, drinking at the best bars, spending the evenings in the best night spots of your choice, and buying the best gifts and souvenirs in the best shops." The 1959–60 edition of Temple Fielding's annual, the one my parents used on their first trip to Europe, closes with an equally telling "L'Envoi":

> I hope that your trip gave you pleasure beyond price—that you had happiness and a bounty of thrills—that it will always pay you off in the currency of cobwebs and dreams. I hope, too, that both Europe and this little book were faithful when called upon for your friendship. . . . But let's share a last secret. Now that we've slipped off our shoes, hung up our clothes, taken a real American shower, raided that familiar refrigerator, and sat down to relax—isn't it wonderful to be able to say those magic words "I'm home again"?

Norman Ford might not have known what he was saying, but Temple Fielding certainly did; he had been inventing the American postwar guide for a dozen years. Thirty years later, his successor, Joe Raff, writes to substantially the same audience, though with slightly more restraint: "Europe is a different creature every year. Economies waver, democracies are born, coronations occur, borders open or close, fads evolve—but always with a pageantry, a zest and a glamour that makes Europe the ultimate travel destination." Other recent guides are even more careful to entice an audience without insulting its intelligence. R. W. Apple, Jr., states his case directly: "Wherever possible, I have looked for the offbeat, the out-of-the-way, the places that the locals know about but visitors often do not. It seems to me that too many Americans save their money for a big trip to Europe only to find themselves steered, by ignorant travel agents or careless tourist operators, into places that exist largely for foreigners. This book is an attempt to do something about that." Michael Spring also begins a recent guidebook with disarming simplicity: "I wrote this guide for those of you who hate rubbing suitcases with strangers on guided tours, but who need help in deciding where to go and how to organize your time."

Spring's final phrase reflects a central preoccupation of European guidebooks for the past century: the traveler, unlike his Victorian predecessor, had no vast colonnades of time to fill during several years of the grand tour, so the guidebook had to help him use what time he had efficiently. Baedeker's *Greece* (1894) begins with "practical hints" suggesting that "a journey to Greece no longer ranks with those exceptional favours of fortune which fall to the lot of but few individuals" and then describes how one can get from London to Athens in just sixty hours. By the fifties, counting hours had extended from transportation to touring itself and had become an obsession in American guidebooks, leading to absurdly compressed itineraries. Frederic Tyarks's *Europe on a Shoestring* (1954) lists "tourist magnets of the first order" throughout the whole of Western Europe in less than two pages, with the following explanation: "In the list below are none of the time wasting suggestions often mentioned by people who know each country overly well but who unconsciously neglect the problems of an American vacationist with none too much time on his hands." In "Tips on Highspots," the 1959–60 Fielding guide carries the same impulse to extremes with an elaborate set of charts, allocating cities one to five days and countries no less than two nor more than ten days. Readers are invited to interpret the chart through a schematic key:

$	Costs Comparatively High	L	Local Color
c	Costs Comparatively Low	Q	Specialized Interests
C	Outstanding Cultural Interest	R	Strictly Routine
E	Excursion Only, Not Overnight	S	Scenic Interest
H	Especially Hospitable to	T	Tourist Trap Atmosphere
	Americans	X	Americans Swarm in Season
J	Outstanding Joie de Vivre		

In this scheme the whole of Baedeker's Greece gets four days, two of which are spent in Athens, while Corinth, Delos, Delphi, Mycenae, Olympia, and Santorini rate only excursions. Such timetables parody themselves, but they do respond, however crudely and mechanically, to the realities of jet-age short trips during which, to paraphrase John Fowles, time can no longer be written firmly adagio. R. W. Apple recognizes this new time signature in his opening chapter on packing light, which no Victorian traveler did, and is not embarrassed to make the following comment about visiting Seville, Cordoba, and Granada: "One could easily spend three days in each place without boredom, but five or six days is enough to gain a good feeling for all three."

Like their live counterparts, most guidebooks advise travelers on the mechanics of travel—lodging, food, local transportation, and the like. On the one hand this is the most mundane of the guidebook's tasks, on the other, the trickiest; some of the most respected series, like the Blue Guides and Michelin Greens, opt out of such duties because they want to concentrate on sightseeing. Most of the big American annuals— such as Fielding, Fodor, and Frommer—are structured around the mechanics, defending their honesty and judgment with varying degrees of fervor. In 1959–60

Temple Fielding devoted five full pages to authenticating his work, including very earnest disclaimers: "This book is 100% independent and 100% clean. In its making, we stick by one inflexible rule *always*: no commissions, rake-offs, cuts, kickbacks, or outside compensation in any form— from *anybody*." By 1990, Joe Raff is far more relaxed: "Certainly you will not agree with all of the evaluations, but then, that is what subjectivity is in an impressionistic world." Such disclaimers were assumed rather than expressed in earlier guidebooks. Baedeker's 1894 *Greece* offers "practical hints" on lodging and food, most notably the problems of finding accommodation beyond the main cities:

> At other places in the interior the accommodation for travellers is still of the scantiest description, unless they have the good fortune to bear introductions ensuring the hospitality of some of the well-to-do natives. The inns, sometimes calling themselves *Xenodochia*, but generally content with the humbler title of *Khans*, are usually miserable cottages, with a kitchen and one large common-sleeping-room; nowadays some of them all possess a few separate rooms, which are, however, destitute of furniture, glass windows, and fire-places. . . . The greatest drawbacks the civilized traveller finds in these houses are the dirt and the vermin, which cause many so extreme an annoyance, that their keen enthusiasm in treading classic soil and their deep admiration for Greek scenery become seriously impaired.

Even if this passage lacks the details more recent guidebooks would include—such as pages listing each miserable cottage one by one—it conveys a clear sense of authenticity: Baedeker was there.

In dealing with more civilized territory, the 1900 Baedeker *London* does provide an elaborate list of recommended restaurants, but only after this summary judgment of British cuisine:

> English cookery, which is as inordinately praised by some epicures and *bon vivants* as it is abused by others, has at least the merit of simplicity, so that the quality of the food one is eating is not so apt to be disguised as it is on the Continent. Meat and fish of every kind are generally excellent in quality at all the better restaurants, but the visitor accustomed to Continental fare may discern a falling off in the soups, vegetables, and sweet dishes. At the first-class restaurants the cuisine is generally French; the charges are high, but everything is sure to be good of its kind.

Six decades later the 1966 Baedeker *Great Britain* notes deterioration, but still risks summary judgment:

English cooking, renowned through Europe in the 18th century, has been gradually losing its reputation during the last hundred years. The English-man himself grumbles as much about his food as about the weather, the former apparently as unchangeable as the latter. Nevertheless, English cooking has at least the merit of simplicity, and the raw materials at the cook's disposal are unsurpassed. It is still possible to obtain meals of inimitable quality in England, at private houses and in certain city restaurants and a few country hotels, at commensurate charges. But middle-grade restaurants with good country dishes at moderate prices are far rarer than in continental countries. Somerset Maugham said that to eat well in England one must breakfast three times a day.

The reconstituted and redesigned Baedekers from Prentice-Hall, left purposely dateless to keep them current, mention food not at all and reduce lodging lists to category labels and numbers of beds.

This new Baedeker series is even more interesting as an index of changes in the amount and kinds of information guidebooks provide. The front matter on each country has changed very little in scope, though it now has a different focus. The geography section of the 1913 *Spain and Portugal*, for example, contains nearly a full page on vegetation, which is replaced by sections on geology and climate in the modern edition. The difference in style between 1913 and 198? is more telling, indicating a shift from the slightly fulsome to the flaccid:

> No country has more natural variety than Portugal. On the coast far-projecting promontories (*cabos*) of naked rock alternate with large dunes. The lezirias of the Tagus and the lagoons of Aveiro recall the marshes of Holland. The mountains of N. Portugal and the Serrada Estrella attain an almost Alpine altitude; the rich wine-district of the Douro, with its terraces toilsomely wrung from the clayey soil, reproduces the rocky slopes of the Rhine. The valley of the Tagus near Abrantes recalls the Elbe at Dresden. Lisbon vies in beauty of position with Naples. Coimbra, the Portuguese Athens, gazes down on the banks of the Mondego, famous in history and song. Oporto sits in majesty on the N. bank of the Douro. (1913)

> The Portuguese mainland has an enormously long Atlantic coastline, the finest parts of which are to be found at its climatically favoured southern end, in the Algarve with its beautiful sandy beaches and rugged cliffs. The country's cosmopolitan capital, Lisbon, on the broad estuary of the Tagus, is one of the most strikingly situated cities in the world. In the interior of the country, too, there are numbers of interesting and attractive

towns, villages and old monasteries and a wide range of varied and beautiful scenery—hills, valleys and plateaux—in every region of Portugal; and there is a special interest in getting to know this country which is now preparing to become a member of the European Economic Community. (198?)

Shifts in coverage between old and new Baedekers reveal, almost without exception, compression and elimination, as well as changes in focus. The 1894 *Greece* devoted six pages of small type to Ithaka, complete with Homeric references, and two pages to climbing routes up Parnassos. In the new edition Ithaca rates less than a page of large type, and Parnassos even less, with emphasis on the ski lifts at the top. This kind of shrinkage had begun to occur even before the new Prentice-Hall issues. The 1900 *London* has eleven pages of fine print on St. Paul's, including identification of all the major monuments, and nine on Hampton Court, with a detailed inventory of the contents of each room; by 1966, St. Paul's had been compressed into half a page and Hampton Court to a page and a map. Fodor's 1990 *Europe's Great Cities* confirms the general trend toward streamlining information to prevent overload for jet-age travelers: St. Paul's, within the city, gets two-thirds of a page of fine print, while Hampton Court, apparently beyond the pale of harried businessmen, disappears entirely, except as a terminus for a Thames cruise. It is not clear how much these changes reflect reduced publishing budgets, flagging curiosity in the audience, or both, but they are consonant with the short attention span and restlessness assumed by contemporary media specialists.

Not only the quantity and kind of information, but the whole function of description in guidebooks may be in question. As rapid changes in technology have replaced pages with screens and put pages on screens, making them soft and pliable, the force of verbal mapping at the core of guidebooks may have waned or simply altered in nature. Yet the integrity of style as a way of seeing remains if we listen to three passages on Bath:

Bath, the leading winter resort in Britain and the largest city in Somerset, with a mild and sedative climate, is situated in the deep and sheltered valley of the river *Avon* and on the slopes of the surrounding hills. . . . Unrivalled in the English provinces for its combination of architectural, social, and scenic interest, Bath is largely a city of squares, crescents, and terraces, built in a substantial Palladian style in Bath stone and rising tier above tier to heights of 600 ft. An incomparable example of 18th c. architecture and town planning, it owes its external appearance to the architects John Wood (d. 1754) and his son of the same name (d. 1782), who worked under the patronage of Ralph Allen, leaving many details to the local builders. (Baedeker, *Great Britain*, 1966)

Bath has never been a great city at all, and stands provincially aloof to the European mainstream. . . . Bath too [like the Severn] is small, inconsequential, and altogether English. It is true that the Romans, exploiting the hot springs in this valley made Aquae Sulis one of the best-known of their colonial spas, and that the medieval Abbey, like all the great English churches, grew up in close communion with its peers across the Channel. But Bath itself, Bath of the Georgian splendours, Bath of the golden stones of the Pump Room minuet, the Bath that Jane Austen knew and loathed, that Sheridan eloped from, that Gainsborough learnt his art in, that Clive, Nelson, Pope and Mrs. Thrale retreated to—Bath of the Bath buns and the Bath chairs, Bath of the dowagers, Bath that greets the visitor terraced and enticing as the train swings into Spa Station down Brunel's line from Paddington—the Bath of persistent legend is a Somerset borough of the middle rank, rather bigger than Annecy, say, about the size of Delft. Its contacts with the greater world have been frequent, but tangential. (Jan Morris, *Among the Cities*, 1985)

Bath has been there, astride the Avon, clinging to the hillsides, for more than two thousand years. . . . The city's golden era came, however, in the late eighteenth century, when a succession of gifted architects gave it a Georgian splendour and order—a kind of serenity in stone—that happily survives. . . . If there [in the Pump Room] on a weekday morning, sit at one of the tables in the vast room, with its Corinthian columns, and order coffee. You will find yourself surrounded by a vanishing culture of innocence: a string trio on the stage, with potted palms on the balcony above their heads, playing show tunes; a brace of elderly gentlewomen at the next table, complaining about change; and from his niche on the back wall, Beau Nash watching imperturbably. (R. W. Apple, *Apple's Europe*, 1986)

Each reader must ask, "Which Bath do I see?" and each traveler might answer, "All three."

Such an answer begs the question, however, because it avoids the complications of what current jargon calls "information overload." How to handle the traveler's need for information is the principal dilemma of those who write and publish modern guidebooks. The sheer quantity of information desired is staggering, both in geographical scope and in special subjects. With virtually the whole world in purview as a destination for touring, and with almost every activity from chasing butterflies or collecting Indian artifacts to white-water rafting or mountain trekking of possible interest, travel guidebooks have lost any natural outer boundaries. Gone are the old guidelines decreeing that "complete" guidebooks need touch only familiar bases of information on weather, visas, local customs, lodging, dining, nightlife, shopping, transportation, currency, prices, and more or less generous doses of background on history, culture, architecture, museums, and ancient sites. The hunger for information has led to fragmentation of the guidebook model. In a 1987 article in *Publisher's Weekly*, Gayle Feldman observed, "All booksellers agree, in fact, that more and more independent travelers—and those are the people who more than most buy guidebooks—are looking for books with a narrower focus." The trend toward specialization is represented in a random sample of 1987 issues—the Blue Guide's *Victorian Architecture in Britain*, John Muir's *Indian America: A Traveler's Companion*, Globe Pequot's *American Institute of Architects Guide to Boston*, or Hunter's *Eperon's French Wine Tour*.

Expansion and fragmentation of content are matched by dispersion of form. Travel guides have always come in odd shapes, sizes, and colors—from long, thin Michelin greens and reds to Baedeker guides for large pockets and American Express and Berlitz guides for small ones. External packaging and internal design, however, are increasingly important marketing tools as a flood of new titles overwhelms limited shelf space in bookstores. Frommer reportedly will spend two million dollars redesigning its series in the next several years.

Recognizing that many travelers never reach the bookstores, publishers are marketing through direct mail, special sales, book warehouse outlets, and special interest stores. In content, some guidebooks, like those in the Birnbaum series, share material with travel magazines, and others have connections with travel newsletters or travel videos. Some forms of travel narrative, like adventure travel, are linked to tours, reminding us of all the anomalies built into prepackaged and guided "adventure" in exotic terrain, where one can travel up New Guinea rivers in perfect air-conditioned luxury or take a comfortable cruise to Antarctica. There is also a curious split consciousness in this reinvented genre, which includes both books keyed to specific tours, pioneered by Banana Republic, and reissues of nineteenth-century classic travel narratives that have no connection with guidebooks, like those in the Atlantic Monthly Press Traveler Series. New media also threaten the long-term viability of guidebooks in interesting ways: travel videos, pioneered by eager chambers of commerce and placed in house on hotel TV channels, for instance, visually encapsulate the content of a guidebook. The demand for up-to-date information in an industry that has a normal lead time of nine months suggests that the guidebook of the future may be an on-line computer directory.

The guidebook writer faces a multitude of problems beyond a perennial lack of clout with publishers, underpayment and an inability to control the shape of the final product, which is largely determined by salesmen rather than editors. Some are caught in the twentieth-century version of Grub Street, as more guidebooks are assembled from disparate, geographically separable parts. In these conditions the "writer" is given a territory, a formula, and a fixed fee, becoming a word processor in the worst sense of that term, and not a wholly reliable one at that. (One offer I know of asked for copy in two months; when the prospective writer objected that there would be no time to visit sites, she was told, "that doesn't matter, just call them.")

In an age of publisher buyouts, writers still fortunate enough to earn royalties must face conglomerate lawyers to negotiate increasingly complex contracts or pay those agents who are willing to deal with travel books up to 15 percent commission. They must also struggle against the shift from list price to "net price after expenses" as the basis for royalties, which places the burden of risk that publishers used to take squarely on writers. They also suffer the vagaries of unpredictable royalties because the computer-controlled stocking of major chains like B. Dalton or Waldenbooks has further reduced the limited, seasonal shelf life of guidebooks and made it easy to return them after a scant forty to sixty days. Thus guidebook writers face special difficulties in keeping their work on the shelves and are often dismayed at the delicate balance between sales and returns on royalty statements.

Most of all, guidebook writers face massive overhead problems in financing the travel necessary to produce a good book, because neither adequate advances nor subsidies are usually available for books, though they often are for articles. And even if it is available, subsidized travel has become the storm center of swirling debate among travel writers and editors. A recent article in the *Condé Nast Traveler* carried the subhead: "Paul Grimes, tagging along on a subsidized tour, finds that when the writer goes free, the reader often gets taken." In the next issue, however, Janet Groene, a well-known free-lance writer, responded: "If Paul Grimes has a *Condé Nast Traveler* expense account, he too travels free." As turmoil in the publishing world continues, none of these problems is likely to disappear, though the free-lance guidebook writer might.

The guidebook may never have been a many-splendored thing, but it did have less protean forms for many generations of travelers. There were also more or less accepted standards by which to judge it: accuracy of detail, a refusal to crib from other guides, few overblown descriptive passages, some control over the amount of information presented, clear organization for reference, and a lively but unaffected style. Guidebook writers have always had difficulty with the latter, trying to find at least an echo of the distinguishing inner voice of travel narratives while presenting obligatory information and avoiding tonal pitfalls ranging from excessive sanguinity to Puritan earnestness, or the self-parody implicit in both. When the "writer" is really a team working for hire to compile a volume, as is often the case in many major series, these problems are exacerbated. It remains unclear whether rapid mutations in the guidebook will produce new forms, each with its own possibilities for usefulness and excellence, or whether it will disintegrate into a set of amorphous products for specialized consumption.

WORKS CITED

Apple, R. W., Jr. *Apple's Europe: An Uncommon Guide.* New York: Atheneum, 1986.

Baedeker, Karl. *Great Britain.* Vol. 1: *Southern England, East Anglia; Handbook for Travellers.* 10th ed. Freiburg, London, and New York: Karl Baedeker, George Allen & Unwin, and Macmillan, 1966.

———. *Greece: Handbook for Travellers.* 2nd rev. ed. Leipsic and London: Karl Baedeker & Dulau, 1894.

———. *London and Its Environs: Handbook for Travellers.* 12th rev. ed. Leipsic: Karl Baedeker, 1900.

———. *Spain and Portugal: Handbook for Travellers.* 4th ed. Leipsic, London, and New York: Karl Baedeker, George Allen & Unwin, and Charles Scribner's Sons, 1913.

Baedeker's Greece. Englewood Cliffs, N.J.: Prentice-Hall, n.d.

Baedeker's Portugal. Englewood Cliffs, N.J.: Prentice-Hall, n.d. (198?).

Casson, Lionel. *Travel in the Ancient World.* London: George Allen & Unwin, 1974.

Chrichton, Jean. "Travel USA." *Publisher's Weekly,* 4 May 1990, 17–30.

Feldman, Gayle. "The Widening World of Travel Books." *Publisher's Weekly,* 13 February 1987, 31–57.

Fielding, Temple. *Fielding's Travel Guide to Europe.* 1959–60 ed. New York: William Sloan, 1959.

Fodor's 90. *Europe's Great Cities: A Complete Guide to 20 Cities*. New York: Fodor's Travel, 1990.

Ford, Norman D. *Where to Stay, Eat and Sleep in Western Europe*. Greenlawn, N.Y.: Harian, 1954.

Fussell, Paul. *Abroad: British Literary Traveling Between the Wars*. New York: Oxford UP, 1980.

———. "The Quest for Reality." *The Guardian*, London, 18 October 1990, 21–22. Condensed from "Travel, Tourism, and 'International Understanding,' " in *Killing in Verse and Prose and Other Essays*. London: Bellew, 1990, 148–73.

Fussell, Paul, ed. *The Norton Book of Travel*. New York: W. W. Norton, 1987.

Grimes, Paul. "Travel Writing with Fear and Favor." *Condé Nast Traveler*, April 1989, 70–80.

Groene, Janet. "Letters: Truth in Travel." *Condé Nast Traveler*, May 1989, 11.

Morris, Jan. *Among the Cities*. New York: Oxford UP, 1985.

Raff, Joseph. *Fielding's Europe 1990*. New York: William Morrow, 1990.

"Snowflake Survey." *Sunday Times*, London, 14 October 1990, 5.11.

Spring, Michael. *Great European Itineraries*. New York: Doubleday, 1987.

Tyarks, Frederic E. *Europe on a Shoestring*. Greenlawn, N.Y.: Harian, 1953.

‹ ‹ ‹ ‹ ‹ ‹

American Detours

> > > > > > **Romancing the Facts
in American
Travel Writing**

TERRY CAESAR

By chapter seven of *Death in the Afternoon* (1932), Ernest Hemingway is ready to describe a bullfight. He doesn't. Instead he begins, "At this point it is necessary that you see a bullfight," and then explains in the following way:

> There are two sorts of guide books; those that are read before and those
> that are to be read after and the ones that are to be read after the fact are
> bound to be incomprehensible to a certain extent before; if the fact is of
> enough importance in itself. . . . there comes a place in the guide book
> where you must say do not come back until you have skied, had sexual
> intercourse, shot quail or grouse, or been to the bullfight so that you will
> know what we are talking about. So from now on it is inferred that you
> have been to the bullfight.

It would appear on the basis of the way Hemingway situates his reader here that he is not, whatever else, writing a guidebook. As Paul Fussell notes, "A travel book, at its purest, is addressed to those who do not plan to follow the traveler at all." A guidebook, in contrast, is addressed to those who do plan to follow its author.

The guidebook model, however, is not so easily banished from Hemingway's text. He concludes *Death in the Afternoon* with an eighty-page glossary of bullfight terminology, followed by several pages of dates when bullfights are normally held in the various parts of the world. And all this practical annotation and data clarifies the purpose of many passages in the main body of the text which precedes them—notations on the best bullfight to see first or the best route by road from Seville to Madrid, criticisms of previous books on Spain, descriptions of the Spanish countryside and so on. Hemingway has written a guidebook.

Or rather, he has written on the model of a guidebook in order to produce what one may call a travel book. The artfully personal, idiosyncratic presence of the author, within an accommodating framework of anecdote and memoir, is clear from the very first page of *Death in the Afternoon*, and this framework (as Fussell also suggests) easily makes available the sort of essayistic asides that characterize travel books just as much as the manner in which they authenticate themselves by actualities. In one chapter, for example, Hemingway romps into a mock-sermon—complete with a dialogue between himself and an old lady—about the dangers of syphilis. In another (again with the old lady for comic relief) he reminisces about the various horrors of death under the guise of "a natural history of the dead." "If I could have made this enough of a book it would have had everything in it," Hemingway begins his last chapter, which proceeds to range freely over the sights, sounds, human texture, and irretrievable memories of the whole Spanish landscape, until the following, very canny conclusion: "No. It is not enough of a book, but still there were a few things to be said. There were a few practical things to be said." It is a beautifully polished performance. I believe no better example of travel writing has been done by an American author in this century. One crucial reason for this is that Hemingway derives his supple and distinctive form from the static and predictable model of the guidebook. Of the various kinds of book *Death in the Afternoon* engages, none proves more influential than the guidebook.

The model of the guidebook—more often the anti-model, whether explicitly invoked or not—appears everywhere in American travel writing since 1915. "Having begun my book with the statement that Morocco still lacks a guidebook, I should have wished to take a step toward remedying that deficiency," writes Edith Wharton in her preface to *In Morocco* (1920). She fails, however, and writes, more or less, a travel book—though two of her concluding sections (a "sketch" of Moroccan history and a "note" on Moroccan architecture) best disclose the practical purpose of her initial project. William Carlos Williams, on the other hand, so disdains guidebook accuracy in *A Voyage to Pagany* (1928) that he gets Santa Croce confused with the Duomo in Florence, has Dante buried in the wrong city, and writes the following sort of thing: "But there—just there the delight of Venice got him. Venice is Venice. It has no antiquity, really; they were just swampy islands; and no future; just a middle greatness of ships. And now it lies like an artificial pearl in a modern shop window. Fragile, useless; used for international swimming lessons."

Yet disdain did not constitute the only form of American response to the guidebook. There was also the literary rejoinder of parody, one whose loony, burlesque quality is suggested in Williams's last phrase here. The straightforward practicalities of the guidebook prose (and pose) against which Williams writes can easily be imagined. They have not changed very much since the twenties and thirties although, as with any utilitarian writing, they become obsolete once their original purpose expires. We can further assume, merely from the spoofs, squibs, and sport from this period still readily available today, something of the influence the guidebook model had in these two decades, when it still claimed more or less exclusive sway about what was abroad and how one should travel there.

The readiest examples can be found in various collections by Robert Benchley. Consider the conclusion to his essay, "Browsing Through the Passport": "Of course, this reading over of a passport will not take up all the time between quarantine and the pier. You will still have opportunity to walk around the deck eight or ten times and go back to your stateroom to pick up the things you forgot to pack. But it will help to while away a little of the tedium, and also may make you more reconciled to staying home next summer." Benchley mimics here the instructional earnestness of the guidebook, ever anxious that there may be some time in a traveler's itinerary that is not calibrated. In another piece, "How to Travel in Peace," after romping through various possibilities for avoiding the distractions and the boors to which oceanic transportation is heir, Benchley concludes: "However it worked out, you would have had a comparatively peaceful voyage, and no price is too high to pay for escaping the horrors that usually attend commuting across the Atlantic Ocean." Besides the distinctively American note of dismissing the value of travel itself, Benchley again fixes on a subject guidebooks do not discuss and (albeit more implicitly here) uses it to mock the subjects they do, as well as, by extension, the dutiful readers of these subjects.

What to do with such people? Benchley has a lively send-up, in "French for Americans," of the "language tips" that were a standard feature of guidebooks by the thirties. The very idea of such a parody cuts into the unstated ideal of personal development, not to say ethical cultivation, that the careful itinerary of the guidebook holds forth as the ultimate justification of travel. Alas for Benchley, these people could not be kept home, and so their insufferably acquired mock-sophistication upon their return is something with which he is forced to come to grips. "Throwing Back the European Offensive" proposes that since "very few travelers know anything more about the places they have visited than the names of one hotel, two points of interest, and perhaps one street," someone who did not go to Europe last summer can "bluff them into insensibility by making up a name and asking them if they saw that when they were in Florence."

It is not my intention to survey all this parody. One of its most compelling instances, even today, is Walcott Gibbs's *Bird Life at the Pole* (1931). In it the ostensible author, "Commander" Christopher Robin, is contacted in the first chapter (concerning "the strange relationship between publicity and poles") by the newspaper magnate, Mr. Herbst. Herbst wishes to have Robin explain the grand prospects of "polar exploration in the terms of the man in the street." Robin's crew includes a glamorous woman and two cameramen. There is little clear sense to the dispatches Robin sends back to Herbst or what Herbst is doing with them. At the Pole the explorers discover that they have been preceded by Popular Polar Tours, Inc. Only at the end does Robin understand that the whole trip has been the inspiration for a love-and-adventure feature film which, of course, fantastically misrepresents everything that has happened.

Gibbs, I think, is only incidentally parodying tourism. He simply takes it for granted that travel has been thoroughly commodified. But it does not seem—yet—to have been thoroughly misrepresented, a job movies can be trusted to accomplish better. Any such falsification could not have been successful, perhaps even quite conceivable, however, had travel not been first transposed into a higher key and reborn as Adventure. Furthermore, it is arguable that the adventure text is inseparable from that of the guidebook, which envisions travel as collective, functional, and predictable, all qualities exactly the opposite of adventure. One can see the nature of the relay between tourism and adventure in Richard Halliburton's *The Royal Road to Romance* (1925), one of the most popular travel books of any kind ever published in the United States.

Halliburton and his one friend arrive in New Delhi, "ticketless as usual." The trees are flaming, the stars hang like lamps in the heavens, and so on. Lying in bed on his first night, Halliburton muses: "What was to come now? Whither would the road to romance lead me?—to Kabul, as I hoped?—or to Argentina? It gave me no small satisfaction to realize that this question could not be answered, and it was just as well, for had I known then what adventures I was to have in another ten months I should not have slept a wink that night." He and his friend are off before sun-up the next morning, and make a complete tour of all the "sights." The "famous" Kartub Tower is first—"its great height and odd conical shape cause it to be visited by every tourist that comes to Delhi." There are four hundred pages of this sort of thing. Eventually Halliburton climbs Mt. Fuji. He ends: "There is no place like home."

Here and nearly everywhere, Halliburton sees and values the same sights as a tourist. The only difference is that he responds to them—and to his experience of getting to and from them—in an entirely different emotional register. When Halliburton mentions something specifically he either resorts to guidebook literalism (as above) or effuses in language taken from a venerable repository of romantic formulas and cliches. Halliburton appears to have become aware of this, as well as of his own ambiguous identity (as both "vagabond" and "journalist" in his first book) and of the uncertain nature of the travel texts he can produce.

His next book, *The Glorious Adventure* (1927), is organized around the travels of Ulysses, although the pattern is most seriously disrupted when he gets smitten by an English girl. His next after that, *New Worlds to Conquer* (1929), forms a bizzare account of how he tried to recreate famous "imaginative exploits" (swimming the Panama Canal, donning the uniform of a prisoner on Devil's Island, even dressing up as Robinson Crusoe on Tobago—all complete with pictures). After his accidental death by drowning just before the onset of World War II, his mother edited a collection of his letters home. In one of them he writes:

> I've thought over your Oxford suggestion seriously and can foresee what would happen. I'd become academic and critical and self-conscious and write refined essays that nobody would read and anybody else could write as well, and I'd lose the one thing that makes me individual—zest and illusions. . . . I must fight an over-artistic conscience and keep my faith in the popularity and value of romanticism.

This disclaimer does more than simply maintain an excellent distinction between the adventure writer and the travel writer (with the latter writing or aspiring to write "refined essays"). It also expresses a faith in the "romantic" illusions that were crucial for a traveler such as Halliburton because his world was imperiled by *facts*. What facts? The kind enshrined in guidebooks that challenged the very heart of Halliburton's project. As he himself puts it in *The Glorious Adventure*: "I realized I didn't want knowledge. I only wanted my senses to be passionately alive and my imagination fearlessly far-reaching."

As I have argued elsewhere, American travel writing until 1915 manifests a formal division that has governed it ever since: that between fact and fiction. This division is apparent in English travel writing as well, but in American works it takes on a particular emphasis. There is a chapter in Peter Fleming's *Brazilian Adventure* (1933) that begins with the matter of "accurate observation." His book, Fleming contends, "is all truth and no facts. It is probably the most veracious travel book ever written; and it is certainly the least instructive." This last statement in particular, I would claim, is what makes Fleming a British travel writer. To an American writer, the question of instruction remains ineluctable—no matter if truth gets converted into higher facts (the pulse of life on the senses, the evil of Communism) or into the more mundane realm of "mere" journalism. There is always something that needs to be *learned*, and even adventure— that heedlessly *useless* affair—emerges out of a distinctly American way of understanding it. Just at the time Halliburton was having his adventures, Fleming was asserting that "adventure—adventure in the grand old manner—is obsolete, having been either exalted to a specialist's job or degraded to a stunt."

I wish to draw a comparison with British practice only insofar as it clarifies the American. There are many ways to discuss the difference itself, the British tradition of "skepticism and empiricism," which Fussell mentions at one point, being perhaps most germane to the one manifestation I have been stressing. There is another I want to mention, and British travel writing in this century affords few better examples of explaining it than Fleming's text. This is parody. The American satirists wished to *expose* something about travel writing by parodying it. The British, instead—as if to prove the truth of Halliburton's fear of becoming "academic"—work parody into the very subject of travel itself. Their playfulness can thus seem truer because, as it were, its falsity can be conceded, if only by overtly marking its "literary" dimensions. As Fleming puts it, "the whole technique of exploring is overlaid with conventions so unmistakable and so often mocked—has a jargon so flashily impressive and so easily guyed— that the man who at his first essay adopts the conventions and employs the jargon must lack both shame and humour."

It is not easy to demonstrate this parodic sense without extensive quotation. It has to do, for instance, with beginning a chapter by saying "São Paulo is like Reading, only much farther away" or by noting the highly conventional nature of a friend's departure by asserting that "the partings of explorers are sweet sorrow for the reading public" and then immediately recovering: "I am happy to say that in this respect, if in no other, our expedition was meticulously loyal to the best traditions." Neither is it easy to explain why Fleming writes this way. I believe it has to do with his exquisite sense of how bookish his experience is—either in terms of the popular press (several times periodicals such as *Wide World Magazine* are jokingly mentioned) or a broader literary tradition (e.g., Elizabethan drama or the writings of W. H. Hudson). Taking his leave of yet another

Indian tribe in Matto Grosso, Fleming begins by stating: "Enchantment has, I suppose, its drawbacks; there are penalties for dealing in magic. On the whole the Tapirape let us off very lightly. Trespassers in fairyland, we were cautioned and discharged." Yet immediately following this warning is some of the loveliest writing in *Brazilian Adventure*. Describing what he elsewhere terms "something of that *Lost World* atmosphere for which we secretly yearned," Fleming invokes Spenser and Milton only in order to suggest how this fairyland remains strangely distinct from theirs and yet mysteriously similar as well. In passages such as these (to paraphrase an axiom of Wallace Stevens), Fleming reveals why literature is the better part of life, provided that life is the better part of literature. Parody offers merely another way of registering the presence of the one in the other.

An American travel text more similar to *Brazilian Adventure* at its most parodic than any I've mentioned is S. J. Perelman's *Westward Ha! or Around the World in Eighty Clichés* (1947). Perelman, at his most adventurous, visits Macao, "widely acclaimed as the wickedest city in the East." But this proves to be simply another illusion. "On the basis of an overnight sojourn, I can report that I found the Pearl of the Orient slightly less exciting than a rainy Sunday evening in Rochester." His Central Hotel meal "was constructed around a chicken that had accompanied Vasco da Gama on his earliest voyage of exploration," and at the cabaret with a rooftop gambling casino, "the half dozen sleepy Chinese girls presiding over the fan-tan tables eyed me with a pronounced lack of interest and returned to their dog-eared movie magazines." Back at his hotel Perelman undresses, he says, without "a single shaft of a knife protruding from the small of my back." Once back on ship, he gives but a knowing wink to all who inquire of his experience, and one morning he overhears one sailor whisper to another, "That's the man who spent the night in Macao."

Yet any similarity between these two writers only belies far more striking differences, for Fleming is simply not as parodic as Perelman. Or rather, Perelman does not write parody in the same way as Fleming. There is no model that *Westward Ha!* can both imitate and mock—except, fatefully, but very broadly, the guidebook. Everywhere Perelman goes is smeared by tourism, everything he sees he sees only to see through. *Westward Ha!* forms a burlesque version of travel as antitravel. It comes as no surprise that on the last page of the book, Perelman and his companion Hirschfield reject an offer from a stranger to go around the world and decide instead to merge with the rest of their fellow Americans in Times Square.

The most interesting moments in Perelman's book occur when the author appears to lose his poise and records what seems to be travel that was actually taken, or perception that was really felt on the senses. Take, for example, his encounter with the Temple of the Emerald Buddha in Bangkok, which is, we read, "mandatory sightseeing":

> Its flaunting, sportive improvisations of gilt and lacquer, the glass-and-tile mosaics, the bronze Garudas, and the rows of colossal, multi-colored divinities guarding its approaches dazzle an Occidental accustomed to the severity of Greek and Roman architecture. Surrounding the temple, under an arcade extending for a few blocks, is an extraordinary mural of the Ramayana; one may be forgiven for gushing shamelessly over the taste and technical skill of the artists who wrought it.

It is possible to discern Perelman's uneasiness here before something factual. It is almost as if the temple is too haplessly *there*. Even putting down facts about it (which may as well be culled from a guidebook) sounds like gushing. Yet curiously enough, Perelman does not gush.

In his critical study, *The Rhetoric of American Romance*, Evan Carton begins by quoting some lines from Emerson, finding them to be akin to either "a disingenuous exercise or a hoax," and then goes on to explain his stronger claim for them as self-parody. Self-parody, Carton avers, "is the way in which Emerson's fundamentally ambivalent, or 'inwardly disrupted,' enterprise sustains and regulates its animating tension (and thus preserves itself) against both the impulse to eliminate that tension and the danger of being overwhelmed by it." To apply these terms to the above passage, we can say that Perelman refuses to gush because he fears he will parody himself. Yet he fears he is already gushing, so there is a very real sense in which he *is* parodying himself. Perelman has become dispossessed of his persona as a guide precisely at the moment when his text can be located as a guidebook. How can we account for this division? It is not completely explained as that between fact and fiction, which I have been examining. This division, in turn, is a function of the way American travel writing has absorbed the assumptions and conventions of American romance.

What does it mean for one not native to a country to be "inside" it? What of oneself does one have to keep out? What has to be brought in? How much does one need to know? What can one assume? These are the kinds of questions John Gunther faced each time he heaved into print another huge volume of his once-famous *Inside* series. By the time of *Inside Africa* (1955) he could not get very far under way before mentioning conundrums such as the following, as he is about to venture into Morocco:

I will not have to define the Nile. But I am not sure that I can mention the Atlas, which is almost as important to Morocco as the Nile is to Egypt, without having to take time out to explain what the Atlas is. We will constantly be impaled on a vexing dilemma—whether to take practically nothing for granted and risk being otiose by describing what the reader already knows, or to irritate and puzzle him by using words like 'Sherifian' without explanation, and driving him to an encyclopedia.

Few things about Gunther's practice are more American than his concern about accuracy; the basic function of each of the *Inside* books was as a guidebook. Few things about Gunther's practice are yet more American than how he proceeds by writing right through insoluble dilemmas caused by too many facts.

The *Inside* books remain accessible even today, when in practical terms they are virtually obsolete, and in my opinion the ones on Asia and Africa are uncategorizable masterpieces. But all of the *Inside* series burst with potted history, political commentary, biographical sketches, interviews, and narrative segments. "Now we tackle geography," begins a chapter in his massive volume on Russia. If it seems relevant, Gunther takes it on, and over and over again he distinguishes himself by generously and indefatigably accommodating as much as he can. He quotes from every sort of document (local pamphlets, newspapers), he explains evenhandedly the most strange religious practices, he even includes a note on camels. There are obligatory destinations: besides all the major cities and all the major sights, Gunther sees Mahatma Gandhi in India, General Alfredo Stroessner in South America, and Albert Schweitzer in Africa. Yet his pages are never closed to any number of far more minor, unintegrated items, so he mentions that a woman can be arrested in Caracas for wearing shorts or that some Arab boys tell him they are skinning alive a hedgehog "to hear it cry." Anecdotes, jokes, even gossip—it is as if Gunther wishes to print *everything*.

In his *A Fragment of Autobiography* Gunther is unable to account for a series (there were eventually eight *Inside* books) that eventually obliged him to represent the entire earth. After his first three he says, "Books were no longer a crazy lark," and so he becomes "less newsy," "broader," "less interested in personalities." None of this is very helpful, for Gunther's background as a journalist and foreign correspondent does not permit him to speak very confidently about himself. "But I continue to be astonished," he states in discussing his penchant for saving clippings from all manner of sources, that "I was systematically assembling material for books that

I had no idea I would ever write, in a pattern that did not even begin to become clear until *Inside Europe* ten years later."

This is one of the few times a reader gets any indication from the author of what a profoundly imaginative effort the *Inside* books are. The most suggestive moment comes when Gunther describes his effort to write up Africa (his hardest book) and especially the night he had to face Kenya. He broke down his notes, he faced his clippings and articles, and then he tossed them all in a trunk and wrote his chapter. Few writers besides Gunther have so labored to get the facts straight. (He mentions at one point in *Inside Africa* that some metal greaves he was once given in the Congo weigh ten and a half pounds each, a weight he has just confirmed on his kitchen scale.) Certainly few have so labored under the fiction that factual accuracy formed the motive force behind what they were doing. What I want to claim instead is that what Gunther is doing is travel writing—but travel writing so unusual, so various, so saturated with fact and grounded in history that it has hardly any precedent, at least on such a scale. The truest successor to Gunther's work may be the bloated, round-the-world (Israel, Poland, Alaska) tomes of James Michener, which are now conveniently marketed as fiction.

"This book, I repeat, is not a record of travel or personal experience; it is a book of politics and information," disclaims Gunther at one point in *Inside Africa.* "But it is impossible to give a fair picture of some African countries without a brief description of some trips we took." Indeed. This had been Gunther's practice since he began the series. It is most obviously present in the "We Visit a Collective Farm" section in *Russia* and the "Indian Village" segment in *Asia.* But any number of Gunther's thousands of pages could be shown to possess exactly the character that he claims they do not, or do only occasionally. Gunther's last *Inside* book, for example, *Inside South America* (1966), includes a stop he makes at a community called Puerto Williams:

> Puerto Williams, the population of which is about three hundred is a Chilean naval and meteorological station. No doubt it was set up partly as a bit of flag-waving vis-à-vis the Argentines across Beagle Channel. It was named, oddly enough, not for an Englishman but for a Chilean admiral whose name was Williams and who first claimed the Magellan territory for Chile. . . . The original name of Puerto Williams was Puerto Luisa. I do not know who Luisa was. Puerto Williams is inexpressibly remote and forlorn. We hiked from the airstrip to a shaky dock and, going down an

even shakier gangplank, boarded a 'papa' boat, or LCVP, a small landing craft used by the U.S. Navy during World War II. No object whatever was to be seen except another landing craft marooned nearby. We crossed an estuary, and on the mainland—or was it the mainland?—we strode up a steep muddy path toward the commandant's house.

Hundreds of paragraphs from the *Inside* books are worked out the same way as this one. They begin with a clear factual statement, then build up a concise block of interpretation, emotional tone (especially the use of "oddly" here), unacknowledged authority (if he didn't find out who Luisa was, how did he find out who Williams was?), and personal impression—all within a basic narrative frame. Gunther's prefatory notes, however, describe a quite different framework. In *Inside Africa*, for example, he mentions his systematic collection of material, the fact that he took fifty-four different air trips, and so on, until the following assurance: "During the course of our trip I worked hard with my ears and took notes on conversations with 1,503 people. I was not looking for adventure. I was looking for facts." The last sentence could well serve as an epigraph for a study of the American travel writer in this century. In both cases here, Gunther validates his personal experience by providing the conventional contract of the American travel text: the Author was There.

The only sanction available for Gunther was factual, and the only textual model for that sanction was the guidebook. No matter that Gunther violates this sanction on every page and engorges the model in every book. Inside each *Inside* is a guidebook. Gunther may never have wanted it out, and as I have suggested, he might never have written any of the several kinds of book he in fact did write had he not worked within the conceptual boundaries of guidebooks. Certainly by *Inside South America* there were more practical "tips" than ever before and more actual citations of information from guidebooks; the very frame that had released such enormous textual energy was now shutting it off. (Even earlier, in *Inside Africa*, there were textual tags, like "French Morocco—To Sum Up," that suggested a guide.) Ironic in one sense, this development was appropriate in another. To the end, Gunther's practice was an expression of one continuous struggle with and transformation of facts, not a transcription or even a "record" of them.

"The Sudan is the last important Moslem country we shall encounter until this long book nears its end," Gunther says on page 242 of *Inside Africa*. On page 705 we read: "About the Cameroons I can write little. This is a pity, because few places in Africa are more fascinating. But this book is getting to be uncomfortably long, and we still have a great deal of territory to cover." All the *Inside*s contain such statements. Gunther's primary, if not most singular struggle was the material fact of his books themselves, which were so large, so various, so intractable that they came to reproduce the very world of which they could only be and remain a representation.

Among American travel writers in this century, Gunther is unusual not only in the scale of his work but in the fidelity of his care about the world. He wants to see it all for himself; he wants to write it all down; he wants to get it *right*. Another way to emphasize this is to refer to one of the most celebrated passages by an American author about a writer's relation to the world: "The balloon of experience is in fact of course tied to the earth, and under that necessity we swing, thanks to a rope of remarkable length, in the more or less commodious car of the imagination; but it is by the rope we know where we are, and from the moment that cable is cut we are at large and unrelated. . . . The art of the romancer is 'for the fun of it,' insidiously to cut the cable, to cut it without our detecting him."

Gunther never cuts the Jamesian cable. But as with any travel writer, he wishes to be "at large and unrelated" in order to have the experience that is given over to us when we read, to possess the same sort of experience. Gunther appears to have moved very fluidly among people because he genuinely liked them; hundreds are mentioned by name in the *Inside* books, and he seldom has a critical word to say about any of them. Yet he traveled very much "at large," with only the most transitory relations to those he met. In some respects he thus resembles Henry Miller. But unlike Gunther, Miller freely cuts the romancer's cable. His *The Colossus of Maroussi* (1941) is one glorious slice, as with the following passage when he gets to Crete:

> Every inch of Herakleion is paintable; it is a confused, nightmarish town, thoroughly anomalous, thoroughly heterogeneous, a place-dream suspended in a void between Europe and Africa, smelling strongly of raw hides, caraway seeds, tar and sub-tropical fruits. It has been brutalized by the Turk and infected with harmless rosewater vapourings of the back pages of Charles Dickens. It has no relation whatever to Knossus or Phaestos; it is Minoan in the way that Walt Disney's creations are American; it is a carbuncle on the face of time, a sore spot which one rubs like a horse while asleep on four legs.

We can, of course, still see the earth here. Miller, as any travel writer, always needs it, if only the better to watch it recede as his imagination soars. Indeed in *The Colossus of Maroussi*, the landscape is seldom seen for any other reason. Miller's romance with Greece is more on the Jamesian model than on that of Hawthorne. The latter defines his domain of romance in the famous passage from "The Custom House": "a neutral territory, somewhere between the real world and fairy-land, where the Actual and the Imaginary may meet, and each imbue itself with the nature of the other." There is nothing neutral about Miller's Greece. Either he is overcome with visionary wonder or he is not, and even if he is, his awareness of the Actual never leaves him, as in the following tribute to Eleusis:

> One must come to Eleusis stripped of the barnacles which have accumulated from centuries of lying in stagnant waters. At Eleusis one realizes, if never before, that there is no salvation in becoming adapted to a world which is crazy. At Eleusis one becomes adapted to the cosmos. Outwardly Eleusis may seem broken, disintegrated with the crumbled past; actually Eleusis is still intact and it is we who are broken, dispersed, crumbled to dust. Eleusis lives, lives eternally in the midst of a dying world.

One could say that it is the presence of the Actual, experienced as pain—but still experienced—that makes it possible to describe Miller's book as an example of travel writing.

Unlike Gunther, Miller is gloriously alienated—most simply from American society, but more profoundly from any society. The relation Miller desires is with the cosmos and it would be well to recall again how this differs from British practice. Fussell quotes a reaction to a garden perceived as anomalous in Peter Quennell's book on China and Japan and then explains the very act of noticing such a thing: "There's a supreme confidence that one knows what is 'normal' and can gauge an anomaly by its difference from the socially expected. . . . Perhaps it's the homogeneity of British culture, compared, say, with American. Whatever the reason, it is an unquestioned understanding of the norm and an unapologetic loyalty to it that underlies the perceptual and expressive techniques of the British travel book." American practice is in one sense what happens when there is not such a norm. Thus Hemingway's measured comment, in *Green Hills of Africa* (1935), that "I had loved my country all my life; the country was always better than the people. I could only care about the people a very few at a time."

Gunther off the mainland, Miller at Eleusis: it does not so much matter what the truths are as that the disaffected American writer sacrifices the social relation to the country itself in order to endure either isolation or alienation or both, so that truths of some normally unspeakable kind can be uttered. In fact, one perspective on American travel writing would mark the recurrent gesture whereby any social relation at all has been gladly sacrificed. I believe the American travel writer has turned to romance (and been turned into something of a fictional romancer) more for the sacrifice than the relation. Of course, to paraphrase one of James's celebrated pronouncements, ideally relations stop nowhere (which represents a superb mandate for a traveler, especially one who perpetually lives abroad). Yet even in James, who is arguably America's greatest travel writer, it seems imperative to see the same sort of ambivalences about other Americans expressed by, say, Paul Theroux and the far more genial Gunther. For all of them, travel is a matter of finding insides turn into outsides and outsides into insides. Travel is about boundaries, boundaries that Romance makes fluid. Society fears acts of transgression and trespass, especially when those activities come to seem like the definition of that impossibly liberated society, a community of one.

Is there a "self" in travel? Suppose one took it upon oneself to travel free of a specific identity and tried instead to experience travel as an impossibly pure, unindividuated experience. That is, what would it be like to travel as the personification of "travel itself"? American travel writers record an abiding fascination with such questions because they promise ways to elude problems of national definition as well as social or generic definition. "Are there not some states of consciousness," Richard Poirier asks, "that resist dramatic formulation, regardless of the genre in which the effort is made, because in dialogue or in actions they automatically become 'like' some conventional states of consciousness that are less transcendental than perverse?" James may have discerned this dilemma in Hawthorne's work. In his book on him, after criticizing *Our Old Home* as "the work of an outsider," James says: "This seems to me to express very well the weak side of Hawthorne's work—his constant mistrust and suspicion of the society that surrounded him, his exaggerated, painful, morbid national consciousness."

James is responding here not only to an objectionable national representation but also, I think, to the representation of what Poirier calls "states of consciousness," which are too careless of either exactitude or responsibility. We can see how generic, social, and national constraints are inseparable. Yet we can also see in James himself the full, destabilizing force of travel, both as a subject itself and as a resource for the representation of other subjects. Free of the social accountability of the British text, American travel narratives are at liberty to migrate.

The first paragraph of John Krich's *Music in Every Room* (1984) offers a paradigmatic example of how many American travelers wish to oppose the idea of travel as a systematized activity and to reject its coherence as a subject or project:

> Day one. Iris and I are real vagabonds now. . . . With free hands, we clutch the permits to trek. Available at a nominal fee, they must serve as passports to Himalayaland. . . . Is that why we keep them in view, bearing them like amusement ride tickets to be punched, scorecards to be filled out with logged mileage? Our names are somewhere inside the gray booklets, above dotted lines printed faintly on coarse parchment specked with the pubic hair of serfs. The script is ancient, the regulation indecipherable, as befits good bureaucratic forms. His Majesty Birendra, King of Nepal, grants us this license to get lost in the hills.

Officially represented, Krich invokes his permits in order to suggest another form of desire altogether. It is hard to say what it is exactly. His figurative language suggests several possibilities, though none of them have any "clear formulation" (to echo Poirier again). And therein lies their logic. Aloft in its balloon of experience, at once infantile and dutiful, with just enough of the cable still tied down in Kathmandu, Nepal, this remains a very American paragraph, as if the enthusiasm of a Halliburton and the burlesque of a Perelman could be fused together.

Such a fusion, I want to claim, is the very stuff of romance: the romance and travel writing are each convertible terms for the other. If formal classification there must be, then it can be accurately enough stated that travel writing forms a vital part of the romance genre. But it seems more important, finally, to locate travel writing—which is sponsored by the mobile provocations of its subject—as a practice that writes across generic boundaries, whether those of memoir or essay, journalism or pastoral, fiction or ethnography. In America it has been grounded in one primary substitution, that of Abroad for home. And it continues to be most acutely performed with fluid transformations of and quick negotiations between the governing polarities of propriety and deviancy, fact and fiction.

WORKS CITED

Benchley, Robert. "Browsing Through the Passport." In *Chips Off the Old Benchley*. New York: Harper & Bros., 1949, 109–13.

———. "French for Americans." In *The Benchley Round-Up*. New York: Harper & Row, 1954, 71–75.

———. "How to Travel in Peace: The Uncommercial Traveler and His Problems." In *Chips Off the Old Benchley*, 134–38.

———. "Throwing Back the European Offensive." In *The Benchley Round-Up*, 103–7.

Caesar, Terry. " 'Counting the Cats in Zanzibar': American Travel Abroad in American Travel Writing to 1914." *Prospects* 13 (1988): 95–134.

Carton, Evan. *The Rhetoric of American Romance*. Baltimore: Johns Hopkins UP, 1985.

Fleming, Peter. *Brazilian Adventure*. New York: Charles Scribner's Sons, 1933.

Fussell, Paul. *Abroad: British Literary Traveling Between the Wars*. New York: Oxford UP, 1980.

Gibbs, Walcott. *Bird Life at the Pole*. New York: William Morrow, 1931.

Gunther, John. *A Fragment of Autobiography: The Fun of Writing Inside Books*. New York: Harper & Row, 1961.

———. *Inside Africa*. New York: Harper & Bros., 1955.

———. *Inside South America*. New York: Harper & Row, 1966.

Halliburton, Richard. *The Glorious Adventure*. Indianapolis: Bobbs-Merrill, 1927.

———. *Letters Home: His Story of His Life's Adventures*. New York: Bobbs-Merrill, 1940.

———. *New Worlds to Conquer*. Garden City, N.Y.: Garden City, 1929.

———. *The Royal Road to Romance*. Garden City, N.Y.: Garden City, 1925.

Hawthorne, Nathaniel. *The Scarlet Letter*. 1850. Rpt. New York: Holt, Rinehart & Winston, 1961.

Hemingway, Ernest. *Death in the Afternoon*. New York: Charles Scribner's Sons, 1932.

———. *Green Hills of Africa*. New York: Charles Scribner's Sons, 1935.

James, Henry. *Hawthorne*. 1879. Rpt. New York: Macmillan, 1966.

———. "Preface" to *The American*. In *Henry James: European Writers and Other Prefaces*. Ed. Leon Edel. New York: Library of America, 1984, 1053–69.

Krich, John. *Music in Every Room: Around the World in a Bad Mood*. 1984. Rpt. New York: Atlantic Monthly P, 1988.

Miller, Henry. *The Colossus of Maroussi*. 1941. Rpt. London: Penguin, 1979.

Perelman, S. J. *Westward Ha! or Around the World in Eighty Clichés*. New York: Simon & Schuster, 1947.

Poirier, Richard. *A World Elsewhere: The Place of Style in American Literature*. 1966. Rpt. London: Chatto & Windus, 1967.

Wharton, Edith. *In Morocco*. New York: Charles Scribner's Sons, 1920.

Williams, William Carlos. *A Voyage to Pagany*. 1928. Rpt. New York: New Directions, 1970.

ROBERT VON HALLBERG

In 1951 Charles Olson left the nation's capital, where he had worked since 1942 in the government and the Democratic Party, for a year in the Yucatán, and that was about half-typical. Many of Olson's contemporaries traveled in the decade following the war, but not many explored North America. In 1949 W. S. Merwin left America to live in France. A year later Robert Lowell took his first trip to Europe and stayed for three years. Elizabeth Bishop had been traveling since the mid thirties; in 1951 she settled in Petropolis, near Rio de Janeiro. James Merrill was living in Rome then too. In 1952 James Wright took a Fulbright to Vienna, Richard Howard went to study at the Sorbonne, and Adrienne Rich had a Guggenheim year in Europe. The following year Charles Gullans went to England on a Fulbright, and Olson's friend Robert Creeley moved to Mallorca. Then in 1954 Richard Wilbur won the Prix de Rome Fellowship. And in 1955 John Ashbery left New York to study in Paris on a Fulbright, not to return for a decade.

Of course poems were spun off these centrifugal circuits. In fact, three conventional poetic subjects dominated the decade: animals (almost always referred to by the more evocative biblical term "beasts"), the fine arts (mainly this meant poems on past European painters and sculptors), and travel. Olson was severely critical of poets who stayed within those conventions. W. S. Merwin was obviously accomplished in just these terms; his second book was entitled *The Dancing Bears* (1954), the third, *Green with Beasts* (1956). Olson insisted that Merwin's poetry showed none of the force and scope of American culture of the early fifties. Like William Carlos Williams, he felt that poets writing about English gardens, French

From *American Poetry and Culture, 1945–1980* (Cambridge: Harvard University Press, 1985), 62–92. © 1985 by Harvard University Press. Reprinted by permission.

boulevards, and Italian piazzas were begging off the challenge of a dramatically expanding American culture. In this respect he was quite wrong, though thoroughly American.

The disapproval of travel writing, even of travel, was not new to American thought. Olson's puritanical censure of travel poetry had little to do with the strictly literary merits of such writing. Rather, his complaint was that a nobler subject—"the Americanization of the world"—was waiting in the wings, and not being called. Travel poems were just not serious enough. And he had a point. Henry James, no mean travel writer, said, "Our observation in any foreign land is extremely superficial." Emerson was especially strenuous on this score: "For the most part, only the light characters travel." Melville, a vigorous advocate of American travel, claimed that to travel well one must be "a good lounger," "care-free." American writers are slow to defend lightness; earnestness is more their game. Travelers are first struck by what is different, new, or odd. Melville understood that the experience of such differences in itself has a liberalizing effect on the sensibility. But for a writer, American or not, this subject has a special danger. Travel is the most difficult subject, Auden said, because it restricts freedom of invention while it offers the lure of journalism, of superficial "typewriter-thumping." All that a journalist requires to create interest is "the new, the extraordinary, the comic, the shocking"; travel supplied these in abundance. The danger is that the serious writer, whose work is not done until the meaning of new experiences has been suggested, will, like a reporter, be too quickly satisfied.

Most of the tourist poems of the fifties work the traditional themes and concerns of travel poems, English and American; not all of them seem timely. This uneasiness about superficiality, for instance, shows up without surprise when poets approach the moral fringes, the lustiness of tourists, say. John Hollander is simply playful about all of this:

> O for the perfumes that arise
> From all those extra-specialty shops
>   In Copenhagen!
> O for the welcome looks from eyes
> Like blue, unbuyable lollipops
>   In Copenhagen!
> —"Non Sum Qualis Eram Bona in Urbe Nordica Illa" (1960)

But this is admittedly light verse and barely counts. More commonly, American poets grow rather serious when they consider the freedom of a tourist; "Nothing in transit need be done by thirds," Anthony Hecht once remarked. Adrienne Rich is rather melancholy and *perdue* about a traveler's promiscuity:

> You will perhaps make love to me this evening,
> Dancing among the circular green tables
> Or where the clockwork tinkle of the fountain
> Sounds in the garden's primly pebbled arbors.
> Reality is no stronger than a waltz,
> A painted lake stippled with boats and swans,
> A glass of gold-brown beer, a phrase in German
> Or French, or any language but our own.
> Reason would call us less than friends,
> And therefore more adept at making love.
> —"The Kursaal at Interlaken" (1951)

American travelers fear tawdriness and decadence. Speaking a foreign language, dancing with an almost-stranger, giving free rein to circumstance ("perhaps")—these are the things that make American poets sense duplicity, even if they consent to it for the moment. Charles Gullans consents, but with tight-lipped self-reproach:

> The fugitive acquires enduring shape,
> The resonance of all that it might be:
> The freedom of assault, the blow, the rape,
> For this is without responsibility.
> —"The Traveler in the Hotel Bar" (1962)

Gullans writes as one trapped and ashamed by transient desire. Along with Edgar Bowers and Turner Cassity, Gullans helped this traveler's theme, the degradation of eros, to evolve into a subgenre, the barroom poem of jaundiced courting. And James Merrill, in "The Thousand and Second Night," wrote a masterpiece on this tourist's subject.

A great many tourist poems have been written by American poets who were simply glad for the chance to write descriptive poetry—poems that are traditionally supposed to be superficial. These are easy to identify, and the motive comes naturally to a stranger in a new place. Every tourist knows that feeling of greater intimacy with the flowers, pavement, and air of a foreign city than with its natives, one's fellow souls. These poems express a loneliness that has more to do with uncertainty and an attendant quick exuberance than with sadness.

I went out at daybreak and stood on Primrose Hill.
It was April: a white haze over the hills of Surrey
Over the green haze of the hills above the dark green
Of the park trees, and over it all the light came up clear,
The sky like deep porcelain paling and paling,
With everywhere under it the faces of the buildings
Where the city slept, gleaming white and quiet,
St Paul's and the water tower taking the gentle gold.
And from the hill chestnuts and the park trees
There was such a clamour rose as the birds woke,
Such uncontainable tempest of whirled
Singing flung upward and upward into the new light,
Increasing still as the birds themselves rose
From the black trees and whirled in a rising cloud,
Flakes and water-spouts and hurled seas and continents of them
Rising, dissolving, streamering out, always
Louder and louder singing, shrieking, laughing.
—W. S. Merwin, "Birds Waking" (1956)

The sharpest criticism of this sort of exercise in elaborate description is
Ashbery's mock-tourist poem, "The Instruction Manual" (1956):

Around stand the flower girls, handing out rose- and lemon-colored
    flowers,
Each attractive in her rose-and-blue striped dress (Oh! such shades of rose
    and blue),
And nearby is the little white booth where women in green serve you green
    and yellow fruit.
The couples are parading; everyone is in a holiday mood.

Those bright colors glare a bit desperately, as though all that Merwin or
Ashbery can see should be registered, almost labeled, since what cannot
be understood looms so large for a tourist. Merwin strains a bit ("streamering"!) for his joy. He draws the poem to a close by asking that the world
explode, perhaps even atomically ("Explosion of our own devising"), right
now when the birdsong is at its highest pitch.

It can be tricky to end a poem that is motivated only by a desire to
describe, because description often does not lead to a take-home message.
American poets, writing in a tradition that disapproves of superficiality,
sometimes have guilty consciences over such things. After giving himself

over to seven elaborate stanzas describing the fauns in a Roman fountain in "A Baroque Wall-Fountain in the Villa Sciarra" (1955), Richard Wilbur draws himself up short to ask, "Yet since this all / Is pleasure, flash, and waterfall, / Must it not be too simple?" This is the moralist's question, though Wilbur is enough of a poet to know how to escape: "Are we not / More intricately expressed / In the plain fountains that Maderna set / Before St. Peter's . . ." Then follow seven more elaborate stanzas on the fountains at St. Peter's. That time Wilbur got away from the puritanical conscience, but few of his contemporaries did and even he is nabbed badly when, at the end of a poem in which he figuratively consumes, with the zest of a connoisseur, an entire landscape, he reflects morosely:

> And we knew we had eaten not the manna of heaven
> But our own reflected light,
> And we were the only part of the night that we
> Couldn't believe.
> —"The Terrace" (1950)

However urgent the impulse just to describe all that is strange, the sanction of an earnest literary tradition, the wagging finger of Emerson, has its way almost every time. The best descriptive tourist poems take sides with that tradition.

Easy joy is only a small part of the tourist's life. Those flashy surfaces seem sometimes to stretch without end. In "Waiting for Ada" (1970), Richard Howard writes about sitting out a rainy day in the lobby of "Rimini's Grand Hotel du Miroir," eager to get beyond the "panoramas and preconceptions" and back home to the deeper pleasure of reading Nabokov's *Ada*. Wilbur and Merwin may usually feel jubilant, but others testify that the interminable spectacle of foreign details—the smaller, the odder—is powerfully unsettling. When tourist-poets begin to elaborate figures, emblems, and allegory, or parable, they are simply wielding the traditional tools for getting the words off the plane of mere circumstance. Gullans writes, in "The Moor, Haworth" (1957), with obvious pleasure, about simply walking across a moor: "The drying goarse, the heather, and the bracken / Move with a brisk confusion, and the sound / Will sometimes deepen and will sometimes slacken." A tourist hears the buzz of insects, and only someone uncertain of his footing, as a tourist often is, notices that this sound is not addressed to him: "Though all about me voices seem to spring, / They are not any voices that I know." Those are not just the voices of insects, of course, but all "The other and the alien tongues" that

leave a "brisk confusion" around even simple acts, like walking across a
field or staring at a brick.

> Neutral and dull, the bricks that serve as shores
> Enforce their color on the channeled water;
> And if a distant movement, as of oars,
> Has made that mirrored brick, its mortar scatter,
> Now, as the soon abated force goes slack,
> A leveling inertia lays them back.
> —Turner Cassity, "A Somewhat Static Barcarolle" (1966)

"Neutral," "dull," "inertia"—these too are the tourist's terms, and it
takes effort and style to get beyond them. Cassity wrote his barcarolle (a
gondolier song) in bourgeois Amsterdam, where the power is oil not oars.
The small disappointment of a tourist (that Amsterdam is not Venice, that
the boats are motored not rowed, that the shore is merely unpicturesque
brick) is dispelled by a hard concentration on nothing more than the old
pun in the word "reflection": the surface of the brick, its image reflected
in the water, and in the mind only intermittently, during calm. With the
last stanza, that concentration, as tough but supple as the rhythm, brings
surface and reflection, these foreign surfaces and this mind bordering on
torpor, together in a quasi-parable (and another pun, on "sense"), where
Venice and Amsterdam are joined (and the last line picks up the gondolier's tread).

> As if our shadows, lengthening below,
> Received us bodily to calm, to vision,
> Always to rock with lifted oars; where, low
> Beside the mirror, sense and its precision
> Give to the arching sky, the dormered town,
> A motion one brick up and one brick down.

For Howard, Gullans, and Cassity, none of them descriptive poets, worries about superficiality are troublesome only momentarily and never really
challenge their poetry in general. But for Elizabeth Bishop, a traveler and
descriptive poet always, the challenge held high stakes—and led to the
best poem on this subject. Here are the opening lines of "Questions of
Travel" (1956):

> There are too many waterfalls here; the crowded streams
> hurry too rapidly down to the sea,

and the pressure of so many clouds on the mountaintops
makes them spill over the sides in soft slow-motion,
turning to waterfalls under our very eyes.
—For if those streaks, those mile-long, shiny, tearstains,
aren't waterfalls yet,
in a quick age or so, as ages go here,
they probably will be.
But if the streams and clouds keep travelling, travelling,
the mountains look like the hulls of capsized ships,
slime-hung and barnacled.

Think of the long trip home.

Bishop knows her most artful moves well, even—as here—to the point of weariness. Those figures, tearstains and hulls, seem to come easily to her, and so does that bird's-eye view, as though from an airplane. Too easily, for the Emersonian: "Where should we be today?" The play of spirit that brightens tourist poems is dazzling but cheap, like sequins. Readers of the *New Yorker*, who first came across this and many of Bishop's poems, might be impressed, but who would be moved? Always to be going on, or over, like the streams and clouds, may only corrupt the soul ("Is it right to be watching strangers in a play / in this strangest of theatres?") and leave a poet stranded like those barnacled ships.

Streams and clouds can be made to stand for travelers, beached ships for dry poets: figures hold the Emersonian at bay with the claim that nothing is merely literal or light. But here that is a debater's defense. Bishop is more a literalist than a fabler; she cannot afford to give away the prerogatives of the descriptive poet.

But surely it would have been a pity
not to have seen the trees along this road,
really exaggerated in their beauty,
not to have seen them gesturing
like noble pantomimists, robed in pink.
—Not to have had to stop for gas and heard
the sad, two-noted, wooden tune
carelessly clacking over
a grease-stained filling-station floor.
(In another country the clogs would all be tested.
Each pair there would have identical pitch.)
—A pity not to have heard

the other, less primitive music of the fat brown bird
who sings above the broken gasoline pump
in a bamboo church of Jesuit baroque:
three towers, five silver crosses.

The first three lines of this strophe, with those homely words that a poet types with terror ("it would have been a pity," "really," "their beauty"), are nothing if not candid. Description and simile (not fable) she needs, even when the language is only amusing, like pantomimists. There are times when a close eye can find the human spirit even in the unfamiliar facets of a tropical gas station. That the music of the clogs is made against the greasy work floor is not exactly an emblematic detail, though that kind of interpretation could be made to work from time to time; it is wonderfully fresh description, with only a restrained hint of some metaphysical fit. The interpretation that counts for more here is the cultural one suggested parenthetically by the contrast between northern European tidiness and South American baroque. One thing a tourist-poet can do naturally is to scrutinize the interfaces of cultures, where the Jesuits meet the jungle.

The imagination that finds "history in / the weak calligraphy of song-birds' cages" is illuminating rather than light. Bishop has set the poem up for a firm, cogent answer to the skeptical charge that travel (and travel writing) is frivolous. All is in place: "*Continent, city, country, society: / the choice is never wide and never free. / And here, or there . . . No. Should we have stayed at home, / wherever that may be?*" What makes the poem genuinely moving is that the well-made argument dissolves into the ellipsis. Differences between continents do in fact count for a great deal, and Bishop is genuinely American whether she chose her nationality freely or not. There can be no relish for the ways that culture shines through bamboo birdcages without the tourist's or expatriate's feeling of estrangement. If the Brazilian character shows in those local details, and if she has faith in the life of those details, why has she given up the physical proximity to American details? This question of travel goes unanswered at the end, which is what makes the poem deadly serious and finally sad.

Bishop asks herself why she is always traveling, traveling, and writing stunning poems about odd details. The question can be put more broadly to a generation of poets. Why in the fifties was such intense concentration brought to this particular genre? Was this just a time, as Olson and James Dickey suggest, of light poetry? No, but it was a traveling time. In the fifties airfares seemed low and the exchange rate favorable to Americans. More

Americans traveled to Europe in that decade than ever before. Poets were addressing a subject that had great pertinence to the time: many Americans were going abroad for the first time, and many of them were the first in their families to conceive of a vacation as a tour of Europe. These travelers can be identified more particularly because the international tourist industry has gone to considerable trouble to locate the spenders. They are spoken of as middle-class, with annual incomes of over $15,000 for the most part, and predominantly white. Poets were giving form to a new cultural experience, or rather to a newly diffused one. They were writing about the class of Americans who conceived of themselves as the center of American social, political, and economic life: these were the Americans whose interests were comprehended within the political consensus of the fifties.

There is more to it, though. With the end of World War II, the United States expressly took on military responsibility for the security of Western Europe. And American economic interests moved into those markets that had formerly been held by French and British firms. After 1945 the United States set about the job of becoming a global power in short order. Exactly when American foreign policy was first directed by the imperialist urge is open to disagreement, but there is no question that the years following the war saw a rapid and immense extension of American power around the world. Most of this was done, it should be remembered, with encouragement of the then withdrawing Western European imperial powers. England, France, and the United States continued after the war to see their interests as allied. Americans had the military and economic strength needed to keep England and France's former political and economic colonies open to western development. So Americans had to take the lead.

Militarily and economically, they were prepared to assume that responsibility: the American army and the major industries were stronger right after the war than they had ever been, though all the other belligerents had been hurt in just those terms by the war. There was a chink, however, in the cultural armor. American artists did not think of themselves as well prepared to assume western leadership in the arts. Many twentieth-century artists, poets most conspicuously, had expatriated, in large measure because America lacked a vital artistic center. Marianne Moore, William Carlos Williams, Georgia O'Keeffe, and many other artists stayed in America, some of them fiercely defending the vigor of the national culture; they were part of an American tradition that reaches back to the first years of nationhood. Noah Webster told schoolchildren, in his

Speller (1783), that "America must be as independent in *literature* as she is in *politics*." Most of the post–World War II poets who wrote tourist poems, however, were not obviously of either camp—neither expatriates nor principled nativists—for the terms of the problem had suddenly shifted with the resolution of the war. The question in the early fifties was no longer whether American culture was fecund enough to produce a world-class literature; that challenge had been plainly met. But could Americans assume the custodianship of European cultural traditions as adroitly as military and economic responsibility was being shouldered?

Even the generals knew that this question would arise. In 1944 Eisenhower warned Patton, Bradley, and other military commanders to move cautiously around the "monuments and cultural centers which symbolize to the world all that we are fighting to preserve." Again and again in the next two decades, Americans would show how eager they were not to proceed too bullishly. In 1956 the largest restoration in the Athenian agora (the Stoa of Attalos, now a museum) was completed by the American School of Classical Studies. Tourists trying to find the narrow pass at Thermopylae, a difficult search after water and earth shifted, are helped by a marker-monument erected by American Friends of the Spartans.

American poets proceeded in a similar fashion. Although poets traveled widely, the poems tend to gather, like pigeons and hawkers, around the sights and monuments: Richard Wilbur on the "Marché aux Oiseaux" (1949), "Wellfleet: The House" (1948), "Piazza di Spagna, Early Morning" (1955), and "A Baroque Wall-Fountain in the Villa Sciarra" (1955); James Merrill on the recovered bronze statue "The Charioteer of Delphi" (1950) and, at Versailles, "In the Hall of Mirrors" (1957); Anthony Hecht at "Ostia Antica" (1967), at the Palazzo Farnese, in "A Hill" (1964), in "The Gardens of the Villa d'Este" (1953); Charles Gullans at "St. John's, Hampstead" (1958); X. J. Kennedy in the "Theater of Dionysus" (1953); Randall Jarrell on "The Orient Express" (1950); W. S. Merwin on "A Sparrow Sheltering under a Column of the British Museum" (1955); John Hollander in "Late August on the Lido" (1958) and on a restored Polish palace, "Lazienka" (1962); Edgar Bowers at St. Mark's, "To Accompany an Italian Guide-Book, 2" (1954); Adrienne Rich at "Versailles (*Petit Trianon*)" (1953), at the "Villa Adriana" (1955), and on "A View of Merton College" (1955); and Paul Blackburn at the Place Dauphine in "La Vieille Belle" (1957). They were all self-conscious tourists, with a mission. By fountain, statue, palazzo, and piazza, the poets were demonstrating their ability to write intelligently, tastefully about the outward signs of the cultural heritage America was taking over after the war. These poems—and most of them are certainly intelligent, tasteful, and worthy of continued attention—are part of America's cultural claim to global hegemony.

Although American poets did not speak about tourist poems in these terms, the ways they wrote about monuments suggest that the poets were somehow aware of the American need for such credentials then. When Keats looked at the Elgin Marbles in the British Museum in 1817, he felt "Like a sick eagle looking at the sky"; he acknowledged that he stood in the "shadow of a magnitude." Rilke, in front of the archaic torso of Apollo in the Louvre in 1908, also felt the sting of comparison: "Du musst dein Leben ändern" (You must change your life). European poets could better afford admissions of inferiority.

American poets customarily maintain equanimity in these circumstances, as though the contemplation of a monument were a test of strength and a flinch could cost the game. American writers (and some tourists too) are painfully aware of the need to prove themselves culturally. In 1959 Allen Tate wrote to the U. S. State Department: "Mr. Lowell is the kind of a man I think we should send abroad more and more in order to eliminate some false impressions that foreigners seem to have about the qualifications of Americans to participate in international cultural life on equal terms with them." Some poems by Americans show tourists reduced by their proximity to the monuments, as when the departing couple Merrill observes in the Hall of Mirrors leaves no trace on the glass. (American poets often establish their own refinement against the background, it must be admitted, of garish compatriots.) More commonly, though, poets overcome distance between themselves and the icons of Europe, though there is little question but that they begin their travels a bit estranged. "Ease is what we lack," Adrienne Rich says ("At Hertford House" [1955]). This is why the poets look around them for some sign of comfort.

> [the sparrow] knows simply that this stone
>
> Shelters, rising into the native air,
> And that, though perhaps cold, he is at home there.
> —W. S. Merwin, "A Sparrow Sheltering Under a Column of the British Museum" (1955)
>
> One is at home here. Nowhere in ocean's reach
> Can time have any foreignness or fears.
> —Richard Wilbur, "Wellfleet: The House" (1948)

These poems aim at that sweet conclusion, of course, because a lack of comfort is the obvious burden the American poet carries through Europe: for the poets, this is as much a test as a vacation. They need to appropriate Europe:

> —The light has changed
> Before we can make it ours. We have no choice:
> We are only tourists under the blue sky . . .
> —Adrienne Rich, "The Tourist and the Town" (1955)

Rich's poem ends with that appropriation achieved, only because she has received a painful letter from home that leaves her feeling common emotions there in San Miniato al Monte, like a normal person more concerned with her own state than with the streets and buildings around her. Anthony Hecht's "A Hill" is a less discursive and more powerful poem on a similar experience. In both poems, memories of American "bitter origins," as Rich puts it, leave the poet with a profound bond to the European landscape. Hecht stands before the Palazzo Farnese transfixed by a vivid boyhood memory of a wintry hill in Poughkeepsie. When the Palazzo becomes that hill, for a moment, it is Hecht's—and Renaissance Rome is his too.

Appropriation occurs in poem after poem, in subtler, more interesting ways. Poets have special methods of establishing their authority over a subject. Often only a few lines setting a tone will do the job, as when Wilbur refers to "a faun-ménage and their familiar goose" in "A Baroque Wall-Fountain in the Villa Sciarra." His ability to be lightly ironic asserts firm self-possession and knowledgeability; here sophistication is power. These lines from Merrill's "The Cruise" (1954) give a sense of the larger dimensions of this procedure:

> Mild faces turned aside to let us fondle
> Monsters in crystal, tame and small, fawning
> On lengths of ocean-green brocade.
> "These once were nightmares," the Professor said,
> "That set aswirl the mind of China. Now
> They are belittled, to whom craftsmen fed
> The drug of Form, their fingers cold with dread,
> Famine and Pestilence, into souvenirs."
> "Well I'm *still* famished," said a woman in red
> From Philadelphia. I wondered then:
> Are we less monstrous when our motive slumbers

> Drugged by a perfection of our form?
> The bargain struck . . .

That woman from Philadelphia could do with some drugging; a little civility would take her a long way. Artistic and social form tend to come together. These Chinese monsters, manageable now, have had their power reduced by being given artistic form. Social form does something similar for the base human drives. A poet's power is form: a subject caught (Europe, say) is tamed. Without the poems, without social manners, mere power is barbaric. The rapid buildup of the American military and the proliferation of defense treaties after 1941 gave this equation particular force in American thought. To prove to others, and perhaps to ourselves too, that this phenomenal power was not monstrously raw and vulnerable to wit and sophistication, monuments had to be restored and written about—preferably with wit and sophistication.

Nearly all the poets who responded to that need by writing tourist poems were conservative in terms of poetic technique. Merrill, Wilbur, Howard, Hecht, Hollander, Rich, Cassity, Gullans, Merwin, Bishop—for most of these poets, Frost, Stevens, Auden, and, a bit anomalously, Eliot were the great masters, not Pound, certainly not Williams. . . . Poets using monuments to write parables or extract a lesson are secure in their authority; this way of writing does not easily admit uncertainty or faintness of voice. The monuments are subordinated somehow, as instances of the poets' general truths. Frost, it should be said, did write mysterious parables that pointed to his own incomplete understanding of particular experiences. These younger poets took to heart the part of Frost that encouraged a more confident "reading" of experience for analogies to the moral life of the individual.

The richest of these poems taking lessons from monuments is John Hollander's "Lazienka" (1962).

> Ruins are what we make of them, and wrecked
> Imaginations could want to do so little
> With any real rubble. Acres of crumbled bricks,
> Painful, cracked chunks of stucco, even, can be
> Reused with the right kind of patience, fitted
>   Back into a fairly free
> Orderliness again. If broken Doric
> Columns look less like finished sculptures now

Than twisted piles of rusty scrap, all stuck
About with dreadful bits of plaster do,
It's not because our own junked age is over
Yet, but that our young sculptors are so clever.

Hollander's subject is the corruption of a culture's imagination, indicated here by paltry misreading of ruins. The reach of the poem can be suggested by noting that responsibility for this sort of failure belongs not only with Poland but with Germany, America, and with the culture too of those people (including Hollander) who, along with various national allegiances, feel loyalty to those lost in the Holocaust. Acres of crumbled brick can be found in the South Bronx, but these are not the ruins that capture the imaginations of Americans. Even the Doric columns are too simple and rudimentary in use and design to fire the imagination of Hollander's overly clever contemporaries. For them, Berlin's Gedächtniskirche is a real ruin because it is properly framed by glittering postwar buildings that stand, really, for a deplorable complacency. Lazienka, the restored palace with its Greek ruins and amphitheater on the water, is as fake a ruin as the Gedächtniskirche: the Polish government uses this monument to proclaim its reverence for history, for those who have served in the past. But the lost Jews of Warsaw are ill remembered, "With no great love." The poem is not strictly a complaint about anti-Semitism. The ruin that commands attention lies closer to home: "Ruination is the ordure / Of violence: a burned-out mattress, still / Stinking of scorch; smashed glass; or the broiled ooze / Of something organic on a plate of dull / Metal. The calyx of no blasted rose, / No shard with a red shape on it, resembles / These portions of a way of life in shambles." That mattress comes from New York, not Warsaw. Urban rubble is the great neglected ruin of Hollander's time— neglected despite polite, abstract talk of the Death of Cities. Hollander acknowledges that he too is caught up in this failure of imagination. He feels "No flaming pains" for the "burnt race" from which he is descended; all he can do is compose "rusty ironies," "Never quite forgetting that every city / Will one day flower in a burning instead of beauty."

No other monument poem is more assured in tone than "Lazienka": the utterance—to call it a "speech" would be misleading—is extraordinarily well composed. Within this twelve-line stanza, Hollander moves his syntax freely over the line breaks so that each pentameter or tetrameter gets a fresh grip on the flow of speech. Hollander is the most accomplished stanzaic craftsman of his generation. The diction is comparably various and free: "Orderliness," "Ruination," "ooze," and "plaster do." Freedom is just the point. The poem is firmly didactic and utterly convincing because the poet shows in his lines that he abides by his own precepts, fitting all sorts of words into a fairly free orderliness, and suffers by his own judgments. For this, after all, is one more American poem on a picturesque and remote monument; this particular New Yorker knows that his attention belongs less in Warsaw than in the south Bronx. . . .

Some of the poets writing about sights and monuments are explicit about the appropriation of icons, though most often the subject is just below the surface, as when Rich ("A View of Merton College" [1955]) and Hecht ("Rome" [1977]) cannot help seeing Europe figuratively as a museum. Just who the custodians of this museum are must be evident by now. In 1950 construction of the Rome Termini was completed, and Richard Wilbur (in "For the New Railway Station in Rome" [1955]) commemorated the achievement five years later: "Those who said God is praised / By hurt pillars, who loved to see our brazen lust / Lie down in rubble, and our vaunting arches / Conduce to dust . . ." Wilbur, who comes from New York, has written no comparably civic poem on an American subject; American poets seldom sing the praises of train stations. (Allen Ginsberg's "In the Baggage Room at Greyhound" [1956] is something quite different.) In fact, American poets seldom take up the civic laurels at all, but for an American to serve, momentarily, as Rome's civic laureate has a special appeal. For a moment, Wilbur could play at being a Roman and speak on behalf of its traditions: those first-person plural pronouns could be said to rest on the sense that all Westerners have a claim to representation in the Foro Romano, and for a moment it seems that bella Roma is Wilbur's, and he, hers.

There are times, though, when poets wanting to speak similarly for monuments build up their own authority by snooty gestures toward others. When Richard Howard's traveling companion asks, "Richard, What's That Noise?"—wondering about the nightingales at the Pozzo di San Patrizio—Howard is quick, and proud, to answer only half-facetiously: "Noise! The natural history of nightingales / comes down to that! and from this: / 'No bird hath so sweet a voice among all silvan / musicians . . .' Sundays, / Milton, Keats to Hollander's / Philomel, nightingales sing with no intermission, / but now, only now, tonight in Umbria, a *noise*." In a poem about the Roman spot most crowded, inch for inch, with American tourists, Wilbur likens a young girl, implausibly pirouetting down 137 steps, to a leaf floating over the lip of a fountain, "Perfectly beautiful, perfectly ignorant of it [the falls]" ("Piazza di Spagna, Early Morning" [1955]). The poets are eager to distinguish themselves, as who would not be, from all those other tourists, ignorant of the ground they tread. The guards at the Palatine doze in amnesia (Hecht, "A Roman Holiday" [1954]), and only an American poet attends to the ritual significance of St. Paul's bells (Wilbur, "Bell Speech" [1947]). The real custodians of all this are of course those responsible for the Pax Americana, or so some would have it.

Many of the poets I have discussed sense a connection between tourism and imperialism, partly because the monuments they write of derive from particular empires. In the fifties, America seemed to be just beginning its reign, as France, England, and Germany retreated. The rise and fall of empires is a subject that comes up often in these poems. John Hollander's "Late August on the Lido" (1958), for instance, is about the end of the Venice season, when the bathers at the Lido cross the Grand Canal and leave for the year. Here is the last stanza:

All this is over until, perhaps, next spring;
This last afternoon must be pleasing.
Europe, Europe is over, but they lie here still,
While the wind, increasing,
Sands teeth, sands eyes, sands taste, sands everything.

Hollander expresses no hope for what is to come, only disgust at what is being lost. The last thing the wind erodes, before everything is lost, is taste. The European sense of value, discrimination, propriety—in short, civilization—is passing. Europe is already only a bathing beach. In Merrill's "Three Sketches for Europa" (1954–55), Henry Adams' aunt explains to her departing nephew, "The Tourist," that Europa, "Poor soul, she's peevish now, an invalid, / Has lost her beauty, gets things wrong. / Go now. But do not stay too long."

The Americans are taking over. "All her [Europa's] radiant passage known," Merrill says, "Lamely as Time by some she dreamt not of." Part of what had passed, poets had a stake in believing, was imaginative vision, just what they might provide for American culture. Rich remarks in "Villa Adriana" (1955) of the Roman emperor and poet Hadrian (bound to her in name), who planned rooms of his villa to reproduce some of the exotic places he had seen as a traveler: "Dying in discontent, he must have known / How, once mere consciousness had turned its back, / The frescoes of his appetite would crumble, / The fountains of his longing yawn and crack." Consciousness, more than brick and mortar, built the great villa; the remaining ruins are "artifacts of thought." Poets are not only, as Rich suggests, the archaeologists of thought, they are, like Hadrian, its architects too. For them, empires and the flow of wealth offer opportunities, commissions, subjects.

Not that opportunities are innocent. When Edgar Bowers looked at St. Mark's and the gondolas crossing from the Lido, he was reminded of how

> The Slavic fleet crept toward it from the sea
> With muffled oars, concealed by mist and rain
> And early morning darkness, silently,
>
> Past Arsenal and *dromi* anchored near,
> Feeding their pirate cunning on the rich
> Shadow of treasure glimmering in the air,
> And waiting for the drag of hull on beach.
> —"To Accompany an Italian Guide-Book" (1954)

In the seventeenth century, Slavs from the Dalmatian coast periodically raided Venice with encouragement from the Austrian empire. In 1954 Bowers sees an analogy between those raiders and the American tourists of his own party. (And, of course, the irony that the Venetian treasures themselves were stolen from Constantinople is also part of the circle.) Strangers all come to take what they can carry away, Venetians, Slavs, and Americans alike, pirates and poets.

Empires run on rapine, and poets follow empires—the plunder sometimes being imaginative. Elizabeth Bishop's *Questions of Travel* (1965) opens with "Arrival at Santos," dated January 1952, about her own disembarkation in South America. Next comes "Brazil, January 1, 1502," about the Portuguese colonization of Brazil. Bishop focuses on the way that the Portuguese projected onto this foreign landscape the imaginative structures of their belief. Birds were seen as symbolic, lizards as dragons, or simply "Sin, / and moss looked like hell-green flames."

> Just so the Christians, hard as nails,
> tiny as nails, and glinting,
> in creaking armor, came and found it all,
> not unfamiliar:
> no lovers' walks, no bowers,
> no cherries to be picked, no lute music,
> but corresponding, nevertheless,

to an old dream of wealth and luxury
already out of style when they left home—
wealth, plus a brand-new pleasure.
Directly after Mass, humming perhaps
L'Homme armé or some such tune,
they ripped away into the hanging fabric,
each out to catch an Indian for himself—
those maddening little women who kept calling,
calling to each other (or had the birds waked up?)
and retreating, always retreating, behind it.
—Originally in *New Yorker*, 2 January 1960

The connections among Christianity, empire, and Brazil are there in the area's first name: Vera Cruz, the true cross. In the sixteenth century, the Portuguese community that controlled the port of Santos was based in São Paulo; the *paulistas* were pathfinders to the interior, and they were slaves too. Many of them had children by the captive Indian women, but an off-shoot of this community, the *bandeirantes*, lived in free union with the Indian women, or married them, though the *bandeirantes* were special-ists in seizing slaves. Jesuit missions were established along the Amazon in the seventeenth century, which were then raided by *paulistas* looking for slaves, as well as gold and precious stones. The slave traffic survived until 1853.

Bishop attends to the way that the Christian framework was brought down on the backs of the South American Indians. Brazil was an Eden for the Portuguese. They could play at being Adam, while taking those "mad-dening little women," whose calls seemed as provocative as the erect tail of the female lizard. This is mainly an ugly business, the way the imagination can disguise rape and plunder, but for a poet from a Christian country it is perfectly understandable. The poem's first words point to what she can understand, a fresh landscape: "Januaries, Nature greets our eyes / exactly as she must have greeted theirs." Setting up these two poems, "Arrival at Santos" and "Brazil, January 1, 1502," as the coordinates of Brazilian history is meant to implicate Bishop herself in the appropriation of that ter-ritory. She comes out of a culture that reaches right back to those Christian imperialists. Horrifying as their actions were (the poem captures that), she can understand their way of seeing. An empire does rest, as Rich suggested in "Villa Adriana," on lively imagination.

As poets follow the rise of empire, so too they sink with its decline, and the dark fate of empires is a wonderful subject for poets. Perhaps Bishop's best tourist poem, "Over 2000 Illustrations and a Complete Concordance" (1948), raises just this point, in an oblique, desperate fashion.

> Thus should have been our travels:
> serious, engravable.
> The Seven Wonders of the World are tired
> and a touch familiar, but the other scenes,
> innumerable, though equally sad and still,
> are foreign. Often the squatting Arab,
> or group of Arabs, plotting, probably,
> against our Christian Empire,
> while one apart, with outstretched arm and hand
> points to the Tomb, the Pit, the Sepulcher.

Bishop seems to be writing playfully about a nineteenth-century Book of the World ornamented by predictably postured illustrations. She describes the black-and-white engravings until they ignite into colorful memories of her own travels in the West Indies, Rome, Mexico, and French Morocco. The poem begins to pull toward its close when these two tours coalesce in one scene:

> It was somewhere near there
> I saw what frightened me most of all:
> A holy grave, not looking particularly holy,
> one of a group under a keyhole-arched stone baldaquin
> open to every wind from the pink desert.
>
> An open, gritty, marble trough, carved solid
> with exhortation, yellowed
> as scattered cattle-teeth;
> half filled with dust, not even the dust
> of the poor prophet paynim who once lay there.
> In a smart burnoose Khadour looked on amused.

These lines, recalling an actual experience, are a color version of the first engraving ("Arabs, plotting, probably, / against our Christian Empire"). Bishop imagines a death (a prophet's, her Christian empire's, her own) that leaves the cultural stranger, the Muslim, amused as he stands near the Tomb, even the tomb of a muslim prophet; for the faithful, death avails not. (Khadour, or al-Khadir, is an Islamic figure of immortality who was protector of mariners and river travelers. In an Urdu poem [1924] by

Muhammed Iqbal, he is the guide who asks the most serious questions of travel and has the answers. . . . The poem is obviously personal—about the fear of death without faith—but two kinds of culture, secular and sacred, are also compared; when East and West face each other, in this poem, the West blinks in empty terror.

In the fifties few American poets wrote with a sense of imperial doom (only Bishop and Lowell come to mind); then there was mainly earnest optimism among intellectuals about the expansion of American industry and the obvious accomplishment of the military. Bishop did not criticize her government; she rather wrote of an intuition that those cultures regarded as weak may stand amused before what causes the rich and strong to quake. . . . American poets are usually aware, painfully so, of being the unacknowledged representatives of national culture, or vulgarity, wealth, and power, and implicated in the expansion of empire. Abroad, America equals money, a simple and binding relationship. When Stanley Kunitz's pocket was picked on a Roman tram, he felt oddly debased, humiliated:

> More even than my purse,
> And that's no laughing matter, it is my pride
> That has been hurt: a fine Italian hand,
> With its mimosa touch, has made me feel
> Blind-skinned, indelicate, a fool Americano
> Touring a culture like a grand museum,
> People and statues interchangeable shows,
> Perception blunted as one's syntax fails.
> —"The Thief" (1956)

Entitled to outrage, he feels guilty instead; his coarseness has been exposed and its center has been touched—the cash. Even after living more than fifteen years in Brazil, Bishop felt the same onus. "Going to the Bakery" ends with an encounter between Bishop and a black man begging a token of sympathy for a recent wound. Suspecting that her alms will go only for liquor, she can do little but play her role:

> I give him seven cents in *my*
> terrific money, say "Good night"
> from force of habit. Oh, poor habit!
> Not one word more apt or bright?

Americans are the world's consumers. "Buy, buy, what shall I buy?" she asks, only half-ironically. Forgiveness, perhaps for incomprehension: "He speaks in perfect gibberish," trying to explain what has happened to him.

When Bishop's readers saw this poem in the *New Yorker* in March 1968, they would have known, from the newspapers, that Rio too was on the slide of that year's catastrophes. The preceding year had seen 30 percent inflation, and in March there were violent demonstrations there. Three days before the poem appeared, New Yorkers read that the American consulate in São Paulo had been bombed. The familiar properties were in place for the South American scenario that would come as no surprise to New Yorkers. A week after the poem appeared, one demonstration in Rio left a student dead. By the end of the year, the turmoil had led to the arrest of former President Juscelino Kubitschek, the suspension of constitutional guarantees, the dissolution of congress, and a declaration of martial law. Less than a year later, the military was back in control. Writing as these events were just beginning to slip into their relentless cycle, Bishop felt helpless, tainted, and estranged, an American with no more to offer than seven luckless pennies and a banality.

Affluence and a favorable exchange rate (in 1968 those seven pennies would buy a pound of sugar) give a tourist a sense of power; everyone has felt that and, however guilty or embarrassed at times, gratitude too for immunity from the small confusions and uncertainties that dog a tourist. But when a nation counts on that immunity and power (or, worse still, when one's hosts presume that such power is real), its humanity is endangered. Richard Wilbur has a poem on this theme, a fable about the birds for sale in Paris.

> Hundreds of birds are singing in the square.
> Their minor voices fountaining in air
> And constant as a fountain, lightly loud,
> Do not drown out the burden of the crowd.
>
> Far from his gold Sudan, the travailleur
> Lends to the noise an intermittent chirr
> Which to his hearers seems more joy than rage.
> He batters softly at his wooden cage.
>
> Here are the silver-bill, the orange-cheek,
> The perroquet, the dainty coral-beak
> Stacked in their cages; and around them move
> The buyers in their termless hunt for love.
>
> Here are the old, the ill, the imperial child;
> The lonely people, desperate and mild;

The ugly; past these faces one can read
The tyranny of one outrageous need.

We love the small, said Burke. And if the small
Be not yet small enough, why then by Hell
We'll cramp it till it knows but how to feed,
And we'll provide the water and the seed.
—"Marché aux Oiseaux" (1949)

Those picturesque birds have been brought from exotic places to the capital, where they can be bought and sold by those who want to feel loved as well as powerful. This, Wilbur suggests, is the psychology of imperialism, but its basis in human nature generally is firm: affection is extended easily to the weak because it is self-serving; kindness to those who might be squashed suggests restraint and generosity. So powerful is the need to be regarded as beneficent that the mighty will reduce the victims of their magnanimity to helplessness. And, as the second quatrain suggests, the imperialist is out to deceive himself as well as others: protests must be heard as songs of joy. At the basis of imperialism (and of tourism too) is a tempting deception that mocks most human interchange.

American poets are commonly thought of as adversaries to political expansion, as advocates of disarmament. But the evidence is abundant that poets, like other observers, were captivated by the proliferation of American interests after World War II. More important, some of these poets, with the interests of the capital in mind (least of all is this an expatriated literature), have written distinguished poems that set out a sensitive, far-seeing critique of American expansion. Seeing the attractions of expansion, and feeling these attractions powerfully as poets, Bishop, Cassity, and others nonetheless took a critical perspective on expansion. Enthusiastic, implicated, and still critical in a measured way: these are the poets who have written best about the effort to take over where France, England, and Germany left off.

I have stressed the cultural purpose served by tourist poems, rather than what might be spoken of as the intentions of the poets, in order to show that these poems address a major experience shared by many middle-class Americans of the fifties and later. I do not mean to suggest that these writers were State Department agents fulfilling a plan for cultural hegemony; rather few of these poets traveled for the State Department. Nor was there explicit discussion among poets of the offices of tourist poetry. The poets wrote about a subject that was held in focus by some conventions of treatment and elaboration; this was also a subject their own experience brought close to them, and they knew it to be close to the experience of their middle-class readers. This subject held one other attraction for poets then: it enabled them to write poems about social life.

A tourist-poet often writes about people, foreign people, with a fresh eye, and that is a powerful attraction for any poet. Poems about people raise some special problems for postwar American poets. The burden of literary tradition was especially heavy in this area. There were two conventional ways of writing about the social activities of Americans after World War II: one was the type-poem in which a character was drawn of a representative type, not of an individual (Wilbur's "He Was" [1950] and Merwin's "The Master" [1956] are examples). The second method was to write with irony turned against a vulgar or crass American character (the bounder in Merrill's "Charles on Fire" [1960] is the best example). But poems written about middle-class American social behavior from a sympathetic viewpoint were more unusual. Immediate literary precedents, the weight of avant-garde scorn for the bourgeoisie, made it difficult to write poems of observation, curiosity, and sympathy or respect about Americans who have claim to social normality; certain literary attitudes, such as the fear of sentiment, or of naïveté, were strongly exclusive, especially in the fifties. Tourist poems offered poets a quick way around conventional attitudes. Although it might be difficult to write admiringly of the social activity of Americans in the fifties—poets being too ironic and sophisticated to show sympathy so close to home—it was relatively easy to write warmly of foreigners.

Many of these poets tended to admire the same human aspects that would set clicking the shutters of any busload of foreigners. Paul Blackburn writing about the instinctive tenderness of a class-conscious sailor in the Adriatic ("The First Mate" [1955]) or the spirited gesture of a gypsy ("Whee!" [1956])—these are pleasant but unremarkable contributions to the genre. What is noteworthy, though, is some rather pointed agreement among poets as to the particular European traits worthy of American admiration. Merwin wrote (in "In the Heart of Europe" [1956]) about the bond between European farmers and the land they till: "You feel they would never / Say the place belonged to them: a reticence / Like love's delicacy or its quiet assurance."

How very un-American, which is exactly the point. These farmers represent an acknowledged core of European values: respect for the tacit, the calm, the refined, and the confident. On the contrary, Americans are typically quick to say proudly that the land they occupy is their own. They prefer relationships to be explicitly defined, partly because their history inspires no particular assurance about the future. In "St. John's, Hampstead," Gullans admires the "style of calm and dignified restraint" expressed in British funerary monuments. Those who repose there were public men who held a "common hope."

A sense of shared fate, of being a member of a group, was regarded by these poets as particularly European and, for obvious reasons, quite distinct from the American ethos. Writing about the small ways that Europeans instinctively know that their lives are tied to a collective civic life provided a means of urging moderation on those Americans of the fifties who thought that the world was theirs. Merwin's poem begins: "Farmers hereabouts, for generations now / Have owned their own places"; any midwestern American would hear compatriots being addressed with that idiom. From its first lines, the poem draws an implicit contrast between European and American ways, though no invidious comparison is actually spelled out. The second line of Gullans's poem—"Of this smooth Georgian pomp none was ashamed"—makes clear too that he writes with an awareness of how embarrassing American pomp can be. Blackburn, in "Affinities II" (1956–57), asks quite directly: "When will we learn / so naturally to / quit, when what we have to do / is done?" Even poems that purport to describe fondly the distinctly European ways of these travelers' hosts are in fact turned to American utility: the tourist poem allowed American poets to write, often obliquely, as social observers, yes, but also as critics of the extreme individualism of their own nation.

Sometimes too the barb was turned back against the pretensions of cultivated tourists.

> Oh, tourist,
> is this how this country is going to answer you
>
> and your immodest demands for a different world,
> and a better life, and complete comprehension
> of both at last, and immediately,
> after eighteen days of suspension?
> —Elizabeth Bishop, "Arrival at Santos"

Even poet-tourists, Bishop suggests (addressing herself), may imagine that they get (and still worse, are entitled to) more from their travels than in fact they do. Cultivation? Neither Bishop nor Merrill are so sure about that. Compared to the Caspar Goodwoods who know their limits, sophisticated travelers are not uniformly charming. These are the opening stanzas of Merrill's "Words for Maria":

> Unjeweled in black as ever comedienne
> Of mourning if not silent star of chic,
> You drift, September nightwind at your back,
> The half block from your flat to the Bon Goût,
> Collapse, order a black
> Espresso and my ouzo in that Greek
> Reserved for waiters, crane to see who's who
> Without removing your dark glasses, then,
> Too audibly: "Eh, Jimmy, qui sont ces deux strange men?"
>
> Curiosity long since killed the cat
> Inside you. Sweet good nature, lack of guile,
> These are your self-admitted foibles, no?
> My countrymen, the pair in question, get
> Up, glance our way, and go,
> And we agree it will not be worthwhile
> To think of funny nicknames for them yet,
> Such as Le Turc, The Missing Diplomat,
> Justine, The Nun, The Nut— . . .

These poems by Bishop and Merrill set seasoned travelers next to perhaps simpler Americans: Bishop and Miss Breen from Glens Falls, New York; Merrill and "ces deux strange men." Moreover, both poems invoke those camp idioms ("So that's the flag. I never saw it before. / I somehow never thought of there *being* a flag") that most call into question the worth of sophistication. The critique of tourism suggested by these two poems is rather different from Emerson's: the issue here is not whether one skates on surfaces or dives for meaning. Bishop and Merrill set the terms instead for a social critique of tourism and sophistication. Maria and Bishop ("Please, boy, do be more careful with that boat hook!") are impolite. Miss Breen has "Beautiful bright blue eyes and a kind expression"; the two Americans in Athens move on discreetly, perhaps to another café. Melville seems to have been not entirely correct: a great deal of travel may not in fact have a liberalizing effect on the spirit. The sophistication that extended travel brings may not have much to do with genuine *bon goût*. And where then do the tourist-poets end?

Tourist poems represent a self-conscious kind of art, though for good, unusual, and (one might say) subtly patriotic reasons. The adequacy of

American high culture was in serious question after World War II, exactly because the nation's economic and military institutions were moving into many of the places left unattended by the European powers. For poets to feel upon them the questioning eyes of fellow citizens, as well as of Europeans, was natural, and to concentrate their energies on those types of poems that display taste, sophistication, intelligence, and inventiveness was, after all, responsible. The still greater responsibility of writing critically as well as patriotically these poets have managed admirably. I have not tried to suggest that only a new imperial power will produce tourist poetry; British poets too, as John Press has shown in *Rule and Energy* (1963), were writing tourist poems by the score during the fifties. A number of different impulses (some strictly literary—the desire to write descriptive or social verse; some economic and circumstantial—the favorable exchange rate and low cost of air fare, the availability of travel fellowships) coincided to produce the tourist poetry I have described. My point is only that these poems performed a special service for the nation in the fifteen years or so following the war. That the responsiveness of poets to the needs of the national culture should issue in poems on the order of Hollander's "Lazienka," Bishop's "Questions of Travel," and, best of all, Merrill's "Thousand and Second Night" is proof enough that even the timeliest of what I have called, after Karl Shapiro, culture poetry has shown extraordinary literary distinction in the last thirty-five years.

WORKS CITED

Ashbery, John. *Some Trees.* 1956. Rpt. New York: Corinth, 1970.

Auden, W. H. *The Dyer's Hand.* New York: Vintage, 1962.

Bishop, Elizabeth. *Complete Poems.* New York: Farrar, Straus & Giroux, 1969.

Blackburn, Paul. *The Cities.* New York: Grove, 1967.

Bowers, Edgar. *Living Together.* Manchester, Eng.: Carcanet, 1977.

Cassity, Turner. *Watchboy, What of the Night?* Middletown, Conn.: Wesleyan UP, 1966.

Eisenhower, Dwight D. Quoted in Stephen E. Ambrose, *Rise to Globalism: American Foreign Policy Since 1938.* Baltimore: Penguin Books, 1971.

Emerson, Ralph Waldo. Quoted in Morton Dauwen Zabel, ed. Introduction. *The Art of Travel: Scenes and Journeys in America, England, France and Italy from the Travel Writings of Henry James.* Garden City, N.Y.: Doubleday, 1958.

Gullans, Charles. *Arrivals and Departures.* Minneapolis: U of Minnesota P, 1962.

Hecht, Anthony. *Millions of Strange Shadows.* New York: Atheneum, 1977.

———. *A Summoning of Stones*. New York: Macmillan, 1954.

Hollander, John. *A Crackling of Thorns*. New Haven: Yale UP, 1958.

———. *Movie-Going and Other Poems*. New York: Atheneum, 1962.

———. *Town and Country Matters: Erotica and Satirica*. Boston: D. R. Godine, 1972.

Howard, Richard. *Fellow Feelings*. New York: Atheneum, 1976.

———. *Findings*. New York: Atheneum, 1971.

James, Henry. Quoted in *The Art of Travel*. Ed. Morton Dauwen Zabel. Garden City, N.Y.: Doubleday, 1958.

Keats, John. *The Poems of John Keats*. Ed. Jack Stillinger. Cambridge: Harvard UP, 1978.

Kunitz, Stanley. *Poems, 1928–1978*. Boston: Atlantic/Little, Brown, 1979.

Melville, Herman. "Traveling." In *Melville as Lecturer*. Ed. Merton M. Sealts, Jr. Cambridge: Harvard UP, 1957 181–85.

Merrill, James. *The Country of a Thousand Years of Peace*. Rev. ed. New York: Atheneum, 1970.

———. *The Fire Screen*. New York: Atheneum, 1969.

———. *Nights and Days*. New York: Atheneum, 1966.

Merwin, W. S. *Green with Beasts*. London: Rupert Hart-Davis, 1956.

Rich, Adrienne. *A Change of World*. New Haven: Yale UP, 1951.

———. *The Diamond Cutters*. New York: Harper, 1955.

Rilke, Rainer Maria. *Selected Poems of Rainer Maria Rilke*. Trans. Robert Bly. New York: Harper & Row, 1979.

Tate, Allen. Letter to Frederick A. Colwell, 30 July 1959. Allen Tate Collection, Princeton U Library.

Wilbur, Richard. *Poems*. New York: Harcourt, Brace & World, 1963.

> > > > > > **Paul Theroux and the Poetry of Departures**

ELTON GLASER

Charles Dickens in America, Henry James in France, Anthony Trollope on his swing from the Middle East to California: nineteenth-century novelists who traveled found it natural to write about the places they had visited, the people they had seen. The recent resurgence of travel literature again seems to be driven by fiction writers who have turned their hands to travel writing, most prominent among them V. S. Naipaul and Paul Theroux; and no one has been more alert to the principles and practices of the genre than has Theroux. Particularly in *The Old Patagonian Express* (1979), but also in *The Great Railway Bazaar* (1975), *The Kingdom by the Sea* (1983), and some of the short pieces in *Sunrise with Seamonsters* (1985), Theroux has not simply recounted his adventures in foreign and familiar places, he has also reflected on the meaning of travel and travel writing.

There is, however, an irony in the self-reflexive nature of Theroux's travel writings: while many of the twentieth century's most celebrated literary works come with a built-in analysis of their own composition, Theroux's novels and short stories have resolutely followed the conventions of realistic fiction. The stories in *The Consul's File* (1977) and *The London Embassy* (1983), for example, are entertainingly old-fashioned chapters in the life of a junior American diplomat, an intelligent scrapbook of Asia and England compiled with a straightforward and low-key realism. Even when a novel threatens to become self-reflexive, as does *Saint Jack* (1973), the book soon reverts to a traditionally unobtrusive narrative style. Jack Flowers, the book's eponymous sadsack hustler, begins his tale self-consciously: "In any memoir it is usual for the first sentence to reveal as much as possible of your subject's nature by illustrating it in a vivid and memorable motto, and with my own first sentence now drawing to a finish I see I have failed to do this!" After that brief nod to metafiction, however,

A version of this essay appeared first in *Centennial Review* 33, no. 3 (Summer 1989): 193–206.

153

the novel, or "memoir," soon settles into an easy lope that leaves behind all speculations about genre conventions: Flowers—or Theroux—has a story to tell, and does not further interrupt the narrative with questions about how that story might be told. The irony deepens when we note that, for Theroux, travel and fiction writing are closely related activities. His essay "Discovering Dingle" begins by asserting that the "nearest thing to writing a novel is traveling in a strange country" and then develops that conceit for a full paragraph. In *The Great Railway Bazaar*, Theroux hears "strangers' monologues framed like Russian short stories" and understands that a "railway was a fictor's bazaar, in which anyone with the patience could carry away a memory to pore over in privacy. The memories were inconclusive, but an ending, as in the best fiction, was always implied." Later, surveying the passengers on a train leaving Saigon, he sees in them "a fictional possibility, a situation containing both a riddle and some clues for solving it."

The "fictional possibility" sometimes becomes fact, as Theroux draws on his travel experiences to compose his novels. For example, on his journey through the Americas, Theroux visits the sandy coast of Costa Rica and notes that it is "wild and looks the perfect setting for the story of castaways." Later, when he meets a group of Baptist missionaries gourmandizing at a fancy restaurant in Colombia, he suddenly realized "who those castaways might be." A few years later, Theroux does write his novel about castaways, *The Mosquito Coast* (1982), making one of the important characters a missionary. Like his friend and one-time mentor, V. S. Naipaul, Theroux seems to need the stimulation of travel, the glimpse of an alien life, in order to construct a fictional world.

Another element that the travel book shares with many novels is the foregrounding of the narrator. The travel writer, telling the story of his journey, becomes the central character in the book; we respond as much to his personality as to the details of the journey that he reports to us. Otherwise, we might as well be sitting through another droning slideshow on Tahiti or the Taj Mahal. When we read Eric Newby's *A Short Walk Through the Hindu Kush* (1958) we center our pleasure in the author-narrator, just as we enjoy *Huckleberry Finn* because we are moved and amused by Huck's blend of backwoods innocence and shrewdness. While other aspects of these books also hold our attention, the only narrative constant is the revealing voice of the traveler.

Every travel book is a trip through two dimensions, the external world and an internal world. The reader takes interest both in the facts the author includes—everything from the traveler's intestinal calamities to the scientific name for a rare orchid hanging in the rain forests of Brazil—as well as in his reactions to these facts. This interior journey through a writer's mind, in which the reader notes the contours of the traveler's mental landscape, is like looking through a train window at dusk, at just that moment when our own reflection is superimposed on the world outside the glass, and suddenly object and subject exist on the same plane, the perceived and the perceiver a single intelligence in an eerie rapprochement.

Throughout his travel books, Theroux halts his narrative to consider the nature of travel, its drawbacks and optimal conditions, the unstated rules and the unavoidable effects of a journey. One dictum stressed by Theroux is that the serious traveler, as he puts it in *The Old Patagonian Express*, always journeys alone: "Travel is at its best a solitary enterprise: to see, to examine, to assess, you have to be alone and unencumbered. Other people can mislead you; they crowd your meandering impressions with their own; if they are companionable they obstruct your view, and if they are boring they corrupt the silence with non-sequiturs, shattering your concentration."

Seeking freedom from any entanglements that would impede his journey or blunt his perceptions, Theroux even refuses to contact people who have been recommended by friends back home: "I had been offered the addresses of people, but one of my rules of travel was to avoid looking up my friends' friends. In the past I had done so reluctantly, and the results had been awkward, not to say disastrous." The solitary traveler, though, is still vulnerable to unwanted ministrations, a source of both annoyance and satisfaction. "In travel," he says in *The Kingdom by the Sea*, "you meet people who try to lay hold of you, who take charge like parents, and criticize. Another of travel's pleasures was turning your back on them and leaving and never having to explain."

But even a successful escape from boorish interruptions can turn against the traveler, leaving him too much alone, trapped in a paradox of his own making: "I sat and wrote; I read and went to sleep; I drank; and often I would look up and be incapable of remembering where I was, the concentration of writing or reading bringing on a trancelike state. Extensive traveling induces a feeling of encapsulation; and travel, so broadening at first, contracts the mind."

For Theroux, the ideal mode of travel is by train, partly because it affords him enough distractions to occupy his mind, but not so many distractions that he loses touch with his inner self. "Train travel," he says in *The Great Railway Bazaar*, "animated my imagination and usually gave me the solitude to order and write my thoughts: I traveled easily in two directions, along the level rails while Asia flashed changes at the window, and at the interior rim of a private world of memory and language."

In these asides on the nature of travel, Theroux reports on the landscapes and societies he encounters and extrapolates from these experiences some general rules or qualities of travel, often in such aphorisms as "travel, above all, is a test of memory" or "travel itself was a sort of optimism in action." For the most part, we trust the conclusions he comes to, because we can see their basis in the particular scene or event he has just experienced. And Theroux also takes pains to convince us that he is a traveler in the grand tradition of philosopher-observers, set far apart from other characters who temporarily share his journey on the open road.

In his essay "Strangers on a Train," Theroux recognizes that there are "two sort of travelers." In the first group "are those whom we instantly recognize as clinging to the traditional virtues of travel, the people who endure a kind of alienation and panic in foreign parts for the aftertaste of having sampled new scenes." This type of traveler journeys alone and willingly suffers deprivations, discomforts, and dangers in order "to make interesting discoveries about oneself and one's surroundings." Travel, Theroux insists, "has less to do with distance than with insight."

The second group of travelers wants no part of the strangeness, the disorientation, the hazards so appealing to the true traveler. Instead, this group engages in what Theroux has called "mock-travel" or "Travel As A Version Of Being At Home." What these people want to see in "foreign surroundings is familiar sights;" they want the glamor of exotic places without the hassle of traditional travel; they want to tour Istanbul with all the amenities available in their Atlanta suburb. The problem, according to Theroux's diagnosis, is that this group has confused "travel" with "vacation," so that travel becomes "a form of repose" instead of an opportunity for insight, an arrival at a new knowledge of the self and of the world.

Three years after that essay, Theroux further refined his distinctions in *The Old Patagonian Express*. Near the end of his trip to the bottom of Argentina, Theroux puts himself into a class apart from his fellow train riders: "I had decided quite early in my trip that I was an implausible traveller—no credit cards, no rucksack. I was not well dressed enough to be a tourist on a ten-day jaunt through ruins and cathedrals; nor was I dirty or frazzled enough to be a wanderer. . . . Tourists regarded me as a backslider, wanderers seemed to think I was an intruder, and natives did not understand me."

Theroux, with "neither a tourist badge nor a rucksack," locates himself somewhere between these two groups, a true traveler looking neither to exploit the society he travels through, nor to ignore it, but to learn from it. He is neither a free spender nor a freeloader: he does not travel in a group or adhere to the tourists' immutable schedule, and neither does he simply follow the wanderers' habit of hunkering down wherever the exchange rate is favorable and the food cheap.

While Theroux has little use for his fellow passengers, he does welcome one kind of traveling companion: books. Authors and titles and literary allusions appear regularly in his pages, and he seems lost whenever he has nothing to read. In South America, Theroux uses books as a survival mechanism. James Boswell's *Life of Johnson* becomes his "lifeline": "There was no landscape in it. I had all the landscape I wanted out the window. What I lacked was talk, and this was brilliant talk, sage advice, funny remarks. . . . I think if I had not had that book to read as I made my way through Colombia, the trip would have been unendurable."

To read Theroux is to listen to a running commentary on the books that accompany him on the trip or that spring to his mind as he passes through some apposite location: "For railway reading, the best book is the plottiest, a way of endowing the haphazardness of the journey with order." We are even, on occasion, offered lessons in literary criticism, as when Theroux, in *The Old Patagonian Express*, runs afoul of the "torrential irrelevance" and "confederate metaphysics" of Faulkner's *The Wild Palms*. Faulkner's style becomes not only an irritant but a soporific: "What had put me to sleep? Perhaps this sentence, or rather, the tail end of a long straggling sentence: '. . . it was the mausoleum of love, it was the stinking catafalque of the dead corpse borne between the olfactoryless walking shapes of the immortal unsentient demanding ancient meat.' " After such rhetoric, what forgiveness? Theroux deflates the sentence with this comment: "I was not sure what Faulkner was driving at, and yet it seemed a fair description of the sausage I was eating that early morning in Ohio."

Besides the books that Theroux brings with him to break the monotony of the journey—books that range from Browning's poems to Paranhansa Yogananda's *Autobiography of a Yogi*—he also frequently mentions writers or books connected with the country he happens to be traveling through. Sometimes these are used as a background against which to measure Theroux's own experience, as when he explains that his "image of the Indian city derives from Kipling," or when he recognizes that V. S. Naipaul's "loathing of Argentina" might be partly attributed to Naipaul's being a vegetarian in a country devoted to beefsteaks the size of footballs.

Sometimes these authors and books are brought in to supply information that Theroux needs to understand current attitudes and conditions.

He turns to David McCullough's *The Path Between the Seas*, for instance, to learn how the history of the Panama Canal resulted in the present antagonism between the Panamanians and the Americans in the Canal Zone. Sometimes these books are called to mind because their settings happen to be the places through which Theroux is traveling. This is most clearly seen on Theroux's excursion around the coast of Great Britain, where he complains that "England was so hard to describe" because "much of it had been written about by great men, and the very mention of a place in a literary work tended to distort the place, for literature had the capacity to turn the plainest corner of England into a shrine." Other parts of the world also call up associated books. Traveling through Switzerland, Theroux notes, "At Vevey, I thought of Daisy," an allusion not only to Henry James's novella *Daisy Miller*, whose first part is set in Vevey, but also—and more playfully—to Edmund Wilson's novel, *I Thought of Daisy*. Perhaps this kind of cultural knee jerk is inevitable when educated people are let loose on the world.

The most important variety of book that Theroux mentions is the travel book. These references serve two functions. First, they show that Theroux has thoroughly prepared for his journeys by reading the relevant guidebooks or memoirs. For example, in Guatemala, Theroux cites a passage from Arthur Morelet's 1871 volume, *Travels in Central America*, and when he is touring the periphery of Great Britain, he frequently alludes to Henry James's *English Hours* (1905).

The second function of these references is to indicate that Theroux is a student of travel writing as a literary art. He demonstrates his familiarity with obscure pieces like Archibald Little's *Through the Yangtse Gorges* (1888), as well as with acknowledged masterpieces like Robert Byron's *The Road to Oxiana* (1937) or Alexander Kinglake's *Eothen* (1844). These constant references to travel literature represent Theroux's way of establishing his credentials with the reader. Thus, when he speaks to us about the genre of travel writing, we accept his authority on two counts: he has made the journeys, and he has studied the exemplary works in this form.

As a student of travel writing, Theroux understands the mixed nature of the genre. "Travel writing," he says in *The Great Railway Bazaar*, "which cannot but be droll at the outset, moves from journalism to fiction, arriving as promptly as the Kodama Echo [a Japanese train] at autobiography. From there any further travel makes a beeline to confession." In other words, travel writing moves from the objective to the subjective, from the fact to the feeling, from a plot determined by events to a plot shaped by the reaction to events. What all of these forms of writing have in common is *narrative*. For Theroux, a travel book typifies "the loner bouncing back bigger than life to tell the story of his experiment with space. It is the simplest sort of narrative, an explanation which is its own excuse for the gathering up and the going. It is motion given order by its repetition in words."

Though the travel narrative may be simple, it still presents difficulties for the writer. In *The Kingdom by the Sea,* for example, Theroux begins by surveying the problems he will have writing a book about a country as tramped-over and dog-eared as Great Britain, and then he extends his personal difficulties to travel writers as a group, who will always have to confront questions of perspective, tone, and itinerary. The problem of perspective, of course, is related to the fiction writer's concern with point of view. For the travel writer, however, this question is practical as well as literary: "How and where to go to get the best view of the place?" The problem of tone also has a double level: the attitude one takes toward the people among whom one is traveling will determine the attitude one strikes when recounting the experiences in a book. And the last problem, that of itinerary, has practical and literary aspects, too: "My route was crucial. It was the most important aspect of travel. In choosing a route, one was choosing a subject." This point may be stated almost tautologically: where a writer travels will determine what a traveler writes about. Itinerary becomes plot.

Sometimes, as in *The Old Patagonian Express,* we are actually allowed to observe Theroux practice his craft, to look over his shoulder as he jots impressions in a notebook: "*policeman's face like salami . . . inky water . . . flags.*" In this instance, the scribbled notes are introduced to us only after they have been transformed into shapely passages—a policeman "whose puffy face was chilled the color of salami," several icy streams whose "moving water turned to ink by the twilight," a puzzling display of American flags "flying over gas stations and supermarkets and in numerous yards"— the way an artist might invite us into his workshop to explain how he has fashioned a piece we admire. This glimpse into Theroux's working methods, his processing of raw material into a finished product, is similar to the effect John Barth creates in "Lost in the Funhouse," where the narrator tries out various phrasings or abandons thoughts half-formed as he tells his story. In both cases, we are permitted to watch the writer explore his material, moving from rough notes to the polished expressions that will preserve for readers his experience.

While Theroux is interested in the demands of his genre, he is not always satisfied with the solutions other travel writers have found for these problems. He is disturbed, for example, by the opening gambits of many travel books. As he notes in *The Old Patagonian Express*, "the convention is to telescope travel writing, to start—as so many novels do—in the middle of things, to beach the reader in a bizarre place without having first guided him there." Particularly irritating to Theroux is the aerial perspective with which many contemporary travel books begin: "The literature of travel has become measly; the standard opening, that farcical nose-against-the-porthole view from the plane's tilted fuselage. The joke opening, that straining for effect, is now so familiar it is nearly impossible to parody."

Theroux does offer a remedy for the *in medias res* beginning of travel books in the Air Age: explain *why* you began the journey and *how* you arrived at your destination. "Even without a motive," he says, "a prologue is welcome, since the going is often as fascinating as the arrival." Because travel, by its nature, is motion and not stasis, the travel writer should be more concerned with the sweep of the journey than with frozen set-pieces of description. On his trip to Patagonia, Theroux muses: "I had known all along that I had no intention of writing about being in a place—that took the skill of a miniaturist. I was more interested in the going and the getting there, in the poetry of departures." The shock and ambiguities of action, the details of mobility, are what sustain a travel book. As Theroux recognizes, the writer faces his most difficult moments when the journey is interrupted: "Nothing seems longer than the unexpected delay. Nothing is harder to describe or more boring to read."

But travelers do eventually reach their destinations, experiencing the relief and disappointment inherent in a journey's end, the post-travel *triste* that is simultaneously satisfying and unfulfilling. For the travel writer, however, all events are recoverable: the journey need not end as long as a text preserves it. On the final page of *The Great Railway Bazaar*, Theroux recognizes this paradox of endless completion: "The trip is finished and so is the book, and in a moment I will turn to the first page, and to amuse myself on the way to London will read with some satisfaction the trip that begins, *Ever since childhood. . .*"

The travel writer can savor his experiences once again in the telling and the reading. But this literary delectation of travel is not for everyone. In Japan, Theroux meets a fellow train passenger who tells him that travel books are useless " 'Because everyone travels. . . . So who wants to read about it?' " In Scotland, Theroux encounters another skeptic, who complains " 'There's too many bloody travel books,' " a charge that Theroux "did not deny." Though Theroux does not answer his critic, we might supply a response for him by recognizing those readers for whom travel literature is still valuable.

In the broadest terms, travel books can be said to attract several different kinds of readers. The first type includes those who travel frequently and want to test their own experiences in Paris or Cairo against the adventures and insights of the travel writers. Sometimes this experienced reader amuses himself by filling in the blanks, by noting what the travel writer has decided not to include in his book. Henry Miller devotes a chapter of *The Air-Conditioned Nightmare* to his stay at The Shadows, an old mansion built on the banks of Bayou Teche in New Iberia, Louisiana. Miller relates this anecdote: "The next morning, after breakfast, as I was about to open a door which had blown shut, I saw to my astonishment the signatures in pencil on the back of the door of hundreds of celebrities, written in every scrawl imaginable. Of course we had to add our own to the collection. I signed mine under that of a Hungarian named Bloor Schleppey."

What Henry Miller does not say is that many of the signatures were attached to a brief remark, as if the door were a larger edition of a high-school yearbook. But anyone who visits the Shadows could supply the missing information, including Miller's own scribbled caption: "I expect to be back and write a book here—the book of camellias and hallucinations. 1/26/41." Perhaps Miller omitted that message because, by the time his book was published in 1945, he had not returned to Louisiana to write the expected book—though one might argue that all of Henry Miller's books have in them some share of hallucination, if not magnolias.

A second group of readers are the "armchair travelers," people who find reasons to remain at home instead of visiting Venice or Mozambique or the Cajun parishes of Louisiana. They prefer to experience these places vicariously, through the senses of the travel writers. Seated comfortably in their armchairs, they travel through the printed page, their favorite mode of transportation, where they do indeed fly by the seat of their pants.

Other readers may be drawn to travel books because they offer a kind of recovery of innocence, a childlike reentry into a world that again seems alive with possibilities. If we think of our earliest years as a time of discovery, when every sight was new and every sensation promised terror or delight, then we can understand how reading a travel book is a return to a life when the world was slowly opening before us, not closing after us as it does now, the decades trailing and fading behind our lives like the wake of a ship. Travel books bring us new data that enable us to confirm, modify, or reject our visions of the world. But their appeal goes beyond the earnestness of self-education, beyond our fumbling attempts to patch together a philosophy of life. Travel books have the capacity to bring us back to original awe, to make us feel again the world that surprised us every morning we awoke, each new day an unpredictable adventure. Travel books can make us feel, in the only redeeming sense of the word, our enormous ignorance. As Wallace Stevens says at the end of "The Sense of the Sleight-of-Hand Man":

> It may be that the ignorant man, alone,
> Has any chance to mate his life with life
> That is the sensual, pearly spouse, the life
> That is fluent in even the wintriest bronze.

One of the peculiarities of travel books is their ability to make us feel the strangeness of the world without making us feel like strangers in it.

A fourth type of reader, represented by the essayists in this volume, seems to be emerging: the student of travel writing, whose emphasis is more on the *writing* than the *travel*. In travel books—as in all successful writing—we find a literal "authorizing" of experience, which we judge not by its mimetic value, not by how accurately it presents a picture of the world out there, but by its internal consistency, its artistic manipulation of language, detail, and structure.

That Theroux does not include photographs in his travel books is no accident; he means for readers to look at the world through his precise and pungent style, not through the falsely factual lens of a camera. In *The Old Patagonian Express*, for instance, Theroux finds a kind of railway romanticism even at Ponca City, Oklahoma, where the countryside was "flat and barren; but the traces of snow—pelts of it blown into ruts and depressions, like the scattered carcasses of ermine—were not enough to keep me sulking in bed." On that same journey, he turns the sardonic accuracy of his style on the American missionaries mentioned earlier in this essay, ten of them indulging their appetites at "an expensive Sunday-night buffet at one of the fancy restaurants" in Cali, Colombia, a city prostrate with poverty:

> There were two enormous men and two fat women, a pot-bellied boy and some smaller children; they were the sort of Bible-punching Baptists who are sometimes found bristling with poisoned arrows on a tributary of the upper Amazon, meddlesome Midwesterners groping and preaching their way through the blankest part of the South American map, only to meet,

just in time for the church newsletter back home, a peculiarly gruesome martyrdom. But tonight they were having a whale of a time.

The best travel books do not simply report on a world we can verify by retracing the author's journey; they recreate the world we travel through, as author and reader become companions carried forward on a flow of wit and insight.

If travel writing is to assume an important position in the canon and curriculum of literature, a position at least as important as that of science fiction or the western novel, then it must be identified as a distinct genre with its own laws and amendments. Paul Theroux, as a noted practitioner and a sometime theoretician of travel writing, offers this new group of readers an intelligent and entertaining entry into the genre, an appropriate departure point for anyone interested in the poetry—and the poetics—of departure.

WORKS CITED

Miller, Henry. *The Air-Conditioned Nightmare*. New York: Grove, 1945.

Stevens, Wallace. *The Collected Poems of Wallace Stevens*. New York: Random House, 1954.

Theroux, Paul. *The Consul's File*. New York: Pocket, 1977.

———. "Discovering Dingle." In *Sunrise with Seamonsters: Travels & Discoveries, 1964–1984*. Boston: Houghton Mifflin, 1986, 140–45.

———. *The Great Railway Bazaar*. New York: Ballantine, 1975.

———. *The Kingdom by the Sea*. Boston: Houghton Mifflin, 1983.

———. *The London Embassy*. New York: Pocket, 1983.

———. *The Old Patagonian Express*. New York: Pocket, 1979.

———. *Sailing Through China*. Boston: Houghton Mifflin, 1984.

———. *Saint Jack*. New York: Pocket, 1973.

———. "Stranger on a Train: The Pleasures of Railways." In *Sunrise with Seamonsters*, 126–35.

> > > > > > The Wilds of New Jersey: John McPhee as Travel Writer

DAVID ESPEY

Is John McPhee really a travel writer? And if he is, am I doing him any favors by calling him one? He is usually viewed as a higher journalist, a naturalist, a nonfiction writer in the *New Yorker* mode. Those kinds of writers don't get a lot of respect from literary critics, but they do better than travel writers, who are generally considered lightweight—like vacations and guidebooks. As the late Bruce Chatwin, a premier British travel writer, once complained, he wanted his books shelved alongside those of Geoffrey Chaucer on the literary shelves, but he invariably ended up next to *Czechoslovakia on $10 a Day*.

If we compare McPhee with Paul Theroux, who more obviously fits the category of travel writer, we will find significant differences in the way they structure trips and books. Theroux plots a general journey (by rail through Asia, for example) and proceeds in leisurely fashion, looking for the chance encounter, the noteworthy, the seedy. He reads widely on the region through which he will travel, but he has only a loose idea about what he is after. The form of his writing—chronological, episodic, and picaresque, reflects the casual style of his actual travel. He travels alone, and he is the major character in his writing. As Paul Fussell notes in "The Stationary Tourist," Theroux writes "real" travel literature precisely because he doesn't plan, but rather courts the unexpected.

Theroux travels almost exclusively abroad, but John McPhee generally stays at home in North America. He plans meticulously and focuses his attention less on himself and more on some technical expert with whom he travels. The tight, deliberate structure of his writing reflects his fascination with the expert's control of knowledge—be it geology or forestry or canoe construction.

Yet travel is essential to McPhee's work—and not merely because he has to take planes or Land Rovers to the sites about which he wishes to write. Travel literature constitutes one form of the literature of fact, a term associated particularly with McPhee because he has taught a writing course under that title at Princeton. He seeks out areas that are remote and unspoiled, and facts that are important but little known. He interviews natives, and explores canyons, rivers, and basins. Discussing the history of travel, Fussell explains that "travel was conceived to be like study . . . the traveler was a student of what he sought." In this sense, McPhee is as much a travel writer as anyone. If he sounds more like a journalist on a business trip than a traveler, remember, as travel writers are quick to insist, that travel is work. William Least Heat-Moon reminds us that the word *travel* comes from *travail*. Or, as another authority on this matter, Henry David Thoreau, puts it, "True and sincere travelling is no pastime, but it is as serious as the grave, or any part of the human journey."

Given this more substantive view of travel, one might call McPhee a travel writer without doing him a disservice. But like most travel writers, he has more than travel on his agenda. Travel writing is a genre that can accommodate enormously varied subject matter. McPhee can be a nature writer, a writer of profiles, a technical writer, and a sports writer, and at the same time be a travel writer.

To be a travel writer, you have to get away from home—even if, like Thoreau, you don't go very far away. The distinction between home and non-home is essential to travel writing. McPhee uses his home state, New Jersey, as a reference point against which to compare the places where he travels; his writing on New Jersey itself reflects in miniature his writing on the world outside his home state. Whether he is in Alaska, or the canyons of the Colorado River, or the Pine Barrens of New Jersey, McPhee has the same preoccupation—the clash between man's exploitation of the land and his reverence for the wilderness.

Nature writing and travel writing have, of course, a great deal in common, especially in America. American travel writers are like Huck Finn: they light out for the territory. Ernest Hemingway's assertion that modern American literature proceeds from Mark Twain's novel applies especially to American travel writing. Whether they go off to the American wilds or to more exotic destinations, American travel writers like Edward Abbey and Peter Matthiessen flee the confining routines of modern industrial civilization in America. My favorite image of John McPhee captures this sense of escape. In his essay, "Travels in Georgia," he describes being stuck in a traffic jam outside the airport in Newark, New Jersey, in that waste land around the smelly refineries. McPhee dons his hiking gear, climbs over lanes of cars, scales the airport fence, and just makes the flight that allows him escape to rural Georgia.

The subtitle of my essay might have been "John McPhee: Between Thoreau and Theroux," but I place McPhee closer to Thoreau, who represents a union of American travel writing and nature writing and is central to both traditions. Like Thoreau, McPhee is a river traveler, a naturalist, and a fact gatherer. This similarity is seen most strongly in McPhee's book, *The Survival of the Bark Canoe* (1975), which covers the same territory that Thoreau visited in the nineteenth century and wrote about in *The Maine Woods* (1864).

McPhee's use of Thoreau exemplifies how travel writers travel their source books in addition to reading them. Going beyond the ordinary vicarious experience of literature, the travel writer puts other travel books to the test of travel. The French critic Michel Butor argues that reading, writing, and travel are all modes of each other. Reading is travel (across and beyond the printed page), travel is a reading of signs, maps, landscapes, and writing is marking that landscape with language.

McPhee reads Thoreau's book even as he sits in a canoe retracing Thoreau's Maine journey. The backwoodsmen he travels with are "saturated with Thoreau. In every segment of the river, they remember things Thoreau did there—places where he camped, where he collected flora, where he searched for moose." In effect, the travelers read the Maine landscape through Thoreau.

Besides retracing Thoreau's itinerary, McPhee retraces Thoreau's methods of composition, his habits of travel writing. McPhee remarks that while traveling in Maine, Thoreau "made condensed, fragmentary notes. . . . weeks later, when he had returned home to Concord, he composed his journal of the trip, slyly using the diary to gain immediacy, to create the illusion of paragraphs written . . . virtually in the moments described. With the journal as his principal source, he later crafted still another manuscript in which he further shaped and rearranged the story." William Howarth's account in *The John McPhee Reader* (1976) of how McPhee himself composes—working slowly from copious notes, shaping and reshaping, creating a sense of immediacy in the narrative—attests to the similarities between Thoreau's methods of travel writing and McPhee's.

Virtually all of McPhee's books feature at least one character, an expert like the canoe builder Henry Vaillancourt in *The Survival of the Bark Canoe*, with whom he travels and through whom he reads the terrain and understands the journey. McPhee gets closer to his characters than formal interview would allow. (Nothing beats traveling with your subjects as a way of getting to know them.) The trip becomes a journey into the character as well as a movement through space and time. McPhee's experience writing the kind of lengthy character sketch that constitutes a *New Yorker* "profile" has undoubtedly influenced his particular mode of travel writing.

A *New Yorker* piece on Euell Gibbons, published in 1968 and later included in *A Roomful of Hovings* (1968), exemplifies McPhee's approach to travel writing as the character study of an expert combined with an exploration of the expert's terrain. McPhee plotted a journey down the Susquehanna River with Gibbons, a connoisseur of wild vegetable food and author of *Stalking the Wild Asparagus*. The very structure of the trip shows McPhee's characteristic emphasis on deliberate planning. The pair subsisted for several days on the weeds and wild plants that Gibbons could forage. Then they allowed themselves the addition of salt, the next day cooking oil, then sugar, flour, and finally baking powder to supplement their wild diet. They celebrated the end of their meatless journey with a steak dinner garnished with wild vegetables.

During the trip, Gibbons began to open up and talk about his Depression-era adolescence as the son of a dreamer and drifter. Gibbons learned to forage for wild food to help himself and his family survive in New Mexico during the hard times when his father was away. He grew up to lead a vagabond life as itinerant worker, cowboy, tramp, and beachcomber. He got the kind of excitement from finding edible wild plants that a hobo gets from finding a coin. Searching for wild food became a natural outgrowth of his nomadic existence.

McPhee interweaves the story of Gibbons' life with accounts of their Susquehanna journey—which results in a kind of nature travel as "weed watching." He learns to appreciate Gibbons' sharp eye, his ability to translate the terrain into a catalog of edible plants. "He read the landscape as if it were language," McPhee observes in a statement that supports Butor's argument that travel represents a mode of reading. By the end of the journey, McPhee has learned to read wild plants well enough to appreciate what Gibbons means when he says, "There is nothing I would rather do than eat my way through a roadside ditch."

This habit of traveling with companions puts McPhee outside another tradition of travel writing—that of the solitary journey. For the travel writer, traveling is usually a solo act, a chance for reflective solitude and self-reliance, a challenge to individual wit and will. Travel writers tend to face travel as they face writing—alone. They become introspective and write of themselves; they become part of the subject of their journey. But McPhee avoids much revelation about himself; he focuses instead on the character of the expert, his traveling companion.

Traveling with naturalists like Gibbons, who exemplifies living with nature rather than exploiting it, McPhee inevitably raises environmental questions. *Encounters with the Archdruid* (1971), a subsequent book on the conflict between wilderness preservers and land developers, joins nature writing and travel writing in the form of an environmental debate personified in the characters he profiles. The book climaxes in another river trip, this time down the Colorado with *two* experts, philosophically opposed: federal dam builder Charles Dominy and environmentalist David Brower, leader of Friends of the Earth. McPhee organizes the journey with his usual eye to literary structure, so that the trip downriver forms the moving stage for the endless debate of his travel companions. At issue are the dams, present and future, on the river. The journey shapes the narrative, within which the profile of each character is developed and his arguments dramatized. William Howarth finds the climax of this book to be one of McPhee's best endings: "Brower and his opponent Dominy ride through the Colorado River's Lava Falls, their ceaseless quarrel silenced momentarily by the roar of pounding water." McPhee lets nature have the last word.

The trips down the Colorado and the Susquehanna are recreational outings. They contain a strong element of play, which McPhee mirrors in the play of his prose. (This association of travel with play and recreation no doubt leads critics to undervalue travel literature, partly because they tend to invoke a specious distinction between work and play.) Given McPhee's Puritan strain and the characteristic intensity with which he pursues any activity, it is difficult to distinguish between work and play in his writing.

Since McPhee studies most terrains with the aid of a professional, we might say that he takes field trips rather than "real" trips. A field trip smacks of work rather than play, and geology is among the foremost of the disciplines that require field trips. Several of McPhee's recent books have come from extensive geological field trips and have produced some of his most technical prose. In his earlier works, McPhee examines the surface of the earth, and his interest in the landscape leads deeper to a study of what shaped the terrain, what lies beneath the skin of the planet. Looking over the course of his journey as a writer, one can see the science of geology becoming a natural destination for him.

McPhee puts even geology into the framework of travel writing. The enormous amount of scientific information in his geology books necessitates some dramatic narrative structure to ensure interest. Travel supplies that structure. In *Basin and Range* (1980), for example, the rock strata exposed by the construction of Interstate 80, all the way from New Jersey to California, make the highway both a stage and a backdrop for geological study. McPhee is bemused by the juxtaposition of time and space; as he examines roadside formations from millions of years ago, traffic speeds by on Route 80. To make the inhuman dimensions of geological time comprehensible, he imagines a kind of time travel—a trip, for example, from New Jersey to California, 200 million years ago in the Triassic era: "You would move west from the nonexistent Hudson River with the Palisades Sill ten thousand feet down. The motions that will open the Atlantic are well under way. . . . Behind you, where the ocean will be, are several thousand miles of land. . . . You cross the Newark Basin. It is for the most part filled with red mud. In the mud are tracks that seem to have been made by a two-ton newt."

McPhee's writing on geology represents a kind of time travel that occasionally suggests the mood of fiction, as seen in the passage above. Grasping the dimensions of geological time necessitates an imaginative leap that approximates fiction. No wonder McPhee's favorite passage in fiction is from Joseph Conrad's *Heart of Darkness*, a narrative that combines a literal journey up the Congo River with a figurative trip back into the primitive: "Going up that river was like travelling back to the earliest beginnings of the world, when vegetation rioted on the earth and the big trees were kings." Metaphorically, says McPhee, Conrad "traveled back to the Carboniferous [Age], when the vegetal riot occurred."

McPhee's traveling expert in *Basin and Range*, a geologist named Karen Kleinspehn, imagines the other way—into the future, after we have used up fossil fuels and cross-country car travel on Interstate 80 is no longer possible: "Before long, to go all the way across the country by yourself will be a fossil experience. A person or two. One car. Coast to coast. . . . It's a most unusual kind of personal freedom, particular to this time span, the one we happen to be in. It's an amazing, temporary phenomenon that will end." The fact that oil motivates much modern geological inquiry makes for an ironic connection between geology and travel. Interstate 80 runs through McPhee's geology books not only because the rock cuts along the way conveniently expose strata. They also remind one that automobile travel is as transient as the dinosaur.

McPhee's geology books demonstrate another basic appeal of travel and travel writing. Travel represents a kind of intellectual conquest, an expansion of knowledge, the marking of the heretofore unknown with words. As Butor says of exploration, in a passage that could well describe McPhee and the geologists who initiate him into the terrain he is exploring: "Usually it is a settled native who teaches the explorer to recognize the trails, to identify landmarks. . . . The unknown land is elaborated like a text . . . the explorer seizes with his language the land he enters." This kind of conquest is metaphorical rather than literal, intellectual rather than material. It is to be distinguished from the economic conquest of nature, the kind of exploitation and development that environmentalists deplore. David Love, the Wyoming geologist with whom McPhee travels in *Rising from the Plains* (1986), experiences both kinds of conquest. He has a passion for solving the various geological mysteries that Wyoming represents and for reconstructing the history of how a landscape evolves. "You try to put the petals back on the flower," he says, using a strikingly benign image for this geological sleuthing. And yet as a geologist he is obliged to find substances like oil and uranium. Love himself made the discovery that started the uranium boom in Wyoming and he earned the wrath of environmentalists by finding oil in Yellowstone Park. The book ends on Love's note of regret about the exploitation of Wyoming as McPhee links nostalgia for the conquest of the Old West to the kind of mining he describes as "war damage" to Wyoming.

One way McPhee experiences the satisfaction of conquest without damage to nature is through wilderness sports. McPhee plots many of his trips as challenges, often constructing an elaborate game plan, which involves hardships, tests of skill, competition, and finally triumph and even celebration. In a world where just about every place has been crisscrossed not only by travelers but by tourists as well, wilderness sports offer a way to recreate the challenges of exploration and territorial conquest. Sport becomes a substitute for such conquest, an alternative way to show physical and intellectual mastery of nature.

James Dickey's novel *Deliverance* (1970), which McPhee refers to several times in his own work, has many elements of a McPhee excursion. In the novel, four men take a canoe trip down a wild Georgia river soon to be obliterated by a dam. As with many of McPhee's trips, this one includes an expert, environmentalist sentiments, risks and challenges, a novice who must master the expert's skill, and an underlying sense of male competition. McPhee can joke (in *The Survival of the Bark Canoe*) about the horrors that the men encounter, and he criticizes the wildly impossible canoe scenes in the movie version of *Deliverance*, but he praises the imaginative power of the fiction and its archetypal evocation of man against the wilderness. "I was awed by the power of Dickey," McPhee says in "Travels in Georgia": "He had assembled '*Deliverance* country' from fragments restored and heightened in the chambers of his imagination."

We persist in categorizing travel writing as nonfiction. But the similarities between Dickey's travel fiction and McPhee's nonfiction show once again how travel as a subject crosses the boundaries of literary genre. Much like the character in Dickey's novel who scales a dizzying cliff and kills a human predator with a bow and arrow, the native experts in McPhee's work take on semiheroic proportions. McPhee has the same admiration for forest rangers and canoe builders that he has for such sports heroes as Bill Bradley and Arthur Ashe, whom he has also profiled.

This appreciation of the expert's technical skill runs as a common thread through the varied subjects of McPhee's nonfiction and allows his travel writing to include, simultaneously, sports writing or nature writing or technical writing. McPhee's world is predominantly male, and he celebrates typically male qualities. Yet his experts are occasionally women—such as geologist Karen Kleinspehn or Georgia naturalist Carol Ruckdeschel—and he pays them the same kind of homage he does the men. The frontier women in *Rising from the Plains* earn his admiration because they are as adventurous and as knowledgeable as the men.

McPhee does not merely describe the skill of his hero-experts. They become his teachers, and he often tries to emulate them. At times they seem almost like alter egos for McPhee, especially one Maine forest ranger whose name is also John McPhee. McPhee the writer ponders his relationship with McPhee the backwoodsman in a passage from "North of the C. P. Line," which says much about the writer's identification with the experts he accompanies on his travels: "Whenever I think about him, I feel such a strong sense of identification that I wonder if it is not a touch of envy. . . . As anyone might, I wish I knew what he knows—and wish not merely for his knowledge but for his compatibility with the backcountry and everything that lives there. I envy him his world, I suppose, in the way that one is sometimes drawn to be another person or lives the life of a character encountered in a fiction."

While deferring to his expert, McPhee often engages in a kind of unspoken competition as he strives to keep up with the expert or imitate his skill. His interest in sport and competition takes on an urban quality in "The Search for Marvin Gardens," a travel essay about Atlantic City. His home state of New Jersey is an unlikely arena for wilderness sports, so a more sedentary and commercial game—Monopoly—forms the structure of the travelogue. Since the Monopoly board bears the place names of Atlantic City, it functions as a miniature map of the area. McPhee pictures himself playing a series of fictitious Monopoly games in counterpoint to a documentary visit to Atlantic City. As one of two expert players, he seems almost a parody of his competitive self, and the frantic pace of the game allows him to switch back and forth from Boardwalk and Park Place to the actual sites on the Jersey shore. It is one of his most originally structured and playful travel pieces.

Writing about home might be conceived of as the opposite of travel writing. Home represents the secure, the fixed, the known, while travel offers the mobile, the changing, the unfamiliar. Travel writers need both. A traveler without a sense of home would be a nomad, in a perpetual state of transience. New Jersey is home to McPhee, and he uses it in two ways in his travel writing—as a point of comparison with far-off places like Alaska or Nevada and as an object of travel writing itself. Like Thoreau, McPhee writes of home as a microcosm within which one can travel fruitfully. Princeton is his Concord, New Jersey his New England.

Like many travelers, McPhee keeps home in mind when he travels. References to New Jersey abound in unlikely places, adding both irony and dramatic example to his travel writing. How to communicate the size of Switzerland? It's "two times New Jersey." How do you conceive of the population density of Alaska? "In 10 square miles of New Jersey, there are more people than in all the 576,000 miles of Alaska. Along the salmon streams in Alaska, bears line up, "hip to hip, like fishermen in New Jersey." Overdeveloped Fairbanks, Alaska, is a "portable Passaic." How do you imagine the shape of the world in a much earlier stage of plate tectonics? Imagine Mauritania and New Jersey joined. What is it like to kayak down a homicidal rush of white water in North Carolina? It's "like going down the New Jersey turnpike in a fog."

New Jersey as a travel destination might seem like a joke to the reading public. We envision nightmare urban landscapes, floating masses of garbage polluting the overdeveloped Atlantic shore, the acrid smell of burning chemicals, all lying just beyond each menacing turnpike exit. In the last section of the *Norton Book of Travel* (1987), Paul Fussell expresses a contemporary pessimism about travel, which is grounded upon the disappearance of beauty and wonder, the omnipresence of industrialism, the blight of modern civilization. "Travel at its truest is [now] an ironic experience," he says, citing Paul Theroux as the epitome of the posttouristic spirit.

We can easily imagine Theroux, with his nostalgia for the days of the imperial railroad and the crime-free subway, evoking New Jersey with a kind of black humor, savoring ironically the weed-choked train tracks of Hoboken, the sign-cluttered truck routes, the abandoned warehouses, and the odor of burning tires—the image of New Jersey as back door to the world. McPhee is not blind to urban blight in his state. His description of the ghetto in Atlantic City in "The Search for Marvin Gardens" sounds like vintage Theroux: "It is deep and complex decay. Roofs are off. Bricks are scattered in the street. People sit on porches, six deep, at nine on a Monday morning. When they go off to wait in unemployment lines, they wait sometimes two hours. . . . Block after block there are three-story brick row houses. Whole segments of them are abandoned, a thousand broken windows. . . . A mattress lies in the street, soaking in a pool of water."

Yet McPhee's irony is gentler, more sanguine than that of Theroux. Elsewhere in his writing, McPhee counteracts the common image of New Jersey. He puts the Garden back into the Garden State. He finds true natural wilderness in this overpopulated hub of the eastern urban world. He emphasizes the resilience and vitality of natural forces despite urban encroachment. That's part of the mystique for McPhee of the Pine Barrens of central New Jersey, an island of virgin forest and pure water amid a stretch of the greatest population density in the nation. It forms the subject of one of his most popular books:

> This area, which includes about six hundred and fifty thousand acres . . . is almost identical in size with the Grand Canyon National park. . . . The Pine Barrens are so close to New York that on a very clear night a bright light in the pines would be visible from the Empire State Building. . . . In the sand under the pines is a natural reservoir of pure water that, in volume, is the equivalent of . . . thirty times as much water [as] all the reservoirs . . . in the New York City water system. . . . its chemical purity approaches that of uncontaminated rain water or melted glacier ice.

McPhee's native expert and traveling companion in the Pine Barrens is Fred Brown, a backwoodsman and storyteller whose knowledge of local history and folklore gives this area of New Jersey the quality of Appalachian hinterlands. Brown is the ideal personification of wilderness New Jersey, a "piney" who lives without telephone or electricity on an unpaved road in the trackless woods somewhere between New York and Philadelphia.

The Pine Barrens offer the most dramatic example of wilderness New Jersey, but McPhee finds invasions of nature all over his home state. He likes to inform us that one of the densest concentrations of wild deer in the U.S. inhabits the area around his home. "I saw a buck with a big-eight-point . . . rack looking magnificent as he stood between two tractor trailers in the Frito-Lay parking lot in New Brunswick, New Jersey." If deer seem too suburban, what about the growing numbers of New Jersey bear? McPhee has written about rescuing bear caught in dumpsters in New Jersey shopping malls, stranded on medians in four-lane highways or trapped in culverts below them. To McPhee, a bear more than any other animal embodies the wilderness. In *Coming into the Country* (1977), he eats the meat of an Alaskan bear and remarks, "in strange communion, I had chewed the flag, consumed the symbol of the total wild." New Jersey, of all places, supplies a chance to atone for that act when McPhee restores a bear cub to its hibernating mother in a den near the Pennsylvania border.

McPhee's celebration of natural beauty and wilderness around his home recalls the preindustrial Northeast of Henry David Thoreau. McPhee himself once said wistfully of Thoreau, "Think of what the East would look like if he had been heeded." Thoreau could be considered the archetypal environmentalist in American letters. In Noel Perrin's words, Thoreau was the first American "who publicly concluded that wilderness as wilderness—that is, pure nature—was a good thing to have around."

In his book *Thoreau as World Traveler* (1965), John Christie shows how Thoreau's opinions on travel reflect his views on nature:

> Who should the traveler be? He should be a scientist in sufficient degree to be able to understand natural phenomena. . . . He should travel in a simple, primitive, original way, standing in a true relation to men and nature, able to give an exact description of what he saw. . . . he should travel for the purpose of examining the variety of phenomena, natural, human, and social. . . . he should be more than a traveler, his travels relegated properly to some other natural activity or occupation which he found most meaningful. . . . he should not bear the taint of a "professional" traveler but be a man whose travels relate to his "profession."

Christie's paraphrase of Thoreau could apply equally to John McPhee as traveler in its emphasis on travel as the serious study of nature, the rejection of travel as merely a leisure diversion, and the relation of travel to the work of one's profession. McPhee is not a "professional" traveler. (A good example of the "professional" traveler is Temple Fielding, author of numerous Fielding travel guides, and the subject of a *New Yorker* profile by McPhee entitled "Templex." Fielding—who travels first class, patronizes five-star hotels and gourmet restaurants, and has counseled generations of tourists—typifies the kind of writer who has made the term "travel writing" synonymous with guidebooks.) McPhee earns the title "traveler," in Thoreau's sense of the word, by subordinating travel to the task of studying the disciplines and the characters with whom he journeys. A century after Thoreau, McPhee accurately exemplifies Thoreau's notion of the ideal traveler.

WORKS CITED

Butor, Michel. "Travel and Writing." *Mosaic* 8 (Fall 1974): 1–16. Reprinted in this collection of essays.

Christie, John Aldrich. *Thoreau as World Traveler*. New York: Columbia UP, 1965.

Fussell, Paul, ed. *The Norton Book of Travel*. New York: W. W. Norton, 1987.

———. "The Stationary Tourist." *Harper's Magazine*, April 1979, 31–38.

Heat-Moon, William Least. *Blue Highways*. Boston: Little, Brown, 1982.

Howarth, William. "Introduction." *The John McPhee Reader*. Ed. William Howarth. New York: Farrar, Straus & Giroux, 1976, vii-xxxiii.

McPhee, John. *Basin and Range*. New York: Farrar, Straus & Giroux, 1980.

———. *Coming into the Country*. New York: Farrar, Straus & Giroux, 1977.

———. "A Forager." *New Yorker*, 6 April 1968, 45–104. Rpt. In *A Roomful of Hovings*. New York: Farrar, Straus & Giroux, 1968.

———. "North of the C. P. Line." In *Table of Contents*. New York: Farrar, Straus & Giroux, 249–93.

———. *The Pine Barrens*. New York: Farrar, Straus & Giroux, 1975.

———. *Rising from the Plains*. New York: Farrar, Straus & Giroux, 1986.

———. "The Search for Marvin Gardens." In *The John McPhee Reader*, 473–89.

———. *The Survival of the Bark Canoe*. New York: Farrar, Straus & Giroux, 1975.

———. *Table of Contents*. New York: Farrar, Straus & Giroux, 1985.

———. "Templex." In *A Roomful of Hovings*. New York: Farrar, Straus & Giroux, 1968, 203–50.

———. "Travels in Georgia." In *The John McPhee Reader*, 408–71.

Perrin, Noel. "For Ever Virgin: The American View of America." In *On Nature: Nature, Landscape, and Natural History*. Ed. Daniel Halpern. San Francisco: North Point P, 1987, 13–22.

Thoreau, Henry David. Quoted in John Aldrich Christie, *Thoreau as World Traveler*.

> > > > > > Joan Didion and the Problem of Journalistic Travel Writing

MARK Z. MUGGLI

"Boca Grande is a land of contrasts" is the conventional opening for many a travelogue to many a Boca Grande. How appropriate, then, that a conventionally minded person like Charlotte Douglas, a central character in Joan Didion's *A Book of Common Prayer* (1977), would begin one of her travelogues with these words. And how admirable that the *New Yorker* rejects Charlotte's "Letter from Central America," since, as Didion's narrator Grace Strasser-Mendana says, "Boca Grande is not a land of contrasts. On the contrary, Boca Grande is relentlessly 'the same.'" Charlotte is wrong about Boca Grande, but the novel centers on Grace's desire to understand Charlotte's perspective and to finish for herself the recurring fragment "Boca Grande is."

It is not surprising that the narrator's interests nearly transform *A Book of Common Prayer* into a fictional travelogue. Most of Joan Didion's writing has explored the definition of places and the people who live in them; her obsessions are objects, landscapes, weather, place-names, epiphanic moments of local color. Her fiction and nonfiction are intertwined in other ways as well, exploring the same situations, themes, and stylistic and epistemological questions. Didion's two latest novels are especially helpful in understanding her travel writing, for they expose the fiction-writing process by focusing particularly on the goal of travel writing: the accurate recreation of character meeting place. Both novels explore the problem of accuracy, both suggest the inadequacy of our easy distinctions between tourist, traveler, and resident, and both question travel writers' assumption that they will grow in understanding and wisdom as they self-consciously establish the empirical reality of foreign places. These novels therefore usefully introduce some of the tensions inherent in contemporary travel writing. In turn, Didion's factual works, especially when compared with other writers' treatments of the same subjects, suggest that there are literary solutions to the problems her novels pose.

The sixty-year-old narrator of *A Book of Common Prayer* has been a "prudent traveler" since the death of her parents, when she was ten. She has traveled from Colorado to California to Brazil to Boca Grande. She is a major anthropologist who has "stopped believing that observable activity defined anthropos" and has therefore metaphorically traveled to become a biochemist. But Charlotte Douglas, whom she comes to love and respect, challenges Grace's prudent aloofness, and Grace begins her narrative with a new fixity:

> I WILL BE HER WITNESS.
> That would translate *seré su testiga,* and will not appear in your travelers' phrasebook because it is not a useful phrase for the prudent traveler.

Grace distinguishes herself from Charlotte, who describes herself as "a tourist." "In fact," says Grace, "she came here less a tourist than a sojourner but she did not make that distinction." Because she does not understand her own motives, Charlotte also does not understand that she, and others like her, come regularly to airports "quite as if they were ordinary travelers" with plans and agendas, when they are merely preparing to jettison their recent pasts. (Charlotte's deep desire to move on is similarly suggested by her late-night telephone calls to California, not to connect with her former home, but to hear "the taped 'road condition' report of the California Highway Patrol.")

Charlotte's daughter Marin claims with revolutionary fervor to disdain her mother's bourgeois superficiality, typified by her attitudes towards travel and history. But Marin is as much a tourist as her mother, leaving behind every past as quickly as it can be forgotten. In her self-deceptive— but intuitively correct—way, Charlotte views Marin's political flight as "traveling with friends" and refers to Marin's hijacking an L-1011 as " 'when Marin went to Utah,' as if it had been a tour of National Parks." Charlotte often alludes to her trip with Marin to the Tivoli Gardens, although it is never clear whether this classic tourist's trip actually took place. But "Tivoli" is the word that Grace repeats to a cynical Marin until "she broke exactly as her mother must have broken the morning the FBI first came to the house on California Street": a shared tourist's fantasy most deeply binds mother to daughter.

Thus as *A Book of Common Prayer* defines the Boca Grande the tourists and travelers encounter, it also explores the traveler's urge to leave old worlds behind. But by the novel's end, the two central characters have reversed themselves. Charlotte decides for once to stay. "Not 'stay' precisely. 'Not leave' is more like it," Grace says. After a lifetime of tourism, passivity, and delusion, Charlotte commits herself to the demands of residency by acting with heroic anger to help some people of Boca Grande. That she may still not fully understand her choice is suggested in her words as she is arrested just before being shot:

> *Soy norteamericana,* she said.
> *Soy una turista,* she said. . . .
> "Don't you lay your fucking hands on me," she said in English.

Grace Strasser-Mendana, who had temporarily settled into Boca Grande and hard science, gradually finds her resident certitudes overturned. She realizes that she had not fully understood her husband's political activities, she recognizes the limitations of biochemistry ("Give me the molecular structure of the protein which defined Charlotte Douglas"), and she begins to think that she, rather than Charlotte, has lived the greatest delusions. Recognizing that she has "no business in this place" but has "been here too long to change," and seeing herself now as permanently *de afuera* and as a less good witness than she wanted to be, she stays in Boca Grande, dying of cancer, clearing groves, and recognizing "the equivocal nature of even the most empirical evidence."

The complex relationship between travel, residency, empirical truth, and wisdom are also central to *Democracy* (1984), Didion's most recent novel. The most prominent travelers are Inez Victor and her daughter Jessie. Both are very much like Charlotte Douglas, although Inez is much more aware than Charlotte that she has spent her life moving through new places partly in order to leave the past behind: "Drop fuel. Jettison cargo. Eject crew." In all three cases, the effect of this continual traveling is deep anxiety. Inez and Jessie are contrasted with Billy Dillon and Jack Lovett, who are the ultimate residents, since even though they are constantly on the move, their assured control makes the whole world their home.

Like *A Book of Common Prayer*, *Democracy* charts the way characters move in and out of their roles, even as it shows the slipperiness of the roles themselves. Jack Lovett's secretive twenty-year commitment to Inez suggests that he may be less at home in his larger world than it had seemed, and at the novel's end, Inez settles into a home in Kuala Lumpur. She claims to be an "American national," but says she will continue to work with the people "in Kuala Lumpur until the last refugee was dispatched" (i.e., forever). Like Charlotte, Inez commits herself to a work that gives her her first permanence; ironically, the former refugee and permanent traveler has chosen to help other refugees. The narrator of *Democracy* is a journalist now working on a novel. Like Grace Strasser-Mendana in *A Book of Common Prayer*, she ends her book with a moderate sense of failure: "It has not been the novel I set out to write, nor am I exactly the person who set out to write it."

Didion's factual writing responds to the categories and doubts that her novels raise. Outside of her reviews and personal analytical essays ("On Morality" and "Why I Write," for example), nearly all her factual pieces fall into two categories parallel to the basic distinction her novels make between travel and residency: either her factual pieces are "travelogues" or they are what might be called "domilogues," memoir-like depictions of a resident's experience of "home."

The most obvious of the domilogues are such pieces as "On Going Home" and "Notes from a Native Daughter" in *Slouching Towards Bethlehem* (1968). In these stories, the insider Didion explores for us—the outsiders—the codes that define her home-life. As *A Book of Common Prayer* and *Democracy* would lead us to expect, Didion's residency in these places is complex and shifting. "It should be clear by now," she says in "Notes from a Native Daughter," "that the truth about the place is elusive, and must be tracked with caution." In addition to these memoirs, Didion has written a series of pieces that explore her even more complex insider/ outsider relationship to Malibu, Los Angeles, New York, and Hawaii. "In the Islands," in *The White Album* (1979), establishes her long-standing connection to Hawaii, but in her earlier "Letter from Paradise" in *Slouching Towards Bethlehem*, she comes there mostly as an outsider, almost a tourist, who comes to understand the complexities of war, race, and class that underlie "the peculiar and still insular mythology of Hawaii."

In much of her writing, however, Didion presents herself as pure outsider. She comes to places as close to her original home as Haight-Ashbury or Alcatraz, defines their strangeness, and then establishes a knowing dominion over them. Whether insider or outsider, Didion has much the same agenda for us: she wants to open the cryptogram before us, so that we can share her communion with the secret core of these places. In one of her classic travelogues, "In Bogotá," Didion establishes her status as outsider by placing herself in Cartagena dreaming of a modern Bogotá that could provide "fresh roses," "hot water twenty-four hours a day," "room service and Xerox *rápido* and long-distance operators who could get Los Angeles in ten minutes." Once in the city she is struck by contradictory images of technology, poverty, violence, and myths that suggest the city's darker, more self-deceptive side. Didion stays in Bogotá for an undefined time, unsystematically gathers images and explanations, and in the end articulates for us a sense of the place that we can share.

Travel writing of this traditional sort, critics like Michiko Kakutani have argued, is an endangered genre:

> Though Waugh and the critic Paul Fussell doubtless overstated matters, when they declared that the modern age of tourism and international politics had effectively killed off real travel writing, it's clearly more difficult, in this day and age, to write the sort of essay that Waugh once specialized in. For one thing, mass communication and the spread of American pop culture (from Coca-Cola to Levis) have brought a new measure of homogenization to both distant lands and provincial backwaters. [Fussell, quoting Lévi-Strauss, does in fact identify "monoculture" as destructive of travel writing.] Second, it's harder, given our knowledge of recent history, to indulge in the sort of curmudgeonly wisecracks that Waugh liked to make at the expense of strangers, without sounding irresponsible, ignorant, or downright bigoted.

The causes outlined by Kakutani have surely been at work, but contemporary travel writing has also been greatly shaped—and often weakened—by contemporary journalism. First of all, the print media have become increasingly consumer-oriented. Writing styles, layout, and content are decided by demographic studies; readers, in turn, expect the media to serve their personal needs directly. The media therefore generate much touristic writing that eases the tourist's mind by listing opening times, the best restaurants, and the most collectable items of local culture.

More importantly, contemporary travel writing has been affected by journalistic conventions that run contrary to the patterns of traditional travel writing. Karl Manoff and Michael Schudson correctly observe that although American journalism may have no "coherent ideological structure," it does exhibit "pervasive and powerful uniformities" that are being increasingly studied. Manoff and Schudson's collection *Reading the News* is organized around the "five W's" of modern journalism, but I would suggest that the center of the journalistic ideal, and of each journalistic text, is the reporter, a coolly invisible collector of data-bits, a figure quite unlike the traveler. The journalist's neutral role is neatly capsulized by *Democracy*'s narrator, a writer named Joan Didion, who describes her own work as a reporter: "I spent the summer collecting and collating these versions, many of them conflicting, most of them self-serving; an essentially reportorial technique." In this kind of journalism (which Schudson, in *Discovering the News*, classifies as the "information model"), the audience is also neutral and invisible, and therefore has no easily identifiable effect on a story's content. Didion has never done newspaper writing, but a number of her stories could, by the measure of this model, be called conventional. "Some Dreamers of the Golden Dream" and "Where the Kissing Never Stops" (in *Slouching Towards Bethlehem*) are admittedly untypical in their treatment of detail and structure, but they are quite conventional in their implicit characterization of writer and audience and in their use of sources.

Fussell argues that the best travel writing has been a subspecies of autobiography—at the classic travelogue's center is a self-revealing figure whose passion is to make sense of new experience. The domilogue is similarly related to autobiography, except that the central figure reveals the meaning of a world foreign to us but of which the figure has been an intimate resident. The domilogue is fairly resistant to journalism's influence, because the writer digs into memory rather than gathering outside sources. The travel writer, however, readily becomes an information gatherer, and—depending on the amount of information, the sources, the gathering method, and the writer's self-characterization—the travel piece can suddenly become a subspecies of journalism, shaped by contemporary journalistic conventions.

Would-be travel writers have explored different paths out of this journalistic thicket. The New Journalists, for example, simply rejected objectivity and hoped thereby to evade the problem. They kept their eyes fixed on other models. Tom Wolfe may have correctly surmised in 1973 that "the sort of reporting that one now finds in the New Journalism probably begins with the travel literature of the late eighteenth and early nineteenth centuries (and, as I say, with the singular figure of Boswell)." But contemporary journalism cannot easily be ignored, and the New Journalist's evasionary tactic sometimes produces a self-conscious, naughty rebellion against restraints that has its own limitations, as in some of Wolfe and Mailer and in their spiritual predecessor James Agee. A similar self-conscious defiance weakens Didion's "John Wayne: A Love Song" (in *Slouching Towards Bethlehem*), in which Didion's report on the completion of John Wayne's 165th film at Estudio Churubusco outside Mexico City becomes so unconventionally intimate that it seems self-indulgent.

Another, sometimes overlapping, response to the demands of journalism is for travel writers to provide themselves a nonjournalistic motive for writing. The journalist is paid to write, and therefore must become an invisible reporter. The travel writer begins with a different motive. "To constitute real travel, movement from one place to another should manifest some impulse of nonutilitarian pleasure," Fussell asserts in *The Norton Book of Travel* (1987), and this pleasure allows the writer to become an autobiographer. The example of nonutilitarianism that Fussell cites is Paul Theroux: "Walking all around the British coast in 1982, he knew he was engaged in *travel* in the pure sense because, as he says, 'I was looking hard . . . and because I had no other business there.' " But given the commercial success of *The Great Railway Bazaar* (1975), it seems probable that Theroux walked the British coast with a publisher's contract in mind—if not actually in hand. And Theroux's situation is not new: many writers have traveled on publishers' advances, and many others have had clear prospects of later publication.

What is crucial, then, is not the writer's actual motive, but the effect of the *revealed* motive on the text's form and content. Didion, for example, uses a reshaped motive to free "Slouching Towards Bethlehem" from journalistic constraints. When this title piece of her collection appeared in *The Saturday Evening Post*, it served journalistic purposes: it was a factual, timely report on a topic of importance to its contemporary readers. In her introduction Didion calls herself a "reporter" and she does things that reporters do. She interviews police officers and local organizers, develops an unnamed source within the police department, balances sources against one another, and even travels with a photographer. But in order to leave room for the personal analysis, carefully modulated plot, and treatment of detail possible within travel writing, she emphasizes San Francisco's foreignness and provides herself a personal, nonjournalistic motive: "and because nothing else seemed so relevant I decided to go to San Francisco. . . . When I first went to San Francisco in that cold late spring of 1967 I did not even know what I wanted to find out, and so I just stayed around a while, and made a few friends." (Is it even possible that the deliberate, personal motivation of "I decided to go to San Francisco" is flavored by the wording and literary, nonjournalistic context of Yeats's famous lines, "And therefore I have sailed the seas and come / To the holy city of Byzantium"?)

Salvador (1983) is another triumphant piece of travel writing about a place more obviously foreign than San Francisco. Again, genre is important. Didion implies that she is not writing a tourist's guide by acknowledging her awareness of "the visionary invention of a tourist industry in yet another republic where the leading natural cause of death is gastrointestinal infection." The book is in some sense journalism—despite its literary debts to Conrad's *Heart of Darkness*—since Didion is writing for the *New York Review of Books* on a topic and place of current interest and follows many conventional information-gathering practices. She interviews presidents, aides, and ambassadors, and she is referred to as a "journalist" by a Salvadoran woman at an embassy party. She takes a trip to Gotera with reporters from the *Washington Post* and *Newsweek*. But Didion's response to her journalistic material suggests her distance from conventional reporting. I have in another essay argued that Didion's fixation on the overwhelmingly meaningful image is one of the distinctive features of her journalism, including *Salvador*. By means of what I call her "emblematic method," she teases out the meanings of images and evokes their resonances until the image stands for a large world of meaning beyond its empirical, journalistic reference. (A similar attitude towards imagery leads the narrator of *Democracy* repeatedly to identify the key to her story as "Colors, moisture, heat, enough blue in the air.")

Salvador's success as a literary work derives also from its structure, perhaps the most problematic feature of journalistic writing. "Slouching Towards Bethlehem" is a collage of evocative moments—the open organization mirrors the discontinuities Didion finds in San Francisco life. "The White Album," despite some powerful moments, suggests that the structure of "Slouching Towards Bethlehem" does not transplant easily, since "The White Album"'s ironic juxtapositions are often contrived and rote, while its overall movement is arbitrary. The emblematic method first developed for shorter magazine pieces poses even greater problems for the organization of longer, book-length reporting. Thus Didion wisely imposes a more formal and analytical structure on *Salvador*. The *New York Review of Books* section titles represent the book's three basic divisions: first, "In El Salvador" (the place's essential nature); second, "In El Salvador: Soluciones" (the internal political alignments and external programs, made ironical in the Spanish word for "solutions"); and third, "El Salvador: Illusions" (the United States' role captured in the English subtitle). (These three divisions are less visible in the Simon and Schuster edition, which uses only three oversized initial letters to separate sections, and which begins the second division one chapter later than in the original text.)

In addition, Didion captures in *Salvador* her own experience of the terror that she sees as the essential feature of Salvadoran life. Some reviewers have ridiculed Didion's anxieties. Gene Lyons wrote in *Newsweek* that "ghastliness and pointlessness are Didion's invariable themes wherever she goes." In *Salvador* Didion is actually much more selective than that. She sometimes depicts scenes that are inherently frightening (e.g., the nighttime restaurant scene alone with her husband, often cited by readers and reviewers, and her encounter with young soldiers who are blocking a driveway with their motorcycles). Another device she uses to register terror is to emphasize the disconnection between people and the consequent fears a sensitive individual feels. For example, when she, her husband, and two other reporters are waiting to ferry a river, she doesn't say that all of them realized together how dangerous the return would be. Rather, she makes this her personal, unspoken insight, and thereby makes the situation even more frightening.

This personalization of terror could have broken down in the second and third sections of *Salvador*, where Didion uses more documents and interviews to establish the "Soluciones" and "Illusions" built into the American presence there. But Didion carefully weaves her own experience into her outside sources. She quotes from a 1982 speech of Ronald Reagan, but says that she read the speech in El Salvador while watching an old Reagan movie. She quotes statements of Robert White, former U.S. ambassador to El Salvador, but his comments mirror the mindset of his successor, Dean Hinton, whose embassy china and pampered sheep dog Didion personally encounters and implicitly contrasts with El Salvador's terror. And when Didion quotes texts or speakers, she writes with a shocked tone that suggests she is encountering these things for the first time or in a new way. The whole book vibrates with a unifying immediacy of experience that makes it one of the great pieces of contemporary travel writing.

The coherent blending of emblematic imagery, structure, and persona in *Salvador* provides a useful backdrop for understanding the more limited achievement of Didion's latest travel book, *Miami* (1987). The structures of *Miami* and *Salvador* are remarkably similar. Didion first shows some of Miami's oddities and contradictions. With a precision that out-reports most reporters, she gives the exact location numbers of the mausoleums of two opposing Cuban political leaders whose remains are in the same Miami cemetery. The first part of the book documents other particulars about Miami, shows the details' symbolic dimension, and on a few occasions pushes some small pieces of symbolism toward their emblematic evocation of the place. "In a virtually empty restaurant on top of a virtually empty condominium," she experiences a lightning storm, and "the backlit islands and the fluorescent water and the voices at the table" define Miami for her, just as *Surrounded Islands*—the 1983 conceptual art piece of the Bulgarian artist Christo—defines Miami for others. Similarly, she explains how the architectural separations in the Omni International Hotel present "a social dynamic . . . in a single tableau."

At the same time, Didion develops an image of herself as sensitive enough to register these reverberating nuances, a self-portrayal most obvious in her comment about never passing security "for a flight to Miami without experiencing a certain weightlessness, the heightened wariness of having left the developed world for a more fluid atmosphere." All of this adds up to what an anonymous reviewer in the *New Yorker* (a magazine that has not generally reviewed Didion's work kindly) calls "superb travel—or maybe anti-travel—writing." This section of *Miami* does what Didion claimed (in a 1983 interview with Paul Hendrickson) was her "very limited objective" in *Salvador*: "What I had in mind was to render a place. Render the sense of a place. I wanted to get the physical reality, the way it felt, down."

As with *Salvador*, *Miami*'s structure is most visible in its *New York Review of Books* version. Part one, which I have just characterized, is simply "Miami." The second and third excerpts, "Miami: 'La Lucha' " and "Miami: Exiles," parallel the second section of *Salvador*, in which Didion focuses on internal political complexities. The final excerpt, "Washington in Miami," with its obvious focus on national political policy, is similarly parallel to *Salvador*'s third section on U.S. "Illusions."

But *Miami*'s second half differs from *Salvador*'s. Some of the newspapers Didion quotes in *Miami* go back to the 1970s, and the index, lengthy bibliographic notes, scholarly acknowledgments, and fully articulated, first-chapter thesis suggest long, quiet hours in libraries and well-lit offices. These features of *Miami* may constitute Didion's response to the reviewers who argued that her two-week visit to El Salvador was too brief and impressionistic. In fact, as political reporting the second half of *Miami* is quite convincing, even if Nicholas Lemann is correct in saying that Didion does not go beyond Taylor Branch and George Crile's 1975 *Harper's* article about Miami.

Didion's persona also shifts in the course of *Miami*. Her final critique of American politics is confident and without her earlier weightlessness and fluidity. We are meant to be shocked by certain of her revelations about the Washington manipulations of Cuban Miami but, as she writes, she is herself no longer shocked. Despite occasional self-references, Didion leaves off being a traveler who records Miami's strangeness in these sections. Instead, she becomes a cool, outside collator not unlike the journalism schools' ideal reporter. I am not suggesting that all factual writing with literary ambitions must contain a self-dramatizing central figure. *Miami*'s flaw, rather, is its inconsistency—character change, which is depicted so effectively in Didion's novels, undermines *Miami*'s structure. The *New York Review of Books* cut nearly one-third of Didion's book, including a large section from chapters 3 and 4 that contains the evocative and personal detail I have described above. This *New York Review of Books* version is less powerful as travel literature precisely because it reduces the central registering figure typical of the genre over the last two hundred years. But it is better journalism and a more unified, if more limited, literary work than that in the Simon and Schuster edition.

Two other books on Miami also published in 1987 provide useful material for analyzing Didion's achievement and the state of contemporary travel writing. The copyright notice in David Rieff's *Going to Miami* says, "Portions of this book were first published, in slightly different form, in *The New Yorker*," but the article differs more than "slightly" from the book, and the changes are instructive. The famous *New Yorker* fact-checkers may have been at work: in *Going to Miami*, "six blacks" were killed in Liberty City and a "hundred thousand Nicaraguans" live in South Florida, but in the *New Yorker*, "four blacks" were killed and there are "some seventy thousand Nicaraguans." There are also numerous deletions of transitional adverbs that give the book a tone of progressive, conversational argument: "but," "to be sure," "of course," "certainly," "obviously," "in any case." More visible are the *New Yorker*'s deletions of scores of judgmental phrases: "a rather loony Cuban politico" becomes in the article "a Cuban politico"; "some less well mannered Cubans" become "some Cubans"; an "elderly fellow with a decided proclivity for shiny polyester suiting and wide, resolutely unfashionable ties" simply becomes an "elderly man"; the Cuban middle class's "fatal error" of believing Fidel Castro when he said he was no communist becomes simply an "error"; the "tragic volcano" of Black Miami becomes a "volcano"; and "rabid teenagers" become "teenagers."

The *New Yorker* editors also cut dozens of what English teachers call "topic sentences," those directing, summarizing statements that often begin or end paragraphs. One effect of these deletions is that Rieff's average-length paragraphs get combined into full-column, *New Yorker* paragraphs. The deletions also affect tone, since Rieff's topic sentences are often tendentious. Some examples: "The panic in a Miami reeling from the cocaine wars and hotels suddenly bereft of Venezuelans was considerable and ugly"; "The rhetoric about Prida was extremely stupid"; "It would be lovely, of course, if the man with the portrait were simply a charming fantasist whose views found no graver echo in the larger community"; "Miami, of course, is nothing like the blood-soaked fantasies put out over Radio Havana"; and, "As for America, it seemed to have learned nothing from Prohibition."

In addition, Rieff's book was radically shortened by the *New Yorker*.

Approximately 170 of the book's 230 pages are cut, with the largest chunks disappearing at the beginning (128 of the first 135 pages) and at the end (22 pages). This excised material contains Rieff's dramatically painted scenes from various parts of Miami and his lengthy commentary on his initial and final visits to the city.

At one point in his book, Rieff refers to the *New Yorker*'s "old-fashioned, enviably prudish way" of rejecting certain advertisements—perhaps he was the beneficiary of the *New Yorker*'s similarly old-fashioned editing. Nicholas Lemann shares my feeling that "the edited version of *Going to Miami* that appeared in the *New Yorker* was much more impressive, because somebody took out everything Rieff should have taken out himself." What Rieff's book was before it was transformed into more conventional *New Yorker* reportage might be variously described. Some reviewers commented on Rieff's epigraph from Evelyn Waugh and suggested that Rieff wants to be a literary traveler of an earlier time. In fact, because the sentence from Waugh's diary that Rieff chose as epigraph is quoted in Fussell's *Abroad*, it is tempting to wonder whether Rieff had read *Abroad* and was specifically trying to fulfill the literary requirements of pretouristic travel writing. The first twenty pages of *Going to Miami* consist of a large-eyed, anxious analysis of the three New York airports and their denizens, as though Rieff wishes to counteract Fussell's argument that the shift from travel to tourism coincided with the shift from ocean liners to airplanes. As the book continues there are more of these personal, traveler's judgments—sometimes jejune, often petulant or merely the result of exhaustion—that made many reviewers react with exasperation. Nicholas Lemann complains that "Rieff talks about himself incessantly without having made himself into a character" and Michiko Kakutani is relieved when Rieff finally "stops substituting his moods for a genuine point of view." Stacey D'Erasmo's comment in the *Village Voice* is the harshest: "Every time this persona [as a latter-day Evelyn Waugh] reared its clever little head I wanted to slam it with a brick."

In his "Author's Note," Rieff specifically distances himself from journalistic rules: he explains his decision to "disguise . . . real names and stories" and "conflate incidents," and he calls *Going to Miami* "a book of impressions, not a work of investigative journalism." The book itself also reveals his desire to escape journalistic controls. Rieff places at the book's center a sensitive figure who suffers the emotional ups and downs of his material and who even experiments with the drugs Miami offers. He tries for a jazzed-up, opinionated, and impressionistic style. He allows the plot to grow out of the material rather than imposing a more rigid journalistic structure. That is, the book exhibits many features of the New Journalism—an irony in this context, since Didion, still regularly described as one of the New Journalists, has in the 1980s considerably distanced herself from many of those devices.

Whether literary traveler or New Journalist, Rieff makes a desperate attempt to free himself from modern journalistic conventions, some of which underlie the *New Yorker* version of his book. The *New Yorker*'s writers often appear in their works, but their travel pieces usually feature a much cooler, less vociferous voice than Rieff's in *Going to Miami*. This is partly because so many of the *New Yorker*'s "Letters from . . ." are actually domilogues, written by residents or sojourners, rather than by travelers. Writers like Mollie Panter-Downes and Jane Kramer have become such fixtures in their foreign places that we—not they—are the travelers.

There are, of course, many *New Yorker* travelogues as well, since one of the magazine's distinctive features is that it considers so much of the world a foreign territory that should be explored in a new, more detailed way. The awe that the magazine feels for the world's foreignness is playfully shown up in the travel section of Alfred Gingold and John Buskin's *Snooze* (1986), a book-length parody of the *New Yorker*. Eustace T., the supposed editor of *Snooze*, introduces a 1977 piece entitled "Letter From the End of the Line" with this comment: "Contrary to the japes of our critics, the four outlying boroughs of New York City have long been known to our magazine. . . . This letter, however, is a landmark of sorts, for it represents the first time one of our reporters actually talked with the natives of these wild, exotic lands." The classic *New Yorker* voice coolly documents the newness of the places it discovers. Sometimes, as in an extreme case like John Hersey's *Hiroshima* (1946), the author is invisible and almost exclusively paraphrases and quotes his sources, often without direct attribution. More often, as with Berton Roueché, the author is visible, but unperturbed, a shaping hand that hides its art. (This is perhaps the point of *Snooze*'s comment on "Jane Kramerversuskramer's willingness to receive any sort of injection without tears or a lollipop afterwards.")

The *New Yorker*'s editing of David Rieff's book pushes him closer to the magazine's other writers, and therefore closer to some of the most fundamental journalistic conventions of our time. But Rieff's *New Yorker* piece still has a somewhat untypical, jazzy quirkiness that makes it more like, for example, some of the magazine's reports by A. Alvarez or the comic travel pieces of Calvin Trillin. Whether the *New Yorker*'s dominant style will continue under new owners and editorship is uncertain: the 5 September 1988 issue contained Joan Didion's "Letter from Los Angeles," her first—though rather subdued—appearance in the magazine.

This comparison of Rieff's book and the magazine·version provides a useful way to study the editorial principles operating in 1987 at the *New Yorker*, a magazine of continuing importance for literary journalism and travel writing. The comparison also has the larger purpose of suggesting something about the complex demands that conventional journalism exerts on travel writers. T. D. Allman's *Miami: City of the Future* (1987) offers another instructive example of the difficulty of writing contemporary travel literature. Allman's *Esquire* article on Miami is radically shorter than his book's four hundred pages, but it provides—like Didion's and Rieff's magazine articles—another angle for judgment. Allman's article uses an edited version of the book's "Prologue" and "Epilogue" and parts of approximately ten pages from the book's middle. The effect is a fairly coherent article that spiritedly generalizes about contemporary Miami's cultural importance and that surveys some recent problems in Miami and the metamorphosis that is taking place there. Allman tries to epitomize the city's character in a few key images—such as those of an alligator lumbering daily out of the Everglades National Park, Miami as a microprocessor using Spanish as its language, and a large, gyrating mobile sculpture in a Key Biscayne office. It is a flashier, more symbol-laden version of a piece like the January 1988 *Newsweek* cover-story "Miami: America's Casablanca," which uses an essayistic, audience-addressing tone to piece together its researchers' reports.

And Allman's book? It has telling moments, but overall it shows the difficulty of building a coherent travel book with journalism looming over your shoulder. Like Rieff, Allman struggles with his persona. He begins with a prologue that presents a rather traveled and cocksure analyst capable of surveying the city's checkered history and incorporating the varied judgments of the city he has heard. He ties together his experiences in New York's Grand Central oyster bar and on the Los Angeles freeways to draw some conclusions about Miami's airport. In Miami he finds "the best sushi I've had outside Japan" and says "the richest 'cultural' experience I had there was one you can't find in any concert hall." In his "Epilogue: Good-bye Miami," Allman hopes to show how deeply he understands Miami (and LIFE), so he chronicles post-Miami trips to Paris, Africa, and Asia. In France, he travels to Chartres where he sits within the cathedral for six hours, nearly freezing, but experiencing a mystical "rapture of the deep," "a sad, joyful acceptance of the beauty and transience of life" that he had only before experienced scuba diving off Belize, in Central America. He later feels the same "underlying unity" while sailing off the Florida coast listening to Pachelbel's *Canon*. All these insights are deepened by his reading in quantum mechanics. As this summary suggests, the epilogue contains a mushy, vaguely religious Theory of Life that implicitly claims profundity for Allman's conclusions about Miami and the future.

Allman's final self-portrait as a mystical traveler—although it is wildly overdrawn—provides a plausible extension of the wise man who speaks the prologue. But this Allman clashes with the narrators who pop up in the book's middle 350 pages. When it comes to drugs, for example, he is like a "precocious six-year-old" who cannot understand the oddities of adult behavior. When he talks with an official of the Drug Enforcement Agency, Allman answers "like some slow learner who's finally getting his multiplication tables right." In these cases, Allman takes on a persona that reviewer Jeffrey Cohen found effective in Rieff's book, "a stance of naiveté—the mark of a good travel writer." Sometimes Allman appears as a guide addressing his audience directly: "Whenever I visit Miami, I try to catch up with Bernardo and Laurinda because, like some other people you'll meet in this book, they have a gift not just for knowing, but also for being what Miami is." Sometimes he is a lyricist: "And that awareness was all around you all the time in Miami—along with that glorious sunshine, these interesting people, those curious buildings, that air which, on the good days, caressed you like a fond and complaisant lover." Sometimes he feigns a nonjournalistic inexactitude: "There were, so far as I can remember, about six of us at dinner at Cafe Chauveron that night." Often he broadly theorizes about the city and America.

This partial list of alternate Allmans suggests the problem of continuity—how do you create a single book out of these different speakers? But there is an added problem. If a writer presents himself as a distinctive character who understands Miami and who gradually comes to understand the universe as well, how does he present 180 pages of anecdotes that constitute the rest of the book? The material is essentially journalistic and historical—it derives from interviews and reading rather than from coincidental experience, which is probably what makes J. Anthony Lukas, in his review of *Miami*, refer to Allman as a "reporter." This journalistic material could easily be handled conventionally, with a distanced, invisible narrator working through a patchwork of material as, for example, in Robert Sherrill's July 1987 cover story on Miami for the *New York Times Magazine*. But Allman presumably recognizes how inconsistent that narrative voice would be with his opening and closing persona, so he works to make himself visible in two particular ways, through his theories and his prose style. Both devices weaken Allman's book.

Allman's theories, first of all, tend to be embarrassingly large, as though to make *Miami* as important as possible: "Like all the great heroes of

American nationalism, Kennedy never imagined that reality could permanently bar his way"; "They will recognize that defeat always contains the seeds of victories, and victory the seeds of defeats both stranger and more fertile than we human beings can predict." Unfortunately the theories pop in and out as each anecdote demands, and they inevitably conflict. At one point Allman discovers how hopeful Miami life can be, so that "for every one who does drown, a thousand get through," but a little later he demonstrates the alienation of the old, the hollowness of the American Dream, and the "riches to rags" story so typical of Miami. Throughout *Miami*, there is a looseness about Allman's thinking that comes from his trying to personalize a large and varied history.

Secondly, Allman's attempt to incorporate masses of journalistic and historical material into his travelogue damages his prose style. Perhaps the journalist/traveler's thinking went like this: "I can keep myself visible when I am really invisible by making it sound as though I am still here." The effect is a dramatic style that is often histrionic or merely cute. Lukas refers to Allman's "chronic overwriting" and complains specifically about his incessant adjectives and paradoxes. Allman also depends on composite characterizations that are meant to be evocative. And he often uses similes that are intended simultaneously to make both the object and the writer more visible: "The Neon vacancy signs on the thirty-dollar motels wink on with a leer."

Miami's discontinuity of persona and central thesis, which Allman tries unsuccessfully to bridge with a distinctive prose style, leaves it with a weak plot. Much of the book is a series of newspaper-length set pieces that have their own individual shape—each one introduced, then narrated, then ended with a gnomic bang that is meant to resonate. The problem of plot is not unique to Allman, of course. Reporters often gather material in short snatches with their own emotional life. But Allman's book is so long that his failure to find a forward-moving shape proves deadly. Even though it contains interesting historical material and some striking moments, Allman's book on Miami is the least successful of the three published in 1987.

But since none of these three books was greeted with unmitigated cheers by early reviewers, it would not be worth an essay to demonstrate their inadequacies. Rather, these three books and the three periodical articles based upon them suggest some of the difficulties inherent in contemporary travel writing. Fussell and others have argued that tourism has crippled travel writing, although Jonathan Culler, in a provocative semiotic critique of Fussell that parallels the depiction of travel found in Didion's novels, argues that the terms *tourist* and *traveler* are "not so much two historical categories as terms of an opposition integral to tourism." International politics has had an influence. As Didion's novels suggest, ambiguous terms like *traveler* and *resident* leave us unsure about which worlds are foreign and which are not, and thus sometimes uncertain whether we are reading a travelogue or a domilogue.

Modern journalism has also affected travel writing. Conventional journalistic invisibility has made readers suspicious of individualized travelers and has often made writers overly self-conscious in their self-portrayals. Journalistic neutrality has made some writers sporadic in their opinions, and others overly aggressive. Similarly, short, prepared statements from sources have made readers and writers uneasy about complete character sketches. Journalism's lack of settings has led to compensatory gaudy scene-painting in much travel writing. The curt documentation of conventional journalism has posed an obstacle for writers trying to build greater significance into their details. And the length and structure of news stories, which are partly determined by the typical journalistic interview, have left many writers inadequately prepared to write long stories. The reviews of the three 1987 books on Miami reveal a generic confusion, with some reviewers calling for more reporting and less authorial self-indulgence, others complaining that the writers' autobiographies are incomplete and their personae underdeveloped, some noting the unexplained icons that reappear in the books, and others praising the effective evocation of place. Didion has in her novels and factual pieces explored the epistemology that underlies modern empiricist journalism. But even an experienced and self-conscious writer like her has to struggle with her journalistic environment as she constructs a book like *Miami*. When Didion said in an interview with Leslie Garis, as *Miami* was going to press, "I am not an investigative reporter," she sounded as defensive as David Rieff, who uses nearly the same words in his author's note to *Going to Miami*. Ironically, Didion's *Miami* is weakened precisely by her inability to aesthetically incorporate the investigative journalism she *has* done.

Joan Didion's factual works range widely, from analytical and personal essays to nearly conventional journalism. In the center, as both the epitome and zenith of her factual writing, stands her travel literature. Journalistic conventions have enervated much contemporary factual writing, but Didion has herself demonstrated, in works like "Slouching Towards Bethlehem," "Guaymas, Sonora," "In Bogotá," and *Salvador*, how possible it still is to integrate autobiography and reporting, to capture the enlightening encounter of a writer and a foreign place.

WORKS CITED

Allman, T. D. "The City of the Future." *Esquire*, February 1983, 39–47.

————. *Miami: City of the Future*. New York: Atlantic Monthly P, 1987.

Anonymous. Review of *Miami*, by Joan Didion. *New Yorker*, 25 January 1988, 112.

Cohen, Jeffrey C. "Metaphor for the Future." Review of *Miami*, by T.D. Allman, *Going to Miami*, by David Rieff, and *Miami*, by Joan Didion. *National Review*, 20 November 1987, 54–58.

Culler, Jonathan. "The Semiotics of Tourism." In *Framing the Sign: Criticism and Its Institutions*. Norman: U of Oklahoma P, 1988, 153–67.

D'Erasmo, Stacey. "City in Pink: Slouching Toward Miami." Review of *Miami*, by Joan Didion, *Going to Miami*, by David Rieff, *Miami*, by T. D. Allman, and *The Corpse Had a Familiar Face*, by Edna Buchanan. *Village Voice Literary Supplement*, October 1987, 21–22.

Didion, Joan. *A Book of Common Prayer*. New York: Simon & Schuster, 1977.

————. *Democracy*. New York: Simon & Schuster, 1984.

————. "In Bogotá." In *The White Album*. New York: Simon & Schuster, 1979, 187–97.

————. *Miami*. New York: Simon & Schuster, 1987.

————. *Miami*. In *New York Review of Books*, 28 May 1987, 43–48; 11 June 1987, 15–18; 25 June 1987, 35–39; 16 July 1987, 22–31.

————. *Salvador*. New York: Simon & Schuster, 1983.

————. *Salvador*. In *New York Review of Books*, 4 November 1982, 9–17; 18 November 1982, 31–55; 2 December 1982, 23–31.

————. *Slouching Towards Bethlehem*. New York: Farrar, Straus, 1968.

Fussell, Paul. *Abroad: British Literary Traveling Between the Wars*. Oxford: Oxford UP, 1980.

Fussell, Paul, ed. *The Norton Book of Travel*. New York: W. W. Norton, 1987.

Garis, Leslie. "Didion & Dunne: The Rewards of a Literary Marriage." *New York Times Magazine*, 8 February 1987, 18–26.

Gingold, Alfred, and John Buskin. *Snooze: The Best of Our Magazine*. New York: Workman, 1986.

Hendrickson, Paul. "Joan Didion's Fortnight of Living Dangerously." *Boston Globe*, 16 April 1983, 2.

Kakutani, Michiko. "A Latin Enclave." Review of *Going to Miami*, by David Rieff. *New York Times*, 29 August 1987, 13.

Lemann, Nicholas. "The Mirage of Miami." Review of *Miami*, by T. D. Allman, *The Corpse Had a Familiar Face*, by Edna Buchanan, *Miami*, by Joan Didion, and *Going to Miami*, by David Rieff. *New Republic*, 23 November 1987, 37–42.

Lukas, J. Anthony. "The Whole Place Was Made Up." Review of *Miami*, by T. D. Allman. *New York Times Book Review*, 10 May 1987, 12.

Lyons, Gene. "Slouching Through Salvador." Review of *Salvador*, by Joan Didion. *Newsweek*, 28 March 1983, 69.

Manoff, Karl, and Michael Schudson. *Reading the News*. New York: Pantheon, 1986.

Muggli, Mark Z. "The Poetics of Joan Didion's Journalism." *American Literature* 59 (1987): 402–21.

Rieff, David. *Going to Miami: Exiles, Tourists, and Refugees in the New America*. New York: Little, Brown, 1987.

———. "A Reporter at Large: The Second Havana." *New Yorker*, 18 May 1987, 65–83.

Schudson, Michael. *Discovering the News: A Social History of American Newspapers*. New York: Basic, 1978.

Sherrill, Robert. "Can Miami Save Itself: A City Beset by Drugs and Violence." *New York Times Magazine*, 19 July 1987, 18–26.

Wolfe, Tom, and E. W. Johnson. *The New Journalism*. New York: Harper & Row, 1973.

> > > > > > More Names on Inscription Rock: Travel Writers on the Great Plains in the Eighties

NANCY COOK

As in decades past, in the 1980s dozens of writers packed up their vehicles and headed west, notebooks handy. Several accounts that cover the Great Plains were published, including Mark Abley's account of the Canadian plains, *Beyond Forget: Rediscovering the Prairies* (1986); *Out West* (1987) by Dayton Duncan; *The Solace of Open Spaces* (1985) by Gretel Ehrlich; Ian Frazier's *Great Plains* (1989); *The Necessity of Empty Places* (1988) by Paul Gruchow; British mountaineer Gwen Moffat's *Hard Road West: Alone on the California Trail* (1981); and *The Hidden West* (1983) by Rob Schultheis.

Of the works that made it into print as books, both Dayton Duncan's *Out West* and Ian Frazier's *Great Plains* garnered numerous favorable reviews in magazines and newspapers with large national circulations. Both sold well enough to warrant paperback printings. Situating themselves within a long tradition of travel writing about the American West, Duncan and Frazier write with other texts about the plains in mind. Duncan follows the Lewis and Clark Trail, reading the explorers' journals as he goes, while Frazier uses a variety of historical texts and narratives to create a journey of the imagination through both space and time.

I have paired these two accounts because they represent similar projects. Both men have worked as journalists. Portions of *Out West* originally appeared in the *Boston Globe* and in the *Kansas City Star*. Frazier's work, including sections of *Great Plains*, has appeared in the *New Yorker*. Each man undertook his odyssey alone in a van, camping out for the most part. Both spent more than one summer traveling, between them ranging from 1982 through 1985. They take up similar topics, cite many of the same sources, and relay some of the same historical anecdotes. At times they

A version of this essay first appeared in *Great Plains Quarterly* 11, no. 2 (Spring 1991): 113–26. Reprinted by permission of *Great Plains Quarterly*.

even travel the same roads and encounter the same people, as if making stops on a predetermined Grand Tour.

But though the two books share such similarities, their styles sometimes diverge significantly, as even their covers reveal. In the photograph that constitutes the cover of *Out West*, Dayton Duncan leans against a road marker for the Lewis and Clark Trail, smiling out at his readers. Garbed in Stetson, pearl-snapped denim shirt, faded Levis, and cowboy boots, Duncan occupies more than half the vertical space of the cover. The road sign, with its silhouettes of a pointing Lewis and a gun-toting Clark, towers over Duncan and directs him (and his readers) onward.

On the dust jacket of Frazier's book, the title, *Great Plains*, fills the top half, superimposed over painted clouds in a blue-green sky. Sky and clouds comprise the top three-fourths of the jacket cover. Empty highway stretches up to a vanishing point on the horizon line, less than two inches up from the bottom. In black block letters "IAN FRAZIER" spans the horizon line, poised like an enormous billboard in the distance. In this unpopulated landscape readers are invited either to lose themselves in the vanishing point or to latch onto Frazier's name. The reader's perspective becomes anchored only through Frazier's name as a linguistic construct. Duncan offers himself as a genial guide, humanizing his landscape, and as a result, the cover of *Out West* seems almost cluttered when compared with that of *Great Plains*. The difference in cover art suggests the contrast in styles between the two books. Duncan poses himself in each scene and appears, as it were, in every snapshot, while Frazier constitutes himself as author rather than participant, as distant observer rather than model.

Near the beginning of *Great Plains* Frazier recalls how he came to the Great Plains for an extended tour. After having fantasized about moving from New York to Montana, in 1982 he finally does so. He sublets his apartment, packs his van, and heads west. Ready to abandon the restrictive East for the free West, Frazier finds himself in Ohio for his sister's wedding. In a gesture emblematic of the casting off of eastern strictures, Frazier remembers, "At the reception, to entertain the bridesmaids, I ate a black cricket the size of my thumb." Presumably, this ceremonial act of savagery indicates his readiness to go west. Traveling west, he finally settles not in eastern or even central Montana, on the plains themselves, but in the mountainous western region, in Kalispell, Montana (or rather the resort town, Bigfork, Montana, according to the end-papers map), because he "finally saw a few people who looked kind of like me." Even there he has difficulty adjusting for he does not "know one person in Montana." More importantly, although "for years in New York [he] had dreamed of Montana," once there Frazier realizes: "Suddenly I no longer had any place to dream about. So I started to dream about the Great Plains." Despite his time in the West, his eastern sensibilities remain. The West exists for him as a dreamscape and his view of the region always remains that of the outsider. Three years later he moves back to New York.

Like several of his predecessors Frazier represents the region as empty in many ways, a space that he can now inscribe. On the opening page of *Great Plains* he proclaims that the land is "still-empty," a place where there are often fields of "nothing." Although Frazier may not have the descriptive language or the point of view of the naturalist, the farmer, the Indian, or the local inhabitant (which might enable him to see the space as other than empty), his point of view seems a strategic one. He defines the plains in contrast to an urban East, delighting in the absence on the plains of those things all too common in the East, for now he is "beyond newsstands and malls and velvet restaurant ropes!" Fearing for the Great Plains "because many people think they are boring" and because they "do not ingratiate," Frazier claims that "the beauty of the plains is not just in themselves but in the sky, in what you think when you look at them, and in what they are not."

He proceeds to fill the space selectively and speculatively, for the marvelous feature of the Great Plains, as Frazier represents them, is the room they allow for the imagination to roam. Throughout *Great Plains* he employs the past tense extensively, placing himself imaginatively into the region's past, often with an eye toward correcting old myths and misnomers. His consistent use of the past tense, both for his own travels as well as for the history he recounts, helps blur the distinction between past and present. All becomes part of the same narrative. Even the living persons he encounters talk about the past, though usually at his prompting. He revises stories of Bonnie and Clyde, George Armstrong Custer, Kit Carson, Buffalo Bill, Billy the Kid, Sitting Bull, and Crazy Horse. Frazier reconstructs the history of the Great Plains for those who are not of the place—those who, if they know of the region at all, know it by its myths. Recasting the journalistic "fact piece" as Romantic history, Frazier makes the present serve the past.

Readers are encouraged to place Frazier's account at the top of the literary heap from the book's outset, as soon as they see the end papers. As one opens *Great Plains* one sees two maps: "The Great Plains, c. 1850" on the left and "The Great Plains Today" on the right. Both maps represent the same geographic space, but the names and superimposed boundaries differ. The first map indicates the routes taken by Coronado in 1541; Lewis and Clark, 1804–1806; Stephen Long, 1819–1820; Francis Parkman in 1846; and Zebulon Pike in 1805. Within its boundaries it labels major rivers as well as regions identified with Indian tribes. In addition, a few forts have been indicated along with the Black Hills in what is now South Dakota. Opposite, "The Great Plains Today" shows the boundaries of Montana, Wyoming, Colorado, New Mexico, Texas, Oklahoma, Kansas, Nebraska, South Dakota, and North Dakota. It names some of the rivers shown on the other map, but not all. It indicates one route, Ian Frazier's, and names only those places taken up by his narrative. The second map no longer represents, in any way, the major points of navigation, commerce, or community that were noted on the first map. It represents instead a past and a present determined by Ian Frazier's account of them. Consequently, Last Chance, Colorado, makes the map, but not Denver. Lincoln, New Mexico, makes the map because of its associations with Billy the Kid, but no other spot in the state warrants a mark. "The Great Plains Today" offers a disorienting view of the region—disorienting at least until one has read Frazier's book.

Maps, as Wayne Franklin suggests, have often functioned as "charts of 'idea,' " rather than as charts of geographic data. The map of Frazier's route offers readers a guide to Frazier's attitude toward the Great Plains instead of a road map they might actually follow. Frazier's map, in its refusal to locate places in reference to common landmarks or main thoroughfares, insists that his journey, as exploration, remains idiosyncratic and that it cannot be duplicated, except by means of his text. Yet, "what is lost in the process," in Franklin's terms, "is a sense of the real terrain as a place of action rather than grand plot." In essence, the map guides us not through the Great Plains, but through Frazier's narrative. In this regard, as in many travel books, the author labors so that his readers don't have to. Franklin quotes Hector St. Jean de Crèvecoeur on maps: " 'Nothing is so easy as to travel on a map; actually to traverse a track . . . is to meet with a thousand unforeseen difficulties.' "

The modern traveler's difficulties, to be sure, are slight in comparison to those of the eighteenth-century traveler, but Crèvecoeur's point remains valid. In a sense, readers are encouraged to peruse maps, even trace routes with their fingers, with an ease that duplicates the ease with which they can now fly over the region on transcontinental flights. Frazier himself hints at the problems with such effortless views in the early pages of *Great Plains*, as "most travellers who see the plains do it from thirty thousand feet." He counters the airline view with a description of the means and the time necessary for transcontinental travel in the mid-nineteenth century. The airline view tends to overlook the plains altogether: "Crossing high and fast above the plains, headed elsewhere, you are doing what rain clouds tend to do. You are in a sky which farmers have cursed and blasted with dynamite barrages and prodded with hydrogen balloons and seeded with silver-iodide crystals and prayed to in churches every day for months at a time, for rain. Usually the clouds wait to rain until they are farther west or east."

Both fliers and map readers may remain indifferent to the topographical diversity and human activity that occur on the plains. Frazier promises to deliver what the airline cannot—a closer view. He knows what others do not: "If you ask the flight attendant about those green and brown rectangles, chances are he or she will not say . . . ," and he goes on for over half a page on the development of strip farming on the plains. Yet despite all his good intentions, one consequence of both mapping and Frazier's own means of representation is that (as Franklin puts it) the "human line comes to dominate the natural ones which first engrossed [a traveler's] attention." In his short history of farming developments, as in his map of "The Great Plains Today," Frazier's attention moves to and remains on himself rather than on the plains. For Frazier's *New Yorker* audience, many of whom will see the plains only from "thirty thousand feet" (presumably those addressed as "you" in the passage quoted earlier), the book is appealing because Frazier wrote it, not because it is about the Great Plains.

The human landscape of the contemporary Great Plains is relegated to the background in much the same way. The present in *Great Plains* most frequently serves as a pretext for a discussion of the past and the mythic. One of the greatest myths surrounds the Sioux chief, Crazy Horse, who becomes the center of the text. As Frazier notes, Crazy Horse never told his own story, never allowed himself to be photographed, never traveled to the land of the white men. In fact he never left the plains. He becomes an emblematic figure in Frazier's text precisely because his history leaves so much room for speculation. Crazy Horse, that is, can be imbued with the heroic qualities that meet Frazier's needs and expectations. His mythic stature, unrestrained by consistent historical data, allows Frazier considerable imaginative space. After cataloging at length why he loves Crazy Horse, Frazier concludes his list with the avowal that "in the mind of each person who imagines him, he looks different." He then expands to connect Crazy Horse with broader national and mythic concerns:

> I believe that when Crazy Horse was killed, something more than a man's life was snuffed out. Once, America's size in the imagination was limitless. After Europeans settled and changed it, working from the coasts inland, its size in the imagination shrank. Like the center of a dying fire, the Great Plains held that original vision longest. Just as people finally came to the Great Plains and changed them, so they came to where Crazy Horse lived and killed him. Crazy Horse had the misfortune to live in a place which existed both in reality and in the dreams of people far away; he managed to leave both the real and the imaginary place unbetrayed.

This deification of Crazy Horse removes him from any complex historical analysis, one that might allow for an Indian point of view, and places him in the role of an emblematic noble savage-victim. In the process, Indians come to occupy a timeless place on the plains as a group separate from the "people [who] finally came to the Great Plains and changed them." Frazier, at least temporarily, forgets that the Plains Indians are immigrants and that they modified the environment to meet their needs, changing it in the process. Frazier sets Crazy Horse apart not only from other Indians, who changed their new home (and perhaps even betrayed it), but also apart from all other inhabitants of the Great Plains who have "the misfortune to live in a place which exist[s] both in reality and in the dreams of people far away," even the living people about whom Frazier writes.

Frazier's idealized Crazy Horse, then, sets the standard by which all other Indians are compared and makes the other Indians represented seem to be either pale imitations of the great chief or decayed remnants of those Indians who betrayed Crazy Horse, their people, and their region. While on the subject of hitchhikers, for example, Frazier describes Lydell White Plume, a Fancy Dancer en route from a powwow on the Crow Reservation to a funeral on the Wind River Reservation. White Plume's funeral trip offers a chance to mention the high suicide rate among young men on the reservation, but Frazier provides no space for an adequate discussion of this matter. When they reach his incapacitated car, White Plume shows Frazier his dance costume, but readers get very little of the conversation, and then only via indirect discourse. The subject of tribal dances gets dropped rather quickly, for Frazier seems to have decided that while his readers may wish to know that Indians can still look colorful, they don't really care about any particular Indian or about what life is actually like on a reservation.

While looking for the site of Sitting Bull's cabin, Frazier later encounters hitchhiker Jim Yellow Earring. He shows his readers a Yellow Earring so desperate for booze that he expresses interest in the writer's bottle of gasoline additive. At the cabin site Frazier encounters a rattlesnake, which Yellow Earring goes after "like a man chasing a bus." He then offers to "snap his tongue out of his bone head," but Frazier asks him "please not to." On the way back to the highway Yellow Earring tells Frazier many things, among them "about how the Crow Indians in Montana drink Lysol, also known as 'Montana Gin,' which will sure get you drunk, but which can collapse your lungs if you don't mix it right." When Frazier drops him off, Yellow Earring asks for a "loan" of a few bucks, then asks for more before he sees the denomination of the bill Frazier gives him. Frazier also picks up hitchhiker Doreet, a Hunkpapa Sioux who "was big, pretty, with scars up both arms." Doreet wears a Cornell tee-shirt. He asks her if she went to Cornell and she replies, " 'Where's that?' " He points to her shirt and she responds, " 'Oh, probably—I've been all over the country.' " For Frazier's readers, a joke has been made, possibly at Cornell's expense, but at Doreet's expense as well, for she isn't "in" on the humor. Whether through direct quotation or indirect discourse, Frazier has the Indians he meets indict their contemporary existence, but he leaves out a context for that indictment. He includes no extended interviews, really no interviews at all, with any Indian. Deceased and legendary Indians get far more coverage in *Great Plains* than any living ones.

Through quotation, Indians are given voice to condemn themselves, but never a voice with which to defend, explain, or praise any aspect of their lives. Thus Frazier's encounter with Yellow Earring is intercut with accounts of Sitting Bull, Ghost Dancers, nineteenth-century Indian customs, the rise of the cattle business, and the demise of the buffalo. Against the grand sweep of history, Yellow Earring fares poorly. This technique of juxtaposition, which Frazier uses throughout the book, always serves to diminish the lives of contemporary Indians. For Frazier, contemporary Lysol-swilling, hitchhiking Indians are interesting only to the degree that they invoke irony or (better yet) make a mythic past seem more rich for being unattainable. It is not surprising then, that in the dreamy reverie that ends the book, the Great Plains become "the place where Crazy Horse will always remain uncaptured. They are the lodge of Crazy Horse."

As with most writer-travelers who have represented the Great Plains during the last 150 years, Ian Frazier does not write to or for those who inhabit the region, but primarily for the eastern urban dweller, for readers of the *New Yorker* in this case, where most of his work has appeared.

He allies himself with his readers through a series of narrative maneuvers that foreground his status as an outsider on the Great Plains. Not surprisingly, the book begins with an eastern, rather than a western perspective: "Away to the Great Plains of America, to that immense Western short-grass prairie now mostly plowed under!" The view is distinctly nostalgic, lamenting what has already been destroyed while celebrating, with exclamation points, what remains. The distancing effect here echoes that found in the first edition of Francis Parkman's *The Oregon Trail* (1849). As Carl Bredahl has noted, Parkman's book, which was originally titled *The California and Oregon Trail*, opens chapter 1 with an epigraph from Shelley: "Away, away from men and towns / To the silent wilderness." While Parkman, or those close to him, chose to remove the epigraph (and all others) from subsequent editions because it seemed too romantic, for Frazier the oblique allusion sets an appropriately romantic, even elegiac tone. Although Frazier doesn't cite the first edition in his notes, the first nine sentences in the book begin with "Away," so he aims for a particular rhetorical effect. He flees from others in order to find a contemplative spot, where he can fill the silence as he sees fit.

Like many travelers before him, Frazier tells greenhorn stories on himself. He gets his van stuck in the mud, he gets lost, he gets caught nosing around someone's family homestead. As ruins, abandoned homesteads intrigue him (and, presumably, his readers), for he asserts that "whenever you see an abandoned house, you wonder." The second-person pronoun here allies the reader with Frazier, but it's an alliance, as it turns out, against the locals. When Frazier snoops around one abandoned house in Texas jotting notes, a man who grew up in the house drives up. Frazier is unsettled, even embarrassed by the man's look of "mild, complete puzzlement," for he adds, "as my van pulled out of the driveway, it slunk." Calculated to gain sympathy with one kind of reader, these anecdotes can put off another. To an inhabitant of the region Frazier can seem both invasive and smug.

In one story he tells on himself, he spends an afternoon with Gerard Baker, an Indian Park Service ranger. Baker invites him to share a pipe of "kinnikinnick (a mixture of tobacco and the dried inner bark of the red willow, which Indians used to smoke)." They take turns throwing an ax, with Baker showing Frazier the technique. Later Baker suggests they take a ceremonial sweat bath ("an important part of many Indian religions," Frazier notes), but he declines. Baker tells him that according to family legend, they are near an old Indian burial site. Frazier relates the end of the exchange:

"Really? Could you maybe go up there and find those burials and find beads and pipes and stuff?" I asked.

Behind his brown eye, a shutter dropped.

". . . Well," Gerard Baker said, "I suppose you *could*. . . ."

Baker's response lets us know that Frazier has stepped out of bounds. And in relating the incident Frazier, like precursors Parkman or Custer, seems determined to remind us that he remains an outsider.

Indeed, Frazier seems to relish his outsider status. Often he notes the lack of human contact during his trips. Just before his visit with Baker, he notes, "I had been driving for several days, talking only to order in cafes, and sleeping in my van at night." Frequently he refuses invitations offered him by locals, as if too much contact with inhabitants might upset his reveries about them. Often the excuse he gives is that he must be going. Like some harried businessman, Frazier seems compelled to keep moving. Though he uses Montana as his base of operations, Frazier seems unwilling to surrender either Manhattan's pace or its sensibilities. After turning down an invitation for dinner with a Wyoming ranch couple, Frazier segues into a quotation from Francis Parkman upon encountering emigrants along the Oregon Trail. The quotation recalls Parkman's urban disdain for the common persons, who "tormented" him with questions. In rendering his encounters with assorted locals, Frazier suggests that while the locals may be colorful, one ought to keep one's distance.

In addition to the anecdotes, Frazier's metaphors also depend upon an urban sensibility for their effect. In his postindustrial perspective, western gunfights are "closer in spirit to drug wars in the Bronx than to duels of honor," lightning flashes are "like the Fourth of July in New Jersey seen from an airplane," and Fort Union is "like the Times Square of the plains." Yet despite the proliferation of similes such as these, Frazier ignores the cities of the plains. Only Dodge City, the setting for the television series *Gunsmoke*, merits a write-up. Denver, Bismarck, and Billings have no place on Frazier's plains.

Frazier's scrupulous avoidance of urban areas seems in keeping with the anxieties he shares with many of his literary predecessors. He turns away from large groups of living inhabitants of the plains in favor of the dead, the lonely, or the disenfranchised. These inhabitants are voiceless, or nearly so, and thus they allow "free" space for Frazier's own imagination. In speaking for such voiceless figures he often laments the despoliation of the plains by the white men. This too places Frazier within the tradition of nineteenth-century writer-travelers, for as Lee Clark Mitchell notes in *Witnesses to a Vanishing America*, many travelers were troubled by the destruction of America's vastness. For Frazier, as well as for some of those before him, lamentation serves a strategic purpose. He repeatedly evokes the blankness of the plains, and upon this "piece of paper" he writes his text. Frazier scrawls his particular view of the region in *Great Plains* almost as literally as the travelers he names scrawled their names on Register Cliffs on the North Platte River.

Anxious about the status of his story among all others, as well as against the places themselves, he complains of the defilement of that very space. He bemoans the way modernity evacuates meaning, drains significance, and defaces ruins. Like many of his predecessors, Frazier's lamentations sometimes read like an alibi. He has come to the plains to mine a unique, powerful, even successful narrative from them. If he has failed to inscribe his name there successfully, along with Francis Parkman and Walter Prescott Webb (two precursors with whom he is compared on the book jacket), we might not perceive that he has failed, but rather that the plains have failed him, that the terms of comparison have been stripped away by a coal mine. The tone of regret suggests that what he represents *was* there, and that if we fail to see *his* Great Plains, it isn't because of a failed narrative strategy, or even an inferior facility for description, but because the artifact itself has been exploited or destroyed. Readers who might venture out West can never really compare notes with Frazier, for as he repeatedly suggests, what *he* saw will be radically changed or gone. According to this model, the space represented must always be dying or dead, historical or mythic. By erasing, in effect, a given landscape or artifact and documenting its demise, Frazier strives to leave his own *imaginative* work unassailable. The pedestrian, quotidian, contemporary Great Plains, with their Denvers and Bismarcks, must not be represented, for they survive and invite comparison.

Great Plains offers an imaginative reconstruction of powerful myths, one designed to keep the plains a pastoral space for those who don't wish to be there, but who want it always to remain an imaginative potential. Fittingly, Frazier's book ends with the evocation of an imaginary Great Plains, suitable for his dreams, a space "enormous, bountiful, unfenced, empty of buildings, full of names and stories." Such empty spaces form a literary construct in line with a powerful tradition in American letters. Ian Frazier's Great Plains are "the territory" that promises escape from contemporary urban life: a theme park, a playground, but not a home.

Dayton Duncan utilizes traditional strategies of representation in *Out West*, but for a different effect than Frazier's. Viewed in light of Frazier's book, Duncan's project seems less ambitious and more narrowly focused. To begin with, he has a definite plan—to follow the Lewis and Clark Trail and respond both to the places they encountered and to their narratives of the journey. He chooses to identify with the introspective and troubled Lewis rather than the more stolid Clark. Lewis sometimes becomes a touchstone for Duncan's own responses, which brings a self-consciousness to *Out West* that is missing from *Great Plains*. Lewis's doubts, as recorded in his journals, allow Duncan to question his own motives and methods, and even the project itself. Unlike Frazier's idealization of Crazy Horse, Duncan's clear admiration of Lewis doesn't paint him as a repository of all that remains elusive. In pursuing his task, Duncan writes a travel book in which the past guides the present and provides coherence, but never dominates. The past may frame the present, but unlike in Frazier's book, the present refuses to serve only the past. In Duncan's book, the voices of the living, in direct quotation, take precedence over voices from the past.

Although *Out West* and *Great Plains* share some Library of Congress subject classifications, Duncan's audience is constituted differently from Frazier's. Frazier's audience may well read *Great Plains* because it is written by Ian Frazier rather than because they seek to know more about the plains, whereas Duncan, in his preface to *Out West*, anticipates his readers' interest as being in his topic rather than in his representation of it. He recalls his own entrance into the cult of Lewis and Clark buffs as a motivating force behind his journeys. (Duncan takes three separate trips: during the summer of 1983, the summer of 1985, and in February 1985.) Duncan's readers, as he seems to imagine them, might one day travel his route themselves. Moreover, he situates himself as being on the periphery of the literary profession by noting that he has the time to undertake his journeys because he had worked for a political candidate whose bid for office failed. Unlike *New Yorker* staffer Ian Frazier, Duncan is between jobs when he undertakes to write his book. We might suspect Duncan here as disingenuous, a kind of folksy fraud. But this seems less the case than that Duncan speaks to a largely different audience, both geographically and socially, than that addressed by Frazier. Throughout the book he demonstrates that Lewis and Clark buffs come from different classes and different regions, including the regions he traverses.

Where Frazier implies his sense of audience most frequently through his choice of metaphor, Duncan's subject itself implies his readers. Throughout his journey, Duncan writes about his interactions with the inhabitants of the region. He shows his readers his attempts to move from the position of outsider to that of benign guest within a community. He is successful, in part, because he can read many of the local codes. He pulls off the highway to talk to a farmer driving a team of Belgian horses, figuring "a man using horses instead of a tractor can't be in any hurry." They chat for a while, then the farmer mentions "how his son is participating in some new seed experiment in planting which [he] thinks is just so much foolishness since it takes up too much time. The mention of taking too much time is his way of saying that ours is up." Later that day Duncan stops to watch another farmer with a team of horses. The farmer sees Duncan watching him and stops. They talk, and the farmer indicates that he is Amish. He asks Duncan for news of a movie about the Amish that has just come out (*Witness*), and Duncan assures him that there were no real Amish in the film. The conversation flags and the farmer

> wipes his forehead again and looks down the straight stretch of highway, where a big truck has crested a rise about a mile away, then at my vehicle in the road.
>
>   "He's movin' right along." His signal that I should, too.

They part and Duncan adds, "I return to the road, knowing enough about his faith not to ask for a picture." Not only does Duncan understand the codes well enough not to make himself a nuisance, he transmits that knowledge to his readers, so that they too might be enlightened travelers.

While this strategy imposes certain limitations, it offers his readers a different relation to the inhabitants who are represented. Duncan explains:

> Visitors in the small towns of the Plains are greeted with a friendly curiosity, instead of the suspicion and reticence of an Eastern hamlet, or the callous indifference of a big city, or even the Chamber of Commerce boosterism of a medium-sized Midwestern city ("Let me show you the Eyetalian fountain down at the city park—cost $25,000 and we're *real* proud of her"). Just the same, it's wise to watch what you put on postcards to mail out from the local post office; it might already have become the chief topic of conversation at the cafe when you walk in for supper.

Unlike Frazier, Duncan acknowledges the consequences and responsibilities of his own forms of representation. Duncan recognizes both another point of view and another audience for his writing. This sense of exchange between writer and subject becomes even clearer when he interviews the editor of the *Eagle Butte News*, Helen Clausen. Duncan asks a few questions, scribbling notes as he listens. Then Clausen asks a few questions, taking notes as *she* listens. Duncan's visit, she tells him, will be featured in the next issue.

The difference between Frazier's and Duncan's positions vis-à-vis their subjects is rendered most obvious through their encounters with the same person, National Park Service ranger Gerard Baker. As noted earlier, Frazier's encounter with Baker takes up a portion of one afternoon and ends with uneasiness, on Baker's side at least. Frazier declined an offer to partake in a ritual sweat bath with Baker, then alarmed him by suggesting the possibility of a souvenir hunt on sacred ground. As Frazier describes him, Baker is identified by his knowledge of traditional Indian skills as well as his knowledge of Indian history, both of which are recast for readers in Frazier's own language and which render Baker consistent with the other images of Indians in *Great Plains*.

Duncan introduces Baker with a summary of his background, including his rise through the National Park Service and his college education. Duncan situates Baker's knowledge of "the old Indian ways" as "partly . . . an intellectual inquiry into his own roots but mainly as a conscious decision to lead his life by gleaning what he thinks is best from the two, often contradictory societies." This strategy takes Baker out of the realm of the merely colorful, out of the tradition that presents, in Lee Clark Mitchell's terms, "exotic instances of the American experience to jaded easterners," and begins to suggest the complexities of contemporary Indian culture.

Duncan goes on to describe several adventures with Baker, including a wintertime stay in a replica of a Mandan lodge and a Buffalo hunt. In each case Duncan plays the greenhorn to Baker, but they both participate, *self-consciously*, in the demarcation of the roles they play. Readers discover Baker both through direct quotation and description. As Duncan portrays him, Baker participates in the shaping of *Out West*, both as teacher and as tour guide. Baker teaches Duncan more than a few lessons about quaint Indian ways. He enlightens Duncan by teasing him, an old Indian custom. He often concocts Indian traditions on the spot for Duncan's benefit and amusement.

Duncan learns of a method of incorporating one's heritage into a culture often hostile to it. Baker is no casual antiquarian but rather a man trying to create a space for himself and his people that will allow for future survival. Duncan learns that Indians don't simply go around being colorful. Gerard Baker maintains traditions within the purview of a professional career. As Duncan describes it, "A day in his life might include paperwork at his office, a horse ride to check the park's buffalo herd, scraping and tanning some deer or elk hides, then a nighttime refresher course in cardio-pulmonary resuscitation to maintain his emergency-medical-technician license or a meeting with fellow deputy sheriffs in McKenzie County." Baker wears elkskin leggings and a deerskin shirt on occasion, but often supplements traditional clothing with an Eddie Bauer parka. As Duncan tells it, Baker "hopes his career can be an example and a proof to whites and members of his tribe alike that an Indian is not a caricature." For Baker, as for other Indians Duncan encounters, "the choice is not between a romantic myth or a despairing reality, idealized nobility or disintegrated culture. It's the harder work in between. 'We have to understand where we came from. . . . But we're never going back . . . and we can't stay where we are. We've got to progress—without bitterness, without self-pity.' "

The process Baker describes does not exclude outside help, for many Indians rely upon historical documents of the whites to tell them about their past. Baker learned of his heritage in part from "the Lewis and Clark journals, diaries of fur-company traders, Prince Maximilian's writings, [and] anthropologists' studies." Though the Indians have been victimized both historically and representationally, it has not been passively. In Duncan's narrative, where the appropriation of history and myth changes hands almost from page to page, the Indians too have their turn. In his work, unlike Frazier's, Indians have a chance to respond both in the present and to the past. Duncan and others have noted biased and uncomprehending representations of Indians in historical documents, but he reveals that Indians do more than passively read white histories, they use them for their individual ends.

Throughout his stays (visiting both in summer and in winter) with Gerard Baker, Duncan participates in as well as observes the activities he describes. He sleeps under buffalo robes in sub-zero weather, eats buffalo tripe, takes a sweat bath, and goes on a buffalo hunt. As part of his job, Baker must catch or kill buffalo that stray off the national park and onto private land. Baker and Duncan head off in a pickup truck to a spot where wandering buffalo have been sighted. After an extensive chase, Baker determines that the buffalo have strayed too far to be caught and transported back to the park. They must be killed, but their meat will be given to local charities. Baker shoots them, then begins to skin and clean them, a task in which Duncan joins. Duncan finds the "hot, messy work . . . harder labor than it looked." Baker "slices off a piece of brownish-purple liver and offers it to the bystanders. They all decline . . . so he turns to me." Duncan and Baker first eat slices of the liver, then of the kidney. Duncan expresses the bond created through his participation by a shift in his use of pronouns. By the end of the passage, the experience is no longer rendered in terms of his own individual experience, but as a communal one. As they start to work on the second buffalo he notes: "Our knives are duller, our arms are more tired, the day is hotter, and this bull is bigger than the first. Blood smears our hands, forearms, shirts, and parts of our foreheads where we have tried to wipe the sweat away." If Duncan had any remaining illusions about the "noble savage" and his idyllic way of life, it vanishes when he notices that "blood smears our hands."

In *Out West*, Duncan attempts to let the words of others into his own text. He taped many of his interviews and presents the results by means of direct quotation throughout his narrative. His is a much more expansive text than Frazier's—he covers more ground and the book is 434 pages to 290 in *Great Plains*—yet in some ways their language is similar. Both tend to use metaphor to replace descriptive prose, and both use metaphor to link a natural phenomenon to a postindustrial one. For Duncan, a hen pheasant "rises slowly, like an overloaded jumbo jet," or some flathead buttes look "like a mountain range that has been lopped with a hedge trimmer for neatness' sake." What is suggested in *Great Plains*, but is manifest in *Out West* is that metaphoric language represents an attempt to humanize Western space. Duncan frequently casts the land in human terms, as when he first visualizes a section of the Missouri River as it appears on a map, then notes that on the map, "the Big Bend of the Missouri . . . looks like a big tonsil in the throat of the river." Some hills "look like the deeply lined face of a man who has been poorly shaved the morning after a hard night: stubble in the clefts, smooth on the flat spots, and a few gouges."

If there is a difference between the way Frazier and Duncan use metaphor, it resides in the descriptive weight analogies are asked to carry in each case. Duncan tends to use more concrete, detailed figurative language than Frazier does. Duncan seems to assume that his readers do not need to depend on a metaphor in order to imagine a scene. Like the narrative itself, Duncan's figurative language encourages his readers to linger, while Frazier urges his readers (as he himself does) to move on. Duncan also seems to be aware of the duty metaphoric language sometimes performs for readers who are unfamiliar with a landscape or a particular experience. A dependence on metaphoric language, Duncan suggests, may separate outsider from insider:

I awake the next morning in Gerard's house to the aroma of testes, kidneys, and small buffalo steaks frying in the pan. The smell is distinctive and overpowering, the same smell from the hillside where we skinned the hides.

"I'm trying to decide what that smells like," I tell Gerard, searching for descriptive images and comparisons.

He turns to me from the frying pan and fixes me with a look like Roosevelt's guide must have during their rainy hunt a hundred years ago—a look wondering if Easterners know anything about anything.

"Buffalo," he says. "It smells like buffalo."

Unlike travel writer Duncan, Baker doesn't need to translate his experience verbally, and Duncan too suggests that any attempt to can only fail. Readers who have smelled game may feel that they can intuit the experience Duncan relates, but the expression "it smells like buffalo" can only recall the smell for those who know it already. Duncan's attempt to metaphorize experience forms an act of translation that often fails. Baker does not, obviously, resist verbal description, but he refuses the role of translator. Translation—at least via metaphor—may be necessary for a visitor but it is not necessary within the community being visited.

Duncan suggests that some parts of his experience cannot be adequately conveyed. A given scene may be as ephemeral as any found in Frazier's book, but Duncan seems far less concerned with establishing his own version of it. Moreover, he resists asserting his own definitive version or interpretation of historical events in the way Frazier finds so attractive in favor of a more fluid, contradictory reading of history. Duncan mistrusts the standard version of many of the historical incidents marked on his journey, as when he comments on our notions of Jesse James and Joseph Smith: "We are left today with their myths and museums, monuments not so much to the tumultuous times of the past as to our national desire to sanitize our history." Rather than gather versions of one story and piece together a single cohesive narrative from them, as Frazier does for Crazy Horse, Duncan tends to present competing stories and historical discrepancies as examples of indeterminacy. Often he goes on to show how those versions are manipulated by different interested parties. For example, after having described numerous examples along the Missouri River of grave robbing and contested claims over the bones of famous people, Duncan encounters one more, near the confluence of the Grand and Missouri rivers:

> A hundred yards away is a polished granite base over the grave of Sitting Bull; the stone bust of the Sioux chief that once rested on the granite has been recently vandalized and has been removed for repairs. . . . At Fort Yates, North Dakota (population 771), is another grave marker for Sitting Bull. He was buried here first, but we know by now what happens to famous people buried along the Missouri River. In 1953, a group from Mobridge [S.D.] convinced some of Sitting Bull's descendants to request a reburial in South Dakota. When the requests were rebuffed, the Mobridge group snuck in under the cover of darkness, dug up the skeleton, trucked it across the state line, and buried it securely under a heavy concrete slab. By the next day, stores in Mobridge were selling T-shirts that said: "Mobridge, S.D. Sitting Bull Sleeps Here."

Though the Great Bone Heist occurred in 1953, Duncan clearly indicates that the appropriation of histories, myths and cultures is nothing new. He discusses General Philip Henry Sheridan's plans for the extermination of the buffalo and its link to the demise of the Indian. As Duncan tells it, "Sheridan suggested that instead of being stopped, the [buffalo] hunters should be given bronze medallions 'with a dead buffalo on one side and a discouraged Indian on the other.' Years later, with both Indian and buffalo reduced in number and safely confined, a different version of Sheridan's medallion would be circulated by the government in the form of a nickel coin." Duncan goes on to remind his readers that on the Indian-head nickel, neither the buffalo nor the Indian looks discouraged or dead. American history, he suggests, reveals a series of appropriations whereby, in this case, the demise of the buffalo can be interpreted as beneficial, and later idealized even further.

Both Dayton Duncan and Ian Frazier attempt to depict a region in terms of their own discourse about it, but the effects differ. Frazier provides amusing anecdotes about curious aspects of plains reality, but he maintains the underlying myths. In *Great Plains* past and present meet within Frazier's slick, seamless narrative. Frazier ends with a reverie that delights in the imaginative possibilities of the Great Plains as myth, "bigger than any name people give them. They are enormous, bountiful, unfenced, empty of buildings, full of names and stories. They extend beyond the frame of the photograph. . . . They are the place where Crazy Horse will always remain uncaptured. They are the lodge of Crazy Horse." The ideal plains for him are those that serve as a setting for his dreams. For Duncan, however, the act of inscription (whether physical or imaginative) always leaves a mark. At the close of *Out West*, readers are left to ponder not the lodge of Crazy Horse, but a dinner-cruise meeting of the Lewis and Clark Trail Heritage Foundation on a St. Louis paddlewheeler called the *Huck Finn*. As the great-great grandson of William Clark, whom Duncan informs us, "like his ancestor, [is] always willing to leave his name marked on something," signs another autograph, Duncan sees that a "beacon light at the top of the Rainbow Arch shines in the night." Duncan ends his book not in dreamy idealism, but with an acknowledgment that all travelers, whether explorers, settlers, or writers, leave their mark on the land. For Duncan, the Great Plains continue to change as each generation builds its Rainbow Arch, celebrates its heritage or writes its stories. In Duncan's account, the Great Plains are not, in the end, a blank sheet, but a palimpsest.

WORKS CITED

Bredahl, A. Carl, Jr. *New Ground: Western American Narrative and the Literary Canon*. Chapel Hill: U of North Carolina P, 1989.

Duncan, Dayton. *Out West*. New York: Penguin, 1987.

Franklin, Wayne. *Discoverers, Explorers, Settlers: The Diligent Writers of Early America*. Chicago: U of Chicago P, 1979.

Frazier, Ian. *Great Plains*. New York: Farrar, Straus & Giroux, 1989.

Mitchell, Lee Clark. *Witnesses to a Vanishing America: The Nineteenth-Century Response*. Princeton: Princeton UP, 1981.

Parkman, Francis, Jr. *California and Oregon Trail*. New York: George P. Putnam, 1849.

––––––––––––––––––

≺ ≺ ≺ ≺ ≺ ≺

British Encounters

> > > > > > **Old Journeys Revisited:**
Aspects of Postwar English
Travel Writing

JACINTA MATOS

In the Hellespont we saw where Leander and Lord Byron swam across, the one to see her upon whom his soul's affections were fixed with a devotion that only death could impair, and the other merely for a flyer, as Jack says.
—Mark Twain, *The Innocents Abroad* (1869)

The death of travel writing with World War II was announced as early as 1946 by Evelyn Waugh in his preface to *When the Going was Good*: "I do not expect to see many travel books in the near future. There is no room for tourists in a world of 'displaced persons.'" Closer to our time, Paul Fussell seems to share basically the same opinion. "I am assuming that travel is now impossible and that tourism is all we have left," he concludes in *Abroad* (1980), after a brief survey of the history of travel.

This idea, which reflects what Frank Kermode would call our "hunger for ends and for crisis," has now become something of a commonplace; it is a symptom of an apocalyptic vision that delights in announcing the end of things-as-we-know-them. Since the Modernist movement, we have been told of the death of history, of the individual and, of course, of travel. Waugh's and Fussell's view of the impossibility of travel in the contemporary world clearly shows a nostalgia for a "golden age" of travel, when passports and other restrictions to travel hardly existed, when there were still large chunks of "Terra Incognita" to be explored, when, in short, difficulties and hardships still conferred on a journey the appropriate aura of "adventure."

While such laments for a lost golden age and the belief in a shrinking world can be traced back long before 1945, there is no denying the post–World War II boom in mass tourism, the widespread availability of air travel and the corollary erasure of the "primitive" and the "exotic" brought about by the almost complete Westernization of the globe. These developments have meant that the problem of where to go in searching for "the other" has become particularly acute for postwar travel writers.

Recent developments in literary theory, in linguistics, in historiography and in all the human sciences have also put into question the relation between the individual observer and the external world, and between language and reality. We no longer hold a positivistic view of a nonfictional text as a neutral, objective reproduction of a prelinguistic reality or meaning capable of affording us a value-free knowledge. We no longer write, read, or travel with the unselfconsciousness of our predecessors, for our sense of crisis and endings is, indeed, an integral part of our world view and of our experience of travel.

But despite gloomy predictions, travel writing has not come to an untimely end. The genre is alive and thriving, and looking back at the last two decades, we can even talk of a revival, both in terms of the production and the consumption of travel books. New ones come out in astonishing numbers, and old ones, until recently only to be dug up from obscurity by patient research, are now being reprinted and bought. Phoenix-like, travel books have risen again, but not surprisingly they utilize altered ways of dealing with a new, apparently undifferentiated world. Postwar literary travelers have had to devise new strategies both for traveling and for writing about it—some of which create new points of departure, some of which constitute a reappropriation of older routes.

The question of the difference between travel writing before and after World War II has been discussed by Colin Thubron in a 1984 Royal Society of Literature lecture. For Thubron, the travel writer "has become more subjective, more turned in on himself." Whereas before he exhibited more of an interest in ruins, monuments, and other signs of the past, he now "travels in the present" with "an awakened social consciousness," devoting himself more to the description of people than objects, to the human, rather than the material, landscape. In short, Thubron claims that "we have taken a voyage away from the beautiful, the historical and objective, to something more representative, more immediately human and more subjective."

Thubron is certainly correct in making this distinction, but I find his articulation of it somewhat simplistic in so far as it centers on now outdated distinctions between objective/external and subjective/internal realities and ways of depicting them. The question of continuity or discontinuity in regards to contemporary travel writing must begin with a recognition that neither pre– nor post–World War II travel books are a homogeneous body of texts that can be grouped together and contrasted. The situation is more complex, since many contemporary travel writers continue to work within established traditions (although reshaping and adapting them), while others tend to respond to specific postwar phenomena in innovative ways.

There are, for instance, a number of contemporary travel writers who elect to keep up the tradition of the "adventurer" or "explorer," for whom a concern with the past is still a central motive for their journeys: their search for the "primitive" and the "exotic" is also, in a sense, a search for the past. They may not find it in ruins or monuments, but in remote places and the lives of peoples outside the familiar tourist routes who have so far kept the modern at bay. Thus Eric Newby in the Hindu Kush, Redmond O'Hanlon in Borneo and on the Amazon, Christina Dodwell in Papua New Guinea, and many others. Unlike their predecessors they have to travel further, and unlike them they are not so much opening up the unknown for future appropriation by the West as reminding us that the past has still not been completely erased by the present and that (if you bother to look for it) there is still a great deal of difference in a world of apparent similitude. That they usually evoke these other worlds as ephemeral utopias doomed to destruction, or simply as a different kind of dystopia from the world in which they live, seems to me not to invalidate their continuation of a tradition, but inevitably to redirect it.

In addition to these contemporary explorers abroad, there are also writers who choose to explore the familiar in the form of the city, their own countries, or civilization in some larger sense. This defamiliarizing of the familiar (which, as the Russian Formalists have taught us, is what art is all about), while often presented in aggressively modern dress, resides, again, squarely within an existing tradition. One has only to think of the "Condition of England" tradition, extending as far back as Daniel Defoe and William Cobbett, through Charles Dickens, George Orwell, J. B. Priestley, and others (not to mention writers outside travel writing, such as Engels, Mayhew, and Mastermann). Contemporary texts such as Stephen Brook's *New York Days, New York Nights* (1985) and *Honky Tonk Gelato* (1985), Paul Theroux's *The Kingdom by the Sea* (1983), and Martin Amis's *The Moronic Inferno* (1986) clearly pursue this interest in the social, political, economic, or cultural conditions of the civilized world, and follow the same impulse of exploring what is under our noses.

But the changing conditions of travel in the contemporary world have also meant that some writers have felt the need to develop new strategies of traveling and of writing as a way to respond to such postwar phenomena as the package tour and the availability of cheap and quick travel at any time of the year and to almost every destination anywhere on the globe.

Although modern tourism can be said to have started in 1841 with

Thomas Cook's organized excursion from Leicester to Loughborough, it is now the received view that we live in an age of mass tourism, and that there is a significant quantitative (if not qualitative) difference between tourism before and after World War II. This difference has to do with more than the fact that we can now travel in groups, comfortably, safely, and quickly to our chosen destination, for these concepts are, after all, relative, particularly if we find ourselves in a crowded airport, our flight delayed, and frightening numbers of planes landing and taking off above our heads. It has to do with what a traveler finds when he arrives in a foreign setting: an Avis Car Rental agency, Coca-Cola billboards, and places called "Harry's Bar," which sell American-style hamburgers. The travel writer has to cope not only with the world of mass tourism, but with the world of mass commodity production and mass consumerism as well, a world that in many respects no longer differs significantly from the one he left behind. I cannot explore all of the ramifications of this here, but it clearly represents at least the potential loss of adventure, of the challenging, unique (sometimes dangerous) experience that may, for the travel writer, if not for the holiday-maker, be disastrous. This is perhaps why those who work within the traditional formulas of travel writing tend to become the chroniclers of fugitive utopias or to stay close to home, implying that there is nothing worth traveling for.

Other writers have tried to circumvent this problem by reformulating our traditional assumptions about travel and travel writing. For them, the question has been less one of a destination, the *where* to go, than of the means of conveyance, the *how* to get there. Paul Theroux has explicitly given voice to this new concept of traveling in *The Old Patagonian Express* (1979):

> What interests me is the waking in the morning, the progress from the familiar to the slightly odd, to the rather strange, to the totally foreign, and finally to the outlandish. The journey, not the arrival, matters; the voyage, not the landing. Feeling cheated that way by other travel books, and wondering what exactly it is I have been denied, I decided to experiment by making my way to travel-book country, as far south as the trains run from Medford, Massachusetts; to end my book where travel books begin.

The act and the means of traveling replace the point of arrival as the main goal of the journey for a writer like Theroux: the going not the getting there is what matters.

It should be clear by now why this is specifically a postwar phenomenon, a reaction against the perceived sameness of the contemporary world.

By taking the journey itself as the goal of travel, a writer deals explicitly and centrally with transition and flux; he is in perpetual movement, always going but never quite getting there. In short, the potential disappointment of arrival is endlessly postponed and travel is reduced to its essence, needing nothing beyond itself to make it a fulfilling experience. Like Theroux (who makes train journeys the main concern of his books), other writers have used the same strategy for dealing with a closed world. Gavin Young, for instance, in *Slow Boats to China* (1981) and *Slow Boats Home* (1985), elects to travel only by different kinds of boat and to go wherever they will lead him. Likewise, Alexander Frater in *Beyond the Blue Horizon* (1986) chooses only to travel by plane, avoiding as far as possible scheduled flights, in his pursuit of the old Imperial Airways route to Australia. This is also, in a sense, a return to past forms of travel. By refusing modern facilities, these writers attempt to make their journeys more difficult and to recover a sense of adventure that is now almost irretrievably lost. They are traveling, we might say, against the grain of modern life.

Another interesting phenomenon in the travel writing of the last three decades, and one that will be my central concern in the remainder of this essay, is the reduplication of old journeys. There exists a significant body of writing whose main purpose is to revisit places and retrace journeys made in the past and written about by others. They are, therefore, journeys that deal not only with the present reality of the traveler but also with a past experience encoded in narrative form. Thus a double focus is created: a journey made by somebody in the past is duplicated by a contemporary traveler, and a prior text is articulated with a present narrative. The old journey serves, that is, both as pretext and pre-text.

I have in mind books such as Tim Severin's works on the track of the Argonauts, Ulysses, and Sinbad; Nicholas Coleridge's *Around the World in 78 Days* (1984); Bernard Levin's *Hannibal's Footsteps* (1985); and Nicholas Rankin's *Dead Man's Chest: Travels After Robert Louis Stevenson* (1987). Although these works differ in everything from motive to literary merit, they illustrate the tendency I have here described: an impulse to reopen a world that is perceived as closed. By juxtaposing the past and the present they question our relation to the past, and the possibility of our knowing it either as lived experience or as written history. This is not to say, of course, that before World War II no text glanced back at the past or commented on the analogies or differences between its own and earlier times. What these contemporary texts uniquely do is turn this duplication of former journeys into the raison d'etre of their own trips. These authors do not simply utilize occasional references to other texts or journeys, they deliberately shape their new journeys in terms of previous ones, retracing an already traveled route with the purpose of reliving another's experience.

Looking at the titles quoted, it is worth noting that some of the original journeys that serve as models for later ones are not "real" journeys: some are fictional (such as Phileas Fogg's famous trip round the world, on which Nicholas Coleridge's book is based), while others are mythical, such as the journeys of Ulysses and the Argonauts, or exist in a sort of historical twilight, such as Hannibal's. Many of the original models, that is, belong to literature rather than to life, which, as I shall discuss later, poses interesting epistemological and rhetorical problems about the way in which the past can be recreated.

Fredric Jameson's reflections on postmodernism, in his essay "Postmodernism or the Cultural Logic of Late Capitalism," seem to me to offer a particularly useful perspective on some of the issues raised by these books. Jameson believes that postmodernism is characterized by the "well nigh universal practice of what may be called pastiche," which is distinguished from parody, he argues, by the absence of any subversive or satiric intention. Pastiche is the neutral practice of mimicry—"blank parody." Following from this, the process of "historicism," whereby all the styles of the past are randomly "cannibalized," effaces history and produces a culture of the image or "simulacrum," an "identical copy for which no original has ever existed." This leads to a loss of our sense of history, of our capacity to know the past except through our stereotypes of it. We witness the gradual loss of the past as referent until we are left with "nothing but texts," and this intertextuality is now "a deliberate, built-in feature" of postmodern culture.

What Jameson calls "cannibalization" becomes the predominant means of appropriating a past that no longer stands in any meaningful relation to the present. As a consequence, there now exists a new depthlessness in representation that eliminates the lived context in which objects existed, one which replaces that context with mere surfaces—flat, random collections of images whose only relation to each other comes from the fact that they coexist in a particular spatial framework. These concepts—especially that of "historicism," the "cannibalization" of the past and its gradual loss as a referent, the idea of a copy or simulacrum, and the notion of a self-conscious and deliberate intertextuality—seem to provide a useful way of approaching the central problems raised by these texts.

I shall begin with Bernard Levin's *Hannibal's Footsteps*. Levin is a columnist for the London *Times* and is more usually associated with such sedentary pleasures as opera and good food than with the rigorous life of a pedestrian traveler. *Hannibal's Footsteps* is, as the title indicates, a retracing of Hannibal's journey through the Alps, an episode of the Punic wars that has aroused the interest both of historians and of the general public, and that has gradually acquired an epic status in the popular imagination. Hannibal's brilliant and unorthodox feat in leading an army (and his famous elephants) across such inhospitable terrain, as well as the courage and qualities of leadership that made it possible, have come to be regarded as major examples of the heroic virtues of antiquity.

Levin, however, is not overawed by Hannibal's impressive shadow, and he sets out boldly to recreate his crossing of the Alps, without forsaking such modern amenities as rucksacks, Swiss army knives, and collapsible portable washbasins. But Levin follows a slightly different itinerary than his predecessor: he stops and even turns aside to contemplate much that wasn't there in 218 B.C., and does not, of course, face the dangers that Hannibal did (hostile Gauls, snowstorms, and the threat of starvation). Indeed his trip appears, at first sight, to be little more than a gastronomic tour of the south of France interspersed with gloomy reflections on the decline of the modern world: from politics to cuisine, from religion to hotels, nothing is what it used to be (or should be).

However, despite its somewhat unattractive surface, his book reveals much about the way we respond to history today, and the place of previous narratives in our own discourses about the past. One passage is worth mentioning in this context, that concerning the discovery of the Lascaux prehistoric caves, a site that becomes part of Levin's itinerary. He tells of the process by which, when the caves were discovered and opened to the public, the pictures on the walls began to disintegrate due to the condensation brought about by human breath. The drawings were then X-rayed and photographed, the caves closed and new ones built where an exact replica was exhibited. Levin's comments on this are: "I could not help feeling, when I heard of this project, that somebody had missed the point in a rather extreme way, and I have not ceased to think so since." Although Levin does not make explicit the point that he has in mind, it seems that he is referring to the question of the possibility or rather, impossibility, of preserving the past, and of the process by which our contemporary culture creates its own image of it (Jameson's "simulacrum").

He appears to deplore this state of affairs and, implicitly, to distance himself from it. But when we look at Levin's own work, we notice that he himself is irredeemably part of a world of fakes and that he cannot step outside it. Throughout his text we are, indeed, not so much aware of the meanings afforded us by the setting of one journey against another within their respective historical contexts as we are of the mere spatial superimposition of the second journey on the first. The movement between roughly the same points of departure and arrival in both journeys (their geographical dimension) takes precedence in the narrative over the temporal dimension created by the evocation of a past event. The respective historical contexts of the journeys are, therefore, lost in favor of a simple duplication of a previous itinerary. The old texts are also deprived of any relevance besides that of the guidebook. They tell the present traveler only where to go and what he is likely to find there. The depthlessness that Jameson considers one of the features of postmodernism is here manifested by the representation of the old and the new as equivalent in the narrative: Livy and the Michelin guide have the same "value" for the modern traveler.

Although Levin explicitly invites us to contrast the past and the present and claims historical perspectives for his insights and his conservative world view, in the end he implicitly denies the possibility of a genuinely historical (rather than merely "historicist") perspective on life. We are told, at the end of the book, that Levin, like Hannibal, did not go alone, but was accompanied by quite an entourage—a television film crew, which was recording the journey for future broadcast. What we have, in other words, is an example of a reduction of the past to (in this case literally) our own images of it. This is *Levin's* journey, Hannibal has become little more than a guide for the conducted tour of television history. (He has, in Jameson's words, been "cannibalized.") The hero is displaced by the celebrity, the pre-text becomes merely a pretext, and history is appropriated and consumed as a spectacle. It should be stressed that even without the reference to the television program the text would amply demonstrate that Levin himself has somehow "missed the point."

The second text, or rather group of texts, I wish to discuss are Tim Severin's three reduplications of the voyages of Sinbad, the Argonauts, and Ulysses. They are based, respectively, on traditional Arabian folk tales (written around the ninth century A.D.) and on Greek epics (Apollonius of Rhodes's compilation of the Argonauts' tales and the *Odyssey*). In all these cases, the journeys and the travelers who made them have no certain historical existence. Severin himself points out that the figures of these heroes are probably composite pictures or totally mythic creations and that their adventures subsume the needs, desires and general world view of a culture existing at a particular historical moment. He insists, however, on the "reality" of each journey and sees the hero as a personification of that journey.

When Severin sets out to duplicate these voyages, he is clearly doing something different from Bernard Levin, for he works more within an anthropological and historical framework. Severin defines himself in *The Jason Voyage* (1985) as a "historian of exploration." He explicitly states that his journeys can be seen as a "quest for the truth behind the legend," and, as he puts it in *The Sindbad Voyage* (1982), they attempt "to establish a dividing line between truth and fiction in the adventures." The voyages thus have, as stated, an overt purpose. They aim at some form of knowledge or truth of particular interest to the historian, since they are, on one level, the testing out of a hypothesis from which definite conclusions can be drawn: Would it have been possible for the Argonauts to reach the Caucasus? Does the geography of the *Odyssey* have any bearing on reality? Could an Arab vessel of the eighth century have made a voyage from Arabia to China? I must at this point confess my ignorance concerning the historical validity of Severin's conclusions or even the reliability of his experiment in conventional scientific terms. Whether present and future historians will revise their theses about the ancient world or eighth-century Arab trade due to Severin's findings I do not know, nor does it seem to me a determining factor in the way we can approach his work. I shall, of course, be considering his motives (both implicit and explicit) and the conclusions he reaches, but only in so far as they are realized in his texts and exemplify a postwar change of mood in English travel writing.

Severin's journeys further differ from Levin's in that he not only tries to retrace previous journeys but to recreate as far as possible the immediate context of these journeys—that is, he seeks a greater authenticity. He has, for instance, an exact replica built of the original boats in which the journeys were made, going so far as to use the same type of wood, joining together the parts of the boat in the same fashion and having the same number and type of sails. Apart from some modern emergency equipment, everything is meant to reproduce exactly the conditions in which men traveled by sea in former times. The journeys themselves also follow the same routes, calling at the same ports and dealing with the same currents and winds described in the old narratives.

Severin's ingenuity in this respect is considerable, but the problem goes beyond matters of detail and calls into question the meaning of the whole project. Severin is able to find craftsmen capable and willing to build the vessels in *The Sindbad Voyage* and *The Jason Voyage* (Vasilis in Greece and Indian craftsmen for the Sinbad voyage). These craftsmen are always presented, significantly, as the only ones of their kind left—anomalous, anachronistic, and threatened in the modern world. But what they produce, however closely it may resemble the original, crucially differs from it not only in being a deliberate imitation but in being self-consciously anachronistic as well, constructed against and in opposition to the current of the time.

Jameson has pointed out in *Marxism and Form* that in preindustrial societies physical objects had an immediate meaning; they were "human products, the result of preordained ritual and of an immediately visible hierarchy of village occupations." The link between the object and the human labor responsible for it was the source of its "original meaning-fulness." Ours, however, is a society where such links are no longer directly and clearly visible, and in which the "original meaningfulness" of things appears to have been lost. It should be fairly clear that at one level Severin's voyages represent just such a rejection of the modern and a quest for an "original meaningfulness" above and beyond the specific "original meanings" of a particular Greek or Arabian pre-text. Despite this utopian impulse, Severin's reproductions are, in our terms, simulacra.

I do not wish to condemn Severin's enterprise; after all, simulacra of such journeys are all we can produce, and they are our only means of access to the past. Severin also genuinely attempts to recover that past in a meaningful form, and I do not question either his sincerity or the desirability of what he is trying to do. However, while (unlike Levin) no suspicion of bad faith can be attached to his work, he may fairly be charged with naïveté. His criteria for the discovery of the "truth" about the past are based upon an unproblematic relation between text and reality, and his epistemological model of knowledge does not represent an adequate means of access to that truth. Severin assumes that by empirically recreating these journeys, he can establish what they were like for Sinbad, Jason, and Ulysses. He also seems to believe in the possibility of fixing and stabilizing meaning, of recording a transparent image of the reality that preexisted the prior text.

This is the case, for instance, with his final conclusions on the legend of the Golden Fleece: "The Golden Fleece was precisely that: a fleece from the Caucasus mountains, used in the gold-washing technique, and impregnated with gold dust. . . . Every single element of the legend matched the archeology. What had seemed a farfetched yarn when we began the Jason Voyage had found its solution in Georgia, 1500 miles away from its starting point in Iolcos." Whatever their historical validity, Severin's concluding remarks on this legend must be seen as symptomatic of our contemporary obsession with a sense of unmediated reality that, in the end, represents an attempt to avoid facing man's inevitable condition as a producer (rather than simply a discoverer) of meaning.

The final book I will consider, Nicholas Rankin's *Dead Man's Chest: Travels After Robert Louis Stevenson*, works within still another framework: that of biographical writing. Rankin's purpose is to follow, both temporally and spatially, Stevenson's life, from his early years in Edinburgh to his death in Western Samoa. The book can be seen as giving fresh meaning to the dead metaphor of man's life as a journey, a metaphor that in the case of Robert Louis Stevenson is an appropriate one, since both his life and his work are full of the idea of traveling. Rankin follows Stevenson's itinerary, in several senses of the word—geographical, psychological, literary and political—and his own journey represents the pursuit of a double figure: the man and the writer. Rankin's sense of this doubleness is subtle and complex, and he does not succumb to the temptation of presenting a fixed, stable, and complete recreation of Stevenson, but rather offers us a deliberately fragmented picture. Stevenson is made the "locus" of many different discourses—that of his own novels, of the written testimonies of people who met him, of his letters to friends and of scholarly studies about him. The world of Rankin's book is, indeed, a world of texts, and it is not accidental that so many writers should make an appearance in the narrative: Chesterton comments on Stevenson's literary production; Henry James, a lifelong friend, writes both to and about him; Graham Greene, a distant relative, starts work on a biography of Stevenson; Jorge Luis Borges, it turns out, is an ardent admirer of his work.

Clearly Rankin is not working with the naive notion of an objective reality that preexists these manifold "versions" of Stevenson. He accepts instead the inevitable existence of preproduced meanings that fundamentally determine any attempt to reproduce that reality. What Hayden White says about historical narrative is also relevant for travel writing in general, and for the question I am addressing in particular: "The presumed concreteness and accessibility of historical milieu, these contexts of the texts that literary scholars study, are themselves products of the fictive capability of the historians who have studied those texts. The historical documents are not less opaque than the texts studied by the literary critic. Nor is the world those documents figure more accessible. The one is no more 'given' than the other." Rankin, unlike Levin or Severin, is aware that there is no direct access to the past, nor an empirically restorable "reality," but only (to use White's terminology) encoded configurations of it.

It is interesting in this respect that Rankin should quote a passage from one of Borges's essays about the way writers respond to their literary ancestry: "In a 1951 essay on Kafka, Jorge Luis Borges observes: 'the word "precursor" is indispensable in the vocabulary of criticism, but one should try to purify it from every connotation of polemic or rivalry. The fact is that every writer *creates* his precursors. His work modifies our conception of the past, as it will modify the future.' " Every writer, Borges claims, creates his own past and the same, Rankin suggests, can be said about himself. He necessarily *creates* a precursor for his journey, he does not simply follow somebody's route or transparently reproduce another's existence in time and space.

We are, in fact, warned earlier in the book about the futility of such an endeavor. While visiting the garden at Colinton, where Stevenson used to play as a child, Rankin finds himself "looking for some carved initials in the wall, or even a long lost toy" and remarks that such "an absurdly literal quest had been foreseen by the author of *A Child's Garden of Verses* in the final poem 'To Any Reader.' " Rankin quotes the poem at length, for it precisely summarizes his point (and mine) about the recuperation of the past:

> So you may see, if you but look
> Through the windows of this book
> Another child, far, far, away
> And in another garden, play.
> But do not think you can at all,
> By knocking on the window, call
> That child to hear you. He intent
> Is still on his play-business bent.
> He does not hear, he will not look,
> Nor yet be lured out of this book.
> For long ago, the truth to say,
> He has grown up and gone away,
> And it is but a child of air
> That lingers in the garden there.

As this shows, Rankin is fully aware that we inevitably create images of the past that become inescapable, and he does not seek to ignore or bypass all the implications of this problem.

In his journey, Rankin frequently encounters examples of a cannibalization of the past, usually in museums or other institutions that preserve the relics of Stevenson's life. Of the Monterey Stevenson House he has this to say: "Museums are strange; fictions made of objects, not words. . . . What was 'the real thing' on the heritage trail of objects? Everything in the museum was both solidly real and quite unreal, because divorced from history and function." He understands that our hunger for the past in terms of "the real" is only, in the end, realizable in the creation of fakes, objects that are taken as real but are, in fact, unreal because they are torn from their original context and exhibited for mass consumption. It is a problem we have encountered before in the other authors I have discussed. Nicholas Rankin, however, seems to me to have an altogether more sophisticated view of this issue and a more satisfactory way of dealing with it in his narrative.

He never, for instance, removes objects, events or people, either past or present, from their political, economic, social, or cultural contexts. Quite the opposite, for what we have in the book are two historically rooted figures: Robert Louis Stevenson and Nicholas Rankin. Rankin does not, like Severin, refuse the modern world nor, like Levin, trivialize the past. The past, for him, is not only the isolated figure or event that constitutes the motive for his own journey, but a vast field of interlocking elements and actions whose ramifications extend into the present. The fragmented nature of the narrative—chapters are divided into sections and subsections, some dealing with Stevenson's personal life, some with political events of his day, others with the narrator's own experience of traveling or with contemporary events—serves precisely to create context. The fragmentation of the text should not be taken as signifying discontinuity, rather the use of juxtaposition invites the reader, as it were, to fill in the gaps, to establish links between the past and the present.

When Rankin is following Stevenson's boat trip through the Belgian and French canals, for example, he stops at Landrecies. Section 11 of the chapter entitled "France" starts with the information that it is raining as it had rained during Stevenson's visit to the town. There follows a quotation from Stevenson about the fortifications he found in the place, and its strategic, military importance. We are then reminded that Stevenson's statement was prophetic, since Landrecies was the scene of fierce battles in World War I, which were written about by Kipling. The next subsection begins with Henry James's opinion that Stevenson might have been a military historian, and some quotations from *An Inland Voyage* (1878) are included as proof of his interest in the matter. There is then another subsection dealing with the atmosphere that the present traveler finds in Landrecies: everybody is talking about war, since it is the fortieth anniversary of D-Day and President Reagan has received the veteran vote in the recent elections. Finally, the subsection ends with the statement that the twentieth century is the American century, just as the nineteenth was Britain's—Rankin clearly suggests a contrast between the British imperialism that formed the context of Stevenson's journey, and the American imperialism that forms the background for his own.

This summary of three pages of the book exhibits a wide range of references: the text brings together events both of a private and public nature and interweaves them in such a way as to create a literary, political, and historical context for both visits to Landrecies. The same takes place in the book as a whole, where Rankin weaves together past and present, private and public into a rich texture that creates a meaningful context for each journey and for the relationship between the two. Rankin is aware, that is, of both the fiction-making process by which reality is transformed into narrative and of the futility of attempting a journey back to an unproblematic past beyond our fictive constructions of it. Knowing that language does not unequivocally coincide with the real, he places his own writing in the context of many different discourses about the particular past he explores.

I am not, of course, claiming that Rankin transcends the limitations of the contemporary world view discussed by Jameson, which I have used as a basis for my analysis of postwar travel writing. But Rankin does seem to me more deeply aware of representational limitations. His work includes and explicitly confronts them, and incorporates the problems of recreating the past in his own narrative of recreation. Thus, although Rankin never claims any special status for his book other than that of a historically based image of the past, he does offer a more meaningful mode of access to it than either Levin or Severin.

Rankin's work suggests that while some of the conventions of pre–World War II travel writing are still of service in exploring a rapidly changing world, new directions are being created, and new routes opened up. I have, in this essay, tried to suggest some of the ways in which postwar travel writers have gone beyond the existing traditions of the genre. Their attempts to create new forms appropriate to our contemporary reality seem to me worth investigating, since while there is, in our time, less and less *Terra Incognita* for the actual traveler, travel *writing* of the last three decades is still largely untouched, without landmarks or trails, waiting to be mapped out for the guidance of future literary travelers.

WORKS CITED

Fussell, Paul. *Abroad: British Literary Traveling Between the Wars.* New York: Oxford UP, 1980.

Jameson, Fredric. *Marxism and Form: Twentieth-Century Dialectical Theories of Literature.* 1971. Rpt. Princeton: Princeton UP, 1974.

————. "Postmodernism or the Cultural Logic of Late Capitalism." *New Left Review* 146 (July/August 1984): 53–92.

Kermode, Frank. *The Sense of an Ending: Studies in the Theory of Fiction*. New York: Oxford UP, 1967.

Levin, Bernard. *Hannibal's Footsteps*. London: Jonathan Cape, 1985.

Rankin, Nicholas. *Dead Man's Chest: Travels After Robert Louis Stevenson*. London: Faber & Faber, 1987.

Severin, Tim. *The Jason Voyage: The Quest for the Golden Fleece*. London: Hutchinson, 1985.

————. *The Sindbad Voyage*. London: Arrow Books, 1982.

Theroux, Paul. *The Old Patagonian Express: By Train Through the Americas*. 1979. Rpt. Harmondsworth, Eng.: Penguin, 1987.

Thubron, Colin. "Travel Writing Today: Its Rise and Its Dilemma." In *Essays by Divers Hands: Being the Transactions of the Royal Society of Literature*. New Series, vol. 44. Ed. A. N. Wilson. London: Boydell, 167–81.

Waugh, Evelyn. *When the Going Was Good*. London: Duckworth, 1946.

White, Hayden. "The Historical Text as Literary Artifact." In *The Writing of History: Literary Form and Historical Understanding*. Eds. Robert H. Canary and Henry Kozicki. Madison: U of Wisconsin P, 1978, 41–62.

The Travel Writer and the Text: "My Giant Goes with Me Wherever I Go"

> > > > > >

HEATHER HENDERSON

Travelling is a fool's paradise. Our first journeys discover to us the indifference of places. At home I dream that at Naples, at Rome, I can be intoxicated with beauty, and lose my sadness. I pack my trunk, embrace my friends, embark on the sea, and at last wake up in Naples, and there beside me is the stern Fact, the sad self, unrelenting, identical, that I fled from. I seek the Vatican, and the palaces. I affect to be intoxicated with sights and suggestions, but I am not intoxicated. My giant goes with me wherever I go.

—Ralph Waldo Emerson, "Self-Reliance" (1841)

The giant that accompanies every travel writer is constructed in part by the books he or she has read. As the Victorian traveler Eliot Warburton tells us, he had read the accounts of many previous travelers before setting out on his own journey to Egypt and the Holy Land: "notwithstanding which, I found much novelty, as well as interest, in my own personal experience." The tentative wording of this remark suggests that what he had seen in his imagination, through the words of others, was really more vivid to him than what he had seen for himself. This curious interplay between literary experience and lived experience forms one of the defining characteristics of the genre of travel literature.

There are two kinds of travelers, those who seek to fill in the "white spaces" on the map, and those who travel to see places that have been previously visited and described. Some are looking to inscribe themselves upon a blank page, others to reread an already written landscape. This essay concerns itself with the latter, with the complex responses of travelers for whom the written word interposes between self and sight. As Warburton acknowledges, texts tend to prevail over the material world

A version of this essay first appeared in *New Orleans Review* 18, no. 2 (Summer 1991): 30–40. © 1991 by Loyola University, New Orleans. Reprinted by permission of the *New Orleans Review*.

of real places, real people: past sight dominates present site. Still further complexities are encountered by travelers who then go on to produce their own travel texts. Theoretically, the value of travelers' accounts lies in the opportunity travelers have for first-hand observation: they can lend their eyes to the stay-at-home reader. But what value does reseeing and retelling have? As Mark Twain complained in *The Innocents Abroad* (1869): "What is there in Rome for me to see that others have not seen before me?" For the travel writer, the real question is, What is there for me to write about?

In exploring how landscapes are both read and written, I will refer to a range of works, while examining in some detail three British travel books about the East, two from the nineteenth century, Alexander Kinglake's *Eothen* (1844) and Warburton's *The Crescent and the Cross* (1845), and one from the twentieth, Philip Glazebrook's *Journey to Kars* (1984). For the Victorian traveler to the East, like Kinglake or Warburton, not only the Bible and the classics but also previous travel accounts provided a textual framework that largely determined his experience of travel. For a modern traveler like Glazebrook, the Victorian adventurers themselves contribute significantly to this literary frame of reference: Glazebrook undertakes his journey to Turkey in order to find out why the Victorians traveled, and he confesses that "besides looking through my own eyes . . . I have been . . . in the company of ghosts, the shades of real travellers, whose voices I have tried to overhear, and whose thoughts I have tried to understand."

Initially, a traveler's previous reading may seem relevant only as a motivating factor in the decision to travel: it was "the rapturous and earnest reading of my childhood which made me bend forward so longingly to the plains of Troy," Kinglake explains. Or, as the prolific travel writer Freya Stark puts it in *The Valleys of the Assassins* (1934), "An imaginative aunt who, for my ninth birthday, sent a copy of the *Arabian Nights*, was, I suppose, the original cause of trouble." The notion of a bookishly inspired journey crops up again and again. Sometimes travelers' imaginations are so fired by what they have read that their entire journey attempts to follow in the footsteps of another traveler, real or fictional: Jonathan Raban's *Old Glory* (1981) follows Huck Finn down the Mississippi, Richard Holmes's *Footsteps* (1985) traces the route described by Robert Louis Stevenson in *Travels with a Donkey* (1879), and the title of Israel Shenker's *In the Footsteps of Johnson and Boswell* (1982) speaks for itself.

But the effects of reading go far beyond merely providing the stimulus to travel. For even when the journey is under way, books condition travelers' choices and shape their perceptions. Clearly these literary pilgrimages are examples of mediated desire: the value of a scene, landscape, or monument lies not so much in its own intrinsic qualities as in the pleasure of seeing for ourselves what someone else has seen and described before us. The observer's relationship to the scene is indirect, filtered through the literary representation by which he first came to know it. Kinglake marvels at the "beautiful congruity betwixt the *Iliad* and the material world," for it confirms "that Homer had *passed along here*—that this vision of Samothrace . . . was common to him and to me." Seeing this island near Troy is unimportant in itself, but immensely important because it proves Homer's authenticity and because it establishes a link between Homer and Kinglake.

The pleasure of imagining scenes from the past on the spot where they took place is often greater than the pleasure of witnessing scenes of today. Glazebrook's obsession with this aspect of travel makes *Journey to Kars* one of the most thought-provoking contemporary travel accounts. He suggests that only tourists travel to see the present; "real" travelers search for a glimpse of the past: "The truth is that few individuals have ever travelled, in modern times, to see what other countries are like nowadays; in general people travel in search of traces of past eras." The book opens at Belgrade, with the narrator conjuring up visions of Victorian travelers for whom crossing the Danube was "the frontier between Christendom and Islam." Modern Belgrade interests him not at all: "For there to be any point in travelling, you have always to be looking for things as they were, and dodging things as they are."

Glazebrook is explicit about his preference: "It was Turkey's past that I was interested in—the 'past' which was the contemporary scene to nineteenth-century travellers." His clarification stresses that of course it isn't really *Turkey*'s past but rather the experience of Victorians *in* Turkey that attracts him. The same was true, he argues, for the nineteenth-century traveler: he "didn't come to the East in order to study contemporary Eastern life or character; the contemporary East was just the condition prevailing, like the weather." As a result, the traveler's perceptions are constantly determined by his preconceptions. Warburton, for example, devotes most of his chapter on "The Nile" to recounting Nelson's victory over Napoleon: "as the traveller paces by these silent and deserted shores . . . he lives again in the stirring days when the scenery before him was the arena whereon France and England contended for the empire of the East." Warburton's knowledge of the past—or rather, of a particular past, European and imperialist—colors everything he sees.

Each of these writers prefers the past (Homeric, Napoleonic, Victorian) to the present. In *Tristes Tropiques* (1955) Claude Lévi-Strauss captures that sense of belatedness: "I wished I had lived in the days of *real* journeys, when it was still possible to see the full splendour of a spectacle that had not yet been blighted, polluted and spoilt." But he recognizes that the "modern traveller, chasing after the vestiges of a vanished reality," is succumbing to an insidious illusion, for "a few hundred years hence, in this same place, another traveller, as despairing as myself, will mourn the disappearance of what I might have seen, but failed to see."

The pervasive desire to reimagine the past leads to one of the central preoccupations of travel literature, the search for the lost innocence of a Golden Age. Glazebrook notes that "as persistently as the idea of Eden runs through human history, the existence, and rare attainment, of an Earthly Paradise runs through the books of Eastern travellers." In *Full Tilt: Ireland to India with a Bicycle* (1965), Dervla Murphy thinks she's found paradise in Afghanistan: "I feel I've been privileged to see Man at his best—still in possession of the sort of liberty and dignity that we have exchanged for what it pleases us to call 'progress.' Even a brief glimpse of what we were is valuable to help to understand what we are. Living in the West, it's now impossible for most of us to envisage our own past by a mere exercise of the imagination, so we're rather like adults who have forgotten the childhood that shaped them." Murphy's belief that travel enables us "to envisage our own past" assumes, of course, that foreigners are like the children we once were (an assumption Glazebrook shares with his Victorian predecessors). The insidious consequence of the Westerner's quest for origins is that it negates the foreign present by seeing it merely as a version of our own past, an embodiment of Western myth.

Glazebrook believes, not merely that foreigners are like children, but that travel itself is a process of locating sites marked on "a secret map given him in childhood." That map is created by literature, whether it be the classics or fairy tales, the *Arabian Nights* or boys' books of adventure. Similarly, in *Journey Without Maps* (1936), Graham Greene finds that travel offers a return to both "a personal and racial childhood." He goes to Liberia to get in touch with the primordial infancy of the human race: "there are times . . . when one is willing to suffer some discomfort for the chance of finding—there are a thousand names for it, King Solomon's Mines, the 'heart of darkness' if one is romantically inclined, or . . . one's place in time, based on a knowledge not only of one's present but of the past from which one has emerged." Again, childhood reading—in this case the novels of Rider Haggard and Joseph Conrad—"maps" a foreign place. There is something both naive and solipsistic in the way certain travelers persistently view others through the lens of their own literature. Trekking through the Liberian jungle in search of self-understanding, Greene turns Africa into an imaginative exercise, a literary construct.

Greene seems unconscious of the racist implications of his quest, with his assumption that "darkest Africa" represents mankind at an earlier stage of development. As Patrick Brantlinger argues: "Evolutionary thought seems almost calculated to legitimize imperialism. The theory that man evolved through distinct social stages—from savagery to barbarism to civilization—led to a self-congratulatory anthropology that actively promoted belief in the inferiority, indeed the bestiality, of the African." Furthermore, seeing "Them" as a primitive "Us" enables travelers to overlook "Them" as distinctively and legitimately "Other." Reflecting on his journey, Greene concludes: "But what had astonished me about Africa was that it had never been really strange. . . . The 'heart of darkness' was common to us both. Freud has made us conscious as we have never been before of those ancestral threads which still exist in our unconscious minds to lead us back. The need, of course, has always been felt, to go back and begin again. Mungo Park, Livingstone, Stanley, Rimbaud, Conrad represented only another method to Freud's." Thus travel, for Greene as for Murphy, is primarily a means to self-knowledge ("more costly, less easy" than Sigmund Freud's), rather than knowledge of others. Western exploration of Africa represents merely another form of psychoanalysis. As Glazebrook puts it, what interested the nineteenth-century traveler was "research into his own character and capabilities seen in relief against a background which had passed away in Europe."

Into the Heart of Borneo (1984), the title of a work by a more recent British traveler, suggests the continuing fascination of the "heart of darkness" metaphor, which associates "primitive" peoples with "our" buried instincts and half-forgotten past. Noting that "late nineteenth-century men of science took Borneo very seriously as a possible birthplace of mankind," Redmond O'Hanlon writes: "Joseph Conrad had imagined central Borneo to be the heart of twilight, the home of the 'old mankind'; and a sight of the Ukit, I reflected, might be as close as we could ever hope to come to those imagined ancestors." Like Greene, O'Hanlon reenacts the Westerner's fantasy of discovering an uncorrupted people who will provide us with a glimpse of our lost selves. He romanticizes his native guide, calling him "a Beowulf, or, more accurately, a warrior-king out of Homer," and he depicts the villagers as sexually free and unselfconscious, like Adam and Eve before the Fall. But as we all know, you can't go home again, and so the traveler's search for the past is doomed from the start. O'Hanlon is dismayed to find that the Ukit speak English and demand to be taught the latest disco steps. They reject the past he so ardently desires to recapture, and he takes revenge for his frustrated nostalgia in his mocking portrayal of them as superficial and absurd.

Inevitably, modern reality clashes with literary evocation: in his own eyes, Eliot Warburton insists, Calypso's isle was "still the enchanted island . . . but a fat gentleman in green spectacles . . . declared it was the Botany Bay of Naples." Thus, in travel literature, the narrator moves in a climate of expectation—engendered, usually, by other literature—but the potential for disappointment is so great that it becomes virtually a convention of the genre itself. As Glazebrook observes, "the disappointments are brought about by the mis-preparation of your mind for what really exists; yet it's the mis-preparation—the treasure trove buried in your mind under certain place-names in early days—which draws you on to travel in the first place."

But if this discrepancy between reality and literature is not to be fatal to their dreams, travelers must find a scapegoat. Clearly Homer and the rest of the Western literary tradition cannot be wrong; questioning them would require travelers to question the whole culture that has produced *them*. It is far easier to grumble about the natives: Turks are dirty and immoral, Africans sensual and savage, Ukits ludicrous and corrupt. The need to protect one's literary myths no doubt underlies much of the familiar litany of traveler's complaints. Fanny Trollope, for example, went to America partly because of her friend Fanny Wright's enthusiastic account in *Views of Society and Manners in America* (1821). But, disenchanted with America for not being the democratic Utopia she had read about, Trollope produced *Domestic Manners of the Americans* (1832), a devastating satire of American vulgarity and provincialism.

The fear of being let down leads the traveler to employ bizarre devices in an attempt to salvage the moment. After an elegiac address to the Nile because it now has steamers on it ("Unhappy river! . . . thy old days of glory are gone by; thy veil of mystery is rent away"), Warburton comforts himself with the thought that when it gets dark he can *pretend* that reality lives up to his romantic fantasies: "by the time the evening and the mist had rendered the country invisible, we had persuaded ourselves that Egypt was indeed the lovely land that Moore has so delightfully imagined in the pages of the 'Epicurean.'" The illusion that has been fostered by reading can only be sustained by blotting out the actual landscape.

Mark Twain resorts to the same psychological sleight of hand in *The Innocents Abroad*. First he records his disappointment with Venice: "And

this was the storied gondola of Venice! . . . This the famed gondola and
this the gorgeous gondolier!—the one an inky, rusty old canoe with a
sable hearse body clapped onto the middle of it, and the other a mangy,
barefooted guttersnipe with a portion of his raiment on exhibition which
should have been sacred from public scrutiny." But although Twain sighs
that his "cherished dreams of Venice have been blighted forever," he soon
discovers that if he waits until midnight he can preserve his fantasy intact.
After dark, his imagination soars:

> In the glare of day there is little poetry about Venice, but under the chari-
> table moon her stained palaces are white again . . . and the old city seems
> crowned once more with the grandeur that was hers five hundred years
> ago. It is easy then in fancy to people these silent canals with plumed gal-
> lants and fair ladies—with Shylocks in gaberdine and sandals, venturing
> loans upon the rich argosies of Venetian commerce—with Othellos and
> Desdemonas, with Iagos and Roderigos.

Not only does darkness enable the imagination to transcend mere humdrum reality, but it unleashes a specifically literary flow of Shakespearean
associations. Even those dingy gondolas and gondoliers are forgiven. Twain
now finds the one "as free and graceful in its gliding movement as a serpent" and the other "a picturesque rascal for all he wears no satin har-
ness, no plumed bonnet, no silken tights." The transforming efforts of the
imagination spare Twain any further thought about contemporary Venice,
"decayed, forlorn, poverty-stricken, and commerceless."

The desire to see for oneself is, of course, one of the chief motivations
for travel, and having done so is one of the traveler's chief claims on the attention of readers. Thus, Lady Mary Wortley Montagu frequently reminds
her correspondents of the value of first-hand observation, and Mark Twain
prefaces *The Innocents Abroad* with the claim to have "seen with impartial eyes." But, like Warburton and Twain, travelers often arrive at the
paradoxical conclusion that *not* seeing can be preferable. Kinglake, disappointed by the sight of the river Scamander, happily finds in retrospect that
" 'divine Scamander' has recovered the proper mystery belonging to him,
as an *unseen* deity" (my italics). "Your feelings," Kinglake explains, "are
chilled and borne down for the time under all this load of real earth and
water, but, let these once pass out of sight, and then again the old fanciful
notions are restored." The passage of time accomplishes for Kinglake what
night achieved for Warburton and Twain, the hegemony of the observing subject over recalcitrant reality: "One's mind regains in absence that
dominion over earthly things which has been shaken by their rude con-

tact," he reflects. Absence makes the traveler's heart grow fonder, allowing the imagination to regain its privileged position of "dominion." Seeing things is not as wonderful as dreaming of them.

Glazebrook's approach to travel provides a modern counterpart. Wandering through quiet backstreets in Turkey he is delighted to find that "from that view modern Turkey was eclipsed, and there existed instead the idea of a fruitful and well-watered oasis." Once again, the traveler strives to preserve "the idea" he has arrived with, though it means blocking out the modern country to do so. His defense of his ignorance of the language reveals his priorities: "If I spoke Turkish would I then be able to maintain my view of Turkey as mysterious and hostile territory, which is the tint most useful to my imagination in the task of resurrecting the Turkey of Ottoman rule?" What is striking about these writers is the deliberateness with which they employ a variety of self-insulating strategies designed to keep the contemporary world at a distance; they consciously perform contortions in order to keep their romantic visions alive.

The conviction that such mental gymnastics are incumbent upon the educated traveler oppresses Kinglake at times:

> If one might judge of men's real thoughts by their writings, it would seem that there are people who can visit an interesting locality, and follow up continuously the exact train of thought which ought to be suggested by the historical associations of the place. A person of this sort can go to Athens, and think of nothing later than the age of Pericles. . . . I don't possess this power at all: it is only by snatches, and for a few moments together, that I can really associate a place with its proper history.

Kinglake's light-hearted tone fails to conceal a certain anxiety, evident throughout the book, at not being able to work himself up into the "proper" frame of mind at sites like Troy and Jerusalem, which history and literature have made sacred. Despite his implication that earlier writers have exaggerated their enthusiasm, Kinglake seems to regret his inability to participate fully in the sublime sensations promised by their accounts. Although he warns us in his preface that "there will often be found in my narrative a jarring discord between the associations properly belonging to interesting sites, and the tone in which I speak of them," he adheres to the belief that there are in fact "proper" associations that a gentleman ought to have.

His meditations on the strange interaction of mind and landscape become a recurrent preoccupation in the book. Riding through the Ottoman Empire, he is continually distracted by reminiscences about his schooldays: "As for me and my comrade," he writes, "we often forgot Stamboul, forgot all the Ottoman Empire, and only remembered old times. We went back, loitering on the banks of the Thames . . . the 'old Eton fellow' that wrestled with us in our boyhood." Later, although he struggles to be suitably impressed in Galilee, his thoughts again keep flying home: "instead there came to me a dear old memory from over the seas in England—a thought more sweet than Gospel to a wilful mortal like me." Kinglake's private memories get in the way of literary associations, yet his awareness of the ways in which the landscape is already "written" imposes on him an obligation to think, feel, and see in a particular way.

Kinglake's efforts to connect self to scene illustrate how the landscape of travel is always mediated. For, as Dean MacCannell puts it in his analysis of the phenomenon of tourism, "usually, the first contact a sightseer has with a sight is not the sight itself but with some representation thereof." And, as Jonathan Culler points out, "Tourists want to encounter and recognize the original which has been marked as a sight." Even "getting off the beaten track" is no solution: the very expression has become a cliché. Culler explains: "The authenticity the tourist seeks is at one level an escape from the code, but this escape itself is coded in turn, for the authentic must be marked to be constituted as authentic." Wrestling with this dilemma, George Packer, author of *The Village of Waiting* (1988), relates the attempts of African entrepreneurs to cater to tourists' desire for the authentic: "They put on a tribal dance tape, and serve pounded yams with peanut sauce, and give the traveler their own idea of the traveler's idea of them." Can we avoid this well-intentioned but ridiculous comedy and discover a world that does not insistently mirror our own? "No one knows the answer," Packer says. "On every trip I thought I'd left my cultural baggage at home; on every trip it had been forwarded to my destination."

Yet where the sophisticated semiotician and the politically aware traveler of the 1980s may despair of ever leaving their baggage behind, the Victorian gentleman happily carted it all along with him. As Eliot Warburton complacently remarks: "What a versatile power our mind possesses of adapting nature to its mood! It is not what a country is, but what we are, that renders it rich in interest." Emerson may sigh at not being able to leave Self behind, but Kinglake frankly acknowledges the "egotism of a traveller . . . his habit of referring the whole external world to his own sensations." And Glazebrook welcomes the presence of his Victorian predecessors: although he congratulates himself for his decision to travel alone—"I wanted no one interposed between myself and the scene"—he is delighted to be traveling "in the company of ghosts." Not real people but "real travellers" (that is, dead ones) are his companions of choice.

For these British travelers, mediation is not something to be overcome but rather profoundly desired. Their ability to quote Homer on the spot invests their travels not only with meaning but with status; it distinguishes them as gentlemen, the possessors of a certain kind of education. (Twain, middle-class and American, wavers between contempt and reverence for the past, between daytime denouncing and midnight dreaming.)

But whatever the traveler's attitude toward mediation, the fact of it is unarguable: no one can see with innocent eyes. Glazebrook's reaction to Kars captures this inescapable, overdetermined aspect of travel in a nutshell: "I never was less disappointed with reaching an objective in all my life." Paradoxically, the very structure of his sentence introduces the idea of disappointment into a context in which he claims it was not present. The literate traveler cannot escape the literature that preconditions his experience of travel. Wherever he goes, as Emerson observed in "Self-Reliance," the traveler carries his "giant" with him.

Travel writers, however, carry an additional burden: the necessity of turning their travel experiences into a book. They must go from being readers of texts to producers of them, thus entering the literary tradition that has shaped them. Given the pressures of this situation—to visit places full of associations, to feel the "right thing" when they arrive—how do travel writers go about accomplishing their task?

Kinglake failed twice in his attempt to recount his journey to the East. He explains in the preface to *Eothen* that he only succeeded on his third try, in response to a friend's request. That friend was Eliot Warburton, who was on the point of undertaking a similar journey. Instead of setting himself up as an authority, Kinglake adopts a casual and intimate style, quite unlike that of many earlier travel writers. He admits that he has shirked the traveler's duty to provide factual information, flippantly avowing that "from all details of geographical discovery, or antiquarian research—from all display of 'sound learning, and religious knowledge'—from all historical and scientific illustrations—from all useful statistics—from all political disquisitions—and from all good moral reflections, the volume is thoroughly free." Instead, he confesses, he has produced "a sadly long strain about Self."

Kinglake knows that he has broken with the demands of the genre, and he apologizes for not fulfilling his readers' expectations about what a travel book should be: "My notion of dwelling precisely upon those matters which happened to interest me, and upon none other, would of course be intolerable in a regular book of travels." But only by writing something that was *not* "a regular book of travels" could he write at all.

Eothen is generally regarded as marking a turning point in the history

of the genre. In 1916 F. A. Kirkpatrick described how, in contrast to the
travel writing of the eighteenth century, "the better travel-books of the
nineteenth century . . . deal less with monuments, museums, churches and
institutions: they deal more with men and women in relation to their surroundings. Sometimes, this human interest lies in the pleasant egotism of
the traveller." Many readers have enjoyed this "pleasant egotism": Jan
Morris, for example, remarks that "*Eothen* is a thoroughly self-centred
book, that is half its charm." However, in *Enlightened Observers: British
Travellers to the Near East, 1715–1850* (1979), Anita Damiani criticizes
Kinglake and other Victorian travelers for their retreat into subjectivity
and the personal. She compares them unfavorably with their eighteenth-
century precursors, who not only provided useful information but also
took a less aggressive and imperialistic stance. And in *Orientalism* Edward
Said writes disapprovingly that Kinglake "is more interested in remaking
himself and the Orient . . . than he is in seeing what there is to be seen."

Kinglake's approach to travel, however, has more to do with feeling
than with seeing. "As I have felt," he declares, "so I have written." This
need not make his writing untruthful, he hastens to assure us: "My excuse
for the book is its truth. . . . it conveys, not those impressions which *ought
to have been* produced . . . but those which were really and truly received
at the time." The insistent claim to be telling the truth is characteristic
of travel literature; as Mary Kingsley asserts in the preface to *Travels in
West Africa* (1897), "If you go there you will find things as I have said."
Travel writers, it is worth noting, are in a singular position: they have
great license to write what they please, since readers can hardly check up
on them without undertaking arduous journeys (and even then, no one
could verify a specific incident or reported conversation, much less a feeling). But their reputations depend on convincing a skeptical audience, for
as Percy G. Adams has shown in *Travelers and Travel Liars, 1660–1800*
(1962), travel writing also provides a rich field of opportunity for liars—
who, of course, also claim to be telling the truth.

But Kinglake goes a step further than the usual boast of objectivity
("impartial eyes"). He argues that the traveler's very subjectivity—he calls
it his selfishness—guarantees his truthfulness, for "he tells you of objects,
not as he knows them to be, but as they seemed to him." Making a virtue
of subjectivity, Kinglake's solution to the problem of how to write about
places that had already been much seen and described is to turn inward,
focusing on the impressions received by "Self."

Wildly popular, *Eothen* had an immediate influence upon the style of
other travel writers. When Warburton came to write his own book, he

imitated Kinglake's device and wrote as though he were having "a sort of imaginary conversation with the reader." The reader thus becomes his companion, whom he addresses at the end with the words: "Reader!— you have been my only fellow-traveller through many lands; wherever I have wandered you have been; whatever I have learned you have known." Warburton's emphasis on the seeing "I" illustrates how the intervening presence of the travel writer has become the point of the travel book. Just as he likes to feel that he has seen through the eyes of biblical and classical authors, so Warburton claims that his own readers have seen through his eyes.

Mark Twain, in contrast, is ambivalent about the kind of intimate fellowship Warburton proposes. More antagonistic toward an enshrined literary tradition, he wants to demystify travel by suggesting "to the reader how *he* would be likely to see Europe and the East if he looked at them with his own eyes, instead of the eyes of those who traveled in those countries before him." But of course this attempt to dispense with literary mediation is doomed to failure: *The Innocents Abroad* cannot help but show us Europe and the East through other eyes than our own—Mark Twain's.

The travel writer inevitably interposes his own text between the sight and the reader, just as previous writers interposed their texts between him and the sight. Textual mediation is inescapable: the writer cannot act as a transparent or self-effacing medium. Warburton's assertion that the reader has seen exactly what he did suggests a faith in the power of language to transmute seeing into reading, and reading back into seeing. These nineteenth-century travel writers all seem confident in the ability of their readers to penetrate language, to decode the literary encoding of an experience in order to reexperience it along with them. To suggest that reading is not the same as seeing would be to break the circuit that binds travel writers to their readers, who in turn become writers for others.

But however much they may protest that we are "seeing" along with them, our reading is clearly not the same as their seeing. In *Journey to Kars* Glazebrook shows himself to be more skeptical about the power of language to capture the essence of an experience. "Never mind," he writes, "I'm used to wrecking the magic of things by writing about them: very little of the mystery of a place or an idea survives the scrutiny required to sort out and to put into words what it was about that mystery sufficiently intriguing to have compelled you to write about it."

Although Glazebrook relishes the way literary evocations create mystery in an "empty" landscape, putting the mystery into words is another matter. On a boat nearing the Turkish coast, he contrasts himself to an Australian couple who, lacking his own classical background, appear oblivious to the Homeric associations of the scene. Instead, their attention is occupied with attending to their baby, and Glazebrook remarks, "I couldn't change the baby's nappies out here for fear of storms, monsters, waterspouts, rocks hurled by blinded giants." He adds disdainfully, "I think I probably prefer to travel with my chimeras, and leave the baby behind."

But it turns out not to be so easy to leave the baby behind. Glazebrook carries his own figurative baby—the preoccupation with writing a travel book—that hinders his appreciation of the foreign adventure. The traveler may want to live for the moment and be content with the memory, but the writer is obliged to turn experience into words: "I spend my life trying to squash Spirit into Word, life into sentences, unruly feelings into orderly syntax, trying to get the naked kicking baby into its clothes." Fussing with the baby emerges as a metaphor for that which occupies and distracts the traveling writer. It represents both the embryonic quest that brought him on the journey and the literary creation to which he must give birth through writing about it.

As a traveler Glazebrook sometimes resents and resists the demand that a writer give birth to books; indeed, he sometimes despairs of doing so: "Hardest, because most important, was to find words for the certainty of happiness which had filled me as I had walked away from the ruined city in the dusk. I could not—cannot—crush that kicking baby into its clothes." And so for a time he tries to fool himself into believing that he doesn't have to, that he can find a substitute for words. Speaking of a precious intaglio he has bought from a Turkish shepherd he says, "But I had in my shirt pocket the gem which expressed it all." His desire to believe that the intaglio can contain the essence of his experience better than any words could seems an attempt to evade the burden of being a writer. But this is an illusion—the "gem" eventually turns out to be a worthless fake, expressing nothing, and he throws it away. He wants the easy satisfaction of a tangible memento—revealing his kinship to the souvenir-hunting tourist—but in acquiescing to that self-deception, he is himself deceived.

Kinglake overcomes his writer's block by violating some of the conventions of the genre. Glazebrook, in contrast, writes his travel book by commenting on, and tacitly imitating, the conventions of his Victorian models. Aware that his modern audience is unlikely to be familiar with their works, he even supplies his own frame of reference in the form of lengthy quotations. Although he sometimes pretends to break with earlier conventions, even mocks them outright, he inevitably reproduces them. Thus, the intertext provides not only the motivation for his journey (to see Turkey as the great nineteenth-century adventurers did), but also the structure for his own book (his "re-writing" of their travels). He solves the problem of dressing the baby by using old clothes.

Glazebrook claims the status of the detached critic, analyzing the methods of nineteenth-century travel writers, but not employing their rather obvious devices himself. For example, he points to the way in which it was de rigueur to conjure up a sense of danger so that the writer would appear brave and heroic: "Travellers mentioned only those like themselves, who would hold to the convention that to reach the spot where they had met was a bold and hazardous enterprise, not to be undertaken by mere merchants out for profit. They suppressed the merchants because they got in the way of the sense of adventure they wanted to convey. I would have done better to have suppressed the Australian baby if I was to convey the sense of adventure I really felt as we ran along that wild shore." Yet despite this pose of being above or outside the conventions, Glazebrook actually takes great pains to evoke danger. He builds suspense by describing the unsettled political situation, the recent military takeover, the outbreak of the Iran-Iraq War, and his own uncertainty about whether to break off his journey before reaching Kars.

Similarly, he contrasts his unsuccessful efforts to obtain news with those of the Victorian traveler, who was "given advice in dramatic terms, usually against proceeding, by consuls and pashas and shocked merchants met by chance in khans after alarming experiences." He wonders whether the writer may only have recorded "the advice of those who begged him to turn back . . . so that the traveller's calm pursuance of . . . his plans should seem all the bolder by light of the perils he has leaked into the reader's mind by this device." And he suggests that his own situation is quite different: "There was no one on whom I could lay the responsibility of deciding." But in fact his very first chapter alludes to the warnings he's had: "Objections raised by others—thirty people a day murdered in Turkey that summer, for instance—show them not to be practical travellers." In making light of these dire statistics, while not omitting to mention them to the reader, Glazebrook participates fully in the very tradition he has been gently satirizing.

He makes fun of the vocabulary of the Victorian narrator, who writes in order to "satisfy the romantic expectations of the armchair traveller": "Here the crags 'beetle,' the cliffs 'frown,' heights are 'dizzy,' chasms 'yawn,' and the rivers are all 'cataracts.'" But two pages further on we find Glazebrook's own romantic description of a bus ride at top speed on a winding mountain road: "The scenes of despair were like those between decks in a slaver, the captain crowding on sail to escape the pursuing man-of-war. At last, through mist and darkness, I saw pine trees lit by the headlights, and shrubs clinging amongst the rocks, and many wild briars." Glazebrook is astute about the conventions informing the narratives of Victorian travelers, but without often admitting it, he himself employs precisely the same devices to which he has called our attention. To take a final example, he writes that "it was a convention amongst travellers . . . that when they returned home they closed the door in your face." As a disappointed reader, he bemoans his eviction, saying, "I long to eavesdrop further." Quoting Warburton's dismissal of the reader ("I scarcely venture to hope that you will share in the regret with which I say—Farewell!"), Glazebrook cries, "But I do, Eliot (if I may call you that), I do!" And then Glazebrook closes the door in *our* faces, observing the convention in the same moment that he deplores it.

This foregrounding of literary convention vividly illustrates the extent to which travel writing, though it may present itself as mere factual reportage, is in fact a highly selective and self-conscious genre. Although the casual reader may expect strict truthfulness from travel writers—why read travel books if they aren't "true"?—their works are inevitably circumscribed by text and tradition. Kinglake's answer to this question is to proclaim that subjectivity offers its own kind of truth; Glazebrook's answer is that fiction may be the closest approximation to reality: "The impulse to write fiction is felt strongly, I think, by travellers. . . . Incidents need to be developed or run together, events shaped, characters touched up, drama heightened, if the reader is to appreciate what were the traveller's real feelings at the time." Yielding to literariness ironically serves as his strategy for overcoming the gap between experience and language; his solution is to write a book about writing a book.

Glazebrook, interestingly, shows how fully he has accepted Kinglake's philosophy: he automatically assumes that the reader will be curious about "the traveller's real feelings," rather than, say, accurate descriptions of landscape, monuments, local customs, or political developments. The temptation "to invent, or at least to embellish, so as to convey to others the force of what you have felt yourself" is perfectly permissible, for the traveler is primarily engaged in the production of a literary text: "For the reader's appreciation of the reality of travel, it is more important that the book's author should be a born writer, than that the events narrated should be the literal truth. . . . The narrator must turn himself into the Hero, if readers are to follow his adventures sufficiently eagerly, and to achieve this requires selection and embellishment, even invention, so long as verisimilitude—dramatic truth—is the aim."

Conspicuously missing from such analysis of how travel literature works are the moral and political dimensions of the British presence in the Middle East. "Dramatic truth" cannot be the only aim of texts that present themselves as reliable accounts of foreign places, for they will inevitably influence readers' attitudes, even public policies. As Patrick Brantlinger has shown, "The great explorers' writings are nonfictional quest romances in which the hero-authors struggle through enchanted, bedeviled lands toward an ostensible goal: the discovery of the Nile's sources, the conversion of the cannibals. . . . The humble but heroic authors move from adventure to adventure against a dark, infernal backdrop where there are no other characters of equal stature, only bewitched or demonic savages." The metaphors chosen by travel writers—quest romance, bringers of light—are not as innocent as Glazebrook believes. Turning "himself into the Hero" does not merely liven up a traveler's tale; it also reinforces Western cultural chauvinism.

Glazebrook is aware that in constructing himself as Hero, the nineteenth-century traveler "employed Asiatics as the crowd of extras and bit-players forming a background of atmosphere and Eastern colour whose function was to show off himself as the central figure." He realizes that "of the many hundreds of native servants underpinning these books of travels, very few surface as individuals." Yet here again Glazebrook shares the conventional attitudes even as he exposes them. Reinscribing Victorian racial prejudice, he frequently indulges in condescending generalization, remarking, for example, that "as a race the Turks don't care a jot for preserving what is beautiful, or even what is useful," and that "as with their love of sweets and loud noises, this inquisitiveness makes Asiatics seem to Europeans like children."

Travel writing is in fact a double-pronged quest for domination, not only of actual experience (foreign lands and foreigners) but also of literary experience (prior travel texts and their authors). Glazebrook's tactic for dealing with his precursors, exposing their foibles and tricks, only to reuse them himself, reveals him to be engaged in a power struggle to become as "authoritative" as they. The adversarial nature of the relationship between travel writers and their literary heirs is confirmed by the military imagery Glazebrook uses to describe it: "By buying the man's book of travels you haven't bought access to his confessions, and he doesn't show you his weaknesses any more than he would show them to the enemies he encounters on his road. That isn't to say that weaknesses may not be deduced." Glazebrook puts his predecessors at the mercy of *his* narrative, so that instead of being one more follower in their footsteps, he makes them seem like part of his experience—he is the one who gives them new life. The ambitious travel writer controls his world by becoming master of the texts that describe it.

Such narrative maneuvers seek ascendancy not only over other peoples, but over one another. Thus Glazebrook's approach is not just a matter of "selection and embellishment," of animating a prosaic narrative. Travel literature is so highly intertextual that at times texts are actually substituted for experience itself, and the attempt to control crucial passages, whether in the Bosphorus or in Victorian prose, represents an essential strategy in the campaign to make a place one's own. This appropriation of the texts of others has its Victorian antecedents: when Warburton makes the obligatory pilgrimage to the home of the late Lady Hester Stanhope, he finds he has little to say, so he slots in whole passages from *Eothen*, in which Kinglake relates *his* visit to this unusual woman. Warburton also quotes and thereby recovers from Kinglake a letter of his own—a letter that Kinglake had already printed in *Eothen*—about her death. In later editions Kinglake omitted Warburton's letter, explaining that "I must now give up the borrowed ornament . . . for the rightful owner has reprinted it in 'The Crescent and the Cross.'" At this point the narrative has become a tissue of juxtaposed texts, and almost all attempts at reporting the actual moment are dropped in the effort to annex whichever preexisting words have become, in MacCannell's terminology, markers of "authentic" experience.

Glazebrook even more boldly uses old reading to stand in for new experience: "I saw nowhere I wished I was stopping, though I peered out at Aksehir with interest, thinking of Layard's description of riding into it in 1839." He then quotes Layard at length, rather than get off the bus himself. Similarly, he waits in the bus station at Erzurum instead of going out to explore the town, "content . . . to remember Erzurum by the pictures of it painted into my head by Robert Curzon." Such evasions lay bare the true nature of the genre, a genre in which texts are primary: "new" experiences are not merely conditioned by generic demands and precedents, they are subsumed by them. Russian formalists regarded the bizarre, self-conscious literary devices of *Tristram Shandy* as making it the most, not the least, representative of novels; the same may be said of Glazebrook's flagrant substitution of literature for experience. His textual pilgrimage takes to its logical conclusion the traveler's endeavor to see what he has already read about. The travel book substitutes nicely for the "real" experience: literary passages stand in for physical ones, confirming the authenticity, not of the experience, but of the text itself. Literature does more than motivate travel, it replaces it.

And indeed, when we last see Glazebrook he is writing up his notes and musing about the book he must produce: "Probably I could have written it without leaving Dorset, except to travel to the London Library." Intertextual to the last, he leaves us with a quotation from Alfred Lord Tennyson's "Ulysses" ("There lies the port: the vessel puffs her sail") and the observation that "the journey ahead was writing the book." The author's physical journey was in fact a journey through books, an extended trip to the London Library; and now the book itself has become a journey. A reader's ticket not only enables the energetic traveler to explore Homeric "realms of gold" by embracing the words that constitute foreign lands, it also grants him dominion over all who have written the landscape that he will reframe and rewrite. Travel literature, the genre that by rights seems most likely to take both writer and reader out of their usual surroundings, is actually most at home with itself when it reveals how neither has ever really left the armchair.

WORKS CITED

Brantlinger, Patrick. "The Genealogy of the Myth of the 'Dark Continent.' " *Rule of Darkness: British Literature and Imperialism, 1830–1914*. Ithaca: Cornell UP, 1988.

Culler, Jonathan. "The Semiotics of Tourism." In *Framing the Sign: Criticism and Its Institutions*. Oxford: Basil Blackwell, 1988, 153–67.

Emerson, Ralph Waldo. "Self-Reliance." In *Essays: First Series, The Collected Works of Ralph Waldo Emerson*. Vol. 2. Eds. Joseph Slater, Alfred R. Ferguson, and Jean Ferguson Carr. Cambridge: Harvard UP, 1979, 25–51.

Glazebrook, Philip. *Journey to Kars: A Modern Traveller in the Ottoman Lands*. New York: Holt, Rinehart & Winston, 1984.

Greene, Graham. *Journey Without Maps*. 1936. Rpt. New York: Penguin, 1986.

Kinglake, Alexander. *Eothen, or Traces of Travel Brought Home from the East*. 1844. Rpt. Oxford: Oxford UP, 1982.

Kingsley, Mary. *Travels in West Africa*. 1897. Rpt. London: Virago, 1982.

Kirkpatrick, F. A. "The Literature of Travel, 1700–1900." *The Cambridge History of English Literature*. Vol. 14. Eds. Sir A. W. Ward and A. R. Waller. Cambridge: Cambridge UP, 1916, 240–56.

Lévi-Strauss, Claude. *Tristes Tropiques*. Trans. John and Doreen Weightman. 1955. Rpt. New York: Pocket, 1977.

MacCannell, Dean. *The Tourist: A New Theory of the Leisure Class*. New York: Schocken, 1976.

Morris, Jan. "Introduction." *Eothen, or Traces of Travel Brought Home from the East*, by Alexander Kinglake. 1844. Rpt. Oxford: Oxford UP, 1982, iii–xvi.

Murphy, Dervla. *Full Tilt: Ireland to India with a Bicycle*. 1965. Rpt. Woodstock, N.Y.: Overlook Press, 1986.

O'Hanlon, Redmond. *Into the Heart of Borneo*. 1984. Rpt. New York: Vintage, 1987.

Packer, George. "Travelers in a New Age." *Boston Review*. August 1988, 19, 27.

Stark, Freya. *The Valleys of the Assassins, and Other Persian Travels*. 1934. Rpt. London: Century, 1986.

Twain, Mark. *The Innocents Abroad*. 1869. Rpt. New York: New American Library, 1980.

Warburton, Eliot. *The Crescent and the Cross; or, Romance and Realities of Eastern Travel*. London: H. Colburn, 1845.

> > > > > > **A Boat Swamped
with Abstractions:
Reading Raban's River**

ROGER GEORGE

The essence of being a good tourist lay in ignoring everything you actually saw and listening instead to what the guide told you you should see.

—Jonathan Raban, *Coasting* (1987)

In 1979 English writer Jonathan Raban sailed a sixteen-foot aluminum boat down the Mississippi River from Minneapolis to the Gulf of Mexico, gathering material for his popular 1981 book, *Old Glory*. In the course of sorting, shaping, and organizing that material into a narrative, Raban confronts an unresolved tension between the nature of experience itself and reading about (and writing about) that experience. This tension remains fundamental to most travel narratives. It creates a desire on the part of many readers to share the writer's travel experience while at the same time frustrating that desire, and it compromises a writer's ability to recreate his or her experience in words—to write a work of "nonfiction." In perhaps no other genre of literature do life and art seem to be so much the same thing, yet both those who read a travel narrative as an imitation of life and those who read it as a crafted work of art miss part of the point.

At one point in his journey, Raban meets an earnest couple sailing a home-built boat, who proclaim that they are making the journey as emissaries for the American people; they are demonstrating the possibilities of self-sufficiency and conservation by using wind power. Raban is appalled by them. It seems peculiarly American, he muses, that "anyone should build a boat as beautiful as this, launch it on a long-absorbing voyage, then swamp it with such a dreary cargo of fashionable abstractions. All the grace of the thing itself had been submerged under these abstractions; yet without them, the boat would never have been built, the trip never embarked on." The boat, Raban concludes, is a "classic victim" of the "American language and its fatal preference for theories, principles, concepts over mere material objects and their intractable thinginess."

Raban's own journey down the Mississippi, however, demonstrates that British citizenship provides no immunity from this fatal preference, for he displays it as well, and it originates in his reading of American travel books. His boat, too, is nearly swamped by abstractions. His Mississippi, when he begins his trip, is "more an imaginary river than a real one." Although Raban comes to see the real river in all its "thinginess," he finally produces a book which will create one more imaginary Mississippi for each and every reader.

From the outset, *Old Glory* examines the authenticity of experience. How much of a journey is the traveler's own, and what portion derives from others' insights? Can any narrative recreate that experience, or provide the *illusion* of doing so? These questions are especially important if one is tempted to use travel writing as a blueprint for experience, as is Raban. His trip down the Mississippi begins in reading and in images derived from reading. Long before he ever sees the Mississippi, he creates it in his mind: "Half the luggage in my room was books. For months I'd been collecting them in London. I had found more in New York. They were the stuff out of which I had been making my imagined river." One of the titles he specifically cites is Thoreau's *A Week on the Concord and Merrimack Rivers* (1849); another is an account of a trip down the Mississippi in the early nineteenth century by Reverend Timothy Flint. Most importantly, though, there's Twain, whose own vision of the river and how to "read" it repeatedly influences Raban's own experience. The headwaters of Raban's Mississippi trickle from his first reading of *Huckleberry Finn* at the age of seven. "The picture on its cover," he writes, "crudely drawn and colored, supplied me with the raw material for an exquisite and recurrent daydream. It showed a boy alone, his face prematurely wizened with experience. . . . The sheet of water on which he drifted was immense, an enameled pool of lapis lazuli. Smoke from a half-hidden steamboat hung over an island of Gothic conifers. Cut loose from the world, chewing on his corncob pipe, the boy was blissfully lost in this stillwater paradise."

The cover picture creates a mental image (of being "blissfully lost" in a "stillwater paradise"), which influences the child's interpretation of the novel itself. Years later, these mutually reinforcing elements help create a new perception of a different painting (of a different river, the Missouri) by George Caleb Bingham.

> Its water had a crystalline solidity and smoothness, as if it had been carved from rosy quartz. The river and the sky were one, with cliffs and forest

hanging in suspension between them. In the foreground, a ruffianly trapper and his son drifted in a dugout canoe. . . . The water captured their reflections as faithfully as a film. Alone, self-contained, they moved with the river, an integral part of the powerful current of things, *afloat* on it in exactly the way I had been daydreaming for myself.

In this ideal vision earth, land, and water all merge into one another, demonstrating the essential unity and harmony of nature. The man and his son, too, merge with the water, which reflects their image with such fidelity that it's hard to tell which is "real." Most importantly, they *drift*. They are in harmony with the natural course of the river, free from civilized demands and schedules and duties. Raban has already clearly adopted the fundamental tenets of a romantic ideology. When he goes to the real river, he will be trying to see it as it appears in these images; not as it appears before his eyes. From the very conception of his trip, his experience of the Mississippi is mediated—"prepackaged" to a certain extent—and his observations are to some degree predestined by the observations written (or the images painted) by those who came before him.

There is nothing necessarily wrong and certainly nothing unusual about this process, at least as long as one is aware of one's own perceptual filters. All readers are influenced by previous texts and images and experiences, and all readers interpret new texts according to those influences. At the very beginning of the journey, the river certainly seems to confirm Raban's images of it. For instance, one morning he sees a fisherman in a skiff, casting his line: "As the sun came up, his reflection sharpened until he and it joined to make a single cruciform pattern on the water. For me, the moment was unalloyed magic. The picture in my head had been real after all." But the river, almost immediately, starts asserting its own "thinginess" distinct from Raban's perception of it. He sets sail, not on "an enameled pool of lapis lazuli," but rather on a polluted river buried under bridges and routed through industrial slums. The river and his journey down it assert their own shape and direction, and refuse to allow his perception to be filtered through romantic illusions.

A pilot must learn to navigate the Mississippi according to the river "that's in your head, and never mind the one that's before your eyes." This is the key piece of advice given by the master Mississippi pilot, Horace Bixby, to his young "cub" in Twain's river book, *Life on the Mississippi* (1884) (which, although not cited by Raban, seems as important to *Old Glory* as is *Huckleberry Finn*). Raban, at the outset of the journey, appears to be an apt pupil, for this is exactly what he plans to do. But it's bad advice, at least if Bixby's meaning is not carefully clarified. The shape of the river Bixby refers to in this famous passage is one derived from countless specific observations of concrete details. It is a product of experience—the accumulated observations of repeated journeys up and down the river. The "shape of the river" in Raban's head, on the other hand, is derived from abstractions conveyed through words and images, and it bears no relationship to the real phenomenon. As Twain's cub had to learn to "read" the signs the real river gave him, and thus lose all the "romance" naive passengers experienced, so too must Raban learn to "read" the text before his eyes: "There was a moral for me here somewhere. Like the Reverend Timothy Flint, I was an incorrigibly bookish man. The river in my books was one thing; that sludgy beast beyond the tracks was quite another— and I had better start getting the distinction between the two clear in my head. If I didn't, I was going to run dangerously, perhaps finally, aground."

There is no romance to Raban's river, any more than there is to Twain's when he returns in the 1880s. *This* Mississippi is not an idyllic, slow-flowing prototype of a luminist painting. It is a malevolent, treacherous river, full of sunken wing piers and snags, tricky currents and whirlpools, traffic that could easily overwhelm his tiny boat, and sudden windstorms that could swamp him.

The day Raban begins the trip, he accidentally (and symbolically) leaves his copy of *Huckleberry Finn* in his hotel room. "Slowing on the current, I thought that perhaps my loss wasn't such a bad augury after all. This was a voyage I was going to have to make alone." Like his literary predecessor Twain, Raban has to learn to install a new river in his head; at this moment he begins to change from a naive passenger into a pilot. And to help with the change, he finds his own master pilot.

Raban's Bixby is the man who outfits his boat, Herb Heichert. Heichert gives the writer a quick but intensive course in river reading. He points out floating logs, warns of the dangers of barge traffic and towboats, and alerts Raban to the presence of wing dams: "They run out twenty, thirty yards into the river. You can't see them when she's high as this, but they're there. Maybe six inches underwater. Maybe a couple of feet. They're real *rascals*. They built them out of riprap . . . rocks and stuff. You run into a wing dam, you'll be real lucky if your motor's the only thing you lose— it can take the bottom clean out of the boat. Hey, don't get too close to them buoys, now! See that log? Watch the piles of the bridge!" For the rest of the journey, the Mississippi stubbornly asserts its own reality, shattering Raban's preconceptions and forcing him, despite himself, to actually *see* it as a physical, material phenomenon, a river without any Platonic "riverness," without any harmony or universal moral order or symbolic significance:

> The mist slowly rolled and plumed. A vertical column of it rose over the white shed of Smiley's Fish Market and its waiting line of black women in fur coats and turbans. They'd come from Chicago, in old pickups and sagging, chromium-snouted Buicks and Chevies, to carry off hundredweights at a time of channel catfish, buffalo, crappies, carp, eels and sunfish. The luminous mist flattened them to two dimensions. The fish market, the women, the sprawl of boats drawn up on the shore, the piled hoop nets all came accidentally together in a perfect pictorial composition. . . . I photographed what I believed I was seeing, and was puzzled when the transparency came back from the processor's: it didn't look like a genre painting in refracted Mississippi light; it was a picture of yellowish mist, with the outline of a leaning telegraph pole faintly visible in the background.

This photograph recalls one of the most famous moments in *Life on the Mississippi*, the passage in which Twain describes the same scene as viewed by naive passengers and by an experienced pilot. To the passengers (and to the cub pilot as well), who have been trained to see the river by viewing genre paintings of their own, a sunset is a manifestation of a benevolent, harmonious Nature:

> A broad expanse of the river was turned to blood; in the middle distance the red hue brightened into gold, through which a solitary log came floating, black and conspicuous; in one place a long, slanting mark lay sparkling upon the water; in another the surface was broken by boiling, tumbling rings, that were as many-tinted as an opal. . . . There were graceful curves, reflected images, woody heights, soft distances; and over the whole scene, far and near, the dissolving lights drifted steadily, enriching it, every passing moment, with new marvels of coloring.

As he gains experience, the young pilot comes to see the reality of the river rather than a Romantic image of it: the floating log means that the river is rising, the marks on the surface are produced by steamboat-killing snags and wrecks, the soft colors mean deteriorating weather, and so forth. The romance of the river is forever lost, but the pilot can now safely navigate it. Raban repeats this transformation throughout his own journey.

As the nonfictional truth of the river intrudes upon the genre painting Raban has constructed in his mind, so does the truth of an actual voyage continually intrude upon the conventions of the writing genre. Travel narratives often have a simple plot: the writer, weary of the artificialities of everyday life, sets out to have a "genuine" experience in the wilderness, to lose his self-consciousness, to "suck the marrow out of life," in Thoreau's phrase, and then return safely to civilization, restored and regenerated. The *idea* of the travel narrative necessarily includes a return, so one's loss of self-consciousness and identity is necessarily only temporary; the traveler assumes that a new self will, at the end of the journey, sit down and write a consciously constructed tale—a work of artifice mimicking the spontaneity of the trip. The generic conventions don't, however, imply that the traveler might *really* get lost "out there," either physically or psychically. Yet this can happen quite easily on a real journey, as Raban discovers.

Living in London, Raban had wanted to immerse himself in the "benign emptiness" of the river. At one point he compares himself to a drowned woman who has just been dragged from the Mississippi: "I wanted to lose myself too. I had no intention of landing up in some small Midwestern city morgue, but I ached to run away from the world for awhile, to put myself in the grip of a powerful current which would make my choices for me, to be literally adrift. The woman had gone to the river for solace, and had ended up drowning in it; I was going for much the same motive, but meant to stay afloat." The woman has had a "pure" experience of the river; by immersing herself in it she has successfully escaped all of what sent her there in the first place. The price for this escape, however, has been death. The kind of journey Raban wants to conduct also requires a loss of self-consciousness, which represents a type of death. What happens if the writer succeeds too well in becoming "immersed" in the river, lives only in the present moment, and devotes all his attention to reading the river immediately in front of the prow? Can the travel experience, for a self-conscious writer, become a form of psychic drowning?

It can certainly be terrifying, as Raban learns. The problem is apparent even in the language he uses to discuss the "immersion" experience. In the following passage, for example, his unusual third-person reference to himself creates the effect of a detached observer (the writer) analyzing another's (the unreflective traveler's) performance:

> This long, careless drift through other people's lives, with the boat always moored ready for a fast getaway, and the solitude of the river never more than a stone's throw away from the society of the town would have impressed him as being grander than anything he'd imagined. He hadn't predicted the fright of it. In those days he hadn't been afraid of drowning. I was. I kept on seeing myself dead in the river, a body strewn untidily on a sandbar, its clothes ridden up over its head.

The "I" at the end of this passage is no longer a traveler, at least not in the sense that the generic conventions promised. This is the very consciousness that has to be lost for there to be pure experience, and yet without this detached observer who analyzes, observes, and understands, there can be no writer. If one were truly to cast overboard all of one's boatload of abstractions, the new "pilot" would lose connection with the outside world and wander forever on the river. Twain notes in *Life on the Mississippi* that the pilots are able to speak only to each other and then only about the process of piloting.

As he nears Hannibal, Raban nearly loses his identity (and his life), and the experience is not the blending with the "benevolent emptiness" travel narratives had prepared him for.

> It was almost dark when I made Hannibal. Throughout the day, I had grown more and more suspicious of the river's placidity. I had been lapped in its current, moving from sheet to sheet through the charts, barely awake, letting my head drift as the water drifted. *She'll lull you to sleep, and then she'll do you in.* Something had happened to my vision. There were banks and islands; they were marked on the charts. But all I saw was water, scrolled with hairlines around the bow of the boat, darkening with the sky, slick as the top of a vat of molasses.

This dangerous reverie is broken before disaster strikes; "alarm bells" begin to ring in "some small cavity" of his mind as he finds himself on the point of submitting to the temptation of being "absorbed by the Mississippi," "to feel that I was as much a part of its flow as the logs around which I now steered without consciously noticing them. That afternoon I thought, *I could drown in this river, and it wouldn't matter; I wouldn't mind.* The current would just open to admit one, close seamlessly over one's head, and keep on going. It would all be as easy and idle as a daydream." He comes to himself with a start and finds himself two miles above Hannibal. From the tugs of moored barge fleets he sees lights and senses the presence of other people, a presence which, perhaps, saves him: "I could hear lazy voices coming from the open windows of their galleys. Everyone else had settled down to supper and TV. Shivering, alerted to my own solitude, I hurried on down."

Raban has now undergone another transformation. He began the journey looking backward, toward the books and paintings in his past (a reader). On the river, briefly, he changes his perspective to the present moment, and for that brief and dangerous interval he is a genuine traveler, immersed in raw experience. That experience offers nothing further for him: "The river had, quite literally, put me into a trance. . . . Was I really moving? Surely I'd been here before. There always comes a point in traveling when motion itself has become so habitual that it breeds its own deep stillness. There was no wind, no cloud; nothing except the imperceptible velocity of the current. My wake was fixed on the water like a piece of molded plaster; it supplied the illusion of movement to a journey that had stopped dead still." Now he reestablishes his social ties, and looks both to the past and the future; he is now a writer. The actual journey continues long past this point, but Raban's motivation and perspective are now completely different from what they were prior to reaching Hannibal. Writing his book about the journey, thus, becomes an important antidote *to* the journey, an act of connection with and commitment to others. And in the process of selecting, shaping, and structuring his perceptions into a narrative, that analytical part of Raban's consciousness again predominates.

In this act of turning outward, the experience of travel ends and the *book* about travel begins. The travel experience offers and provides freedom (especially freedom from preconceived and erroneous ideas about the river). But too much freedom, Raban learns, leads to isolation, incoherence, and even death. One cannot travel forever without risking the loss of one's very identity. Writing a book, then, becomes an act of reconstruction, which helps the writer assert a new self. But why should readers read this piece of therapy? What do readers expect from a travel narrative, and how do these expectations shape the form of the narrative?

A stock figure in travel narratives seems to be the wistful, would-be traveler. Raban finds the Mississippi full of them. Another boater observes them too, and, in a conversation with Raban, observes that these characters always have two responses when they hear of what a real traveler is doing:

> "The first is *You must be mad!* and he makes out like he's looking at a maniac. But then there's always the second—you know what that is?"
> "*I envy you.*"
> "Right. Every time. *I envy you.* And the envy's real. They'd kind of like to hear of our family drowning, just to prove that they needn't do it themselves."

But the mere existence of a book demonstrates that the writer *hasn't* drowned, and thus the need for others to "do it themselves" is still there. The travel writer acts as a kind of emissary (a human version of the young couple's sailboat) for all those others who want to travel but who lack the ability or the commitment. As with the young Raban, those who cannot make the trip read books instead, so the travel book can be seen as the experience itself for such people. Yet it's always an unsatisfactory substitute; the narrative reinforces the urge to travel rather than relieving it. It also provides a new vision of the terrain, which can prove quite dangerous if the reader actually ventures out from the library.

Which type of reading is best: reading that mimics the experience itself or reading that mirrors the manner in which the experience is turned into writing? Experience is linear, as is a "naive" first reading. But critical reading is recursive, as is the writing about an experience. On his boat, Raban drifts downstream with the current, in one direction, and so does the reader who reads only for pleasure. But a critical reader repeatedly heads upstream, revisiting literary "landmarks," creating an entirely new "map" by combining elements in thematic patterns and overriding the sequence of events, discovering meaning *in retrospect* in the same way that the traveler discovers meaning and significance in the act of writing about the journey, after the experience is finished. "I suspect that the real secret of its [the voyage's] appeal to the writer is that it provides him with a usable past, a store of memory," Raban writes in an essay entitled "The Journey and the Book."

> Life ravels on, but the trip is over, and it's the writer's business to tease
> its significance out in the long tranquillity of the study. His notebook may
> supply him with cues and prompts, but these bits and pieces of the random
> world are little more than scraps of wool on a barbed wire fence; they're
> there to be collected, spun and woven into the fiction of the book. . . .
> Events which were quite unrecorded because they appeared trifling then
> now turn into structural pillars of the narrative. The relationship between
> *then* and *now,* between the journey and the book, is tricky and paradoxi-
> cal; and as he negotiates it the writer discovers, often to his embarrassment,
> that he is a fabulist who only masquerades as a reporter.

If the writer becomes a fabulist through the distortions inherent in the act of writing, then what of the critical reader who adds even another level of distortion in the act of reading for significance?

On the other hand, is it even possible for a reader to share a writer's journey through reading? If the plot of a journey includes "immersing" oneself, even briefly, and losing self-consciousness, then shouldn't reading provide the same sensation?

"*Travel*. It was an intransitive verb," Raban comments after meeting a waitress who dreams of being an airline stewardess. "It didn't involve any destinations. It was going for the going's sake, to be anywhere but where you were, with the motion itself the only object." Cannot reading, for such people at least, also be an intransitive verb? Finding one's way through a narrative, being surprised with each new page and not knowing what lies ahead, "drifting" through the book—isn't this, in fact, a safe kind of travel, with a guaranteed ending?

If so, if some readers concentrate upon the *reading process* itself as a type of travel, following close in Raban's wake with their forward view blocked by his presence, they can do so only on the first, "naive" reading. Reading analytically, from the end backward, recombining elements and interpreting episodes: this is essentially the same process the writer uses at the end of the journey to shape notes and memory into a narrative. But it is fundamentally different from the journey itself, as is a second reading from the first. The "fellow traveler" reader will expect to read linearly, closing the book as Raban turns around south of New Orleans, and, perhaps, never coming back to it. Like the naive passengers on Twain's steamboat, such readers might be entranced with surface details and oblivious to their hidden significance. But, as Twain himself points out, such an experience has undeniable rewards, rewards that are forever lost as one becomes a "pilot"—or a writer. If such readers are deluded as to the true nature and meaning of the journey, at least their delusion is not life-threatening (unless, of course, they copy Raban too much and actually set out on a *real* journey down the river).

The desire of such readers to share a writer's experience, then, comprises a major factor in shaping the narrative itself. In its pacing and its relationship of time and space, the book should, as faithfully as possible, recreate the journey as it has actually happened. As Raban sets out on his journey, he has a plan for the book that reveals his awareness of these readers. "The book and the journey would be all of a piece," he says.

> The plot would be written by the current of the river itself. It would carry me into long deep pools of solitude, and into brushes with society on the shore. Where the river meandered, so would the book, and when the current speeded up into a narrow chute, the book would follow it. Everything would be left to chance. . . . It was a journey that would be random and haphazard; but it would also have the insistent purpose of the river current as it drove southward and seaward to the Gulf of Mexico.

This kind of narrative resembles that of another writer who stressed the *process* of writing and reading over the *product*: Raban's adopted mentor, Mark Twain. In his autobiography, Twain explains the "law" of narrative, which is, he claims, really no law at all:

Narrative should flow as flows the brook down through the hills and the leafy woodlands, its course changed by every bowlder that it comes across and by every grass-clad gravelly spur that projects into its path; its surface broken, but its course not stayed by rocks and gravel on the bottom in the shoal places; a brook that never goes straight for a minute, but *goes*, and goes briskly, sometimes ungrammatically, and sometimes fetching a horse-shoe three-quarters of a mile around, and at the end of the circuit flowing within a yard of the path it traversed an hour before.

A story should recreate in its shape—the associations of ideas, primarily—the *flow* of concealed thought (or of the experience it represents). "Nothing to do," Twain concludes, "but make the trip; the how of it is not important, so that the trip is made."

Having read Twain's river books before setting out and having adopted his vision, it is hardly surprising that Raban should share his theories of narrative, and even the metaphor of writing as a river: "If riding the river was like anything else in life at all, it was like writing. One could lose oneself in the delicate business of keeping afloat and on course in just the same way as one could lose oneself in the pleasure and hazard of inching along through the words on a page, feeling for the main drift of the current and trying not to run aground. One needed a degree of disengagement to do either." A reader can "drift" through this river, and so can a passenger/traveler. A writer (and an analytical, critical reader), on the other hand, concerned with "staying on course" and concluding the narrative satisfactorily, needs "a degree of disengagement," as Raban develops after Hannibal. The two types of activities are both kinds of "travel," and the superiority of one over the other depends upon the traveler's/reader's/writer's objectives.

This distinction between two types of reading applies, of course, to other genres as well, but it seems particularly relevant to travel writing. If the purpose of reading a travel narrative is to undertake an imaginative journey of one's own, then that purpose would seem to be far better served by a first reading than by subsequent ones. By this criterion, the narrative should be judged by how well it provides the intended reader with a dynamic interaction with the text similar to a voyager's dynamic interaction with, say, a river. An appropriate reading would be characterized by a combination of careful observation and provisional attempts to link past experiences and predict the future, to make meaning of the details observed *at the moment they are, in fact, observed.* To read in such a manner would be to become immersed in the page immediately before your eyes, and to feel as Raban felt as he set out: "I was full of that receptive good humor which marks the beginnings of journeys—a time when everything is coated with the bloom of newness, and one's eyes and ears skitter like minnows, seizing excitedly on every humdrum scrap. A sleeping dog! They have sleeping dogs in Wisconsin! A pile of cut wood! They cut wood here! Look, cows! Look, a water tower! Look, a gas station! Everything shapes up to the same astonishing size."

Unfortunately, this criterion is an impossible one; a narrative that truly recreated the travel experience would be as formless, and meaningless (and, often, as *boring*) as the journey itself. Popular travel narratives like *Old Glory* do, indeed, reward a casual first reading, but only to a point. The receptive good humor described above soon diminishes for the reader as much as for the traveler. Inevitably, form creeps in: some incidents are emphasized and others suppressed, the narrative takes on an overall theme or tone and finally, at the end, the writer draws conclusions that may not have been at all apparent when the actual journey ended. And with these changes, the narrative becomes less mere entertainment and more rhetorical; in some important ways it works to push the would-be traveler out onto the real river.

As Raban confronts the Mississippi through a set of perceptual filters, so too will any reader who has ever so much as heard about this particular river. Many, if not most, travel books open with a map (which may even include brief descriptions of significant incidents) that plants a "shape of the river" in the reader's head even before the text is encountered. Like Raban, that reader begins the book swamped with abstractions—vague expectations and images, remembered episodes from other books, or even memories and personal connotations attached to locations the reader might have visited or lived in. Without these abstractions, in fact, the reading "boat" might never be launched. Just as Raban has to learn quickly that the river under his boat is far different from the river portrayed in Bingham's painting, so the reader has to confront the "true" landscape in the book quickly. To read this ink-and-paper river accurately, to perceive things as they actually are, the reader's own mental copy of *Huckleberry Finn* has to be left behind as well. To be most like Twain on Twain's river, Raban learns, he has to *forget*, at least during the course of the journey, all the Twain he has ever read and pay intense attention to the river at his bow. The same applies to the reader of Raban's book.

The irony is obvious. Raban's Mississippi is not as Twain or Bingham or Flint portrayed it. While encouraging readers to reject all previous representations of a particular landscape, the narrative is at the same time representing this particular version—Raban's image, for instance, of the Mississippi as a sewer running neglected through the industrial heart of Minneapolis—as the truth. The traveler claims to be undertaking the journey to discover the landscape for him or herself (and "seeing for oneself" is thus promoted as a positive value), but the river at the reader's bow is Raban's.

One of the dangers of real travel, as Raban found at Hannibal, is the loss of the self. That too seems a potential danger in reading a travel narrative, for one is likely to become a captive of a writer's vision and not one's own. The experience, no matter how vividly it might be described, is always illusory: no matter how dramatic or threatening events might seem to be, the mere presence of the book and its characterization as "nonfiction," is proof that the writer survived. Riding the river, Raban saw himself "as a sincere traveler, thinking of my voyage not as a holiday but as a scale model of a life. It was different in one essential: I would survive it to give an account of its end. The journey would turn into a complete narrative, where life—my own life—could be only an unfinished story with an inconclusive plot." So, too, with reading.

The book will always end, and readers expect it to end satisfactorily, with the writer aware and articulate, not wandering incoherently in the wilderness or adrift at the mouth of the Mississippi. It is thus impossible to actually lose oneself in the text as the traveler might lose him or herself in the journey itself. But it can seem, for a while, that one does. Thus the narrative provides some of the sensations of travel without any of the risks, and this difference between the experience itself and the representation of the experience is so apparent that the illusion is easily shattered—once the first reading is done. To look back through a travel book one has just read can result in a feeling very much like Raban's own at the conclusion of the journey: "I wasn't a traveler at all; I was just another rubberneck in a city that made its living out of credulous rubbernecks. Go buy a guidebook! Take a buggy ride! Get your picture painted! Eat *beignets!* Listen to the sounds of Old Dixie! Have yourself a relief massage; then *go home,* shmuck!"

Ultimately the reader too is a tourist rather than a traveler, armed with a guidebook and sampling prepackaged sensations. The very presence of the book contradicts its purpose, just as the placid, eternal image presented by Bingham's painting contradicts the fluid, ever-changing reality of the Mississippi. *Old Glory,* like many travel books, is rhetorical, promoting a particular imaginative vision—a vision of an utterly free and unconstrained style of life, where one reacts to a never-ending set of fresh challenges and lives in the moment, free from past and future. Yet the book seems to make it possible for the reader to avoid testing that vision through actual experience. It promotes freshness of perception, and yet it forces the reader to see the Mississippi only through one particular consciousness: Jonathan Raban's. It gives the tangible lie to the writer's assertion that he or she has learned to abandon the self and merge with the environment, because in such a state no verbal communication is possible at all.

All of these paradoxes are readily apparent. In fact, travel writers often explicitly caution readers against mistaking the narrative for the real landscape. *Old Glory* devotes a great deal of space to contrasting Raban's reading-derived images of the river with the river he actually finds, and the warning not to repeat the mistake should be clear enough. Here, perhaps, is where the second type of readers, the analytical readers, may miss the point of travel writing. Critical readers read *Old Glory* as they would read fiction, recombining elements and incidents in order to gain a deeper understanding of the book's theme, structure, meaning, and so forth. In so doing, they add additional levels of fiction to what was already a fiction— an imaginative representation of an actual journey. They, like unwary first readers, are captured by the writer's vision of the river, and are perhaps *more* likely to remain prisoners of it. If a primary goal of travel (and one of the prime motivations for reading travel books) is to experience a landscape directly and freshly, then the proper response to *Old Glory* might be to leave it behind in the hotel room next to *Huckleberry Finn* and go off in one's own boat. Another item on the reader's own manifest of abstractions, a travel book might help launch the reader on a new journey, turning that individual from a deluded (but appreciative) reader, a tourist, into a genuine traveler. That reader might even go on to write a new travel book and affirm his or her membership in the community of travel writers, presenting another vision to new readers, producing a new illusion of experience that will load the holds of future generations. To read critically is to read backwards. But travel looks forward, and perhaps the proper response to accounts of it should be to create new accounts.

So new travelers repeat the process, covering the same ground (or water) as their predecessors, and making the same mistakes by confusing literary accounts with the reality of the journey. A short time ago, as I was working on this essay, the news reported the rescue of four pleasure boaters from a sandbar on the Mississippi River. They had set out to sail the length of the river, imagining, they said, that the river would be smooth and slow-flowing. Instead, they found four-foot waves and treacherous shoals, including the one upon which they ran aground, and they nearly lost their lives. There is some talk about writing a book about the adventure.

WORKS CITED

Raban, Jonathan. "The Journey and the Book." In *For Love and Money, A Writing Life*. New York: Harper & Row, 1989, 231–38.

———. *Old Glory: An American Voyage*. New York: Simon & Schuster, 1981.

Thoreau, Henry David. *Walden, or, Life in the Woods*. 1854. Rpt. New York: New American Library, 1960.

Twain, Mark. *Life on the Mississippi*. 1884. Rpt. New York: Signet/New American Library, 1961.

———. *Mark Twain's Autobiography*. Ed. Albert Bigelow Paine. New York: Harper & Bros., 1924.

> > > > > > **Perspectives on Abroad
in Spender and Hockney's
*China Diary***

CHARISSE GENDRON

In the preface to *When the Going Was Good*, an anthology of his travel
pieces published in 1945, Evelyn Waugh writes, "I do not expect to see
many travel books in the near future." It is over for Waugh, that renaissance of travel writing when many talented writers of his generation—
Lawrence, Graham Greene, Robert Byron—went abroad and wrote artful, entertaining books about their adventures. The war ended it by making
a mockery of adventure and by turning travel writing into journalism,
an illegitimate form whose vaunted objectivity barely hides its hectoring
"political argument." Order, the distinction between the man of culture
and the barbarian, has collapsed in Waugh's world, and with it the innocent fancy that inspired British travelers for generations. "There is no room
for tourists in a world of 'displaced persons,'" he writes. "Never again,
I suppose, shall we land on foreign soil with letter of credit and passport
(itself the first faint shadow of the great cloud that envelops us) and feel
the world wide open before us." The truly foreign territory—storybook
Europe, bizarre Africa—no longer exists; the exotic other is a citizen of
the world, conversant with bureaucracies and ideologies.

Perhaps even more damaging, not just to the fantasy of travel but to
the kind of travel book written by Waugh's generation, is the loss of the
norm that gives significance to the exotic. Noting how his contemporaries
rushed to the "initiation into manhood" represented by the penetration of
South America or the Arctic, he writes that they would have lingered in
Europe "had we known that all that seeming-solid, patiently built, gor-
geously ornamented structure of Western life was to melt overnight like an
ice-castle, leaving only a puddle of mud; had we known man was even then

This essay was written with the help of a Faculty Research Grant from Middle Tennessee
State University during the spring of 1986.

leaving his post." However one might deplore Waugh's Toryism, one must grant that, as the masters of that seemingly solid ice castle, English writers for a hundred years—Kinglake, author of *Eothen* (1844), is preeminent—used their ascendancy as a device of literary detachment, writing travel books that read like comic novels of manners abroad. When the castle dissolved, representing the melt-down not just of the class structure and esthetic hierarchies but of imperial self-assurance, what would supply the travel writer with a norm against which to measure the foreign, should he be lucky enough to encounter it abroad?

Taking his cue from Waugh, Paul Fussell, in *Abroad* (1980), writes an elegy for the travel book, which in the late thirties, he says, was "capture[d] . . . by events" and died in captivity. His metaphor of imprisonment is appropriate to describe the literary activities of a generation that has often testified to feeling forced by the advent of fascism, communism, and world war to incorporate political consciousness in their writing, sometimes against their temperaments (Samuel Hynes has collected this testimony in *The Auden Generation* [1976]). Fussell's examples of failed travel books, Auden and MacNeice's *Letters from Iceland* (1937) and Auden and Isherwood's *Journey to a War* (1939), indicate to him the end of a tradition in their "unraveling" of narrative form, their "self-consciousness" about travel and travel writing and their attempts at political journalism occasioned by the crisis atmosphere of the late thirties. I don't think the books fail: both are entertaining and contain good writing—including Auden's "Letter to Lord Byron" and the sonnet sequence "In Time of War"—while the mixed formats of poetry, prose, photographs, and maps preserve a tongue-in-cheek attitude toward travel writing as a form of documentary.

I do agree with Fussell, however, that these books mark the transition to a more politicized and self-conscious mode of travel writing, expressed, for instance, in sonnet 16 from *Journey to a War* and the verse commentary that follows the sequence:

> But ideas can be true although men die,
> And we can watch a thousand faces
> Made active by one lie:
>
> And maps can really point to places
> Where life is evil now:
> Nanking; Dachau. . . .
>
> While in an international and undamaged quarter
> Casting our European shadows on Shanghai,

Walking unhurt among the banks, apparently immune
Below the monuments of an acquisitive society,
With friends and books and money and the traveller's freedom
We are compelled to realize that our refuge is a sham.

Although ideas are suspect because people kill and die for them, the sonnet intimates, when the fascists are at the door one must choose between two ideas, good and evil. The commentary expresses Auden's consciousness of both his privileged distance from the local struggle, which has not reached the international quarter, and his colonizing presence as an Englishman, which casts a shadow on Asian ground like those of the imperial European buildings in Shanghai. As Fussell suggests, Auden's self-critical approach is not an isolated case. It parallels, for instance, the approach to non-European cultures developed in the thirties by Claude Lévi-Strauss, who says in *Structural Anthropology* (1958) that "research in the field, by which every anthropological career begins, is mother and nurse of doubt, the philosophical attitude par excellence. This 'anthropological doubt' does not only consist of knowing that one knows nothing, but of resolutely exposing what one thought one knew—and one's very ignorance—to buffetings and denials directed at one's most cherished ideas and habits by other ideas and habits best able to rebut them." That both Auden and Lévi-Strauss should begin to cultivate "anthropological doubt" in the thirties is not coincidental, for leftist writers of the period felt something like what Lévi-Strauss calls the "remorse" for the colonial past that motivated anthropologists, who saw their science as "atoning" for a history that went wrong as far back as the Renaissance.

Fussell is right, then, in identifying Auden's collaborations with Mac-Neice and Isherwood as the emergence of political consciousness in the travel book, but wrong, as Stephen Spender and David Hockney's *China Diary* (1982) demonstrates, in predicting that this consciousness could not be reconciled with the personal approach that makes a travel book literature. (Fussell considers *China Diary* to be "only a tourist book" whose author and illustrator were too "decent" to challenge their official guides' interpretation of totalitarian China.) Travel writing currently thrives in the hands of Paul Theroux, V. S. and Shiva Naipaul, Bruce Chatwin, Jonathan Raban, and even Waugh's contemporary Spender. These writers carry as a part of their essential equipment the awareness that history shapes the experience of the observer and the observed, that the perspective of the English traveler (native or adoptive) will differ from that of the foreign native, and that in the postcolonial world the relationship between traveler and native may symbolize the old imperial one. To represent this new truth of the foreign encounter, which has supplanted the old truism of the confrontation of self and exotic "other," current travel writers experiment with relativistic perspectives and analyze the nature of travel writing itself, to one extent or another writing what John Thieme has called "meta-travelogue." Awareness of history on this level does not mean hawking a "political argument"; these writers construct a personal norm out of their earned cosmopolitanism and habit of critical thinking.

For Jonathan Raban, for instance, adventure often lies in traveling the distance between minds holding different world views, a distance that has not narrowed now that people the world over wear business suits, drink Coke, and read newspapers in fractured English. If anything, the foreign "other" grows more enigmatic as it grows less romantic. In his book *Arabia: A Journey Through the Labyrinth* (1979), Raban describes an encounter in a bazaar in Abu Dhabi with an old man reading the Koran, who, the author realizes, would be baffled by Raban's claim to be a "writer," since to the old man the one book—the Koran—has already been written. (Islam's recent persecution of Salman Rushdie's *Satanic Verses* [1988], of course, dramatizes Raban's observation that the old man's culture encourages him to see fictions as lies or blasphemies.) That the old man possesses no mental category for an activity central to the author's thinking—that while sharing a sidewalk the men exist in different worlds—reminds Raban of his Arab neighbors in London, never absorbed into English life, "and of how lightly we were tiptoeing over the top of each other's worlds, traveling freely on passports of ignorance and misunderstanding. Old travelers grumpily complain that travel is now dead, that the world is a suburb. They are quite wrong. Lulled by familiar resemblances between all the unimportant things, they miss the brute differences in everything of importance." A fan who totes *When the Going Was Good* on his journey, Raban contradicts Waugh by affirming that the value of travel and travel writing lies not in escaping politics but in perceiving the "brute differences" between people who hold diverse ideologies.

Stephen Spender and David Hockney's *China Diary* is a travel book in the tradition initiated by Auden, MacNeice and Isherwood and continued by writers such as Raban. It presents a light-hearted appearance in its diary format and charming visuals, but it also attempts to give a just picture of China through the multiple perspectives of its various media and dual, mutually "corrective" authorship. Like *Letters from Iceland* and *Journey to a War*, it betrays the understanding that, no matter how serious the subject, a travel book should present a casual, personal appearance, as if it were dashed off between adventures, while impressions are fresh; a travel book should never smell of the study (where it is invariably revised before publication). "The book should be . . . patched up in some way," Hockney advised in a planning session with Spender eight months after the trip, "as if made by three schoolboys on a tour of a continent for the first time" (the schoolboy touch being, of course, peculiarly Audenesque).

Spender has written the text in diary form, with headings indicating cities on the itinerary. The text and Hockney's drawings, watercolors, and photographs of the trip illustrate and comment on each other. (Spender emphasizes Hockney's autonomy as coproducer of the book, but I intend to focus more on Spender's contribution.) An epilogue comprised of dialogue from the planning session continues the mood of zestful creative cooperation—a mood that also recalls the previous collaborations of the Auden generation, proofs that artists can be social beings as well as isolated prophets. If apparent artlessness is desirable in the finished product, however, the collaborators must still face the problem of how to perceive and organize their perceptions of a foreign place within the limitations of time, the arbitrariness of impressions (some determined by the agendas of official guides) and their various media. The dilemma of how to perceive and represent the vastness of China is dramatized when, lacking time to draw, Hockney begins to photograph the trip, only to find that the more pictures he takes, the less he sees things in context—just as Auden complains in *Letters from Iceland* that the trip has left him with a series of mental film rushes that don't make a book. In the epilogue Hockney admits to having been defeated occasionally: "We can't pretend that we didn't get it—that feeling of deadness. We don't know what we missed, frankly."

Besides these formal concerns, *China Diary* shares with *Letters from Iceland*, *Journey to a War*, and their successors a consciousness of the traveler as an intruder, a tripper from the affluent West who makes snap judgments about complex problems in order to produce a book. While he can't change the nature of this intrusion, Spender tries to be sensitive to it by adopting the native perspective, noting that "those observed are themselves observers of the observers" and that to Chinese eyes the aged, bulbous author, the artist in mismatched socks, and their companion (Gregory Evans) in a Robin Hood jerkin must have looked slightly absurd. A tourist's status as an exotic exhibit to the natives becomes even more questionable when Spender's group joins a clutch of Americans to sail up a canal in Wusih, where the townspeople, dressed in their sober blue pajamas, line the banks: "Our boat was like a cage full of gaudy tropical birds. The spectator stares at the plumage, hears the squawks but sees only the gap which divides different stages of evolution. Did they or we here represent the higher form?" Should this remark leave the impression that Spender and Hockney are in search of a pristine China untrodden by tourist's foot, let me correct it, for they are unromantic travelers at home with anomaly. While Spender, like Theroux in "Memories of Old Afghanistan" (1985) and Shiva Naipaul in *North of South* (1978), observes how Western hippies abroad compete with natives of underdeveloped countries in primitiveness, Hockney blithely comments that when traveling with tourists in Egypt, "after a bit, I found them just as interesting as the antiquities." By acknowledging the commercialization of modern travel, Spender and Hockney—like Raban, Theroux, and the Naipauls—assure that the travel book does not degenerate into a nostalgic literary form.

Travel writers today use various techniques to create a tension between relativism and a cohesive moral perspective on the foreign scene: Raban, for instance, shows himself babbling helplessly among laconic long-time users at a *qat* party in a Middle Eastern village, while Theroux lets us see how riding six thousand miles in trains can put sinister warps in the outlook of the stablest traveler. While such episodes seem to undercut these writers' authority, they actually establish their credibility as students of anthropological doubt, "the philosophical attitude par excellence."

Spender's technique for putting his own biases into the picture, and thus giving himself and his reader a chance to compensate for them, is to create a friendly dialectic between his and Hockney's responses to the conundrum of China—for if the traveler's self is indeterminate, how much more so is a great communist state. Spender and Hockney work as complementary principles, as reason and intuition, duty and pleasure, age and youth, literature and art. This is, I think, part of Spender's design and a product of how he sees himself and Hockney. In an essay on Hockney's stage sets he writes: "Hockney has common sense, is a sharp social commentator, is, in fact, in many ways a representative member of a generation for whom Elvis Presley and the Beatles were heroes." Although Hockney, an opera buff, despised the exclusive, skirt-chasing London club scene of his young manhood, Spender inevitably sees him as a product of the swinging sixties.

Spender and Hockney's dialectic, then, serves as a device for apprehending China, which itself is deeply double. On the simplest level, its history is split into the imperial past and the communist present. The past is constantly repudiated yet spookily extant in ancient monuments, traditional arts such as calligraphy, national characteristics such as the "megalomaniac vastness" and "anonymity" Spender notices in both the pre- and postrevolutionary styles of public architecture. This first level of enigmatic juxtaposition is represented in Peking's two cities, the Imperial City enclosing the palace, where now no one but the tourist goes, and, on the other side of a large red gate, Tien An Men Square, location of the current government. Hockney's schematic painting of the two cities shows on one side a labyrinthine pattern like a rectangle cut from a richly colored textile and on the other a white rectangle with an obelisk in the center, a monumental government building in the foreground, and line formations of antlike cyclists on three sides. Hockney indicates with an empty white square what is actually a looming portrait of Mao mounted over the gate on the side of the current government (a portrait that was defaced during the recent demonstrations for democracy).

The enigma goes beyond the compartmentalization of history to a disjunction in individual discourse between surface and depth, public and private. After talking to poets in Peking about new artistic freedoms, Spender reflects, "a Chinese wall of what is called Marxist-Leninist-Maoist thought surrounds everything. . . . A metaphor formed in my mind of conversation with these Chinese: that of a clear transparent stream with a smiling friendly surface, but a few inches down an opaque floor of stone at the bottom of the stream below which one could not see at all." Spender, of course, does not blame the individuals for maintaining this frustrating wall, for he recognizes that periodically their government, touting new freedoms, has encouraged poets to tear it down, only to insist later that they reconstruct it. Rather than Rimbaud's " 'on me pense' . . . what is required of the Chinese poet," he says, "is that he should say 'Mao me pense.' . . . This is the substitution of political for poetic consciousness." The price of this loss is obvious, even if, as Spender characteristically concedes, "the possibility always exists that only in this way could a country like China achieve social justice for 'the masses.' "

For Spender and Hockney, seeing sometimes through each other's eyes dramatizes the disjunction between smiling surface and stony depth. Hockney explains the perceptual puzzle China offered: "Our mood kept changing: when we'd become convinced at one moment that it was a police state, the next day, we'd look around suspiciously for evidence and find it. The day after, the sun would shine on the lovely mountains of Kweilin and you'd forget all about it and you'd enjoy the nature and the trees." For Hockney the two Chinas alternately replace each other, while for Spender one always lurks beneath the other. The symbol of the puzzle was their chief guide, Mr. Lin. Hockney continues: "with our change of mood, the first person we looked at differently each time was Mr Lin. When we were convinced China was a police state, we saw Mr Lin as a bit of a monster; when we'd forgotten about it, Mr Lin was just the charming man that he appeared to us to be!" Mr. Lin possesses the mock-heroic powers appropriate to an official of a state that takes itself rather seriously: disentangling traffic jams with the wave of a hand, sanctioning with laughter some (not all) of the travelers' jokes, and underscoring the significance of the travelers' reentry into the evil West.

"On our last morning in China," Spender says, "Mr Lin took us to the Canton railway station to catch the through train to Hong Kong. When we got to the customs barrier, he said, rather solemnly, I thought, 'Here my powers end. From beyond that barrier you are on your own.' This reminded me of some guardian spirit in a masque who accompanies and protects the hero through the forest and then has to leave him." Hockney's emblematic photo shows a jovial Mr. Lin standing between two huge painted masks, one smiling, a yin/yang symbol on the forehead, the other frowning with outthrust lower lip. The two sides of Mr. Lin, sensitive humanist and communist official, represent a bifurcation that the Chinese have not been able to eradicate in practical life.

At the jade factory of the Hangchow art school, where objects are made for export and sale to tourists, Spender encounters a contradiction between explicit rejection and implicit acceptance of Western values familiar to readers of Theroux, Raban, and the Naipauls: "The function of the rich as sustainer of values was being recognized here in China where anyone rich enough to buy the perfectly plain jade bowl which I longed for and which was quite beyond my means would be regarded as a class enemy, if not a criminal. Yet by implication the director was also admitting that the rich buy jade objects because they are amateurs of the rare and beautiful, whereas no one in China is able to possess rare and beautiful things." The doubleness of China, then, consists not only of the separation of past and present and of poetic and political consciousness, but of an unspoken dependence on an outside world that sustains cultural values a communist state cannot afford.

The travelers respond to China's dark side—archaic, totalitarian, surreal—with laughter and dismay. At times the country's Kafkaesque quality elicits the conscious paranoia of thirties texts such as Edward Upward's Mortmere stories, as when Spender gleefully notes that two of the Peking poets, who never speak to the travelers, "[whisper] to each other, laughing, and pointing at us occasionally like the mysterious Assistants in Kafka's *The Castle*." On the train to Shanghai,

> Mr Lin . . . said that even at the height of his power Chairman Mao never
> had a salary of more than $500 a month. It struck me that this was a
> little like saying the Queen of England never had money to go shopping
> in a London department store. . . . He told us of statements and ideas put
> forward by the students in the Cultural Revolution. These remind me of
> Surrealist ideas in Auden's *The Orators*: all postmen should wear red uni-
> forms; the police should direct traffic waving not batons, but copies of
> Chairman Mao's *Little Red Book*; no pictures of Chairman Mao should be
> exhibited which did not show both his ears; traffic lights should be altered
> so that *green* signified STOP and *red* FORWARD; no one should be per-
> mitted to put a portait of Chairman Mao on sale, since representations of
> him should not be the objects of mercenary transaction.

If Spender and Hockney can conceive of the police state as high nonsense,
however, they realize that the state's arbitrariness, which reminds them of
public-school life, also lies behind the violence of the Cultural Revolution,
some of whose victims they meet.

Recent Chinese history, indeed, reminds them of school life under a
senile headmaster, one of whose "more eccentric acts was to give the children a year's holiday during which they were free to break the school
windows, desecrate the sacred objects in the chapel, make the masters
scrub floors and clean out lavatories, and, as a final insult, attend courses
given them by their former pupils, become their teachers. That was the impression we had of the Cultural Revolution." Superimposed on the text is
Hockney's line drawing of a frowning, topknotted child in party pajamas.

With the suppression of culture, Spender notes, comes the ironic suppression of a popular art under the style China has caught from the Soviet
Union—or maybe the United States—"like a terminal disease": "It is
strange that the buildings have so much in common with totalitarian architecture elsewhere: Stalin's, Mussolini's, Hitler's and, in capitalist societies,
great industrial concerns and banks. Gregory remarked that the Mao Tse-
tung Memorial Hall reminded him of the Home Federal Savings Bank at
Sunset Boulevard and Vine, in Los Angeles." The Mortmere quality of
arrested development—surreal propaganda, anonymous "modern" architecture—prepares us for the archaic level of certain Chinese arts and
industries described in *China Diary*. One day in Hangchow Spender comes
across Hockney who, watching art students doing an academic drawing
from a bust of an Edwardian lady, claims "he had not drawn from such
a model for over thirty years." Hockney uses a blunt word for the official
effort to impose the rhetoric of a revolutionary "present" forty years old

onto the actual present inhabited by a new generation: "The swindle is that if you have to be told something that happened was heroic, it is not heroic in real terms, certainly not for you, in the way you feel."

Hockney dislikes seeing youth swindled because he loves the resurgent, optimistic aspect of human nature, an attribute that allows him to believe in China's other side, that which is apolitical, universal, or, as he puts it in the epilogue, "neutral":

> For instance, take architecture: it could be Stalinist, or traditionalist or neutral, like the diplomats' quarter and the Friendship Stores! . . . There was also a neutral side to Mr Lin. . . . The categories begin to shift.
>
> SS   The neutral way of seeing Mr Lin would be as someone like Leopold Bloom, wandering through China!
>
> DH   It's a very good idea. . . . Everything's a little more complex . . . the little boy artist—purely neutral. . . . Kweilin seemed touristy, but life also seemed charming. . . . The beauty of it neutralizes it. . . . You can make patterns in different ways now. Madame Sun Yat-sen died while we were there. . . . At first, we didn't quite know who she was; then we found out that her sister was Madame Chiang Kai-shek and that made you think she was probably an opportunist. And yet she might have been a dear, wonderful lady and a deep patriotic Chinese, which is what Mr Lin suggested she was.

In convincing him, even temporarily, that China's sunny surface may possess depth, that the apparent may be real, Hockney probably activates Spender's own wish to transcend frontiers. When at the border with Hong Kong they see "two very young customs officers seated on one chair with their arms around each other," Spender detects China's "note of innocence." In smiling upon such "innocence," Spender chooses to ignore the total suppression of homoeroticism that makes men's public embraces acceptable in China.

Early in *China Diary*, after a skeptical analysis of a 1949 speech by Mao about the necessity for dictatorial methods in establishing a people's government, Spender explains how a generational difference helps distinguish Hockney's point of view from his own. "Thoughts like these," he says of his refutation of Mao's logic,

> pursued me all the time we were in China even in my sleep. . . . They were typical thoughts of someone of my generation. . . . David, being of his gen-

eration and 44 as against my 72, does not have the same tendency to think along lines laid down by the history of power politics in this century. He used, he told me when we talked about this, at one time to vote Labour but today party politics don't interest him. This may be due in part to the fact that, from the point of view of an English painter who divides his life between Los Angeles and London, party politics seem parochial. He looks at life, he says, from the point of view of the imagination. . . . Often he exclaims "Everything is imagination," as though this thought were some touchstone in his mind. . . . On our travels David and I were, I think, corrective to each other because I am able to point out to him that he should not expect everyone in the world to have his capacity for enjoyment; and he corrects in me the tendency to be got down or over-impressed by the sheer weight of seemingly insuperable obstacles and insoluble problems, to live as it were under a dark vague cloud of uncomprehended and, I suspect, incomprehensible statistics.

Trained in the analysis of power politics in the thirties and thereafter, Spender gained a new idea of justice, but he also learned how socialism can, in practice, constrain the imagination. Lacking this historical experience, Hockney approaches the communist world spontaneously, feeling little pressure to be politically correct in his opinions. He disapproves, for instance, of the Chinese policy of encouraging families to have only one child, apparently feeling that sibling play encourages creativity. Spender says, "I understood his feelings but remained convinced that, apart from nuclear war, the greatest danger to the world in the foreseeable future is over-population. . . . Human behavior should not, he thought, be submitted to scientific necessity. . . . I didn't agree, but I saw that I accepted too easily as truth the scientific arguments and that in accepting scientific arguments one may be jettisoning the insight of the imagination into human nature." Hockney's intuitively grounded responses serve Spender as signposts in a thicket of complexities. He may not always follow them, but he is sure they lead somewhere.

In *The Thirties and After* (1979), Spender explains his generation's background in learning to peel away layers of truth—or layers of bias. Although nurtured on modernism and apolitical poetry, young writers felt obliged to make their poetry confront issues of the times: unemployment, Hitler's rise to power, the probability of another world war. This obligation split their natures, rendering them

extremely nonpolitical with half of themselves and extremely political with the other half. With the political half they really did try to see the world

from the ideological viewpoint; that is, with the idea that all those thinking and doing activities which brought one in relation with other human
beings involved, consciously or unconsciously, participation in a struggle
between opposed interests, those of capitalist imperialism and those of
the socialist revolution. Perhaps one might not in past historical situations
have seen this, but in the current situation it was so highlighted by circumstances that, if one belonged to the ruling class, not to see it was to take
the side of the class into which one had been born and which had a definite
interest in one's not seeing it; and if one saw it, one was almost certain to
take sides against one's own class.

Belonging to the ruling class made it possible for writers such as Auden,
Spender, MacNeice, Isherwood, and Day Lewis to repudiate the ruling
class, for it assured them an education in the liberal tradition of self-
criticism. Yet, haunting working-class bars in Berlin and giving up material
advantages with comparative ease, they grew anxious about the esthetic
costs of such choices: "poets of my own generation were full of doubts
mostly due to the fact that in varying and different ways they distrusted
the involvement of art in politics." They found a middle ground writing a
variety of anti-Fascist war poetry—such as Auden's sonnets from China—
which was distinct from the communist writings of younger authors such
as John Cornford and Julian Bell.

When their allegiance to antifascist causes demanded the repudiation,
not just of ruling-class privileges but of critical thinking itself, the writers
of Spender's generation could accept the irony for only so long. "I think
one might sum up reasons for the disruption of the anti-Fascist popular
front of the intellectuals in a phrase," Spender writes. "It was a refusal on
behalf of all but the most convinced ideologists to tell the lies required by
the Stalinist Communists. In face of Stalinist propaganda and methods it
was a reversion to the view that individual conscience is the repository of
witnessed truth." This reversion carried thirties writers to a new level of
critically examining received ideas, so that they had to steer narrowly between notions possibly rooted in class privilege and those possibly derived
from liberal guilt. The habit of placing one's ideas in a context meant to
reveal their potential errors stuck with Spender. In writing about China, he
again strives for candor, using his diary as a place to register the reactions
of a mind shaped in the thirties to a great communist state and relying on
his younger companion to expose the limitations of such a mind.

At the office of *Poetry Magazine* in Peking, when a young poet tells the
visitors that, "after smashing up the Gang of Four, we had the opportunity
to study the criterion of truth," Spender presses the poets to define "the

criterion of truth." The poets explain that the new freedom means poets can choose among more subjects to "educate people and enhance their ideological role"; poetry is to be judged by poets rather than officials. One young man, who likes Donne, Eliot, and Auden's poems in *Journey to a War*, and Spender's "Landscape Near an Aerodrome," shows the author a poem of his praising the present over the past or future, which another reader might interpret as a typical poem about the allegiance of youth to its own moment. Spender, however, alert to political nuance, finds the poem but one more "suggestion of the Gang of Four and the suffering caused during the Cultural Revolution." That surely "is the 'yesterday' referred to in the poem. Today is an era of comparative freedom, a budding. At the same time, the mood of the poet reflects a certain uneasiness about tomorrow, as he well may feel, I thought."

Spender's political consciousness leads him actually to internalize the situation of the Chinese poet. In Kweilin, he writes,

> I was feverish throughout the night and had what I can only describe as a political nightmare. . . . I dreamed that I had to write a poem in traditional form about a classical subject, Anchises. . . . After a time, a gap seemed to widen between idea and form, like a space that I could not fill. Besides, I had forgotten who Anchises was. I could not breathe, I felt that I was going to die. Even when I woke I had the sense of something deeply, even terribly, unsatisfactory, this failure on my part to perform a task, and the inability to fill a space between the wish to do something and the conditions under which it could be done.

In this dream dramatizing the creative strain of artists whose subject and form are dictated to them, Spender's empathy, I think, is aided by the fundamentally apolitical temperament that underlies his thirties training and which surfaces intermittently in *China Diary*, as when he admits that on a visit to a communal farm near Shanghai he must take careful notes "because I seem temperamentally incapable of understanding terms such as 'brigade,' 'cadre' etc." Similarly, he finds "chilling" the director's interpretation of a friendly visit to the art school at Hangchow as an act of diplomacy. "I don't like being thought of as a nation," he writes, recalling Auden's dedicatory poem to *The Orators* (1932): "Private faces in public places / Are wiser and nicer / Than public faces in private places." E. M. Forster's desire to transcend class, nationality, and ideology echoes in Spender's query, after a meeting with a group of calligraphers at Nanking, as to "whether there is a composite character meaning hail/farewell [capable of] cancelling geography and ideology—leaping over and ignoring our repulsive political systems—with friendship."

Elsewhere, tellingly, Spender finds a way out of the maze of political discourse through the language of art, indicating that direction with rhetorical brevity. At a poetry recital given for the travelers' benefit in Kweilin, a Maoist poem is "applauded only in perfunctory fashion. One had the feeling: 'It's already too late for this kind of thing.' . . . I said . . . that I thought the best message I could give them was simply to write on the blackboard, three names: W. B. Yeats, T. S. Eliot, W. H. Auden." Spender's trilogy of apolitical modernist poets here serves as his version of an ideogram, "a composite character meaning hail/farewell cancelling geography and ideology . . . with friendship."

Ideogrammatic directness of communication is one thing Spender probably admires in Hockney, whose language of images looks innocent of ideological conflict. But if Hockney serves as Spender's "corrective" in *China Diary*, the former is sufficiently the cultural heir of the thirties for the dialogue between them to be meaningful. Spared the prewar pressure to make leftist art, he explains in his autobiography, *David Hockney* (1977), that he had his own modern orthodoxy to confront, that of abstract expressionism. Ironically, as a student in the late fifties he began to resist the imperative to do nonfigurative painting by depicting his interests in subjects with political implications: vegetarianism, pacifism, and homosexuality. His early paintings contain references to his heroes, the anti-imperialist Gandhi and the democrat Whitman, although in the beginning of his rebellion he used writing rather than figurative images to sneak in subject matter. Hockney, afraid of his own inclination toward illusionism, would put a border around a figurative painting to emphasize the picture plane and make it suitably modern. With experience he freed himself from the party line laid down by Paul Cézanne, that the figure is simply a cone, cylinder, and sphere, and explored the figure's psychological and esthetic associations. He quotes Auden's lines from "Letter to Lord Byron": "To me art's subject is the human clay / Landscape but a background to a torso; All Cézanne's apples I would give away / For a small Goya or a Daumier." In short, in the words of his friend Henry Geldzahler, curator of twentieth-century art at the Met, "Hockney still judges and loves like an old humanist."

Hockney's humanist legacy is evident in his willingness, atypical of many contemporary artists, to see the past as a continuum, each period possessing an idiom from which one can learn a particular mode of perception. As Spender writes of Hockney's stage designs for Igor Stravinsky's *A Rake's Progress* for the Glyndebourne production of 1975, "Stravinsky and Hockney have it in common that they can both make a completely modern work most recognizably their own out of the elements of some past work which arouses their admiration." Yet unlike Stravinsky, Spender contends, Hockney wears his erudition lightly:

> Hockney knows a lot about painting, a lot about music, and quite a lot else though he has the appearance of the self-educated. One is, in fact, always a bit surprised at how much he knows, for example how much poetry he has read and can recite. For he does not strike one as being a learned artist—in the way, say, that Eliot and Auden were learned and looked it. Under his considerable sophistication, he remains fundamentally naive, childlike even—a fact of which he is aware in a way that shows loyalty to childhood.

This tenacious innocence is itself a kind of political stance, one that allows Hockney to appreciate esthetically a past that was, doubtless, corrupt.

In addition to his being a cultural heir, Hockney's experience as an artist, individualist, and homosexual has encouraged him to live out tropes established by the thirties generation. When Hockney won a prize at art school he used the money to go to New York—not to see art, but to go to gay bars and meet boys. As for Auden and Isherwood, America for Hockney meant anonymity, egalitarianism and sex. Like Auden also, Hockney found that to create he needed distance from the expectations of provincial, idolatrous England. As Hynes has pointed out, England's repressive atmosphere preceding the war assured that "the journey itself [was] the most insistent of 'thirties metaphors." Even in the supposedly liberated sixties, however, Hockney found England classbound and insular and joined the long lineage of British writers and artists who have sought new worlds abroad. Like that of his forebears, Hockney's attraction to foreign places is inspired by their associations: he went to Berlin in 1962 partly because of Isherwood's stories and to Alexandria in 1963 partly because of Constantine Cavafy's poems, which he later illustrated. The associations aren't always literary, and are sometimes attached to a personal myth of the exotic no doubt nurtured by the collective fantasy of artistic Englishmen about warm, free places.

Hockney's fascination with the history of style, so evident in the California paintings, makes him a born travel illustrator, as his photos, drawings, and paintings of Egypt and China demonstrate. The Egyptian series made for the *Times* in 1963, Geldzahler asserts, shows "the artist as a sharply observant tourist collecting information for the benefit of the Home Counties—the Englishman abroad. Like Edward Lear or Graham Greene, he displays an affectionate yet wrily ironic view of the exotic."

Hockney, defining himself as cosmopolitan, remains sufficiently English to discern the foreign anomaly from the English norm.

In *China Diary* Hockney, himself from the working class, exhibits optimism about people's ability to communicate and create, but few illusions about communism. Spender welcomes his opinions, which derive authority from their pungency and directness, even when they contradict his own, as when Hockney counters the truism about China's being a classless society: "Actually, nothing could be further from the truth. There is more difference here between the peasants, who, we are told, form 80% of the population, and the townspeople than anything you'll find in England." And at a market outside Peking where peasants are allowed to sell a few surplus goods, he remarks: "You see, they're happier here. They're hustling." On his own turf, meeting officially appointed art teachers and students from the Central Academy of Fine Arts, Peking, he insists even more firmly that the system cannot determine the nature of the individual: "David asked rather pointedly: 'Do you notice that certain artists are very good at painting—better than others?'"

The opposite of orthodoxy is naïveté, which for Hockney is closely identified with esthetic vision. He finds them combined in a boy painter at Kweilin who sulks when asked to perform for guests: "He's the most interesting painter we've seen yet in China. He knows exactly what he's doing. Naturally he doesn't want to bother with us." Hockney gives him some art materials and shows him how to use them. "From that moment," Spender records, "it was as though the two of them were at one, children or artists, or both." Encapsulating his approach to experience, Hockney recalls a children's park in Canton, which "had an unbelievable innocence about it, more so than you would find here in L.A. The simplification of the forms of those animals [painted on the playground equipment]. . . . It was the most human part of China, the real people, like all human beings, brothers really, and it gave you that feeling. And it gave you it in a simple childlike way which the political way, trying to do something similar, does not." Hockney's simplicity of esthetic apprehension is, of course, deceptive. While manifesting an immediate delight in seeing, making images, and handling materials, his illustrations play with layers of representation as complex as Spender's verbal analyses.

The visuals in *China Diary* illustrate the celebrated *faux naïveté* of Hockney's vision. In a colored drawing of two poets and two guides sitting around a coffee table at the office of *Poetry Magazine* in Peking, he provides journalistic information in the guides' watchful body language, the editor's mature expression compared to the student poet's inchoate one, and the utilitarian sparseness of the symmetrically arranged room. Dominating the picture, however, is a large, oblong, peagreen thermos bottle, sitting among blue and white china mugs and a sugarbowl on the table. True, the thermos conveys journalistic information by showing the entry of Western convenience into this already anomalous combination of gracious tradition and communist earnestness. Yet it dominates almost irrelevantly because Hockney seems to have fallen in love with its shape and color.

Hockney's fascination with the history of style and layers of representation emerges in these images of China. At the Great Wild Goose Pagoda in Sian, part of a seventh-century Buddhist monastery, Spender reports that below "the stone-coloured pagoda towering rather gloomy in the distance, there was a table with a vase of flowers and a solitary chair about a foot away, to one side. The top of the hedge was a light-yellowish green, with shadow below that. David took a photograph of what seemed very much a David Hockney arrangement." The photo is a still life true to the Chinese penchant for symmetry, the step-sided pagoda centered so that the windows in the middle of each story line up like buttons, the table and chair directly below. The furniture, however, although deliberately arranged down to the flowerpot, introduces a recreational touch into the scene of monastic austerity.

Here visitors to the pagoda are photographed, Hockney explains in his book entitled *Photographs* (1982), "as it used to be in Europe by the seaside, [by] a man with a big camera. . . . it was absolutely charming." Result: a photograph of an old-world European portrait setting in the middle of "modern" China which, because no one is sitting in it, changes from representational prop to represented subject. The photograph captures a natural Hockney scene, not only because it contains the formal elements suggested by Spender, but because it juxtaposes two very different works of "art"—the ancient Chinese temple and the "old-world" European portrait setting—within one frame.

Hockney shows the same ability to isolate images, play with abstractions and convey a sense of place in three photographs taken at the bridge across the Yangtze at Nanking. The first shows the shadow cast on the river's surface by Gregory Evans smoking a cigarette. A leafy twig floats by his head, which emphasizes that the river surface is also a picture plane; the elegant shadow implies the proximity of Evans who is contingent with but separate from the picture. The next is a photograph of a sign bearing Chinese characters and the translation NO SMOKING! NO PICTURE! which has no framing device except the tacks that probably attach the sign to the bridge where Evans stands smoking and where Hockney photographs him. The third is a shot of Evans through a plexiglass case enclosing a scale-model of the bridge. To analyze fully Hockney's play here with surface planes and natural and artificial objects would be to kill it, if I haven't already; I'll just point out that the harmless subversion of official rules narrated in the series is de rigueur for literary and artistic Englishmen abroad.

Neither elegists of empire nor apologists for capitalism, Spender and Hockney exhibit in mild form what Fussell considers the characteristic trait of English travelers, "a powerful strain of lawless eccentricity and flagrant individualism." That is, they entertain the reader by defining themselves whimsically against the foreign place: sensual, irreverent humanists with a detached view of history, they wander through an earnest, teleological China. When a guide in Peking scoldingly relates how a nineteenth-century empress built a marble replica of a steamboat with embezzled public monies, Spender writes, "David and I could not help feeling a little sympathy for the Empress Dowager . . . this Sitwellian ghost. To us . . . there was something about the atmosphere of the Summer Palace that made it feel like many Victorian parks and gardens: that it was presided over by some fairy godmother, perhaps wicked but with a magic wand just the same." This is the mildly subversive, imaginative spirit that allows Hockney, the working-class artist, to create stage designs for the "ludicrously anachronistic" Glyndebourne festival and Spender, the old leftist poet, to feel in Glyndebourne's aristocratic fantasy setting that perhaps "the past has established a just claim to criticize the present."

The frontispiece photograph shows Hockney photographing Gregory Evans, Mr. Lin, Spender, and himself in a mirror somewhere near the Great Wall. Hockney seems to be suggesting that travelers of today, like those of the romantic age of travel regretted by Waugh, seek abroad the image of themselves superimposed against an exotic backdrop. Yet Spender and Hockney's evident purpose is to travel beyond the self, to reveal in a dual perspective something of China's complex actuality. If the book entertains with their distance from puritan China—toward the end of the trip, "a bit ashamed, we admitted to each other that we were looking forward to the fleshpots of Hong Kong"—it also instructs with their attempt to raise the question, all joking aside: "Which do we prefer? The People's Republic of China or Hong Kong?"

The question is left open because Spender and Hockney's ideal city would combine Peking's civic responsibility with Hong Kong's individual freedom. That they leave the question open is a sign of their sophistication as travel writers: they have avoided the trap Waugh deplored of writing propaganda and also the trap he fell into of writing an elegy for the romantic age of travel, before the foreign "other" wore Communist Party pajamas. Instead, they have written a travel book for an age of anthropological doubt, one that registers the complex reality of the foreign place and the uncertainty of a traveler's interpretations. Trained though he may be in the liberal tradition of critical thinking, Spender has not entrusted the task to himself alone, but relies on the younger Hockney's intuition to "correct" his own thirties-style political analysis. Though still too enmeshed in European prejudices for some readers' tastes, perhaps, *China Diary* nonetheless presents a lively and candid view of China and of Spender and Hockney in collaboration.

WORKS CITED

Auden, W. H. *The English Auden: Poems, Essays, and Dramatic Writings, 1927–1939.* Ed. Edward Mendelson. New York: Random House, 1977.

Auden, W. H., and Christopher Isherwood. *Journey to a War.* 1939. Rpt. New York: Octagon-Farrar, 1972.

Auden, W. H., and Louis MacNeice. *Letters from Iceland.* New York: Random House, 1937.

Fussell, Paul. *Abroad: British Literary Traveling Between the Wars.* New York: Oxford UP, 1980.

———. "Shadows on Tour." Rev. of *China Diary*, by Stephen Spender and David Hockney. *Times Literary Supplement*, 26 November 1982, 1294.

Hockney, David. *David Hockney.* Ed. Nikos Stangos. Introd. Henry Geldzahler. New York: Harry N. Abrams, 1977.

———. *Photographs.* London: Petersburg, 1982.

Hynes, Samuel. *The Auden Generation: Literature and Politics in England in the 1930s.* 1976. Rpt. Princeton: Princeton UP, 1982.

Lévi-Strauss, Claude. *Chaire d'Anthropologie sociale: Leù inaugurale fait le 6 janvier 1960 par M. Claude Lévi-Strauss, Professor.* No. 31. Paris: Coll. de France, 1960. Rpt. as "The Scope of Anthropology." In *Structural Anthropology.* Vol. 2. Trans. Monique Layton. New York: Basic, 1976, 3–32.

Naipaul, Shiva. *North of South: An African Journey.* 1978. Rpt. Harmondsworth, Eng.: Penguin, 1984.

Raban, Jonathan. *Arabia: A Journey Through the Labyrinth.* New York: Simon & Schuster, 1979.

Spender, Stephen. "Text to Image." In *Hockney Paints the Stage*. Ed. Martin Friedman. New York: Abbeville, 1983, 61–75.

————. *The Thirties and After: Poetry, Politics, People 1933–1970*. New York: Vintage–Random House, 1979.

Spender, Stephen, and David Hockney. *China Diary*. New York: Harry N. Abrams, 1982.

Theroux, Paul. *The Great Railway Bazaar: By Train Through Asia*. 1975. Rpt. New York: Random House–Ballantine, 1983.

————. "Memories of Old Afghanistan." In *Sunrise with Seamonsters: Travels and Discoveries 1964–1984*. Boston: Houghton Mifflin, 1985, 109–22.

Thieme, John. "Authorial Voice in V. S. Naipaul's *The Middle Passage*." In *The Art of Travel: Essays on Travel Writing*. Ed. Philip Dodd. Towata, N.J.: Frank Cass, 1982, 139–50.

Waugh, Evelyn. *When the Going Was Good*. 1946. Rpt. Boston: Little, Brown, 1962.

≺ ≺ ≺ ≺ ≺ ≺

Travel Writing Since 1900: A Selective Chronology and Bibliography

> > > > > > **A Note About**
the Chronology
and Bibliography

There is at present no accessible general bibliography of twentieth-century travel writing. This bibliography, while not exhaustive, is designed to convey a sense of the range, diversity, and multicultural richness of travel writing in this century. It includes both well-known and obscure works and authors, and it offers readers several ways of finding (and thinking about) them.

The books in this century falling under the rubric "the literature of travel" number in the thousands. My decisions about which texts to include have thus been guided by certain principles of selection. A few collections of poetry have been listed, but I have not included any fiction. Nor have I included autobiographies, memoirs, or collections of personal essays unless they include a significant number of travel essays.

Among the nonfictional narratives that form the bulk of the material listed, I have included only books in which travel itself plays a significant role. If travel simply provided the precondition for a writer's extended sojourn in a place that he or she then describes, I have not included it. Thus, such otherwise estimable works as E. M. Forster's *Alexandria: A History and Guide* (1922), Isak Dinesen's *Out of Africa* (1937), Marjorie Kinnan Rawlings's *Cross Creek* (1942), V. S. Pritchett's *London Perceived* (1962), Andrea Lee's *Russian Journal* (1981), Terry Tempest Williams's *Pieces of White Shell* (1984), and George Packer's *The Village of Waiting* (1988) have not been included here. The exception to this rule is that I have included a few works (e.g., Vera Brittain's *Thrice a Stranger* [1938] and Jonathan Raban's *Hunting Mister Heartbreak* [1990]) in which each writer describes living in several different places.

I have refrained from including straightforward autobiographies or works in which "travel" signifies primarily a spiritual or metaphoric journey rather than an actual one. Therefore books such as Paul Zweig's *Three Journeys: An Automythology* (1976) have not been included in this bibliography. I have also not listed "picture books" in which the text serves only as an adjunct to the photos; nor have I included books about sailing, mountaineering, or sporting or scientific expeditions when they have appeared too specialized or too technical. Even with this proviso, works about adventure travel make up a sizable portion of this list.

The chronology includes all the works (except anthologies and critical studies) listed in the bibliography. Together these two listings provide three separate ways to search for a book: by date of original publication (in the chronology, arranged alphabetically by title for each year), by the author's last name (arranged alphabetically within the bibliographic entries for each country) and by the author's nationality (in the bibliography). The cross-referenced chronology is meant to offer a preliminary chronological/contextual perspective on material that the bibliography alone could not provide.

My reference source for copyright and title information on works before 1956 was the *National Union Catalog (Pre-1956 Imprints)*. Information on works published after that date has been culled, in the majority of cases, from the books themselves. The bibliography contains several books by authors writing in languages other than English, but I have included only those that have been translated into English. If there was a difference of more than a year between the copyright date of the original and that of the translation, this has been noted parenthetically in the chronology. All other parenthetical references to date in the chronology refer to the date of publication when there was a significant discrepancy between that date and the time at which the work was actually written. (The letters included in *Willa Cather in Europe*, for instance, were not published until 1956. But because they were written in 1902, I have listed the book under the latter date in the chronology.) The secondary bibliography is limited to book-length critical studies or collections of essays. References to most of the recent critical essays of note on travel and travel writing can be found in the "Works Cited" pages of contributors' essays.

I have listed authors by their nationality, but "nationality" has proven in some cases to be a problematic term. Take the case of Peter Goullart, for instance, author of *Land of the Lamas* (1959). Born in Moscow in 1902 and educated privately at home by tutors, he fled with his mother from the Russian Revolution into China in 1919. He learned Chinese, studied in Taoist monasteries and was a cooperative expert for Chinese Industrial Co-operatives in China and Eastern Tibet from 1939 to 1949. He later lived in Switzerland for nine years but also in England. He continued to travel, work, and live in southeast Asia for much of his life. He was a member of the Society of Authors in London, and the reference work *Contemporary Authors* specified his address as "c/o John Murray (Publishers) Ltd." I have listed Goullart as an English writer; it was clearly a judgment call. Similar decisions have been made with a number of the authors listed below.

> > > > > > Travel Writing Since 1900:
A Selective Chronology

1900	*Sailing Alone Around the World*, Joshua Slocum
	A Sportswoman in India, Isabel Savory
	3800 Miles Across Canada, J. W. C. Haldane
1901	*Afoot Through the Kashmir Valleys*, Marion Doughty
1902	*The Path to Rome*, Hilaire Belloc
	Seventy-One Days' Camping in Morocco, Agnes Grove
	Through Hidden Shensi, Francis Nichols
	Willa Cather in Europe (1956), Willa Cather
1903	*Cities*, Arthur Symons
	In the Tail of the Peacock, Isabel Savory
	Old Time Travel, Alexander Innes Shand
	Travels in Europe and America, Charles Edward Bolton
	Two Country Walks in Canada, Arnold Haultain
1904	*Highways and Byways of the South*, Clifton Johnson
	The Old Road, Hilaire Belloc
	Through the Lands of the Serb, Edith Durham
1905	*English Hours*, Henry James
	Italian Backgrounds, Edith Wharton
	London Films, William Dean Howells
	Two Years in the Antarctic, Albert B. Armitage
1906	*Certain Delightful English Towns*, William Dean Howells
	Highways and Byways of the Mississippi Valley, Clifton Johnson
	Hills and the Sea, Hilaire Belloc
	On Tramp Among the Mongols, John Hedley
	Ten Thousand Miles in a Yacht, Richard Arthur
1907	*The American Scene*, Henry James
	In Other Lands than Ours, Maud Gage Baum
	Pekin to Paris, Luigi Barzini
	Syria: The Desert and the Sown, Gertrude Bell
1908	*The Cruise of the Snark*, Jack London
	En Route, Roy Trevor
	A Motor-Flight Through France, Edith Wharton

Et Nos in Arctis, Adelaide M. Gerard
Familiar Spanish Travels, William Dean Howells
A Woman's Winter in Africa, Charlotte Cameron
1914   *Abroad at Home*, Julian Leonard Street
Adventures of the Far North, Stephen Leacock
The Ascent of Denali, Hudson Stuck
On Old-World Highways, Thomas D. Murphy
Ten Thousand Miles with a Dog Sled, Hudson Stuck
Through the Grand Canyon, Ellsworth L. Kolb
1915   *Australian Byways*, Norman Duncan
The Conquest of Mt. Cook and Other Climbs, Freda
Du Faur
Old Calabria, Norman Douglas
Travels in Alaska, John Muir
Two Vagabonds in Serbia and Montenegro (1939), Jan
Gordon and Cora Gordon
1916   *A Handy Guide for Beggars*, Vachel Lindsay
Letters from America, Rupert Brooke
A Thousand-Mile Walk to the Gulf, John Muir
Through Russian Central Asia, Stephen Graham
Twilight in Italy, D. H. Lawrence
1917   *American Adventures*, Julian Leonard Street
*Tramping Through Mexico, Guatemala and Hon-
duras*, Harry A. Franck
Voyages on the Yukon, Hudson Stuck
1918   *Cities and Sea-Coasts and Islands*, Arthur Symons
Oriental Encounters, Marmaduke Pickthall
Steep Trails, John Muir
1919   *California Desert Trails*, John Smeaton Chase
In Morocco, Edith Wharton
Unconducted Wanderers, Rosita Forbes
What to See in America, Clifton Johnson
White Shadows in the South Seas, Frederick O'Brien

1920   *A Canadian Tour*, Edward W. Watt
A Cheechako in Alaska and Yukon, Charlotte
Cameron
Hither and Thither in Germany, William Dean
Howells
Vagabonding Through Changing Germany, Harry A.
Franck
Westward with the Prince of Wales, W. Douglas
Newton
1921   *Down the Columbia*, Lewis R. Freeman

Down the World's Most Dangerous River, Clyde Eddy
Jungle Days, William Beebe
Mt. Eryx and Other Diversions of Travel, Henry
   Festing Jones
Mystic Isles of the South Seas, Frederick O'Brien
Sea and Sardinia, D. H. Lawrence
The Secret of the Sahara: Kufara, Rosita Forbes
Where the Strange Trails Go Down, E. Alexander
   Powell
Working North from Patagonia, Harry A. Franck

1922   *Across the Prairie in a Motor Caravan*, Eva Hasell
Atolls of the Sun, Frederick O'Brien
Canadian Cities of Romance, Katherine Hale
Cannibal-Land, Martin Johnson
A Motor Scamper 'Cross Canada, Percy Gomery
Mountain Madness, Helen Hamilton
My Discovery of England, Stephen Leacock
Over Prairie Trails, Frederick Philip Grove
The Peaks of Shala, Rose Wilder Lane
The Track of the "Typhoon," William Washburn
Tramping with a Poet in the Rockies, Stephen Graham
What I Saw in America, G. K. Chesterton
The Worst Journey in the World, Apsley Cherry-
   Garrard

1923   *American Travels of a Dutch Hobo* (1984), Gerard
   Leeflang
By Camel and Car to the Peacock Throne, E. Alexan-
   der Powell
Hilltops in Galilee, Harold Speakman
In Quest of El Dorado, Stephen Graham
Roman Pictures, Percy Lubbock
The Southern Sierras of California, Charles Francis
   Saunders
Wandering in Northern China, Harry A. Franck
Wide Seas and Many Lands, Arthur Mason

1924   *Camera Trails in Africa*, Martin Johnson
From China to Hkamti Long, F. Kingdon Ward
Glimpses of Japan and Formosa, Harry A. Franck
Grecian Italy, Henry James Forman
Pearls and Savages, Frank Hurley
The Road to Timbuktu, Dorothy Mills
Through Central France to the Pyrenees, Maude Speed
Tidemarks, H. M. Tomlinson

In Egypt, John C. Van Dyke
In the World's Attic, Henrietta Sands Merrick
Jungle Ways, William B. Seabrook
The Macadam Trail, Mary Day Winn
Paradise Quest, Lee Saunders Crandall
Pigs in Clover, Frances Noyes Hart
Remote People, Evelyn Waugh
The Spring Journey, Alan Pryce-Jones
They Were Still Dancing, Evelyn Waugh

1932   *Across Lapland with Sledge and Reindeer*, Olive
        Murray Chapman
        Afloat and Aflight in the Caribbean, Lewis R. Freeman
        Death in the Afternoon, Ernest Hemingway
        Etruscan Places, D. H. Lawrence
        Filibusters in Barbary, Wyndham Lewis
        The Flying Carpet, Richard Halliburton
        In the West Indies, John C. Van Dyke
        Iorana! Robert Gibbings
        Lower California: A Cruise, Griffing Bancroft
        Olivia's African Diary (1980), Olivia Stokes Hatch
        A Superficial Journey Through Tokyo and Peking,
        Peter Quennell
        Three Lands on Three Wheels, Jan Gordon and Cora
        Gordon
        Winters of Content, Osbert Sitwell

1933   *Air Adventure*, William B. Seabrook
        Brazilian Adventure, Peter Fleming
        Down and Out in Paris and London, George Orwell
        First Russia, Then Tibet, Robert Byron
        In Scotland Again, H. V. Morton
        Journey to Armenia (1979), Osip Mandelstam
        Raggle Taggle, Walter Starkie
        A Scamper Tour to Rhodesia and South Africa,
        Maude Speed
        Solo (1983), Wright Morris
        South African Summer, Dorothy Una Ratcliffe
        Spoken in Tibet, Henrietta Sands Merrick
        Tschiffely's Ride, Aimé Felix Tschiffely

1934   *Beyond the Mexique Bay*, Aldous Huxley
        Derby Day and Other Adventures, Alfred Edward
        Newton
        English Journey, J. B. Priestley
        A Girl Before the Mast, Betty Jacobsen

In All Countries, John Dos Passos
Ninety-Two Days, Evelyn Waugh
North to the Rime-Ringed Sun, Isobel Wylie
    Hutchison
One's Company, Peter Fleming
Suburban Columbus, John Gibbons
Tents in Mongolia, Henning Haslund
Turkestan Solo, Ella Maillart
The Valleys of the Assassins, Freya Stark

1935   *Africa Dances*, Geoffrey Gorer
Arctic Adventure, Peter Freuchen
Green Hills of Africa, Ernest Hemingway
A Journal of a Voyage, Dora Birtles
Men Against the Clouds, Richard Burdsall and Arthur
    Emmons
Scottish Journey, Edwin Muir
Seven League Boots, Richard Halliburton
Spanish Adventure, Norman Lewis
Speak to the Earth, Vivienne De Watteville
Trailing Cortez Through Mexico, Harry A. Franck
The Two Roads of Papua, Evelyn Cheesman

1936   *Aerial Odyssey*, E. Alexander Powell
The Ascent of Mt. Stalin, Michael Romm
Don Gypsy, Walter Starkie
Equatorial Dawn, Dorothy Una Ratcliffe
Green Mountains to Sierras, Zephine Humphrey
Journey Without Maps, Graham Greene
News from Tartary, Peter Fleming
No Place Like Home, Beverley Nichols
Sailing South American Skies, James Saxon Childers
South African Summer, Dorothy Una Ratcliffe
The Southern Gates of Arabia, Freya Stark
Travels in Two Democracies, Edmund Wilson
Waugh in Abyssinia, Evelyn Waugh
Where Life Is Better, James Rorty

1937   *Across Cyprus*, Olive Murray Chapman
An Artist in America, Thomas Hart Benton
The Cruise of the Bouncing Betsy, J. N. Darling
Discovering South America, Lewis R. Freeman
Forbidden Journey, Ella Maillart
Forbidden Road, Rosita Forbes
Great Trade Route, Ford Maddox Ford
Journey to the Morea (1965), Nikos Kazantzakis

Laughing Odyssey, Eileen Bigland
Letters from Iceland, W. H. Auden and Louis Mac-
  Neice
My Discovery of the West, Stephen Leacock
Northward Ho! Harold Nossiter
Return from the U.S.S.R., André Gide
The Road to Oxiana, Robert Byron
The Road to Wigan Pier, George Orwell
Spain, Nikos Kazantzakis
Stepping Stones from Alaska to Asia, Isobel Wylie
  Hutchison
Where Seldom a Gun Is Heard, Anthony Jenkinson
You Have Seen Their Faces, Erskine Caldwell and
  Margaret Bourke-White

1938   *Blue Angels and Whales*, Robert Gibbings
Canoe Errant on the Mississippi, Rowland
  Raven-Hart
Homage to Catalonia, George Orwell
I Crossed the Minch, Louise MacNeice
Japan/China, Nikos Kazantzakis
Journey to Manáos, Earl Parker Hanson
Journeys Between Wars, John Dos Passos
Just for the Hell of It, Kenneth Collings
Lodging for a Night, Duncan Hines
The Other Side of the Mountain, James Ramsey
  Ullman
Sand and Sea in Arabia, Norman Lewis
Thrice a Stranger, Vera Brittain
Through the Kitchen Door, Grace Smith et al.
Voyaging Down the Thames, Clyde Eddy
With Malice Towards Some, Margaret Halsey

1939   *Eastern Visas*, Audrey Harris
Going Places, Colin Hood
Hell! I'm British, Andrew George Elliot
I Went to the Soviet Arctic, Ruth Gruber
Journey to a War, W. H. Auden and Christopher
  Isherwood
The Lake of the Royal Crocodiles, Eileen Bigland
The Lawless Roads, Graham Greene
News of Persephone, Dorothy Una Ratcliffe
Outboard Cruising, Don Waters
Red Horizons, George Digby
Seven Seas on a Shoestring, Dwight Long

A Unicorn in the Bahamas, Rosita Forbes
Wind, Sand and Stars, Antoine de Saint-Exupéry

1940   *The "Argonauts,"* Lillian E. Ross et al.
A Doctor's Holiday in Iran, Rosalie Slaughter Morton
Helvellyn to Himalaya, F. Spencer Chapman
Into China, Eileen Bigland
An Irish Journey, Sean O'Faolain
Land Without Laughter, Ahmad Kamal
Sweet Thames Run Softly, Robert Gibbings
A Winter in Arabia, Freya Stark

1941   *Black Lamb and Grey Falcon*, Rebecca West
The Colossus of Maroussi, Henry Miller
England (1965), Nikos Kazantzakis
Last Man Around the World, Stephen Longstreet
Let Us Now Praise Famous Men, James Agee
Middle East, H. V. Morton
Places, Hilaire Belloc
Sea of Cortez, John Steinbeck and Edward F. Ricketts

1942   *Coming Down the Wye*, Robert Gibbings
Cruises and Caravans, Ella Maillart
The Gobi Desert, Mildred Cable and Francesca French
Gypsy A-Float, Ella Maillart
I Saw Two Englands, H. V. Morton
The Last Cannibals, Jens Bjerre
The Last Man Comes Home, Stephen Longstreet
Letters from Syria, Freya Stark
Saddlebags for Suitcases, Mary Bosanquet
The Unknown Country, Bruce Hutchison
West with the Night, Beryl Markham

1943   *Across Madagascar*, Olive Murray Chapman
A Picture Book, Frank O'Connor

1944   *American Trails*, J. B. Murray
People on Our Side, Edgar Snow

1945   *African Journey*, Eslanda Goode Robeson
The Air-Conditioned Nightmare, Henry Miller
Lovely Is the Lee, Robert Gibbings
Prospero's Cell, Lawrence Durrell

1946   *Mongolian Journey* (1949), Henning Haslund
When the Going Was Good, Evelyn Waugh

1947   *The Cruel Way*, Ella Maillart
Europe Without Baedeker, Edmund Wilson

Home Country, Ernie Pyle
Irish Miles, Frank O'Connor
1948   *From the Heart of Europe*, F. O. Matthiessen
In Search of South Africa, H. V. Morton
Journey to the Alcarria (1964), Camilo José Cela
Journey to Egypt, Eileen Bigland
A Russian Journal, John Steinbeck
1949   *The Condor and the Cows*, Christopher Isherwood
Fabled Shore, Rose Macaulay
Six-Legged Snakes in New Guinea, Evelyn Cheesman
The Sugar Islands, Alec Waugh

1950   *The Face of the Earth*, H. M. Tomlinson
Jungle Journey, Ethel Edith Mannin
Kon-Tiki, Thor Heyerdahl
Leinster, Munster and Connaught, Frank O'Connor
The Traveller's Tree, Patrick Leigh Fermor
1951   *Beyond Euphrates*, Freya Stark
Caucasian Journey, Negley Farson
A Dragon Apparent, Norman Lewis
Hands Across the Pacific, Frank Clune
I Cannot Rest from Travel, Willard Price
I'll Fly No More, Ursula Barnett Potter
Last Voyage, Ann Davison
The Log from the "Sea of Cortez," John Steinbeck
North with the Spring, Edwin Way Teale
Sails and Whales, Harry Allen Chippendale
Ti-Puss, Ella Maillart
A Western Journal, Thomas Wolfe
1952   *American Days*, Phiroze Dustoor
The Dragon and the Unicorn, Kenneth Rexroth
A Forgotten Journey, Peter Fleming
Golden Earth, Norman Lewis
A Pattern of Islands, Arthur Grimble
A Sabine Journey, Anthony Rhodes
Tents and Towers of Arabia, Robert Shaffer
Where the Clocks Chime Twice, Alec Waugh
1953   *The Coast of Incense*, Freya Stark
Coming Down the Seine, Robert Gibbings
Exploration Fawcett, P. H. Fawcett
The Hill of Devi, E. M. Forster
The Overloaded Ark, Gerald Durrell

Lost World of the Kalahari, Laurens Van Der Post
Love and the Caribbean, Alec Waugh
Mani, Patrick Leigh Fermor
A Short Walk in the Hindu Kush, Eric Newby
The Spirit of Mediterranean Places (1986), Michel
    Butor

1959   *Arabian Sands*, Wilfred Thesiger
The Bridge of the Brocade Sash, Sacheverell Sitwell
The Desperate People, Farley Mowat
The Flight of Ikaros, Kevin Andrews
Get Up and Go, Don White
Land of the Lamas, Peter Goullart
Land of the Lotus Eaters, Norman Bartlett
The Light of Common Day, Diana Cooper
A Passage to England, Nirad C. Chaudhuri
Riding to the Tigris, Freya Stark
The Stones of Florence, Mary McCarthy
A Train to Tarragona, Anthony Carson

1960   *Follow the North Star*, Tay Thomas
Goodbye to a River, John Graves
Journey into Summer, Edwin Way Teale
Lonesome Traveler, Jack Kerouac
Offbeat in Asia, Michael Alexander
Tourist in Africa, Evelyn Waugh

1961   *Blue Skies, Brown Studies*, William Sansom
The Buffalo Head, Raymond M. Patterson
The Cloud Forest, Peter Matthiessen
The Forgotten Peninsula, Joseph Wood Krutch
Golden Wall and Mirador, Sacheverell Sitwell
In Search of a Character, Graham Greene
In Search of Sheba, Barbara Toy
The Lonely Land, Sigurd F. Olson
The Lost Towns & Roads of America, John R. Hum-
    phreys
Winter Shoes in Springtime, Beryl Smeeton

1962   *Brazil*, Elizabeth Bishop
By Gemini, Ann Davison
The Middle Passage, V. S. Naipaul
Travels, Anthony Carson
Travels with Charley, John Steinbeck

1963   *An African Abroad*, Olabisi Ajala
Brazil on the Move, John Dos Passos

Mobile, Michel Butor

Their Heads Are Green and Their Hands Are Blue,
   Paul Bowles

Two Middle-Aged Ladies in Andalusia, Penelope
   Chetwode

Under a Lilac-Bleeding Star, Lesley Blanch

1964   *An Area of Darkness*, V. S. Naipaul

Florida Junket, Ann Davison

Home Is a Tent, Myrtle Simpson

Journey into Russia, Laurens Van Der Post

The Marsh Arabs, Wilfred Thesiger

Next Generation, David Pryce-Jones

The Offensive Traveller, V. S. Pritchett

Road to Volgograd, Alan Sillitoe

Round the World in 70 Days, Bernard Newman

This Is My Country Too, John A. Williams

The Thousand-Mile Summer, Colin Fletcher

Tracking Marco Polo, Tim Severin

A Traveller in Italy, H. V. Morton

The Way of the Chariots, Barbara Toy

1965   *Full Tilt*, Dervla Murphy

I See By My Outfit, Peter Beagle

Questions of Travel, Elizabeth Bishop

Strange Island, Arvid Klemensen

Wandering Through Winter, Edwin Way Teale

1966   *All the Time in the World*, Hugo Williams

Journey About Myself, Félix Martí-Ibáñez

Journey to the East (1987), Le Corbusier

Roumeli, Patrick Leigh Fermor

Slowly Down the Ganges, Eric Newby

Trail to the Interior, Raymond M. Patterson

1967   *Gipsy Moth Circles the World*, Francis Chichester

The Man Who Walked Through Time, Colin Fletcher

The Voices of Marrakesh (1978), Elias Canetti

The Waiting Land, Dervla Murphy

White Horizons, Myrtle Simpson

Who Needs a Road? Harold Stephens and Albert
   Podell

1968   *The Highway of the Three Kings*, Barbara Toy

In Ethiopia with a Mule, Dervla Murphy

Journey Through Britain, John D. Hillaby

Trip to Hanoi, Susan Sontag

1969   *As I Walked Out One Midsummer Morning*, Laurie
        Lee
        Notes from the Century Before, Edward Hoagland
        Odd Way Round the World, Willard Price
        Seven League Boots, Wendy Myers
        Spirit of Place, Lawrence Durrell
        The Sun in My Eyes, Beverley Nichols
        Voyage to Atlantis, James W. Mavor

1970   *Due North*, Myrtle Simpson
        The Mexican Night, Lawrence Ferlinghetti
        The Minaret of Djam, Freya Stark
        Springtime in Britain, Edwin Way Teale
1971   *Across a Darkling Plain*, Marshall Frady
        Britannia, John Fairfax
        The Ra Expeditions, Thor Heyerdahl
        Voyage by Bus, Leonard Wibberley
        The Winds Call, Carleton Mitchell
1972   *Amazon Journey*, John Ridgway
        Among the Believers, V. S. Naipaul
        For Better, For Worse, Marika Hanbury-Tenison
        The Light Garden of the Angel King, Peter Levi
        Oars Across the Pacific, John Fairfax and Sylvia Cook
        Places, James Morris
1973   *A China Passage*, John Kenneth Galbraith
        But I Wouldn't Have Missed It for the World, Peg
        Bracken
        Manscapes, Colin Henfrey
        Masquerade, Sarah Hobson
1974   *Cutting Loose*, James Lipscomb
        Fatu-Hiva, Thor Heyerdahl
        The Fearful Void, Geoffrey Moorhouse
        Florida Ramble, Alex Shoumatoff
        High Time, Louise Hillary
        The Scent of India (1984), Pier Paolo Pasolini
        A Slice of Spice, Marika Hanbury-Tenison
        Through Black Eyes, Elton C. Fax
        A Traveler's Tale, Enid Saunders Candlin
        Winter in Castille, Honor Tracy
        Zen and the Art of Motorcycle Maintenance, Robert
        Pirsig
1975   *The Dancing Waiters*, Joseph Hone

The Great Himalayan Passage, Michel Peissel
The Great Railway Bazaar, Paul Theroux
Narrowgauge to Riobamba, John Brandi
Passage to Ararat, Michael J. Arlen
Run, River, Run, Ann Zwinger
The Survival of the Bark Canoe, John McPhee
1976   *Afternoons in Mid-America*, Erskine Caldwell
Airborne, William F. Buckley, Jr.
Indian Action, Stuart Mitchner
Journey into Silence, Jack Denton Scott
On a Shoestring to Coorg, Dervla Murphy
To Jerusalem and Back, Saul Bellow
Travels Around America, Harrison E. Salisbury
1977   *Coming into the Country*, John McPhee
A Drive Across Africa, Ferenc J. Bodó
Grand and Private Pleasures, Caskie Stinnett
The Hidden Canyon, John Blaustein
The Incredible Voyage, Tristan Jones
India: A Wounded Civilization, V. S. Naipaul
In Patagonia, Bruce Chatwin
The Journey Home, Edward Abbey
Sicilian Carousel, Lawrence Durrell
Storm Passage, Webb Chiles
A Time of Gifts, Patrick Leigh Fermor
Where the Indus is Young, Dervla Murphy
1978   *The Big Red Train Ride*, Eric Newby
The Brendan Voyage, Tim Severin
Diary from Baja California, John Brandi
Mountain Passages, Jeremy Bernstein
North of South, Shiva Naipaul
The Rivers Amazon, Alex Shoumatoff
The Snow Leopard, Peter Matthiessen
The Starship and the Canoe, Kenneth Brower
Travels with Myself and Another, Martha Gellhorn
Wind in the Rock, Ann Zwinger
1979   *African Calliope*, Edward Hoagland
Arabia, Jonathan Raban
Chinese Encounters, Arthur Miller and Inge Morath
Dateline America, Charles Kuralt
Diary from a Journey to the Middle of the World, John
        Brandi
Journeys Through the South, Fred Powledge
Jupiter's Travels, Ted Simon

The Old Patagonian Express, Paul Theroux
Saga of a Wayward Sailor, Tristan Jones
"Seraffyn's" European Adventure, Lin Pardey and
    Larry Pardey
Travels with Fortune, Christina Dodwell
A Walk Across America, Peter Jenkins

1980   *Annapurna*, Arlene Blum
Destinations, Jan Morris
Going to Extremes, Joe McGinniss
The Hidden West, Rob Schultheis
The Hill of Kronos, Peter Levi
States of Desire, Edmund White and Adam Mars-Jones
Stones of Silence, George Schaller
Third-Class Ticket, Heather Wood
Tracks, Robyn Davidson

1981   *An African in Greenland* (1983), Tété-Michel Kpo-
    massie
The Fortunate Traveler, Derek Walcott
Gone Tomorrow, Joseph Hone
Halfway Around the World, Gavin Young
Hard Road West, Gwen Moffat
A Journey Through Afghanistan, David Chaffetz
Letters from the Antipodes, Michel Butor
Mucking Around, Naomi Mitchison
No Particular Place to Go, Hugo Williams
Old Glory, Jonathan Raban
Rowing Toward Eden, Ted Morgan
Sand Rivers, Peter Matthiessen
Slow Boats to China, Gavin Young
The Walk West, Peter Jenkins and Barbara Jenkins

1982   *Atlantic High*, William F. Buckley, Jr.
Blue Highways, William Least Heat-Moon
China Diary, Stephen Spender and David Hockney
In the Footsteps of Johnson & Boswell, Israel Shenker
Journeys into Britain, Robin Page
Scenes in America Deserta, Reyner Banham
The Sindbad Voyage, Tim Severin
The South Seas Dream, John Dyson
Special Places, Berton Roueché
Steaming to Bamboola, Christopher Buckley
Words for My Brother, John Staley

1983   *Africa Alone*, Sandy McMath

Dead Man's Chest, Nicholas Rankin
Displaced Person, John Clellon Holmes
Down in the Free State, Sam McAughtry
Downriver, Dean Krakel
Dreams of the Peaceful Dragon, Katie Hickman
Duck Soup in the Black Sea, Joseph Hone
East Along the Equator, Helen Winternitz
Elvis Presley Boulevard, Mark Winegardner
Everest Grand Circle, Ned Gillette and Jan Reynolds
Fall Out of Heaven, Alan Cheuse
First Light, Ethan Hubbard
The Good Red Road, Kenneth Lincoln and Al Logan
    Slagle
The Great Divide, Stephen Pern
Heidi's Alp, Christina Hardyment
In the Footsteps of Scott, Roger Mear and Robert
    Swan
It's a Long Road to Comondu, Everett Gee Jackson
The Jaguar Smile, Salman Rushdie
Journey to the Crest, Cindy Ross
The Life of My Choice, Wilfred Thesiger
Maple Leaf Rag, Stephen Brook
Miami, Joan Didion
New York to Nome, Rick Steber
North to the Pole, Will Steger and Paul Schurke
One for the Road, Tony Horwitz
Out West, Dayton Duncan
Over the High Passes, Christina Noble
Racing Through Paradise, William F. Buckley, Jr.
Ram Ram India, Alex Thomson and Nick Rossiter
Reach of Tide, Ring of History, Sam McKinney
A Ride Along the Great Wall, Robin Hanbury-Tenison
Riding the Dragon's Back, Richard Bangs and Chris-
    tian Kallen
Round Ireland in Low Gear, Eric Newby
The Song-Lines, Bruce Chatwin
To the Navel of the World, Peter Somerville-Large
Touch the Happy Isles, Quentin Crewe
Traveling the Trans-Canada, William Howarth
A Traveller on Horseback, Christina Dodwell
Travels with My Sketchbook, Nicholas Garland
Two Roads to Dodge City, Nigel Nicolson and Adam
    Nicolson

Stranger in the Forest, Eric Hansen
Trainsong, Jan Kerouac
Travels, Michael Crichton
Travels in Nepal, Charlie Pye-Smith
Two Against the Sahara, Michael Asher
Vanished Empire, Stephen Brook
Video Night in Kathmandu, Pico Iyer
Where the Spirits Dwell, Tobias Schneebaum
Zanzibar to Timbuktu, Anthony Daniels

1989   *An Adventure on the Old Silk Road*, John Pilkington
All the Right Places, Brad Newsham
At Home and Abroad, V. S. Pritchett
Baja Journey, Robin Carey
Behind the Mountain, Peter Conrad
Beyond the Silver River, Jimmy Burns
Cameroon with Egbert, Dervla Murphy
Crusader, Tim Severin
The Deluge and the Ark, Dale Peterson
Dust of the Saints, Radek Sikorski
El Beisbol, John Krich
Europe, Europe, Hans Magnus Enzensberger
Footloose in the Himalaya, Mike Harding
From Cape to Cairo, David Ewing Duncan
God's Dust, Ian Buruma
Great Plains, Ian Frazier
In Bolivia, Eric Lawlor
In the Himalayas, Jeremy Bernstein
In the North of Our Lives, Christopher Norment
In the Realms of Gold, Quentin Crewe
In Xanadu, William Dalrymple
Italian Days, Barbara Grizzuti Harrison
Journey Across Tibet, Sorrel Wilby
A Long Road Home, Geoffrey O'Gara
The Lost Continent, Bill Bryson
Malaria Dreams, Stuart Stevens
My Father's Island, Johanna Angermeyer
My Time in Hawaii, Victoria Nelson
On the Narrow Road, Lesley Downer
Our Grandmothers' Drums, Mark Hudson
Outposts of Eden, Page Stegner
Paddle to the Amazon, Don Starkell
Poisoned Arrows, George Monbiot
Ronda Gorge and Other Precipices, Aidan Higgins

Running in Place, Nicholas Delbanco
Running the Amazon, Joe Kane
A Scot Returns, Alastair Scott
A Singular Country, J. P. Donleavy
Sons of the Moon, Henry Shukman
The Storm Seekers, Gwen Moffat
Ticket to Latvia, Marcus Tanner
Time Among the Maya, Ronald Wright
Timeless Towns and Haunted Places, John R. Humphreys
To Run Across the Sea, Norman Lewis
Travels with Alice, Calvin Trillin
Travels with Pegasus, Christina Dodwell
A Turn in the South, V. S. Naipaul
Walking the Line, Marian Botsford Fraser
Water and Sky, Alan S. Kesselheim
A Wolverine Is Eating My Leg, Tim Cahill

1990   *Apples in the Snow*, Geoffrey Moorhouse
Boomer, Linda Niemann
Camping with the Prince, Thomas A. Bass
Caprock Canyonlands, Dan Flores
Coming Home Crazy, Bill Holm
Delta Time, Tony Dunbar
Expats, Christopher Dickey
The Good Rain, Timothy Egan
Hunting Mister Heartbreak, Jonathan Raban
Last Places, Lawrence Milliman
Magnetic North, David Halsey
Making Tracks, Terry Pindell
Middle East Journal, Laila Abou-Saif
Midnight Wilderness, Debbie S. Miller
One Dry Season, Caroline Alexander
Reflections, Graham Greene
Riding North One Summer, Bettina Selby
The Saddest Pleasure, Moritz Thomsen
Shopping for Buddhas, Jeff Greenwald
A Shout in the Street, Peter Jukes
Small Places, Thomas H. Rawls
Tracks Across Alaska, Alastair Scott
Travels in San Francisco, Herbert Gold
Tuning the Rig, Harvey Oxenhorn
Tuturani, Scott L. Malcomson

> > > > > > Travel Writing Since 1900: A Selective Bibliography

Anthologies

Crossley-Holland, Kevin, ed. *The Oxford Book of Travel Verse*. New York: Oxford UP, 1987.

Eisenberg, Lee, and Phillip Moffitt, eds. *"Esquire's" The Soul of America*. New York: Charles Scribner's Sons, 1986.

Fraser, Keath, ed. *Bad Trips*. New York: Vintage, 1991.

Fussell, Paul, ed. *The Norton Book of Travel*. New York: W. W. Norton, 1987.

Marsden-Smedley, Philip, and Jeffrey Klinke, eds. *Views From Abroad: The "Spectator" Book of Travel Writing*. London: Grafton, 1988.

Massingham, Hugh, and Pauline Massingham, eds. *The Englishman Abroad*. London: Phoenix House, 1962.

Newby, Eric, ed. *A Book of Travellers' Tales*. New York: Penguin, 1985.

Newcombe, Jack, ed. *Travels in the Americas*. New York: Weidenfeld & Nicolson, 1989.

Norwich, John Julius. *A Taste for Travel*. New York: Knopf, 1987.

Rosenthal, A. M., and Arthur Gelb, eds. *The Sophisticated Traveler: Beloved Cities, Europe*. New York: Villard, 1984.

———. *The Sophisticated Traveler: Enchanting Places and How to Find Them: From Pleasant Hill to Katmandu*. New York: Villard, 1986.

———. *The Sophisticated Traveler: Great Tours and Detours*. New York: Villard, 1985.

———. *The Sophisticated Traveler: Winter Love It or Leave It*. New York: Penguin, 1985.

Thorn, John, and David Reuther, eds. *The Armchair Traveler*. New York: Prentice Hall, 1988.

Vermeulen, James P., ed. *Mountain Journeys: Stories of Climbers and Their Climbs*. Woodstock, N.Y.: Overlook P, 1989.

Journals (Special Issues)

Biguenet, John, and John Mosier, eds. *New Orleans Review* 18, no. 2 (Summer 1991). Special issue on travel.

Buford, Bill, ed. "Travel Writing." *Granta* 10 (Winter 1981).

———. "In Trouble Again: A Special Issue of Travel Writing." *Granta* 20 (Winter 1986).

———. "Travel." *Granta* 26 (Spring 1989).

Dodd, Philip, ed. "The Art of Travel: Essays on Travel Writing." *Prose Studies* 5, no. 1 (May 1982). Reprinted in book form as *The Art of Travel* (1982).

Lewis, Robert W., ed. "Travel/Travail: A Special Issue." *North Dakota Quarterly* 54, no. 4 (Fall 1986).

MacLaren, Ian, ed. "The Literature of Travel." *Ariel* 21, no. 4 (October 1990).

Rudman, Mark, ed. "Secret Destinations: Writers on Travel." *Pequod* 19/20/21 (1985).

American Works

Abbey, Edward. *Beyond the Wall: Essays from the Outside.* New York: Holt, Rinehart & Winston, 1984.

———. *The Journey Home: Some Words in Defense of the American West.* New York: Dutton, 1977.

Ackermann, Jessie A. *Australia from a Woman's Point of View.* London: Cassell, 1913.

Agee, James. *Let Us Now Praise Famous Men.* Boston: Houghton Mifflin, 1941.

Alexander, Caroline. *One Dry Season: In the Footsteps of Mary Kingsley.* New York: Knopf, 1990.

Alexander, Lamar. *Six Months Off: An American Family's Australian Adventure.* New York: William Morrow, 1988.

Anaya, Rudolfo A. *A Chicano in China.* Albuquerque: U of New Mexico P, 1986.

Angelou, Maya. *All God's Children Need Traveling Shoes.* New York: Random House, 1986.

Angermeyer, Johanna. *My Father's Island: A Galapagos Quest.* New York: Viking, 1989.

Arlen, Michael J. *Passage to Ararat.* New York: Farrar, Straus & Giroux, 1975.

Arthur, Richard. *Ten Thousand Miles in a Yacht Round the West Indies and Up the Amazon.* New York: Dutton, 1906.

Bancroft, Griffing. *Lower California: A Cruise; The Flight of the Least Petrel.* New York: G. P. Putnam's Sons, 1932.

Bangs, Richard, and Christian Kallen. *Islands of Fire, Islands of Spice: Exploring the Wild Places of Indonesia.* San Francisco: Sierra Club, 1988.

———. *Riding the Dragon's Back: The Race to Raft the Upper Yangtze.* New York: Atheneum, 1987.

———. *Rivergods: Exploring the World's Great Rivers.* San Francisco: Sierra Club, 1985.

Barich, Bill. *Traveling Light.* New York: Viking, 1984.

Bass, Thomas A. *Camping with the Prince and Other Tales of Science in Africa.* Boston: Houghton Mifflin, 1990.

Baum, Maud Gage. *In Other Lands than Ours.* Chicago: M. G. Baum, 1907.

Beagle, Peter. *I See By My Outfit.* New York: Viking, 1965.

Beasley, David. *Through Paphlagonia with a Donkey: A Travel Journal.* New York: Davus, 1983.

Beebe, William. *Jungle Days.* New York: Putnam, 1921.

Belcher, Wendy Laura. *Honey from the Lion: An African Journey.* New York: Dutton, 1988.

Bellow, Saul. *To Jerusalem and Back: A Personal Account.* New York: Viking, 1976.

Benton, Thomas Hart. *An Artist in America.* New York: R. M. McBride, 1937.

Bernstein, Jeremy. *In the Himalayas: Journeys Through Nepal, Tibet and Bhutan.* New York: Simon & Schuster, 1989.

———. *Mountain Passages.* Lincoln: U of Nebraska P, 1978.

Bishop, Elizabeth. *Brazil.* New York: Time, 1962.

———. *Questions of Travel.* New York: Farrar, Straus & Giroux, 1965.

Blanchard, Smoke. *Walking Up and Down in the World: Memories of a Mountain Rambler.* San Francisco: Sierra Club, 1985.

Blaustein, John. *The Hidden Canyon: A River Journey.* New York: Viking, 1977.

Blum, Arlene. *Annapurna: A Woman's Place.* San Francisco: Sierra Club, 1980.

Bockstoce, John. *Arctic Passages: A Unique Small-Boat Voyage in the Great Northern Waterway.* New York: Hearst Marine, 1991.

Bolton, Charles Edward. *Travels in Europe and America.* New York: Thomas Y. Crowell, 1903.

Bordewich, Fergus M. *Cathay: A Journey in Search of Old China.* New York: Prentice Hall P, 1991.

Bowles, Paul. *Their Heads Are Green and Their Hands Are Blue.* New York: Random House, 1963.

Bracken, Peg. *But I Wouldn't Have Missed It for the World: The Pleasures and Perils of an Unseasoned Traveler.* New York: Harcourt Brace Jovanovich, 1973.

Brandi, John. *Diary from Baja California.* Oakland, Calif.: Christopher's, 1978.

———. *Diary from a Journey to the Middle of the World.* Berkeley: The Figures, 1979.

———. *Narrowgauge to Riobamba.* Oakland, Calif.: Christopher's, 1975.

Brower, Kenneth. *A Song for Satawal.* London: André Deutsch, 1983.

———. *The Starship and the Canoe.* New York: Holt, Rinehart & Winston, 1978.

Broyles, William. *Brothers in Arms: A Journey from War to Peace.* New York: Knopf, 1986.

Buckley, Christopher. *Steaming to Bamboola: The World of a Tramp Freighter.* New York: Congdon & Lattes, 1982.

Buckley, William F., Jr. *Airborne: A Sentimental Journey.* New York: Macmillan, 1976.

———. *Atlantic High.* Garden City, N.Y.: Doubleday, 1982.

———. *Racing Through Paradise: A Pacific Passage.* New York: Random House, 1987.

Burdsall, Richard, and Arthur B. Emmons. *Men Against the Clouds: The Conquest of Minya Konka.* New York: Harper & Bros., 1935.

Cahill, Tim. *Road Fever: A High-Speed Travelogue*. New York: Random House, 1991.

————. *A Wolverine Is Eating My Leg*. New York: Vintage, 1989.

Caldwell, Erskine. *Afternoons in Mid-America: Observations and Impressions*. New York: Dodd, Mead, 1976.

Caldwell, Erskine, and Margaret Bourke-White. *You Have Seen Their Faces*. New York: Viking, 1937.

Candlin, Enid Saunders. *A Traveler's Tale: Memories of India*. New York: Macmillan, 1974.

Carey, Robin. *Baja Journey: Reveries of a Sea-Kayaker*. College Station: Texas A & M UP, 1989.

Cather, Willa. *Willa Cather in Europe: Her Own Story of the First Journey* [1902]. Ed. George N. Kates. New York: Knopf, 1956.

Chaffetz, David. *A Journey Through Afghanistan: A Memorial*. Chicago: Regnery Gateway, 1981.

Cheuse, Alan. *Fall Out of Heaven: An Autobiographical Journey Across Russia*. Salt Lake City: Gibbs M. Smith, 1987.

Childers, James Saxon. *Sailing South American Skies*. New York: Farrar & Rinehart, 1936.

Childress, David Hatcher. *A Hitchhiker's Guide to Africa and Arabia*. Chicago: Chicago Review P, 1984.

Chiles, Webb. *Storm Passage: Alone Around Cape Horn*. New York: Times, 1977.

Chippendale, Harry Allen. *Sails and Whales*. Boston: Houghton Mifflin, 1951.

Clark, Eleanor. *Tamrart: Thirteen Days in the Sahara*. New York: Stuart Wright, 1984.

Collings, Kenneth Brown. *Just for the Hell of It*. New York: Dodd, Mead, 1938.

Conover, Ted. *Rolling Nowhere: A Young Man's Adventures Riding the Rails with America's Hoboes*. New York: Viking, 1984.

Crandall, Lee Saunders. *Paradise Quest: A Naturalist's Experiences in New Guinea*. New York: Charles Scribner's Sons, 1931.

Cravath, Paul Drennan. *Letters Home from India and Irak, 1925*. New York: J. J. Little & Ives, 1925.

Crichton, Michael. *Travels*. New York: Knopf, 1988.

Darling, Jay N. *The Cruise of the Bouncing Betsy: A Trailer Travelogue*. New York: Frederick A. Stokes, 1937.

Davenport, Homer. *My Quest of the Arabian Horse*. New York: B. W. Dodge, 1909.

Davidson, James West, and John Rugge. *Great Heart: The History of a Labrador Adventure*. New York: Viking, 1988.

Delbanco, Nicholas. *Running in Place: Scenes from the South of France*. New York: Atlantic Monthly P, 1989.

Dickey, Christopher. *Expats: Travels in Arabia, from Tripoli to Teheran*. New York: Atlantic Monthly P, 1990.

Didion, Joan. *Miami*. New York: Simon & Schuster, 1987.

————. *Salvador*. New York: Simon & Schuster, 1983.

Donleavy, J. P. *A Singular Country*. Peterborough, Eng.: Ryan, 1989.

Dos Passos, John Roderigo. *Brazil on the Move*. Garden City, N.Y.: Doubleday, 1963.

————. *In All Countries*. New York: Harcourt, Brace, 1934.

————. *Journeys Between Wars*. London: Constable, 1938.

————. *Orient Express*. New York: Harper & Bros., 1927.

Dunbar, Anthony P. *Delta Time: A Journey Through Mississippi*. New York: Pantheon, 1990.

Duncan, David Ewing. *From Cape to Cairo: An African Odyssey*. New York: Weidenfeld & Nicolson, 1989.

————. *Pedalling the Ends of the Earth*. New York: Simon & Schuster, 1985.

Duncan, Dayton. *Out West: American Journey Along the Lewis and Clark Trail*. New York: Penguin, 1987.

Ebener, Charlotte. *No Facilities for Women*. New York: Knopf, 1955.

Eddy, Clyde. *Down the World's Most Dangerous River*. New York: Frederick A. Stokes, 1921.

————. *Voyaging Down the Thames: An Intimate Account of a Voyage 200 Miles Across England, Down "the River of Liquid History"—the Thames*. New York: Frederick A. Stokes, 1938.

Egan, Timothy. *The Good Rain: Across Time and Terrain in the Pacific Northwest*. New York: Knopf, 1990.

Fax, Elton C. *Through Black Eyes: Journeys of a Black Artist to East Africa and Russia*. New York: Dodd, Mead, 1974.

Ferlinghetti, Lawrence. *The Mexican Night: Travel Journal*. New York: New Directions, 1970.

————. *Seven Days in Nicaragua Libre*. San Francisco: City Lights, 1984.

Finkelstein, Dave, and Jack London. *Greater Nowheres: A Journey Through the Australian Bush*. New York: Harper & Row, 1988.

Fisher, Harriet. *A Woman's World Tour in a Motor*. Philadelphia: J.B. Lippincott, 1911.

Flagg, James Montgomery. *Boulevards All the Way—Maybe: Being an Artist's Truthful Impression of the U.S.A. from New York to California and Return, by Motor*. New York: George H. Doran, 1925.

Flandrau, Charles Macomb. *Viva Mexico!* New York: Appleton, 1908.

Flores, Dan. *Caprock Canyonlands: Journeys into the Heart of the Southern Plains*. Austin: U of Texas P, 1990.

Fons, Valerie. *Keep It Moving: Baja by Canoe*. Seattle: Mountaineers, 1986.

Forman, Henry James. *Grecian Italy: Adventures of Travel in Sicily, Calabria and Malta*. New York: Boni & Liveright, 1924.

————. *In the Footprints of Heine*. Boston: Houghton Mifflin, 1910.

Frady, Marshall. *Across a Darkling Plain: An American's Passage Through the Middle East*. New York: Harper & Row, 1971.

Franck, Harry A. *The Fringe of the Moslem World*. New York: Century, 1928.

———. *Glimpses of Japan and Formosa*. New York: Century, 1924.

———. *Trailing Cortez Through Mexico*. New York: Frederick A. Stokes, 1935.

———. *Tramping Through Mexico, Guatemala and Honduras*. New York: Century, 1917.

———. *Vagabonding Through Changing Germany*. New York: Harper & Bros., 1920.

———. *A Vagabond Journey Around the World: A Narrative of Personal Experience*. New York: Century, 1910.

———. *Wandering in Northern China*. New York: Century, 1923.

———. *Working North from Patagonia: Being the Narrative of a Journey, Earned on the Way, Through Southern and Eastern South America*. New York: Century, 1921.

Frazier, Ian. *Great Plains*. New York: Farrar, Straus & Giroux, 1989.

Freeman, Lewis R. *Afloat and Aflight in the Caribbean*. New York: Dodd, Mead, 1932.

———. *Discovering South America*. New York: Dodd, Mead, 1937.

———. *Down the Columbia*. New York: Dodd, Mead, 1921.

Fritz, Jean. *China Homecoming*. New York: G. P. Putnam's Sons, 1985.

Galbraith, John Kenneth. *A China Passage*. Boston: Houghton Mifflin, 1973.

Gellhorn, Martha. *Travels with Myself and Another*. New York: Dodd, Mead, 1978.

Gillette, Ned, and Jan Reynolds. *Everest Grand Circle: A Climbing and Skiing Adventure Through Nepal and Tibet*. Seattle: Mountaineers, 1987.

Gold, Herbert. *Travels in San Francisco*. New York: Arcade, 1990.

Graves, John. *Goodbye to a River*. New York: Knopf, 1960.

Greenwald, Jeff. *Mister Raja's Neighborhood: Letters from Nepal*. Ed. Jim Cook. Santa Barbara, Calif.: J. Daniel, 1986.

———. *Shopping For Buddhas*. San Francisco: Harper & Row, 1990.

Gruber, Ruth. *I Went to the Soviet Arctic*. New York: Simon & Schuster, 1939.

Gruchow, Paul. *The Necessity of Empty Places*. New York: St. Martin's P, 1988.

Hall, Brian. *Stealing from a Deep Place: Travels in Southeastern Europe*. New York: Hill & Wang, 1988.

Halliburton, Richard. *The Flying Carpet*. Indianapolis: Bobbs-Merrill, 1932.

———. *The Glorious Adventure*. Indianapolis: Bobbs-Merrill, 1927.

———. *New Worlds to Conquer*. Garden City, N.Y.: Garden City, 1929.

———. *The Royal Road to Romance*. Garden City, N.Y.: Garden City, 1925.

———. *Seven League Boots*. Indianapolis: Bobbs-Merrill, 1935.

Halsey, David. *Magnetic North: A Trek Across Canada from the Pacific to the Atlantic by Foot, Dogsled and Canoe*. San Francisco: Sierra Club, 1990.

Hansen, Eric. *Motoring with Mohammed: Journeys to Yemen and the Red Sea*. Boston: Houghton Mifflin, 1991.

———. *Stranger in the Forest: On Foot Across Borneo*. New York: Houghton Mifflin, 1988.

Hanson, Earl Parker. *Journey to Manáos.* New York: Reynal & Hitchcock, 1938.

Harris, Eddy L. *Mississippi Solo: A River Quest.* New York: Nick Lyons, 1988.

Harrison, Barbara Grizzuti. *Italian Days.* London: Weidenfeld & Nicolson, 1989.

Hart, Frances Noyes. *Pigs in Clover.* New York: Doubleday, Doran, 1931.

Hatch, Olivia Stokes. *Olivia's African Diary: Cape Town to Cairo, 1932.* Washington, D.C.: A.C.E. Distribution Center, 1980.

Heat-Moon, William Least. *Blue Highways: A Journey into America.* Boston: Little, Brown, 1982.

Hemingway, Ernest. *Death in the Afternoon.* New York: Charles Scribner's Sons, 1932.

———. *Green Hills of Africa.* New York: Charles Scribner's Sons, 1935.

Hemphill, Paul. *Me and the Boy: Journey of Discovery: Father and Son on the Appalachian Trail.* New York: Macmillan, 1986.

Henson, Matthew A. *A Negro Explorer at the North Pole.* New York: Frederick A. Stokes, 1912. Republished as *A Black Explorer at the North Pole.*

Higginbotham, Jay. *Fast Train Russia.* New York: Dodd, Mead, 1983.

Hines, Duncan. *Lodging for a Night.* Bowling Green, Ky.: Adventures in Good Eating, 1938.

Hoagland, Edward. *African Calliope: A Journey to the Sudan.* New York: Random House, 1979.

———. *Notes from the Century Before: A Journal from British Columbia.* New York: Random House, 1969.

Holm, Bill. *Coming Home Crazy: An Alphabet of China Essays.* Minneapolis: Milkweed Editions, 1990.

Holmes, John Clellon. *Displaced Person: The Travel Essays.* Fayetteville: U of Arkansas P, 1987.

Horwitz, Tony. *One For the Road: Hitchhiking Through the Australian Outback.* Sydney: Harper & Row, 1987.

Howarth, William. *Traveling the Trans-Canada.* Washington, D.C.: National Geographic Society, 1987.

Howells, William Dean. *Certain Delightful English Towns: With Glimpses of the Pleasant Country Between.* New York: Harper & Bros., 1906.

———. *Familiar Spanish Travels.* New York: Harper & Bros., 1913.

———. *Hither and Thither in Germany.* New York: Harper & Bros., 1920.

———. *London Films.* New York: Harper & Bros., 1905.

———. *Roman Holidays, and Others.* New York: Harper & Bros., 1908.

———. *Seven English Cities.* New York: Harper & Bros., 1909.

Hubbard, Ethan. *First Light: Sojourns with People of the Outer Hebrides, the Sierra Madre, the Himalayas, and Other Remote Places.* Chelsea, Vt.: Chelsea Green, 1987.

Hughes, Langston. *I Wonder As I Wander: An Autobiographical Journey.* New York: Rinehart, 1956.

Humphrey, Zephine. *Green Mountains to Sierras.* New York: Dutton, 1936.

Humphreys, John R. *The Lost Towns and Roads of America.* New York: Harper & Row, 1961. Revised edition, 1967.

——. *Timeless Towns and Haunted Places from Florida to Maine.* New York: St. Martin's P, 1989.

Jackson, Everett Gee. *Burros and Paintbrushes: A Mexican Adventure.* College Station: Texas A & M UP, 1985.

——. *It's a Long Road to Comondu: Mexican Adventures Since 1928.* College Station: Texas A & M UP, 1987.

Jacobsen, Betty. *A Girl Before the Mast.* New York: Charles Scribner's Sons, 1934.

James, Henry. *The American Scene.* London: Chapman & Hall, 1907.

——. *The Art of Travel: Scenes and Journeys in America, England, France and Italy from the Travel Writings of Henry James.* Ed. Morton Dauwen Zabel. Garden City, N.Y.: Doubleday, 1958.

——. *English Hours.* Boston: Houghton Mifflin, 1905.

——. *Italian Hours.* Boston: Houghton Mifflin, 1909.

Jeffers, Una. *Visits to Ireland: Travel-Diaries of Una Jeffers.* Los Angeles: Ward Ritchie P, 1954.

Jenkins, Peter. *Across China.* New York: William Morrow, 1986.

——. *A Walk Across America.* New York: Ballantine, 1979.

Jenkins, Peter, and Barbara Jenkins. *The Road Unseen.* New York: Ballantine, 1985.

——. *The Walk West: A Walk Across America 2.* New York: Ballantine, 1981.

Johnson, Clifton. *Highways and Byways of the Mississippi Valley.* New York: Macmillan, 1906.

——. *Highways and Byways of the Rocky Mountains.* New York: Macmillan, 1910.

——. *Highways and Byways of the South.* New York: Macmillan, 1904.

——. *What to See in America.* New York: Macmillan, 1919.

Johnson, Martin. *Camera Trails in Africa.* New York: Century, 1924.

——. *Cannibal-Land: Adventures with a Camera in the New Hebrides.* Boston: Houghton Mifflin, 1922.

Kamal, Ahmad. *Land Without Laughter.* New York: Charles Scribner's Sons, 1940.

Kandell, Jonathan. *Passage Through El Dorado: Traveling the World's Last Great Wilderness.* New York: William Morrow, 1984.

Kane, Joe. *Running the Amazon.* New York: Knopf, 1989.

Keely, Robert N. *Paris and All the World Besides.* Philadelphia: Howard C. Myers, 1930.

Kerasote, Ted. *Navigations.* Harrisburg, Pa.: Stackpole, 1986.

Kerouac, Jack. *Lonesome Traveler.* New York: McGraw-Hill, 1960.

Kerouac, Jan. *Trainsong.* New York: Henry Holt, 1988.

Kesselheim, Alan S. *Water and Sky: Recollections of a Northern Year.* Golden, Colo.: Fulcrum, 1989.

Klinkenborg, Verlyn. *Making Hay.* New York: Nick Lyons, 1986.

Knight, Kathryn Lasky. *Atlantic Circle.* New York: W. W. Norton, 1985.

Kolb, E. L. *Through the Grand Canyon from Wyoming to Mexico.* New York: Macmillan, 1914.

Krakel, Dean. *Downriver: A Yellowstone Journey.* San Francisco: Sierra Club, 1987.

Krich, John. *El Beisbol: Travels Through the Pan American Pastime.* New York: Atlantic Monthly P, 1989.

————. *Music In Every Room: Around the World in a Bad Mood.* New York: McGraw-Hill, 1984.

Krutch, Joseph Wood. *The Forgotten Peninsula: A Naturalist in Baha.* New York: William Sloane, 1961.

Kuralt, Charles. *Dateline America.* New York: Harcourt Brace Jovanovich, 1979.

————. *On the Road with Charles Kuralt.* New York: G. P. Putnam's Sons, 1985.

Lane, Rose Wilder. *The Peaks of Shala: Being a Record of Certain Wanderings Among the Hill-Tribes of Albania.* London: Chapman & Dodd, 1922.

Lighty, Kent, and Margaret Lighty. *Shanty-Boat.* New York: Century, 1930.

Lincoln, Kenneth, and Al Logan Slagle. *The Good Red Road: Passages into Native America.* San Francisco: Harper & Row, 1987.

Lindsay, Vachel. *A Handy Guide for Beggars, Especially Those of the Poetic Fraternity: Being Sundry Explorations, Made While Afoot and Penniless in Florida, Georgia, North Carolina [etc.].* New York: Macmillan, 1916.

Lipscomb, James. *Cutting Loose.* Boston: Little, Brown, 1974.

London, Jack. *The Cruise of the Snark.* New York: Regent P, 1908.

Long, Dwight. *Seven Seas on a Shoestring: Sailing All Seas in the "Idle Hour."* New York: Harper & Bros., 1939.

Longstreet, Stephen. *Last Man Around the World.* New York: Random House, 1941.

————. *The Last Man Comes Home: American Travel Journals, 1941–1942.* New York: Random House, 1942.

Lopez, Barry. *Arctic Dreams: Imagination and Desire in a Northern Landscape.* New York: Charles Scribner's Sons, 1986.

Lynch, Kermit. *Adventures on the Wine Route: A Wine Buyer's Tour of France.* New York: Farrar, Straus & Giroux, 1988.

MacCreagh, Gordon. *White Waters and Black.* New York: Century, 1926.

MacMillan, Donald Baxter. *Etah and Beyond, or Life Within Twelve Degrees of the Pole.* Boston: Houghton Mifflin, 1927.

McAdoo, Richard B. *Eccentric Circles: Around America in a House of Wheels.* Boston: Houghton Mifflin, 1991.

McCarthy, Mary. *The Stones of Florence.* New York: Harcourt, Brace, 1959.

————. *Venice Observed.* New York: Reynal, 1956.

McGinniss, Joe. *Going to Extremes.* New York: Knopf, 1980.

McKinney, Sam. *Reach of Tide, Ring of History: A Columbia River Voyage.* Portland: Oregon Historical Society, 1987.

McMath, Sandy. *Africa Alone: Odyssey of an American Traveler*. Little Rock, Ark.: August House, 1983.

McPhee, John. *Coming into the Country*. New York: Farrar, Straus & Giroux, 1977.

———. *In the Highlands and Islands*. London: Faber & Faber, 1986.

———. *The Survival of the Bark Canoe*. New York: Farrar, Straus & Giroux, 1975.

Madson, John. *Up on the River: An Upper Mississippi Chronicle*. New York: Schocken, 1985.

Malcomson, Scott L. *Tuturani: A Political Journey in the Pacific Islands*. New York: Poseidon P, 1990.

Martí-Ibáñez, Félix. *Journey About Myself: Impressions and Tales of Travel Around the World [etc.]*. New York: Clarkson N. Potter, 1966.

Matthiessen, F. O. *From the Heart of Europe*. New York: Oxford UP, 1948.

Matthiessen, Peter. *African Silences*. New York: Random House, 1991.

———. *The Cloud Forest: A Chronicle of the South American Wilderness*. New York: Viking, 1961.

———. *Sand Rivers*. New York: Viking, 1981.

———. *The Snow Leopard*. New York: Viking, 1978.

Mavor, James W. *Voyage to Atlantis*. New York: G. P. Putnam's Sons, 1969.

Merrick, Henrietta Sands. *In the World's Attic*. New York: G. P. Putnam's Sons, 1931.

———. *Spoken in Tibet*. New York: G. P. Putnam's Sons, 1933.

Mewshaw, Michael. *Playing Away: Roman Holidays and Other Mediterranean Encounters*. New York: Atheneum, 1988.

Miller, Arthur, and Inge Morath. *Chinese Encounters*. New York: Farrar, Straus & Giroux, 1979.

Miller, Debbie S. *Midnight Wilderness: Journeys in Alaska's Arctic National Wildlife Refuge*. San Francisco: Sierra Club, 1990.

Miller, Henry. *The Air-Conditioned Nightmare*. New York: New Directions, 1945.

———. *The Colossus of Maroussi*. San Francisco: Colt P, 1941.

Miller, Tom. *The Panama Hat Trail: A Journey from South America*. New York: William Morrow, 1986.

Milliman, Lawrence. *Last Places: A Journey in the North*. Boston: Houghton Mifflin, 1990.

Mitchell, Carleton. *The Winds Call: Cruises Near and Far*. New York: Charles Scribner's Sons, 1971.

Mitchner, Stuart. *Indian Action: An American Journey to the Great Fair of the East*. Boston: Little, Brown, 1976.

Morgan, Ted. *Rowing Toward Eden*. Boston: Houghton Mifflin, 1981.

Morris, Mary. *Nothing to Declare: Memoirs of a Woman Traveling Alone*. New York: Houghton Mifflin, 1988.

———. *Wall to Wall: From Beijing to Berlin by Rail*. New York: Doubleday, 1991.

Morris, Wright. *Solo: An American Dreamer in Europe, 1933–34*. New York: Harper & Row, 1983.

Morton, Rosalie Slaughter. *A Doctor's Holiday in Iran*. New York: Funk & Wagnalls, 1940.

Mosher, Steven W. *Journey to the Forbidden China*. New York: Free P, 1985.

Muir, John. *Steep Trails: California, Utah, Nevada, Washington, Oregon, the Grand Canyon*. Boston: Houghton Mifflin, 1918.

———. *A Thousand-Mile Walk to the Gulf*. Boston: Houghton Mifflin, 1916.

———. *Travels in Alaska*. Boston: Houghton Mifflin, 1915.

Murphy, Thomas Dowler. *On Old-World Highways: A Book of Motor Rambles in France and Germany and the Record of a Pilgrimage from Land's End to John O'Groats in Britain*. Boston: L. C. Page, 1914.

Neihardt, John G. *The River and I*. New York: G. P. Putnam's Sons, 1910.

Nelson, Victoria. *My Time in Hawaii: A Polynesian Memoir*. New York: St. Martin's P, 1989.

Newsham, Brad. *All the Right Places: Traveling Light Through China, Japan and Russia*. New York: Villard, 1989.

Newton, A. Edward. *Derby Day and Other Adventures*. Boston: Little, Brown, 1934.

———. *A Tourist in Spite of Himself*. Boston: Little, Brown, 1930.

Nichols, Francis H. *Through Hidden Shensi*. New York: Charles Scribner's Sons, 1902.

Niemann, Linda. *Boomer: Railroad Memoirs*. Berkeley: U of California P, 1990.

Norment, Christopher. *In the North of Our Lives: A Year in the Wilderness of Northern Canada*. Camden, Maine: Down East, 1989.

Nugent, Rory. *The Search for the Pink-Headed Duck*. Boston: Houghton Mifflin, 1991.

O'Brien, Frederick. *Atolls of the Sun*. New York: Century, 1922.

———. *Mystic Isles of the South Seas*. New York: Century, 1921.

———. *White Shadows in the South Seas*. New York: Century, 1919.

O'Gara, Geoffrey. *A Long Road Home: Journeys Through America's Present in Search of America's Past*. New York: W. W. Norton, 1989.

Olson, Sigurd F. *The Lonely Land*. New York: Knopf, 1961.

O'Rourke, P. J. *Holidays in Hell*. New York: Atlantic Monthly P, 1988.

Oxenhorn, Harvey. *Tuning the Rig: A Journey to the Arctic*. New York: Harper & Row, 1990.

Palmer, Tim. *The Sierra Nevada: A Mountain Journey*. Washington, D.C.: Island P, 1988.

Pardey, Lin, and Larry Pardey. *"Seraffyn's" European Adventure*. New York: W. W. Norton, 1979.

Parfit, Michael. *Chasing the Glory: Travels Across America*. New York: Macmillan, 1988.

————. *South Light: A Journey to the Last Continent*. New York: Macmillan, 1985.

Peissel, Michel. *The Great Himalayan Passage: The Story of an Extraordinary Adventure on the Roof of the World*. Boston: Little, Brown, 1975.

Perkins, Robert. *Into the Great Solitude: An Arctic Journey*. New York: Henry Holt, 1991.

Peterson, Dale. *The Deluge and the Ark: A Journey into Primate Worlds*. Boston: Houghton Mifflin, 1989.

Pindell, Terry. *Making Tracks: An American Rail Odyssey*. New York: Grove Weidenfeld, 1990.

Pirsig, Robert. *Zen and the Art of Motorcycle Maintenance: An Inquiry into Values*. New York: William Morrow, 1974.

Powell, E. Alexander. *Aerial Odyssey: Cuba, Haiti, Dominican Republic, Porto Rico [etc.]*. New York: Macmillan, 1936.

————. *By Camel and Car to the Peacock Throne*. Garden City, N.Y.: Garden City, 1923.

————. *In Barbary: Tunisia, Algeria, Morocco and the Sahara*. New York: Century, 1926.

————. *Where the Strange Trails Go Down*. New York: Charles Scribner's Sons, 1921.

Powledge, Fred. *Journeys Through the South*. New York: Vanguard P, 1979.

Preschel, Pearl L. *Travels in Jewish Europe*. New York: Moznaim, 1985.

Price, Lucien. *Winged Sandals*. Boston: Little, Brown, 1927.

Pyle, Ernie. *Home Country*. New York: William Sloane, 1947.

Pyne, Stephen J. *The Ice: A Journey to Antarctica*. Iowa City: U of Iowa P, 1986.

Rawls, Thomas H. *Small Places: In Search of a Vanishing America*. Boston: Little, Brown, 1990.

Reiger, George. *Wanderer On My Native Shore*. New York: Simon & Schuster, 1983.

Rexroth, Kenneth. *The Dragon and the Unicorn*. Norfolk, Conn.: New Directions, 1952.

Robeson, Eslanda Goode. *African Journey*. New York: John Day, 1945.

Rorty, James. *Where Life Is Better: An Unsentimental American Journey*. New York: Reynal & Hitchcock, 1936.

Ross, Cindy. *Journey to the Crest: Walking 2,600 Miles from Mexico to Canada*. Seattle: Mountaineers, 1987.

Ross, Lillian E., George Whitman, Joe Wershba, Helen Ross, and Mel Fiske. *The "Argonauts."* New York: Modern Age, 1940.

Rothchild, John. *Up For Grabs: A Trip Through Time and Space in the Sunshine State*. New York: Viking, 1985.

Roueché, Berton. *Sea to Shining Sea: People, Travels, Places*. New York: Dutton, 1985.

————. *Special Places: In Search of Small-Town America*. Boston: Little, Brown, 1982.

Salisbury, Harrison E. *Travels Around America*. New York: Walker, 1976.

Salzman, Mark. *Iron and Silk*. New York: Random House, 1986.

Saunders, Charles Francis. *The Southern Sierras of California*. Boston: Houghton Mifflin, 1923.

Savage, Barbara. *Miles From Nowhere: A Round-the-World Bicycle Adventure*. Seattle: Mountaineers, 1983.

Schaller, George B. *Stones of Silence: Journeys in the Himalaya*. New York: Viking, 1980.

Scheer, George F., III. *Booked on the Morning Train: A Journey Through America*. Chapel Hill, N.C.: Algonquin, 1991.

Scherman, Katharine. *Spring on an Arctic Island*. Boston: Little, Brown, 1956.

Schneebaum, Tobias. *Where the Spirits Dwell: An Odyssey in the New Guinea Jungle*. New York: Grove P, 1988.

Schultheis, Rob. *The Hidden West: Journeys in the American Outback*. New York: Random House, 1980.

Scott, Jack Denton. *Journey into Silence*. New York: Reader's Digest P, 1976.

Seabrook, William B. *Adventures in Arabia: Among the Bedouins, Druses, Whirling Dervishes, and Yezidee Devil Worshipers*. New York: Harcourt, Brace, 1927.

————. *Air Adventure: Paris—Sahara—Timbuctoo*. New York: Harcourt, Brace, 1933.

————. *Jungle Ways*. New York: Harcourt, Brace, 1931.

Shaffer, Robert. *Tents and Towers of Arabia*. New York: Dodd, Mead, 1952.

Shenker, Israel. *In the Footsteps of Johnson and Boswell*. Boston: Houghton Mifflin, 1982.

Shoumatoff, Alex. *Florida Ramble*. New York: Harper & Row, 1974.

————. *The Rivers Amazon*. San Francisco: Sierra Club, 1978.

————. *In Southern Light: Trekking Through Zaire and the Amazon*. New York: Simon & Schuster, 1986.

Simetti, Mary Taylor. *On Persephone's Island: A Sicilian Journal*. New York: Knopf, 1986.

Slocum, Joshua. *Sailing Alone Around the World*. New York: Century, 1900.

Smith, Grace, Beverly Smith, and Charles Morrow Wilson. *Through the Kitchen Door: A Cook's Tour of the Best Kitchens of America*. New York: Stackpole Sons, 1938.

Snow, Edgar. *People On Our Side*. New York: Random House, 1944.

Snyder, Gary. *Passage Through India*. San Francisco: Grey Fox, 1983.

Sontag, Susan. *Trip to Hanoi*. New York: Farrar, Straus & Giroux, 1968.

Speakman, Harold. *Hilltops in Galilee*. New York: Abingdon P, 1923.

————. *Mostly Mississippi*. New York: Dodd, Mead, 1927.

Starkell, Don. *Paddle to the Amazon*. Rocklin, Calif.: Prima, 1989.

Steber, Rick. *New York to Nome: The Northwest Passage by Canoe*. New York: Simon & Schuster, 1987.

Steger, Will, and Paul Schurke. *North to the Pole*. New York: Times, 1987.

Stegner, Page. *Islands of the West: From Baja to Vancouver*. San Francisco: Sierra Club, 1985.

——. *Outposts of Eden: A Curmudgeon at Large in the American West*. San Francisco: Sierra Club, 1989.

John Steinbeck. *The Log from the "Sea of Cortez."* New York: Viking, 1951.

——. *A Russian Journal*. New York: Viking, 1948.

——. *Travels with Charley: In Search of America*. New York: Viking, 1962.

Steinbeck, John, and Edward F. Ricketts. *Sea of Cortez: A Leisurely Journal of Travel and Research*. New York: Viking, 1941.

Stephens, Harold, and Albert Podell. *Who Needs a Road? The Story of the Trans-World Record Expedition*. Indianapolis: Bobbs-Merrill, 1967.

Stevens, Stuart. *Malaria Dreams: An African Adventure*. New York: Atlantic Monthly P, 1989.

——. *Night Train to Turkestan: Modern Adventures Along China's Ancient Silk Road*. New York: Atlantic Monthly P, 1988.

Stinnett, Caskie. *Grand and Private Pleasures*. Boston: Little, Brown, 1977.

Street, Julian. *Abroad at Home: American Ramblings, Observations, and Adventures*. New York: Century, 1914.

——. *American Adventures: A Second Trip "Abroad at Home."* New York: Century, 1917.

Sullivan, William L. *Listening for Coyote: A Walk Across Oregon's Wilderness*. New York: William Morrow, 1988.

Teale, Edwin Way. *Autumn Across America: A Naturalist's Record of a 20,000-Mile Journey Through the North American Autumn*. New York: Dodd, Mead, 1956.

——. *Journey into Summer: A Naturalist's Record of a 19,000-Mile Journey Through the North-American Summer*. New York: Dodd, Mead, 1960.

——. *North With the Spring: A Naturalist's Record of a 17,000-Mile Journey with the North American Spring*. New York: Dodd, Mead, 1951.

——. *Springtime in Britain: An 11,000-Mile Journey Through the Natural History of Britain from Land's End to John o' Groats*. New York: Dodd, Mead, 1970.

——. *Wandering Through Winter: A Naturalist's Record of a 20,000-Mile Journey Through the North American Winter*. New York: Dodd, Mead, 1965.

Theroux, Paul. *The Great Railway Bazaar: By Train Through Asia*. Boston: Houghton Mifflin, 1975.

——. *The Kingdom by the Sea: A Journey Around Great Britain*. Boston: Houghton Mifflin, 1983.

——. *The Old Patagonian Express: By Train Through the Americas*. Boston: Houghton Mifflin, 1979.

————. *Riding the Iron Rooster: By Train Through China*. New York: Putnam, 1988.

————. *Sailing Through China*. Boston: Houghton Mifflin, 1984.

Thomas, Lowell. *Beyond Khyber Pass*. New York: Century, 1925.

————. *India: Land of the Black Pagoda*. New York: Century, 1930.

Thomas, Tay. *Follow the North Star*. Garden City, N.Y.: Doubleday, 1960.

Thompson, Era Bell. *Africa, Land of My Fathers*. Garden City, N.Y.: Doubleday, 1954.

Thompson, Hunter S., and Ralph Steadman. *The Curse of Lono*. New York: Bantam, 1983.

Thomsen, Moritz. *The Saddest Pleasure: A Journey on Two Rivers*. Minneapolis: Graywolf P, 1990.

Trillin, Calvin. *Travels with Alice*. New York: Ticknor & Fields, 1989.

Ullman, James Ramsey. *The Other Side of the Mountain: An Escape to the Amazon*. London: Gollancz, 1938.

Van Dyke, John C. *In Egypt: Studies and Sketches Along the Nile*. New York: Charles Scribner's Sons, 1931.

————. *In Java, and the Neighboring Islands of the Dutch East Indies*. New York: Charles Scribner's Sons, 1929.

————. *In the West Indies: Sketches and Studies in Tropic Seas and Islands*. New York: Charles Scribner's Sons, 1932.

Walker, Dale. *Fool's Paradise*. New York: Random House, 1988.

Warner, Arthur. *A Landlubber's Log: Around the World as Sailor and Tramp*. Boston: Little, Brown, 1930.

Washburn, William. *The Track of the "Typhoon."* New York: Motor Boat, 1922.

Waters, Don. *Outboard Cruising*. New York: L. Furman, 1939.

Weller, James Marvin. *Caravan Across China: An American Geologist Explores the Northwest, 1937–38*. San Francisco: March Hare, 1984.

Wells, Frederick DeWitt, *The Last Cruise of the Shanghai: Being the Story of the Teakwood Boat over the Viking Trail*. New York: Minton, Balch, 1925.

Wells, Linton. *Around the World in Twenty-Eight Days*. Boston: Houghton Mifflin, 1926.

Wharton, Edith. *Italian Backgrounds*. New York: Charles Scribner's Sons, 1905.

————. *In Morocco*. New York: Charles Scribner's Sons, 1919.

————. *A Motor-Flight Through France*. New York: Charles Scribner's Sons, 1908.

White, Edmund, and Adam Mars-Jones. *States of Desire: Travels in Gay America*. New York: Dutton, 1980.

Wibberley, Leonard. *Voyage By Bus*. New York: William Morrow, 1971.

Williams, John A[lfred]. *This Is My Country Too*. New York: New American Library, 1964.

Williams, William Carlos. *A Voyage to Pagany*. New York: Macaulay, 1928.

Wilson, Edmund. *Europe Without Baedeker: Sketches Among the Ruins of Italy, Greece, and England*. Garden City, N.Y.: Doubleday, 1947.

———. *Travels in Two Democracies*. New York: Harcourt, Brace, 1936.

Winegardner, Mark. *Elvis Presley Boulevard: From Sea to Shining Sea, Almost*. New York: Atlantic Monthly P, 1987.

Winn, Mary Day. *The Macadam Trail: Ten Thousand Miles by Motor Coach*. New York: Knopf, 1931.

Winternitz, Helen. *East Along the Equator: A Journey up the Congo and into Zaire*. New York: Atlantic Monthly P, 1987.

Wolfe, Thomas. *A Western Journal*. Pittsburgh: U of Pittsburgh P, 1951.

Zalis, Paul. *Who Is the River: Getting Lost and Found in the Amazon and Other Places*. New York: Atheneum, 1986.

Zwinger, Ann. *Run, River, Run: A Naturalist's Journey Down One of the Great Rivers of the West*. New York: Harper & Row, 1975.

———. *Wind in the Rock*. New York: Harper & Row, 1978.

English Works

Alexander, Michael. *Offbeat in Asia: An Excursion*. London: Weidenfeld & Nicolson, 1960.

Allen, Benedict. *Mad White Giant*. London: Macmillan, 1985. Reprinted in the United States as *Who Goes Out in the Midday Sun?*

Andrews, Kevin. *The Flight of Ikaros: Travels in Greece During A Civil War*. London: Weidenfeld & Nicolson, 1959.

Armitage, Albert B. *Two Years in the Antarctic: Being a Narrative of the British National Antarctic Expedition*. London: Edward Arnold, 1905.

Asher, Michael. *In Search of the Forty Days Road*. London: Longman, 1984.

———. *Two Against the Sahara*. London: Viking, 1988. Republished as *Impossible Journey: Two Against the Sahara*.

Auden, W. H., and Christopher Isherwood. *Journey to a War*. London: Faber & Faber, 1939.

Auden, W. H., and Louis MacNeice. *Letters From Iceland*. London: Faber & Faber, 1937. Rev. ed., 1973.

Bailey, Anthony. *Spring Jaunts: Some Walks, Excursions and Personal Explorations of Town, Country and Seashore*. New York: Farrar, Straus & Giroux, 1986.

Bailey, F[rederick] M[arshman]. *No Passport to Tibet*. London: Rupert Hart-Davis, 1957.

Banham, Reyner. *Scenes in America Deserta*. Salt Lake City: Gibbs M. Smith, 1982.

Bedford, Sybille. *The Sudden View: A Mexican Journey*. London: Gollancz, 1953. Republished as *A Visit to Don Otavio*.

Bell, Gertrude Lowthian. *Amurath to Amurath*. London: William Heinemann, 1911.

———. *Syria: The Desert and the Sown*. London: William Heinemann, 1907.

Belloc, Hilaire. *The Cruise of the "Nona."* London: Constable, 1925.

———. *The Four Men: A Farrago*. London: Thomas Nelson & Sons, 1912.

———. *Hills and the Sea*. London: Methuen, 1906.

———. *The Old Road*. London: A. Constable, 1904.

———. *The Path to Rome*. London: George Allen, 1902.

———. *Places*. New York: Sheed & Ward, 1941.

Betham-Edwards, [Matilda Barbara]. *In the Heart of Vosges and Other Sketches by a "Devious Traveller."* London: Chapman & Hall, 1911.

———. *Unfrequented France: By River, Mead and Town*. London: Chapman & Hall, 1910.

Bigland, Eileen. *Into China*. London: Collins, 1940.

———. *Journey to Egypt*. London: Jarrolds, 1948.

———. *The Lake of the Royal Crocodiles*. London: Hodder & Stoughton, 1939.

———. *Laughing Odyssey*. London: Hodder & Stoughton, 1937.

Blair, Lawrence, and Lorne Blair. *Ring of Fire: Exploring the Last Remote Places of the World*. New York: Bantam, 1988.

Blanch, Lesley. *Under a Lilac-Bleeding Star: Travels and Travelers*. London: John Murray, 1963.

Booth, Alan. *The Roads to Sata*. New York: John Weatherhill, 1985.

Bosanquet, Mary. *Saddlebags for Suitcases*. New York: Dodd, Mead, 1942. Reprinted in England as *Canada Ride: Across Canada on Horseback*.

Brittain, Vera Mary. *Thrice a Stranger*. New York: Macmillan, 1938.

Brook, Stephen. *Honky Tonk Gelato: Travels Through Texas*. New York: Atheneum, 1985.

———. *Maple Leaf Rag*. New York: Random House, 1987.

———. *New York Days, New York Nights*. New York: Atheneum, 1985.

———. *Vanished Empire: Vienna, Budapest, Prague: The Three Capital Cities of the Hapsburg Empire as Seen Today*. New York: William Morrow, 1988. Published in England as *The Double Eagle*.

Brooke, Rupert. *Letters from America*. London: Sidgwick & Jackson, 1916.

Bruce, Mildred. *The Bluebird's Flight*. London: Chapman & Hall, 1931.

———. *Nine Thousand Miles in Eight Weeks: Being an Account of an Epic Journey by Motor-Car Through Eleven Countries and Two Continents*. London: Heath, Cranton, 1927.

Bryson, Bill. *The Lost Continent: Travels in Small-Town America*. New York: Harper & Row, 1989.

Burns, Jimmy. *Beyond the Silver River: South American Encounters*. London: Bloomsbury, 1989.

Buruma, Ian. *God's Dust: A Modern Asian Journey*. New York: Farrar, Straus & Giroux, 1989.

Buxton, Noel. *Travel and Reflections*. London: George Allen & Unwin, 1929.

Byron, Robert. *First Russia, Then Tibet*. London: Macmillan, 1933.

———. *The Road to Oxiana*. London: Macmillan, 1937.

———. *The Station: Athos, Treasures and Men*. London: Duckworth, 1928.

Cable, Mildred, with Francesca French. *The Gobi Desert*. London: Hodder & Stoughton, 1942.

——— . *Through Jade Gate and Central Asia: An Account of Journeys in Kansu, Turkestan and the Gobi Desert*. London: Constable, 1927.

Cameron, Charlotte. *A Cheechako in Alaska and Yukon*. London: T. Fisher Unwin, 1920.

——— . *Wanderings in South-Eastern Seas*. London: T. Fisher Unwin, 1924.

——— . *A Woman's Winter in Africa: A 26,000 Mile Journey*. London: Stanley Paul, 1913.

Carrington, Richard. *East from Tunis: A Record of Travels on the Northern Coast of Africa*. London: Chatto & Windus, 1957.

Carson, Anthony. *A Train to Tarragona*. New York: British Book Centre, 1959.

——— . *Travels: Near and Far Out*. New York: Pantheon, 1962.

Chapman, F. Spencer. *Helvellyn to Himalaya: Including an Account of the First Ascent of Chomolhari*. New York: Harper & Bros., 1940.

Chapman, Olive Murray. *Across Cyprus*. London: John Lane, 1937.

——— . *Across Iceland, the Land of Frost and Fire*. London: John Lane, 1930.

——— . *Across Lapland with Sledge and Reindeer*. London: John Lane, 1932.

——— . *Across Madagascar*. London: E. J. Burrow, 1943.

Chase, John Smeaton. *California Coast Trails: A Horseback Ride From Mexico to Oregon*. Boston: Houghton Mifflin, 1913.

——— . *California Desert Trails*. Boston: Houghton Mifflin, 1919.

Chatwin, Bruce. *In Patagonia*. New York: Summit, 1977.

——— . *The Song-Lines*. New York: Viking, 1987.

Chatwin, Bruce, and Paul Theroux. *Patagonia Revisited*. Boston: Houghton Mifflin, 1986.

Cheesman, Evelyn. *Islands near the Sun: Off the Beaten Track in the Far, Fair Society Islands*. London: H. F. & G. Witherby, 1927.

——— . *Six-Legged Snakes in New Guinea: A Collection Expedition to Two Unexplored Islands*. London: Harrap, 1949.

——— . *The Two Roads of Papua*. London: Jarrolds, 1935.

Cherry-Garrard, Apsley. *The Worst Journey in the World*. London: Constable, 1922.

Chesterton, G. K. *What I Saw in America*. London: Hodder & Stoughton, 1922.

Chetwode, Penelope. *Two Middle-Aged Ladies in Andalusia*. London: John Murray, 1963.

Chichester, Francis. *Gipsy Moth Circles the World*. London: Hodder & Stoughton, 1967.

Christmas, Linda. *The Ribbon and the Ragged Square: An Australian Journey*. New York: Viking, 1986.

Churchill, Winston. *My African Journey*. London: Hodder & Stoughton, 1908.

Clarke, Thurston. *Equator: A Journey*. New York: William Morrow, 1988.

Close, Etta. *Excursions and Some Adventures*. London: Constable, 1926.

————. *A Woman Alone in Kenya, Uganda and the Belgian Congo*. London: Constable, 1924.

Coleridge, Nicholas. *Around the World in 78 Days*. London: William Heinemann, 1984.

Conrad, Peter. *Behind the Mountain: Return to Tasmania*. New York: Poseidon P, 1989.

————. *Where I Fell to Earth: A Life in Four Cities*. New York: Poseidon P, 1990.

Cooper, Diana. *The Light of Common Day*. London: Hart-Davis, 1959.

Crewe, Quentin. *In the Realms of Gold: Travels Through South America*. London: Michael Joseph, 1989.

————. *Touch the Happy Isles: A Journey Through the Caribbean*. London: Michael Joseph, 1987.

Cunliffe-Owen, Betty (Ethel Beatrice Bainbridge). *"Thro' the Gates of Memory" (From the Bosphorus to Baghdad)*. London: Hutchinson, 1925.

Daniels, Anthony. *Coups and Cocaine: Two Journeys in South America*. London: John Murray, 1986.

————. *Zanzibar to Timbuktu*. London: John Murray, 1988.

Danziger, Nick. *Danziger's Travels: Beyond Forbidden Frontiers*. New York: Random House, 1987.

Davidson, Basil. *Turkestan Alive: New Travels in Chinese Central Asia*. London: Jonathan Cape, 1957.

Davison, Ann. *By Gemini, Or Marshmallows in the Salad: A Coastwise Cruise from Miami to Miami*. London: Davies, 1962.

————. *Florida Junket: The Story of a Shoestring Cruise*. London: Davies, 1964.

————. *Last Voyage: An Autobiographical Account of All That Led Up to an Illicit Voyage and the Outcome Thereof*. London: Davies, 1951.

De Watteville, Vivienne. *Speak to the Earth: Wanderings and Reflections Among Elephants and Mountains*. New York: Harrison Smith & Robert Haas, 1935.

Digby, George. *Red Horizons*. London: Collins, 1939. Reprinted in the United States as *Under the Redwood Trees*.

Dodwell, Christina. *A Traveller in China*. London: Hodder & Stoughton, 1985.

————. *A Traveller on Horseback: In Eastern Turkey and Iran*. London: Hodder & Stoughton, 1987.

————. *Travels with Fortune: An African Adventure*. London: W. H. Allen, 1979.

————. *Travels with Pegasus: A Microlight Journey Across West Africa*. London: Hodder & Stoughton, 1989.

Doughty, Marion. *Afoot Through the Kashmir Valleys*. London: Sands, 1901.

Douglas, Norman. *Fountains in the Sand*. London: Martin Secker, 1912.

————. *Old Calabria*. London: Martin Secker, 1915.

————. *Siren Land*. London: J. M. Dent & Sons, 1911. Rev. ed. 1923.

Downer, Lesley. *On the Narrow Road: Journey into a Lost Japan*. London: Jonathan Cape, 1989.

Drysdale, Helena. *Alone Through China and Tibet*. London: Constable, 1986.

Durham, Mary Edith. *High Albania*. London: E. Arnold, 1909.

———. *Through the Lands of the Serb*. London: E. Arnold, 1904.

Durrell, Gerald M. *The Overloaded Ark*. New York: Viking, 1953.

Durrell, Lawrence. *Bitter Lemons*. New York: Dutton, 1957.

———. *Prospero's Cell: A Guide to the Landscape and Manners of the Island of Corcyra*. London: Faber & Faber, 1945.

———. *Reflections on a Marine Venus: A Companion to the Landscape of Rhodes*. London: Faber & Faber, 1953.

———. *Sicilian Carousel*. London: Faber & Faber, 1977.

———. *Spirit of Place: Letters and Essays on Travel*. Ed. Alan G. Thomas. New York: Dutton, 1969.

Dyson, John. *The South Seas Dream: An Adventure in Paradise*. Boston: Little, Brown, 1982.

Eden, Emily. *Up the Country: Letters Written to Her Sister from the Upper Provinces of India*. 2 vols. Oxford: Oxford UP, 1930.

Edwards, Ted. *Beyond the Last Oasis: A Solo Walk in the Western Sahara*. London: John Murray, 1985.

———. *Fight the Wild Island: A Solo Walk Across Iceland*. London: John Murray, 1986.

Fairfax, John. *Britannia: Rowing Alone Across the Atlantic*. New York: Simon & Schuster, 1971.

Fairfax, John, and Sylvia Cook. *Oars Across the Pacific*. New York: W. W. Norton, 1972.

Farson, Negley. *Caucasian Journey*. London: Evans Bros., 1951.

Fawcett, Percy Harrison. *Exploration Fawcett*. London: Hutchinson, 1953.

Fenton, James. *All the Wrong Places: Adrift in the Politics of the Pacific Rim*. New York: Atlantic Monthly P, 1988.

Fermor, Patrick Leigh. *Between the Woods and the Water: On Foot to Constantinople from the Hook of Holland, the Middle Danube to the Iron Gates*. London: John Murray, 1986.

———. *Mani: Travels in the Southern Peloponnese*. London: John Murray, 1958.

———. *Roumeli: Travels in Northern Greece*. London: John Murray, 1966.

———. *A Time of Gifts: On Foot to Constantinople: From the Hook of Holland to the Middle Danube*. London: John Murray, 1977.

———. *A Time to Keep Silence*. London: John Murray, 1957. Rev. ed. 1982.

———. *The Traveller's Tree: A Journey Through the Caribbean Islands*. London: John Murray, 1950.

Fitzroy, Yvonne. *A Canadian Panorama*. London: Methuen, 1929.

Flecker, James Elroy. *Some Letters from Abroad*. London: William Heinemann, 1930.

Fleming, Peter. *Brazilian Adventure*. London: Jonathan Cape, 1933.

———. *A Forgotten Journey*. London: Hart-Davis, 1952.

———. *News from Tartary: A Journey from Peking to Kashmir*. London: Jonathan Cape, 1936.

————. *One's Company: A Journey to China*. London: Jonathan Cape, 1934.

Fletcher, Colin. *The Man Who Walked Through Time*. New York: Knopf, 1967.

————. *The Thousand-Mile Summer: In Desert and High Sierra*. Berkeley, Calif.: Howell-North, 1964.

Forbes, Rosita. *Adventure: Being a Gipsy Salad—Some Incidents, Excitements and Impressions of Twelve Highly-Seasoned Years*. London: Cassell, 1928.

————. *Forbidden Road—Kabul to Samarkand*. London: Cassell, 1937.

————. *The Secret of the Sahara: Kufara*. London: Cassell, 1921.

————. *Unconducted Wanderers*. London: John Lane, 1919.

————. *A Unicorn in the Bahamas*. London: H. Jenkins, 1939.

Ford, Ford Madox. *Great Trade Route*. London: George Allen & Unwin, 1937.

Forster, E. M. *The Hill of Devi*. New York: Harcourt, Brace, 1953.

Fraser, David. *The Short Cut to India: The Record of a Journey Along the Route of the Baghdad Railway*. Edinburgh: William Blackwood & Sons, 1909.

Frater, Alexander. *Beyond the Blue Horizon: On the Track of Imperial Airways*. London: William Heinemann, 1986.

Gebler, Carlo. *Driving Through Cuba: An East-West Journey*. London: Hamish Hamilton, 1988.

Gerard, Adelaide M. *Et Nos in Arctis*. London: Ballantyne, 1913.

Gibbings, Robert. *Blue Angels and Whales: A Record of Personal Experiences Below and Above Water*. Harmondsworth, Eng.: Penguin, 1938.

————. *Coming Down the Seine*. London: J. M. Dent & Sons, 1953.

————. *Coming Down the Wye*. London: J. M. Dent & Sons, 1942.

————. *Iorana! A Tahitian Journal*. London: Duckworth, 1932.

————. *Lovely Is the Lee*. London: J. M. Dent & Sons, 1945.

————. *Sweet Thames Run Softly*. London: J. M. Dent & Sons, 1940.

Gibbons, John. *Afoot in Italy*. London: George Newnes, 1930.

————. *Suburban Columbus*. London: George Newnes, 1934. Published in the United States as *Is this America?*

————. *Tramping Through Ireland*. London: Methuen, 1930.

Glazebrook, Philip. *Journey to Kars*. New York: Atheneum, 1984.

Golding, William. *An Egyptian Journal*. London: Faber & Faber, 1985.

Gordon, Jan, and Cora J. Gordon. *On Wandering Wheels: Through Roadside Camps from Maine to Georgia in an Old Sedan Car*. New York: Dodd, Mead, 1928.

————. *Three Lands on Three Wheels*. New York: William Morrow, 1932.

————. *Two Vagabonds in Albania*. London: John Lane, 1927.

————. *Two Vagabonds in Serbia and Montenegro—1915*. Harmondsworth, Eng.: Penguin, 1939.

Gorer, Geoffrey. *Africa Dances: A Book About West Africa Negroes*. London: Faber & Faber, 1935.

Goullart, Peter. *Land of the Lamas: Adventures in Secret Tibet*. New York: Dutton, 1959. Printed in England as *Princes of the Black Bone*.

Graham, Stephen. *The Gentle Art of Tramping*. New York: D. Appleton, 1926.

————. *In Quest of El Dorado*. New York: D. Appleton, 1923.

————. *Through Russian Central Asia*. New York: Macmillan, 1916.

————. *Tramping with a Poet in the Rockies*. New York: D. Appleton, 1922.

————. *A Tramp's Sketches*. London: Macmillan, 1912.

————. *A Vagabond in the Caucasus, with Some Notes of His Experiences Among the Russians*. London: John Lane, 1911.

Greene, Graham. *In Search of a Character: Two African Journals*. London: Bodley Head, 1961.

————. *Journey Without Maps*. London: William Heinemann, 1936.

————. *The Lawless Roads*. London: William Heinemann, 1939. Reprinted in the United States as *Another Mexico*.

————. *Reflections*. London: Reinhardt, 1990.

Grimble, Arthur. *A Pattern of Islands*. London: John Murray, 1952. Reprinted in the United States as *We Chose the Islands*.

————. *Return to the Islands*. London: John Murray, 1957.

Grove, Agnes Geraldine. *Seventy-One Days' Camping in Morocco*. London: Longmans, Green, 1902.

Haldane, J. W. C. *3800 Miles Across Canada*. London: Simpkin, Marshall, Hamilton, Kent, 1900.

Halsey, Margaret. *With Malice Toward Some*. New York: Simon & Schuster, 1938.

Hamilton, Genesta. *A Stone's Throw: Travels from Africa in Six Decades*. London: Hutchinson, 1986.

Hamilton, Helen. *Mountain Madness*. London: William Collins Sons, 1922.

Hampton, Charles, and Janie Hampton. *A Family Outing in Africa*. London: Macmillan, 1988.

Hanbury-Tenison, Marika. *For Better, For Worse: To the Brazilian Jungles and Back Again*. London: Hutchinson, 1972.

————. *A Slice of Spice: Travels to the Indonesian Islands*. London: Hutchinson, 1974.

Hanbury-Tenison, Robin. *A Ride Along the Great Wall*. London: Century Hutchinson, 1987.

Harding, Mike. *Footloose in the Himalaya*. London: Michael Joseph, 1989.

Hardyment, Christina. *Heidi's Alp: One Family's Search for Storybook Europe*. New York: Atlantic Monthly P, 1987.

Harris, Audrey. *Eastern Visas*. London: Collins, 1939.

Harvey, Andrew. *A Journey in Ladakh*. Boston: Houghton Mifflin, 1983.

Hasell, Eva. *Across the Prairie in a Motor Caravan: A 3,000 mile tour by two Englishwomen on Behalf of Religious Education [etc.]*. New York: Macmillan, 1922.

————. *Canyons, Cans and Caravans*. New York: Macmillan, 1930.

————. *Through Western Canada in a Caravan*. London: Society for the Propagation of the Gospel in Foreign Parts, 1925.

Hedley, John. *On Tramp Among the Mongols*. Shanghai: North-China Daily News & Herald, 1906.

Henfrey, Colin. *Manscapes: An American Journey.* Boston: Gambit, 1973.

Herbert, Agnes. *Casuals in the Caucasus: The Diary of a Sporting Holiday.* London: John Lane, 1912.

———. *Two Dianas in Alaska.* London: John Lane, 1909.

———. *Two Dianas in Somaliland: The Record of a Shooting Trip.* London: John Lane, 1908.

Hickman, Katie. *Dreams of the Peaceful Dragon: A Journey Through Bhutan.* London: Gollancz, 1987.

Hillaby, John. *Journey Home: A Walk About England.* New York: Holt, Rinehart & Winston, 1983.

———. *Journey Through Britain.* London: Constable, 1968. Published in the United States as *A Walk Through Britain.*

Hillary, Edmund. *High Adventure.* New York: Dutton, 1955.

Hobson, Sarah. *Masquerade: An Adventure in Iran.* London: John Murray, 1973. Reprinted as *Through Persia in Disguise* and *Through Iran in Disguise.*

Hodson, Peregrine. *Under a Sickle Moon: A Journey Through Afghanistan.* London: Century Hutchinson, 1986.

Holman, Alan. *White River, Brown Water.* London: Hodder & Stoughton, 1985.

Holmes, Richard. *Footsteps: Adventures of a Romantic Biographer.* London: Hodder & Stoughton, 1985.

Hone, Joseph. *Children of the Country: Coast to Coast Across Africa.* London: Hamish Hamilton, 1986.

———. *The Dancing Waiters: Some Collected Travels.* London: Hamish Hamilton, 1975.

———. *Duck Soup in the Black Sea: Further Collected Travels.* London: Hamish Hamilton, 1988.

———. *Gone Tomorrow: Some More Collected Travels.* London: Secker & Warburg, 1981.

Hudson, Mark. *Our Grandmothers' Drums.* London: Secker & Warburg, 1989.

Hudson, Peter. *A Leaf in the Wind: Travels in Africa.* London: Columbus, 1988.

Huxley, Aldous. *Along the Road: Notes and Essays of a Tourist.* New York: George H. Doran, 1925.

———. *Beyond the Mexique Bay.* London: Chatto & Windus, 1934.

———. *Jesting Pilate: An Intellectual Holiday.* New York: George H. Doran, 1926.

Huxley, Elspeth. *Out in the Midday Sun: My Kenya.* London: Chatto & Windus, 1985.

Hyland, Paul. *The Black Heart: A Voyage into Central Africa.* London: Gollancz, 1988.

Isherwood, Christopher. *The Condor and the Cows.* London: Methuen, 1949.

Iyer, Pico. *Video Night in Kathmandu and Other Reports from the Not-So-Far East.* New York: Knopf, 1988.

James, Clive. *Flying Visits.* London: W. W. Norton, 1984.

Jebb, Louisa. *By Desert Ways to Baghdad.* Boston: Dana Estes, 1909.

Jenkins, Catherine Minna. *Sport and Travel in Both Tibets.* London: Blades, East & Blades, 1909.

Jenkinson, Anthony. *Where Seldom a Gun Is Heard.* London: Arthur Barker, 1937.

Jones, Henry Festing. *Diversions in Sicily.* London: A. Rivers, 1909.

———. *Mt. Eryx and Other Diversions of Travel.* London: Jonathan Cape, 1921.

Jukes, Peter. *A Shout in the Street: An Excursion into the Modern City.* London: Faber & Faber, 1990.

Lawrence, D. H. *Etruscan Places.* London: Martin Secker, 1932.

———. *Mornings in Mexico.* London: Martin Secker, 1927.

———. *Sea and Sardinia.* New York: T. McBride, 1921.

———. *Twilight in Italy.* London: Duckworth, 1916.

Lee, Laurie. *As I Walked Out One Midsummer Morning.* New York: Atheneum, 1969.

———. *A Rose for Winter: Travels in Andalusia.* London: Hogarth P, 1955.

Levi, Peter. *The Hill of Kronos.* London: Collins, 1980.

———. *The Light Garden of the Angel King: Journeys in Afghanistan.* London: Collins, 1972. Rev. ed. 1984.

Levin, Bernard. *Hannibal's Footsteps.* London: Jonathan Cape, 1985.

Lewis, Norman. *A Dragon Apparent: Travels in Indo-China.* London: Jonathan Cape, 1951.

———. *Golden Earth: Travels in Burma.* London: Jonathan Cape, 1952.

———. *Sand and Sea in Arabia.* London: G. Routledge & Sons, 1938.

———. *Spanish Adventure.* London: Gollancz, 1935.

———. *To Run Across the Sea.* London: Jonathan Cape, 1989.

Lewis, Wyndham. *Filibusters in Barbary.* London: Grayson & Grayson, 1932.

———. *Journey into Barbary: Morocco Writings and Drawings.* Ed. C. J. Fox. Santa Barbara, Calif.: Black Sparrow P, 1983. Includes most of *Filibusters in Barbary* and *Kasbahs and Souks* (which was previously unpublished).

Linklater, Andro. *Wild People: Travels with Borneo's Head-Hunters.* New York: Atlantic Monthly P, 1990.

Lloyd, Sarah. *Chinese Characters: A Journey Through China.* London: Collins, 1987.

Lubbock, Percy. *Roman Pictures.* London: Jonathan Cape, 1923.

Macaulay, Rose. *Fabled Shore: From the Pyrenees to Portugal.* New York: Farrar, Straus, 1949.

MacNeice, Louis. *I Crossed the Minch.* London: Longmans, Green, 1938.

Mainwaring, Marcus. *Nor Any Drop to Drink: England to Australia, May 1987– January 1988.* London: Bloomsbury, 1988.

Mannin, Ethel. *Jungle Journey.* London: Jarrolds, 1950.

Markham, Beryl. *West with the Night.* Boston: Houghton Mifflin, 1942.

Marnham, Patrick. *So Far from God: A Journey to Central America.* New York: Viking-Penguin, 1985.

Maugham, W. Somerset. *The Gentleman in the Parlour: A Record of a Journey from Rangoon to Haiphong.* London: William Heinemann, 1930.

Maxwell, Gavin. *A Reed Shaken by the Wind*. London: Longmans, Green, 1957.

Mear, Roger, and Robert Swan. *In the Footsteps of Scott*. London: Jonathan Cape, 1987.

Meegan, George. *The Longest Walk: An Odyssey of the Human Spirit*. New York: Dodd, Mead, 1988.

Mills, Dorothy. *The Golden Land: A Record of Travel in West Africa*. London: Duckworth, 1929.

——— . *The Road to Timbuktu*. London: Duckworth, 1924.

——— . *Through Liberia*. London: Duckworth, 1926.

Mitchison, Naomi. *Mucking Around: Five Continents over Fifty Years*. London: Gollancz, 1981.

Moffat, Gwen. *Hard Road West: Alone on the California Trail*. New York: Viking, 1981.

——— . *The Storm Seekers: A Journey in the Footsteps of John Charles Frémont*. London: Secker & Warburg, 1989.

Monbiot, George. *Poisoned Arrows: An Investigative Journey Through Indonesia*. London: Michael Joseph, 1989.

Moorhouse, Geoffrey. *Apples in the Snow: A Journey to Samarkand*. London: Hodder & Stoughton, 1990.

——— . *The Fearful Void*. Philadelphia: J. B. Lippincott, 1974.

——— . *To the Frontier*. London: Hodder & Stoughton, 1984.

Morley, John David. *Pictures from the Water Trade: Adventures of a Westerner in Japan*. Boston: Atlantic Monthly P, 1985.

Morris, Elizabeth Keith. *An Englishwoman in the Canadian West*. London: Simpkin Marshall, 1913.

Morris, James [Jan Morris]. *Coast to Coast*. London: Faber & Faber, 1956.

——— . *Places*. London: Faber & Faber, 1972.

Morris, Jan. *Among the Cities*. New York: Oxford UP, 1985.

——— . *Destinations: Essays from "Rolling Stone."* New York: Oxford UP, 1980.

——— . *Journeys*. New York: Oxford UP, 1984.

Morton, H. V. *The Call of England*. London: Methuen, 1928.

——— . *I Saw Two Englands: The Record of a Journey Before the War, and After the Outbreak of the War, in the Year 1939*. London: Methuen, 1942.

——— . *In Scotland Again*. London: Methuen, 1933.

——— . *In Search of England*. London: Methuen, 1927.

——— . *In Search of Ireland*. London: Methuen, 1930.

——— . *In Search of South Africa*. London: Methuen, 1948.

——— . *Middle East: A Record of Travel in the Countries of Egypt, Palestine, Iraq, Turkey and Greece*. London: Methuen, 1941.

——— . *A Traveller in Italy*. New York: Dodd, Mead, 1964.

Muir, Edwin. *Scottish Journey*. London: William Heinemann, 1935.

Myers, Wendy. *Seven League Boots: The Story of My Seven-Year Hitch-Hike Round the World*. London: Hodder & Stoughton, 1969.

Naipaul, Shiva. *North of South: An African Journey*. London: André Deutsch, 1978.

Naipaul, V. S. *Among the Believers: An Islamic Journey*. London: André Deutsch, 1972.

———. *An Area of Darkness*. London: André Deutsch, 1964.

———. *India: A Wounded Civilization*. New York: Knopf, 1977.

———. *The Middle Passage: Impressions of Five Societies—British, French and Dutch—in the West Indies and South America*. London: André Deutsch, 1962.

———. *A Turn in the South*. New York: Knopf, 1989.

Newby, Eric. *The Big Red Train Ride: A Ride on the Trans-Siberian Railway*. New York: St. Martin's P, 1978.

———. *The Last Grain Race*. Boston: Houghton Mifflin, 1956.

———. *On the Shores of the Mediterranean*. Boston: Little, Brown, 1984.

———. *Round Ireland in Low Gear*. London: Collins, 1987.

———. *A Short Walk in the Hindu Kush*. London: Secker & Warburg, 1958.

———. *Slowly Down the Ganges*. London: Hodder & Stoughton, 1966.

Newman, Bernard. *Round the World in 70 Days*. London: Herbert Jenkins, 1964.

Newton, Wilfrid Douglas. *Westward with the Prince of Wales*. London: Hurst & Blackett, 1920.

Nicholl, Charles. *Borderlines: A Journey in Thailand and Burma*. London: Secker & Warburg, 1988.

Nichols, Beverley. *No Place Like Home*. London: Jonathan Cape, 1936.

———. *The Sun in My Eyes, or How Not to Go Round the World*. London: William Heinemann, 1969.

Nicholson, Michael. *Across the Limpopo: A Family's Hazardous 4,000-Mile Journey Through Africa*. London: Robson, 1988.

Nicolson, Nigel, and Adam Nicolson. *Two Roads to Dodge City*. New York: Harper & Row, 1987.

Nossiter, Harold. *Northward Ho! Being the Log of a 35 Ton Schooner from Sydney to Plymouth*. London: H. F. & G. Witherby, 1937.

O'Brien, Conor. *Across Three Oceans: A Colonial Voyage in the Yacht "Saoirse."* London: Arnold, 1926.

O'Hanlon, Redmond. *In Trouble Again: A Journey Between the Orinoco and the Amazon*. London: Hamish Hamilton, 1988.

———. *Into the Heart of Borneo*. Edinburgh: Salamander P, 1984.

Orwell, George. *Down and Out in Paris and London*. London: Gollancz, 1933.

———. *Homage to Catalonia*. London: Secker & Warburg, 1938.

———. *The Road to Wigan Pier*. London: Gollancz, 1937.

Page, Robin. *Journeys into Britain*. London: Hodder & Stoughton, 1982.

Paxman, Jeremy. *Through the Volcanoes: A Central American Journey*. London: Michael Joseph, 1985.

Perham, Margery. *East African Journey: Kenya and Tanganyika, 1929–30*. London: Faber & Faber, 1976.

Pern, Stephen. *The Beach of Morning: A Walk in West Africa*. London: Hodder & Stoughton, 1983.

——. *The Great Divide: A Walk Through America Along the Continental Divide*. New York: Viking-Penguin, 1987.

Pickthall, Marmaduke. *Oriental Encounters: Palestine and Syria (1894–5–6)*. London: Wm. Collins Sons, 1918.

Pilkington, John. *An Adventure on the Old Silk Road: From Venice to the Yellow Sea*. London: Century Hutchinson, 1989.

——. *Into Thin Air*. London: George Allen & Unwin, 1985.

Portway, Christopher. *Journey Along the Spine of the Andes*. Sparkford, Eng.: Oxford Illustrated P, 1984.

Potter, Ursula Barnett. *I'll Fly No More: An Airwoman's Diary*. London: George Allen, 1951.

Powell, Anthony. *The Empire Revisited*. London: Cleveland P, 1985.

Powell, Sydney Walter. *Adventures of a Wanderer*. London: Jonathan Cape, 1928.

Prentice, James K. *Time, Chance and Change*. Braunton, Eng.: Merlin, 1984.

Priestley, J. B. *English Journey: Being a Rambling but Truthful Account of What One Man Saw and Heard and Felt and Thought During a Journey Through England During the Autumn of the Year 1933*. London: William Heinemann, 1934.

Pritchett, V. S. *At Home and Abroad: Travel Essays*. Berkeley: North Point P, 1989.

——. *Marching Spain*. London: E. Benn, 1928.

——. *The Offensive Traveller*. New York: Knopf, 1964.

Pryce-Jones, Alan. *The Spring Journey*. London: Cobden-Sanderson, 1931.

Pryce-Jones, David. *Next Generation: Travels in Israel*. London: Weidenfeld & Nicolson, 1964.

Pye-Smith, Charlie. *The Other Nile: Journeys in Egypt, the Sudan and Ethiopia*. New York: Viking-Penguin, 1986.

——. *Travels in Nepal: The Sequestered Kingdom*. London: Aurum P, 1988.

Quennell, Peter. *A Superficial Journey Through Tokyo and Peking*. London: Faber & Faber, 1932.

Raban, Jonathan. *Arabia: A Journey Through the Looking Glass*. London: William Collins Sons, 1979.

——. *Coasting*. New York: Simon & Schuster, 1987.

——. *Hunting Mister Heartbreak*. London: Collins Harvill, 1990.

——. *Old Glory: An American Voyage*. New York: Simon & Schuster, 1981.

Rankin, Nicholas. *Dead Man's Chest: Travels After Robert Louis Stevenson*. London: Faber & Faber, 1987.

Ratcliffe, Dorothy Una. *The Babes of the Sea: Being an Account of Their First Voyage in "Sea Swallow."* Leeds, Eng.: North Country P, 1928.

——. *Equatorial Dawn: Travel Letters from North, East, and Central Africa*. London: Eyre & Spottiswoode, 1936.

————. *News of Persephone: Impressions in Northern and Southern Greece with a Car, a Kettle and Cameras.* London: Eyre & Spottiswoode, 1939.

————. *South African Summer: 5,000 Miles with a Car and a Caravan-Trailer.* London: Eyre & Spotiswoode, 1936.

Raven-Hart, Rowland. *Canoe Errant on the Mississippi.* London: Methuen, 1938. Published in the United States as *Down the Mississippi.*

Reynolds, Reginald. *Cairo to Cape Town: A Pilgrimage in Search of Hope.* Garden City, N.Y.: Doubleday, 1955.

Rhodes, Anthony Richard Ewart. *The Dalmatian Coast.* London: Evans Bros., 1955.

————. *A Sabine Journey to Rome in Holy Year.* London: Putnam, 1952.

————. *Where the Turk Trod: A Journey to Sarajevo with a Slavonic Mussulman.* London: Weidenfeld & Nicolson, 1956.

Ridgway, John. *Amazon Journey.* 1972. Rpt. Garden City, N.Y.: Doubleday, 1979.

————. *Road to Elizabeth: A Quest in the Mountains of Peru.* London: Gollancz, 1986. Reprinted in the United States as *Road to Osambre.*

Roome, William J. W. *Tramping Through Africa: A Dozen Crossings of the Continent.* New York: Macmillan, 1930.

Rushdie, Salman. *The Jaguar Smile: A Nicaraguan Journey.* New York: Viking, 1987.

Sackville-West, V. *Passenger to Teheran.* London: Hogarth P, 1926.

————. *Twelve Days: An Account of a Journey Across the Bakhtiari Mountains in South-western Persia.* Garden City, N.Y.: Doubleday, Doran, 1928.

Sansom, William. *Blue Skies, Brown Studies.* Boston: Atlantic Monthly P, 1961.

Sassoon, Philip. *The Third Route.* London: William Heinemann, 1929.

Savory, Isabel. *In the Tail of the Peacock.* London: Hutchinson, 1903.

————. *A Sportswoman in India: Personal Adventures and Experiences of Travel in Known and Unknown India.* London: Hutchinson, 1900.

Selby, Bettina. *Riding North One Summer.* London: Chatto & Windus, 1990.

————. *Riding the Desert Trail: By Bicycle to the Source of the Nile.* London: Chatto & Windus, 1988.

————. *Riding the Mountains Down.* London: Gollancz, 1984.

————. *Riding to Jerusalem.* London: Sidgwick & Jackson, 1985.

Severin, Timothy. *The Brendan Voyage.* New York: McGraw-Hill, 1978.

————. *Crusader: By Horse to Jerusalem.* London: Hutchinson, 1989.

————. *The Jason Voyage: The Quest for the Golden Fleece.* London: Hutchinson, 1985.

————. *The Sindbad Voyage.* London: Arrow Books, 1982.

————. *Tracking Marco Polo.* London: Routledge & Kegan Paul, 1964.

————. *The Ulysses Voyage: Sea Search for the "Odyssey."* London: Hutchinson, 1987.

Sewell, Brian. *South from Ephesus: Travels in Aegean Turkey.* London: Century Hutchinson, 1988.

Shand, Alexander Innes. *Old Time Travel: Personal Reminiscences of the Continent Forty Years Ago Compared with Experiences of the Present Day*. London: John Murray, 1903.

Shukman, Henry. *Sons of the Moon: A Journey in the Andes*. New York: Charles Scribner's Sons, 1989.

Sillitoe, Alan. *Road to Volgograd*. New York: Knopf, 1964.

Simon, Ted. *Jupiter's Travels*. Garden City, N.Y.: Doubleday, 1979.

Simpson, Myrtle. *Due North*. London: Gollancz, 1970.

———. *Home Is a Tent*. London: Gollancz, 1964.

———. *White Horizons*. London: Gollancz, 1967.

Sinclair, Ronald. *Adventures in Persia: To India by the Back Door*. London: H. F. & G. Witherby, 1988.

Sitwell, Constance. *Flowers and Elephants*. London: Jonathan Cape, 1927.

———. *Lotus and Pyramid*. London: Jonathan Cape, 1928.

Sitwell, Osbert. *Discursions on Travel, Art and Life*. London: G. Richards, 1925.

———. *The Four Continents: Being More Discursions on Travel, Art, and Life*. London: Macmillan, 1954.

———. *Winters of Content, and Other Discursions on Mediterranean Art and Travel*. London: Duckworth, 1932.

Sitwell, Sacheverell. *Arabesque and Honeycomb*. London: R. Hale, 1957.

———. *The Bridge of the Brocade Sash: Travels and Observations in Japan*. London: Weidenfeld & Nicolson, 1959.

———. *Golden Wall and Mirador: Travels and Observations in Peru*. London: Weidenfeld & Nicolson, 1961.

Smeeton, Beryl. *Winter Shoes in Springtime*. London: Rupert Hart-Davis, 1961.

Smith, Anthony. *Smith and Son: An Expedition into Africa*. London: Hodder & Stoughton, 1984.

Speed, Maude. *A Scamper Tour to Rhodesia and South Africa*. London: Longmans, Green, 1933.

———. *Through Central France to the Pyrenees*. London: Longmans, Green, 1924.

———. *A Yachtswoman's Cruises and Steamer Voyages*. London: Longmans, Green, 1911.

Spender, Stephen, and David Hockney. *China Diary*. New York: Harry N. Abrams, 1982.

Staley, John. *Words for My Brother: Travels Between the Hindu Kush and the Himalayas*. New York: Oxford UP, 1982.

Stark, Freya. *Alexander's Path: From Caria to Cilicia*. New York: Harcourt, Brace & World, 1958.

———. *Beyond Euphrates*. London: John Murray, 1951.

———. *The Coast of Incense: Autobiography 1933–1939*. London: John Murray, 1953.

———. *Letters from Syria*. London: John Murray, 1942.

———. *The Minaret of Djam: An Excursion in Afghanistan*. London: John Murray, 1970.

———. *Riding to the Tigris*. London: John Murray, 1959.

———. *The Southern Gates of Arabia: A Journey in the Hadhramaut*. London: John Murray, 1936.

———. *The Valleys of the Assassins and Other Persian Travels*. London: John Murray, 1934.

———. *A Winter in Arabia*. London: John Murray, 1940.

Starkie, Walter. *Don Gypsy: Adventures with a Fiddle in Barbary, Andalusia and La Mancha*. London: John Murray, 1936.

———. *Raggle Taggle: Adventures with a Fiddle in Hungary and Roumania*. London: John Murray, 1933.

Stuck, Hudson. *The Ascent of Denali: A Narrative of the First Complete Ascent of the Highest Peak in North America*. New York: Charles Scribner's Sons, 1914.

———. *Ten Thousand Miles with a Dog Sled: A Narrative of Winter Travel in Interior Alaska*. New York: Charles Scribner's Sons, 1914.

———. *Voyages on the Yukon and Its Tributaries: A Narrative of Summer Travel in the Interior of Alaska*. London: T. Werner Laurie, 1917.

Symons, Arthur. *Cities*. London: J. M. Dent, 1903.

———. *Cities and Sea-Coasts and Islands*. London: W. Collins Sons, 1918.

Tanner, Marcus. *Ticket to Latvia: A Journey from Berlin to the Baltic*. New York: Henry Holt, 1989.

Thesiger, Wilfred. *Arabian Sands*. London: Longmans, Green, 1959.

———. *The Life of My Choice*. London: William Collins, 1987.

———. *The Marsh Arabs*. London: Longmans, Green, 1964.

Thomson, Alex, and Nick Rossiter. *Ram Ram India*. London: William Collins, 1987.

Thubron, Colin. *Among the Russians*. London: William Heinemann, 1983. Reprinted in the United States as *Where Nights Are Longest: Travels by Car Through Western Russia*.

———. *Behind the Wall: A Journey Through China*. New York: Atlantic Monthly P, 1987.

Tomlinson, H. M. *The Face of the Earth, with Some Hints for Those About to Travel*. London: Duckworth, 1950.

———. *Gifts of Fortune and Hints for Those About to Travel*. London: Harper & Bros., 1926.

———. *The Sea and the Jungle*. London: Duckworth, 1912.

———. *Tidemarks: Some Records of a Journey to the Beaches of the Moluccas and the Forest of Malaya in 1923*. London: Cassell, 1924.

Torday, Emil. *Camp and Tramp in African Wilds: A Record of Adventure, Impressions, and Experiences During Many Years Spent Among the Savage Tribes Round Lake Tanganyika and in Central Africa, with a Description of Native Life, Character, and Customs*. London: Seeley, Service, 1913.

Toy, Barbara. *Columbus was Right! Rover Around the World*. London: John Murray, 1958.

———. *A Fool in the Desert: Journeys in Libya*. London: John Murray, 1956.

———. *A Fool on Wheels: Tangier to Baghdad by Land-Rover*. London: John Murray, 1955.

———. *A Fool Strikes Oil: Across Saudi Arabia*. London: John Murray, 1957.

———. *The Highway of the Three Kings: Arabia—from South to North*. London: John Murray, 1968.

———. *In Search of Sheba: Across the Sahara to Ethiopia*. London: John Murray, 1961.

———. *The Way of the Chariots: Niger River—Sahara—Libya*. London: John Murray, 1964.

Toynbee, Arnold Joseph. *East to West: A Journey Round the World*. New York: Oxford UP, 1958.

Tracy, Honor. *Silk Hats and No Breakfast: Notes on a Spanish Journey*. London: Methuen, 1957.

———. *Winter in Castille*. New York: Random House, 1974.

Trevor, Roy. *En Route: A Descriptive Automobile Tour Through Nine Countries and Over Nineteen Great Passes of Europe*. London: Edward Stanford, 1908.

Tschiffely, A. F. *Tschiffely's Ride: Ten Thousand Miles in the Saddle from Southern Cross to Pole Star*. New York: Simon & Schuster, 1933. Reprinted as *Southern Cross to Pole Star: Tschiffely's Ride*.

Ward, F. Kingdon. *From China to Hkamti Long*. London: Edward Arnold, 1924.

Waugh, Alec. *Hot Countries*. New York: Farrar & Rinehart, 1930.

———. *Love and the Caribbean: Tales, Characters and Scenes of the West Indies*. New York: Farrar, Straus & Cudahy, 1958.

———. *The Sugar Islands: A Caribbean Travelogue*. New York: Farrar, Straus, 1949.

———. *Where the Clocks Chime Twice*. London: Cassell, 1952.

Waugh, Evelyn. *Labels: A Mediterranean Journal*. London: Duckworth, 1930. Published in the United States as *A Bachelor Abroad*.

———. *Ninety-Two Days: The Account of a Tropical Journey Through British Guiana and Part of Brazil*. London: Duckworth, 1934.

———. *Remote People*. London: Duckworth, 1931.

———. *They Were Still Dancing*. New York: Jonathan Cape & Harrison Smith, 1931.

———. *Tourist in Africa*. Boston: Little, Brown, 1960.

———. *Waugh in Abyssinia*. London: Longmans, Green, 1936.

———. *When the Going Was Good*. London: Duckworth, 1946.

West, Rebecca. *Black Lamb and Grey Falcon: A Journey Through Yugoslavia*. London: Macmillan, 1941.

White, Don. *Get Up and Go: Round the World on Twenty-Five Pounds*. London: Allan Wingate, 1959.

Williams, Hugo. *All the Time in the World*. London: Alan Ross, 1966.

————. *No Particular Place to Go*. London: Jonathan Cape, 1981.

Wilson, Angus. *Reflections in a Writer's Eye: Travel Pieces*. London: Secker & Warburg, 1986.

Winchester, Simon. *Outposts*. London: Hodder & Stoughton, 1985. Published in the United States as *The Sun Never Sets: Travels to the Remaining Outposts of the British Empire*.

Young, Gavin. *Halfway Around the World: An Improbable Journey*. New York: Random House, 1981.

————. *Slow Boats Home*. London: Hutchinson, 1985.

————. *Slow Boats to China*. London: Hutchinson, 1981.

————. *Worlds Apart: Travels in War and Peace*. London: Hutchinson, 1987.

Australian Works

Bartlett, Norman. *Land of the Lotus Eaters: A Book Mostly About Siam*. London: Jarrolds, 1959.

Birtles, Dora. *A Journal of a Voyage*. London: Jonathan Cape, 1935. Republished as *North-West By North*.

Clune, Frank. *Hands Across the Pacific: A Voyage of Discovery from Australia to the Hawaiian Islands and Canada, April to June, 1950*. Sydney: Angus & Robertson, 1951.

Davidson, Robyn. *Tracks*. New York: Pantheon, 1980.

Du Faur, Freda. *The Conquest of Mt. Cook and Other Climbs: An Account of Four Seasons' Mountaineering on the Southern Alps of New Zealand*. London: George Allen & Unwin, 1915.

Hall, Rodney. *Journey Through Australia*. London: John Murray, 1988.

Hurley, Frank. *Pearls and Savages: Adventures in the Air, on Land and Sea in New Guinea*. New York: G. P. Putnam's Sons, 1924.

Law, Phillip. *Antarctic Odyssey*. Melbourne: William Heinemann Australia, 1983.

Lawrence, Murray. *High Times in the Middle of Nowhere: The Misadventures of Murray Lawrence, Compulsive Traveller*. St. Lucia, Brisbane: U of Queensland P, 1986.

Murray, J. B. *American Trails*. Carlton, Victoria: Melbourne UP, 1944.

Murray, Max. *The World's Back Doors*. London: Jonathan Cape, 1927.

Wilby, Sorrel. *Journey Across Tibet: A Young Woman's 1900-Mile Trek Across the Rooftop of the World*. Chicago: Contemporary, 1989.

Austrian Work

Canetti, Elias. *The Voices of Marrakesh: A Record of a Visit*. Trans. J. A. Underwood. London: Marion Boyars, 1978. Originally published in 1967.

Canadian Works

Abley, Mark. *Beyond Forget: Rediscovering the Prairies.* San Francisco: Sierra Club, 1986.

Cameron, Agnes Dean. *The New North: Being Some Account of a Woman's Journey Through Canada to the Arctic.* New York: D. Appleton, 1909.

Duncan, Norman. *Australian Byways: The Narrative of a Sentimental Traveler.* New York: Harper & Bros., 1915.

——. *Going Down from Jerusalem: The Narrative of a Sentimental Traveller.* New York: Harper & Bros., 1909.

Fraser, Marian Botsford. *Walking the Line: Travels Along the Canadian/American Border.* San Francisco: Sierra Club, 1989.

Gomery, Percy. *A Motor Scamper 'Cross Canada: A Human Interest Narrative of a Pathfinding Journey from Montreal to Vancouver.* Toronto: Ryerson P, 1922.

Grove, Frederick Philip. *Over Prairie Trails.* Toronto: McClelland & Stewart, 1922.

——. *A Search for America: The Odyssey of an Immigrant.* Montreal: Louis Carrier, 1928.

Hale, Katherine. *Canadian Cities of Romance.* New York: George H. Doran, 1922.

Haultain, Arnold. *Two Country Walks in Canada.* Toronto: G. N. Morang, 1903.

Hutchison, Bruce. *Canada, Tomorrow's Giant.* New York: Knopf, 1957.

——. *The Unknown Country: Canada and Her People.* New York: Coward-McCann, 1942.

Leacock, Stephen. *Adventures of the Far North: A Chronicle of the Frozen Seas.* Toronto: Glasgow, Brook, 1914.

——. *My Discovery of England.* London: John Lane, 1922.

——. *My Discovery of the West: A Discussion of East and West in Canada.* Toronto: Thomas Allen, 1937.

Mowat, Farley. *The Desperate People.* Toronto: McClelland & Stewart, 1959. Rev. ed. 1975.

Patterson, Raymond M. *The Buffalo Head.* New York: William Sloane, 1961.

——. *Trail to the Interior.* New York: William Morrow, 1966.

Price, Willard. *I Cannot Rest from Travel: An Autobiography of Adventure in Seventy Lands.* New York: John Day, 1951.

——. *Odd Way Round the World.* New York: John Day, 1969.

Wood, Heather. *Third-Class Ticket.* London: Routledge & Kegan Paul, 1980.

Woodcock, George. *Caves in the Desert: Travels in China.* Vancouver: Douglas & McIntyre, 1988.

Wright, Ronald. *Cut Stones and Crossroads: A Journey in the Two Worlds of Peru.* New York: Viking, 1984.

——. *On Fiji Islands.* New York: Viking, 1986.

——. *Time Among the Maya: Travels in Belize, Guatemala and Mexico.* New York: Weidenfeld & Nicolson, 1989.

Chinese Work

Zongren, Liu. *Two Years in the Melting Pot*. San Francisco: China, 1984.

Danish Works

Bjerre, Jens. *The Last Cannibals*. Trans. Estrid Bannister. New York: William Morrow, 1942.
Haslund, Henning. *Mongolian Journey*. Trans. F. H. Lyon. London: Routledge & Kegan Paul, 1949. Originally published in 1946.
————. *Tents in Mongolia: Adventures and Experiences Among the Nomads of Central Asia*. Trans. Elizabeth Sprigge and Claude Napier. New York: Dutton, 1934.
Holdt, Jacob. *American Pictures: A Personal Journey Through the American Underclass*. Copenhagen: American Pictures Foundation, 1985.
Klemensen, Arvid. *Strange Island: The Noona Dan in the South Seas*. Trans. Joan Bulman. London: Souvenir P, 1965.

Dutch Works

Leeflang, Gerard. *American Travels of a Dutch Hobo, 1923–26*. Ames: Iowa State UP, 1984.
Visser, Jeannette (Hooft). *Among the Kara-Korum Glaciers in 1925*. London: Edward Arnold, 1926.

Egyptian Work

Abou-Saif, Laila. *Middle East Journal: A Woman's Journey into the Heart of the Arab World*. New York: Charles Scribner's Sons, 1990.

French Works

Baudrillard, Jean. *America*. Trans. Chris Turner. London: Verso, 1988. Originally published in 1986.
Butor, Michel. *Letters from the Antipodes*. Trans. Michael Spencer. Athens: Ohio UP, 1981. This is a portion of a translation of *Boomerang, le génie du lieu*, originally published in 1978.
————. *Mobile: Study for a Representation of the United States*. Trans. Richard Howard. New York: Simon & Schuster, 1963. Originally published in 1962.
————. *The Spirit of Mediterranean Places*. Trans. Lydia Davis. Marlboro, Vt: Marlboro P, 1986. Originally published in 1958.
David-Neel, Alexandra. *My Journey to Lhasa: The Personal Story of the Only White Woman who Succeeded in Entering the Forbidden City*. London: William Heinemann, 1927.

Gide, André. *Return from the U.S.S.R.* Trans. Dorothy Bussy. London: Secker &
    Warburg, 1937. Originally published in 1936. Republished as *Back from the
    U.S.S.R.*

———. *Travels in the Congo.* Trans. Dorothy Bussy. New York: Knopf, 1929.
    Comprises *Voyage au Congo* (1927) and *Le Retour du Thcad* (1928).

Le Corbusier [Charles Edouard Jeanneret-Gris]. *Journey to the East.* Trans. Ivan
    Zaknić. Cambridge: MIT P, 1987. Originally published in 1966.

Lévi-Strauss, Claude. *Tristes Tropiques.* Trans. John and Doreen Weightman. Lon-
    don: Jonathan Cape, 1973. Originally published in 1955.

Migot, André. *Tibetan Marches.* Trans. Peter Fleming. London: Rupert Hart-
    Davis, 1955.

Saint-Exupéry, Antoine de. *Wind, Sand and Stars.* Trans. Lewis Galantière. New
    York: Reynal & Hitchcock, 1939.

Tazieff, Haroun. *South from the Red Sea.* Trans. Naomi Lewis. London: Travel
    Book Club, 1956.

German Works

Böll, Heinrich. *Irish Journal.* Trans. Leila Vennewitz. New York: McGraw-Hill,
    1967. Originally published 1957.

Cohnstaedt, Wilhelm. *Western Canada, 1909.* Trans. Herta Holle-Scherer. Regina,
    Saskatchewan: Canadian Plains Research Center, 1976.

Enzensberger, Hans Magnus. *Europe, Europe: Forays into a Continent.* Trans.
    Martin Chalmers. New York: Pantheon, 1989.

Helfritz, Hans. *The Yemen: A Secret Journey.* Trans. M. Heron. London: George
    Allen & Unwin, 1958. Originally published 1956.

Ritter, Christiane. *A Woman in the Polar Night.* Trans. Jane Degras. New York:
    Dutton, 1954.

Greek Works

Kazantzakis, Nikos. *England.* Anonymous translation. New York: Simon & Schus-
    ter, 1965. Originally published in 1941.

———. *Japan/China.* Trans. George C. Pappageotes. New York: Simon & Schus-
    ter, 1963. Originally published in 1938.

———. *Journey to the Morea.* Trans. F. A. Reed. New York: Simon & Schuster,
    1965. Originally published in 1937.

———. *Journeying: Travels in Italy, Egypt, Sinai, Jerusalem and Cyprus.* Trans.
    Themi Vasils & Theodora Vasils. Boston: Little, Brown, 1975. Originally pub-
    lished in 1927.

———. *Spain.* Trans. Amy Mims. New York: Simon & Schuster, 1963. Originally
    published in 1937.

Hungarian Work

Bodó, Ferenc J. *A Drive Across Africa*. Hicksville, N.Y.: Exposition P, 1977.

Indian Works

Chaudhuri, Nirad C. *A Passage to England*. New York: St. Martin's P, 1959.
Dustoor, Phiroze E. *American Days: A Traveller's Diary*. Bombay: Orient Longmans, 1952.
Seth, Vikram. *From Heaven Lake*. New York: Random House, 1983.

Irish Works

Fennell, Desmond. *A Connacht Journey*. Dublin: Gill & Macmillan, 1987.
Higgins, Aidan. *Ronda Gorge and Other Precipices: Travel Writing, 1956–1989*. London: Secker & Warburg, 1989.
Lawlor, Eric. *In Bolivia*. New York: Random House, 1989.
McAughtry, Sam. *Down in the Free State*. Dublin: Gill & Macmillan, 1987.
Mason, Arthur. *Wide Seas and Many Lands: An Autobiography*. London: Jonathan Cape, 1923. Published in the United States as *Ocean Echoes*.
Murphy, Dervla. *Cameroon with Egbert*. London: John Murray, 1989.
———. *Eight Feet in the Andes*. London: John Murray, 1983.
———. *Full Tilt: Ireland to India with a Bicycle*. London: John Murray, 1965.
———. *In Ethiopia with a Mule*. London: John Murray, 1968.
———. *Muddling Through in Madagascar*. London: John Murray, 1985.
———. *On A Shoestring to Coorg: An Experience of South India*. London: John Murray, 1976.
———. *The Waiting Land: A Spell in Nepal*. London: John Murray, 1967.
———. *Where the Indus is Young: A Winter in Baltistan*. London: John Murray, 1977.
O'Connor, Frank. *Irish Miles*. London: Macmillan, 1947.
———. *Leinster, Munster and Connaught*. London: R. Hale, 1950.
———. *A Picture Book*. Dublin: Cuala P, 1943.
O'Faolain, Sean. *An Irish Journey*. London: Longmans, Green, 1940.
Somerville, Edith OE. *The States Through Irish Eyes*. New York: Houghton Mifflin, 1930.
Somerville-Large, Peter. *To the Navel of the World: Yaks and Unheroic Travels in Nepal and Tibet*. London: Hamish Hamilton, 1987.

Italian Works

Barzini, Luigi. *Pekin to Paris: An Account of Prince Borghese's Journey Across Two Continents in a Motor-Car*. Trans. L. P. de Castelvecchio. London: E. G. Richards, 1907.

Magris, Claudio. *Danube.* Trans. Patrick Creagh. New York: Farrar, Straus & Giroux, 1986.

Pasolini, Pier Paolo. *The Scent of India.* Trans. David Price. London: Olive P, 1984. Originally published in 1974.

Scarfoglio, Antonio. *Round the World in a Motor-Car.* Trans. J. Parker Heyes. London: G. Richards, 1909.

Japanese Work

Dazai, Osamu. *Return to Tsugaru: Travels of a Purple Tramp.* Trans. James Westerhoven. Tokyo: Kodansha International, 1985.

Lebanese Work

Nasr, Kameel Bassam. *The World Up Close: A Cyclist's Adventures on Five Continents.* Bedford, Mass.: Mills & Sanderson, 1990.

New Zealand Works

Garland, Nicholas. *An Indian Journal.* Chicago: Academy Chicago, 1983.

————. *Travels with My Sketchbook.* London: Harrap, 1987.

Hillary, Louise. *High Time.* New York: Dutton, 1974.

Nigerian Work

Ajala, Olabisi. *An African Abroad.* London: Jarrolds, 1963.

Norwegian Works

Freuchen, Peter. *Arctic Adventure: My Life in the Frozen North.* New York: Farrar & Rinehart, 1935.

————. *Ice Floes and Flaming Water: A True Adventure in Melville Bay.* Trans. Johan Hambro. New York: Julian Messner, 1954.

Heyerdahl, Thor. *Fatu-Hiva: Back to Nature.* London: George Allen & Unwin, 1974.

————. *Kon-Tiki: Across the Pacific by Raft.* Trans. F. H. Lyon. Chicago: Rand McNally, 1950.

————. *The Ra Expeditions.* Trans. Patricia Crampton. London: George Allen & Unwin, 1971.

Skrede, Wilfred. *Across the Roof of the World.* Trans. M. A. Michael. London: Staples P, 1954.

Polish Works

Kapuściński, Ryszard. *The Soccer War*. Trans. William Brand. New York: Knopf, 1991.

Sikorski, Radek. *Dust of the Saints: A Journey to Herat in Time of War*. London: Chatto & Windus, 1989.

Russian Works

Mandelstam, Osip. *Journey to Armenia*. Trans. Henry Gifford. San Francisco: George F. Ritchie, 1979. Reprint of 1933 ed.

Romm, Michael. *The Ascent of Mt. Stalin*. Trans. Alec Brown. London: Laurence & Wishart, 1936.

St. Lucian Work

Walcott, Derek. *The Fortunate Traveler*. New York: Farrar, Straus & Giroux, 1981.

Scottish Works

Dalrymple, William. *In Xanadu: A Quest*. London: William Collins Sons, 1989.

Elliot, Andrew G. *Hell! I'm British: A Plain Man Looks at America, Americans and Englishmen*. London: H. Joseph, 1939.

Hood, Colin. *Going Places: A Tour in North America*. London: Collins, 1939.

Hutchison, Isobel Wylie. *North to the Rime-Ringed Sun: Being the Record of an Alaskan-Canadian Journey Made in 1933–34*. London: Blackie & Son, 1934.

———. *Stepping Stones from Alaska to Asia*. London: Blackie & Son, 1937. Reprinted as *The Aleutian Islands* in 1942.

Noble, Christina. *Over the High Passes: The True Story of One Woman's Year in the Himalayas*. London: Collins, 1987.

Patterson, George N. *Tibetan Journey*. London: Faber & Faber, 1954.

Scott, Alastair. *Scot Free: A Journey from the Arctic to New Mexico*. London: John Murray, 1986.

———. *A Scot Goes South: A Journey from Mexico to Ayres Rock*. London: John Murray, 1988.

———. *A Scot Returns: A Journey from Bali to Skye*. London: John Murray, 1989.

———. *Tracks Across Alaska: A Dog Sled Journey*. London: John Murray, 1990.

Watt, Edward W. *A Canadian Tour*. Aberdeen: Aberdeen Free P, 1920.

South African Works

Van Der Post, Laurens. *Journey into Russia*. London: Hogarth P, 1964. Published in the United States as *A View of All the Russias*.

——. *Lost World of the Kalahari*. London: Hogarth P, 1958.

Spanish Work

Cela, Camilo José. *Journey to the Alcarria*. Trans. Frances M. López-Morillas. Madison: U of Wisconsin P, 1964. Originally published in 1948.

Swiss Works

Maillart, Ella K. *The Cruel Way*. London: William Heinemann, 1947.

——. *Cruises and Caravans*. London: J. M. Dent & Sons, 1942.

——. *Forbidden Journey: From Peking to Kashmir*. Trans. Thomas McGreevy. New York: Henry Holt, 1937.

——. *Gypsy A-Float*. London: William Heinemann, 1942.

——. *The Land of the Sherpas*. London: Hodder & Stoughton, 1955.

——. *Ti-Puss*. London: William Heinemann, 1951.

——. *Turkestan Solo: One Woman's Expedition from the Tien Shan to the Kizil Kum*. Trans. John Rodker. New York: G. P. Putnam's Sons, 1934.

Togolandese Work

Kpomassie, Tété-Michel. *An African in Greenland*. Trans. James Kirkup. New York: Harcourt Brace Jovanovich, 1983. Originally published in 1981.

Welsh Works

Jones, Tristan. *The Incredible Voyage: A Personal Odyssey*. Kansas City: Sheed Andrews & McMeel, 1977.

——. *Saga of a Wayward Sailor*. Kansas City: Andrews & McMeel, 1979.

——. *Somewheres East of Suez*. New York: Hearst Marine, 1988.

Criticism

BIBLIOGRAPHIES

Clark, Thomas D. *Travels in the New South: A Bibliography*. Vol. 2: *The Twentieth-Century South, 1900–1955*. Norman: U of Oklahoma P, 1962.

Cox, Edward G. *A Reference Guide to the Literature of Travel*. Seattle: U of Washington P, 1935–49.

New Cambridge Bibliography of English Literature. Vols. 3–4. 1969. Rpt. Cambridge: Cambridge UP, 1972.

Robinson, Jane. *Wayward Women: A Guide to Women Travellers.* Oxford: Oxford UP, 1990.

GENERAL LITERARY CRITICISM

Adams, Percy G. *Travel Literature and the Evolution of the Novel.* Lexington: U of Kentucky P, 1983.

————. *Travelers and Travel Liars, 1660–1800.* Berkeley: U of California P, 1962.

Anderson, Patrick. *Over the Alps: Reflections on Travel and Travel Writing with Special Reference to the Grand Tours of Boswell, Beckford, and Byron.* London: Rupert Hart-Davis, 1969.

Andrews, Malcolm. *The Search for the Picturesque: Landscape Aesthetics and Tourism in Britain, 1760–1800.* Stanford: Stanford UP, 1989.

Batten, Charles L., Jr. *Pleasurable Instruction: Form and Convention in Eighteenth-Century Travel Literature.* Berkeley: U of California P, 1978.

Bishop, Peter. *The Myth of Shangri-La: Tibet, Travel Writing and the Western Creation of Sacred Landscape.* Berkeley: U of California P, 1989.

Campbell, Mary B. *The Witness and the Other World.* Ithaca: Cornell UP, 1988.

Cheyfitz, Eric. *The Poetics of Imperialism: Translation and Colonization from "The Tempest" to "Tarzan."* New York: Oxford UP, 1991.

Christie, John Aldridge. *Thoreau as World Traveler.* New York: Columbia UP, 1965.

Clifford, James, and George E. Marcus, eds. *Writing Culture: The Poetics and Politics of Ethnography.* Berkeley: U of California P, 1986.

Conrad, Peter. *Imagining America.* New York: Oxford UP, 1980.

Damiani, Anita. *Enlightened Observers: British Travellers to the Near East, 1715–1850.* Beirut, Lebanon: American U of Beirut, 1979.

Dodd, Philip, ed. *The Art of Travel: Essays on Travel Writing.* Totowa, N.J.: Frank Cass, 1982.

Eisner, Robert. *Travelers to an Antique Land: The History and Literature of Travel to Greece.* Ann Arbor: U of Michigan P, 1991.

Fanon, Frantz. *The Wretched of the Earth.* Trans. Constance Farrington. New York: Grove P, 1963. Originally published in 1961.

Franklin, Wayne. *Discoverers, Explorers, Settlers: The Diligent Writers of Early America.* Chicago: U of Chicago P, 1979.

Geertz, Clifford. *The Interpretation of Cultures.* New York: Basic, 1973.

Giltrow, Janet. "North American Travel Writing." Dissertation, Simon Fraser U, 1979.

Greenblatt, Stephen. *Marvelous Possessions: The Wonder of the New World.* Chicago: U of Chicago P, 1991.

Kagle, Steven E. *America: Exploration and Travel*. Bowling Green, Ohio: Bowling Green State U Popular P, 1979.

Leed, Eric J. *The Mind of the Traveler: From Gilgamesh to Global Tourism*. New York: Basic, 1991.

Lowes, John Livingston. *The Road to Xanadu: A Study in the Ways of the Imagination*. London: Constable, 1927.

Michael, Maurice Albert, ed. *Traveller's Quest: Original Contributions Towards a Philosophy of Travel*. Freeport, N.Y.: Books for Libraries P, 1950.

Mulvey, Christopher. *Anglo-American Landscapes: A Study of Nineteenth-Century Anglo-American Travel Literature*. London: Cambridge UP, 1983.

——. *Transatlantic Manners: Social Patterns in Nineteenth-Century Anglo-American Travel Literature*. London: Cambridge UP, 1990.

Ousby, Ian. *The Englishman's England: Taste, Travel, and the Rise of Tourism*. New York: Cambridge UP, 1990.

Porter, Dennis. *Haunted Journeys: Desire and Transgression in European Travel Writing*. Princeton: Princeton UP, 1991.

Rice, Warner G., ed. *Literature as a Mode of Travel*. New York: New York Public Library, 1963.

Robinson, Jeffrey C. *The Walk: Notes on a Romantic Image*. Norman: U of Oklahoma P, 1989.

Russell, Mary. *The Blessings of a Good Thick Skirt: Women Travellers and Their World*. London: Collins, 1986.

Said, Edward W. *Orientalism*. New York: Pantheon, 1978.

Sells, A. Lytton. *The Paradise of Travellers: The Italian Influence on Englishmen in the Seventeenth Century*. Bloomington: Indiana UP, 1964.

Spengemann, William C. *The Adventurous Muse: The Poetics of American Fiction, 1789–1900*. New Haven: Yale UP, 1977.

Stout, Janis P. *The Journey Narrative in American Literature: Patterns and Departures*. Westport, Conn.: Greenwood P, 1983.

Tabachnick, Stephen E., ed. *Explorations in Doughty's "Arabia Deserta."* Athens: U of Georgia P, 1987.

Tidrick, Kathryn. *Heart-Beguiling Araby*. New York: Cambridge UP, 1981.

Walker, Franklin D. *Irreverent Pilgrims: Melville, Browne, and Mark Twain in the Holy Land*. Seattle: U of Washington P, 1974.

LITERARY CRITICISM ON WORKS 1900–PRESENT

Fussell, Paul. *Abroad: British Literary Traveling Between the Wars*. New York: Oxford UP, 1980.

Hassan, Ihab. *Selves at Risk: Patterns of Quest in Contemporary American Letters*. Madison: U of Wisconsin P, 1990.

SINGLE-AUTHOR STUDIES ON WORKS 1900–PRESENT

Goodman, Susan. *Gertrude Bell*. Leamington Spa, Eng.: Berg, 1985.

Hamalian, Leo. *D. H. Lawrence in Italy*. New York: Taplinger, 1981.

Hayashi, Tetsumaro, ed. *Steinbeck's Travel Literature: Essays in Criticism*. Muncie, Ind.: Steinbeck Society of America, 1980.

Moorehead, Caroline. *Freya Stark*. Harmondsworth, Eng.: Penguin, 1985.

Tomlinson, H. M. *Norman Douglas*. London: Chatto & Windus, 1931.

Winstone, H. V. F. *Gertrude Bell*. London: Jonathan Cape, 1978.

STUDIES IN THE HISTORY AND CULTURE
OF MODERN TRAVEL AND TOURISM

Aitken, Maria. *A Girdle Round the Earth*. London: Constable, 1987.

Hokanson, Drake. *The Lincoln Highway: Main Street Across America*. Iowa City: U of Iowa P, 1988.

Hudson, Kenneth. *Air Travel: A Social History*. Bath, Somerset, Eng.: Adams & Dart, 1972.

Jakle, John A. *The Tourist: Travel in Twentieth-Century North America*. Lincoln: U of Nebraska P, 1985.

Lockwood, Allison. *Passionate Pilgrims: The American Traveler in Great Britain, 1800–1914*. East Brunswick, N.J.: Associated University Presses, 1981.

MacCannell, Dean. *The Tourist: A New Theory of the Leisure Class*. New York: Schocken, 1976.

McKinsey, Elizabeth. *Niagara Falls: Icon of the American Sublime*. Cambridge: Cambridge UP, 1985.

Pakenham, Valerie. *The Noonday Sun: Edwardians in the Tropics*. London: Methuen, 1985.

Patton, Phil. *Open Road: A Celebration of the American Highway*. New York: Simon & Schuster, 1986.

Pomeroy, Earl. *In Search of the Golden West: The Tourist in Western America*. New York: Knopf, 1957.

Schivelbusch, Wolfgang. *The Railway Journey: The Industrialization of Time and Space in the Nineteenth Century*. Berkeley: U of California P, 1986.

Schlereth, Thomas J. *U.S. 40: A Roadscape of the American Experience*. Indianapolis: Indiana Historical Society, 1985.

Sears, John F. *Sacred Places: American Tourist Attractions in the Nineteenth Century*. New York: Oxford UP, 1989.

Smith, Valene, ed. *Hosts and Guests: The Anthropology of Travel*. Philadelphia: U of Pennsylvania P, 1977.

> > > > > > **Contributors**

MICHEL BUTOR, a distinguished French novelist and critic of art, literature, and music, is the author of several experimental travel works including *Mobile* (1962; trans. 1963), *Oû* (1971) and *Boomerang* (1978; partially translated as *Letter from the Antipodes*, 1981).

TERRY CAESAR is a professor of English at Clarion University of Pennsylvania. His articles on American travel writing have appeared in *Prospects* and *Arizona Quarterly*, and he has finished a book-length study of the topic. He has also published travel essays himself, on Saudi Arabia in the *Yale Review* and on both China and Brazil in the *Massachusetts Review*.

NANCY COOK is an assistant professor of English at the University of Montana. She has completed a book-length study that examines Mark Twain's travel writing in terms of the literary marketplace.

DAVID ESPEY is the director of freshman English at the University of Pennsylvania. He has published on such topics as American Indian literature, George Orwell, and fiction about the British Empire. In the 1960s he was a Peace Corps volunteer in Morocco, and he has had Fulbright grants to Morocco and Turkey.

ROBERT FOULKE is a professor of English at Skidmore College and has taught at Trinity College (Hartford) and the University of Minnesota. His main scholarly publications have dealt with critical theory, Joseph Conrad, *The Odyssey*, and the literature and history of voyaging. With his wife Patricia he has written four travel guides in the last decade (two on Europe and two on New England and the Mid-Atlantic states), as well as many travel articles in newspapers and magazines.

PAUL FUSSELL is the author and editor of many books on literature and cultural history, including *Abroad: British Literary Traveling Between the Wars*, which was nominated for the award in criticism by the National Book Critics Circle and for an award in general nonfiction by the American Book Awards. A contributing editor of *Harper's* and *New Republic*, he is Donald T. Regan Professor of English at the University of Pennyslvania.

CHARISSE GENDRON, an associate professor of English at Middle Tennessee State University, has published articles on the travel writings of Lucie Duff Gordon, Alexander Kinglake, and D. H. Lawrence. Her article on images of Middle Eastern women in Victorian travel books was published in *The Victorian Newsletter*. She is writing a book on literary personality in British travel books from Smollett to Auden.

ROGER GEORGE teaches composition and literature at Bellevue Community College in Bellevue, Washington. He received his Ph.D. in American Literature in 1986 from the University of Washington. His dissertation, "The Transcendental Traveler," examined the influence of transcendentalist ideas on American travel narratives from the nineteenth century to the present. He has published an article on Twain in *American Transcendental Quarterly*. He is also a freelance journalist and essayist; his work has appeared in *Crosscurrents* and *Arnazella*.

ELTON GLASER is a professor of English at the University of Akron. His poetry, collected in *Relics* and *Tropical Depressions*, has received awards from the National Endowment for the Arts, the Ohio Arts Council, the University of Iowa Press, and several literary magazines.

ROCKWELL GRAY is the author of *The Imperative of Modernity: An Intellectual Biography of José Ortega y Gasset*, and of numerous essays on modern literature and culture. He is writing a study of modern autobiography, of which his thoughts on travel will form a part.

WILLIAM LEAST HEAT-MOON is the author of *Blue Highways*, which has sold more than 1.25 million copies since it appeared in 1982. His second book, *Prairy-Erth*, about the tallgrass country of the Kansas Flint Hills, was published in 1991. His work has appeared in *Atlantic*, *Time*, the *New York Times*, and elsewhere.

HEATHER HENDERSON is assistant professor of English at Mount Holyoke College. She has also taught at Columbia University, where she received her Ph.D in 1986. She is the author of *The Victorian Self: Autobiography and Biblical Narrative* (1989). She is writing a book about travel literature.

MICHAEL KOWALEWSKI is an assistant professor of English at Carleton College. His articles and reviews have appeared in *Raritan*, *Texas Studies in Literature and Language*, *Northwest Review*, *Southern Quarterly*, *Western American Literature*, and *California History*.

JACINTA MATOS is a graduate of the University of Coimbra, Portugal, and also holds an M.A. from the University of Birmingham, England, where she worked on nonfiction narratives under the supervision of David Lodge. She is a lecturer at Coimbra University and is writing a Ph.D. dissertation on English travel writing since World War II.

MARY MORRIS is a novelist whose travel book about Latin America, *Nothing to Declare: Memoirs of a Woman Traveling Alone*, came out in 1988. In 1979 her collection of stories *Vanishing Animals and Other Stories* won the American Academy and the Institute of Arts and Letters' coveted Rome Prize. She is the author of two novels (*Crossroads* [1983] and *The Waiting Room* [1989]) and a second collection of stories, *The Bus of Dreams and Other Stories* (1985). Her travel book, *Wall To Wall: From Beijing to Berlin by Rail*, was published in 1991.

MARK Z. MUGGLI is an associate professor of English at Luther College in Iowa, where he teaches Shakespeare, modern literary journalism, and an interdisciplinary course in literature and history. He has published on Joan Didion's journalism in *American Literature*. His essay "Ben Jonson and the Business of News" combines his interests in Renaissance literature and the history of factual writing.

ROBERT VON HALLBERG is a professor of English at the University of Chicago. He has published several books on modern American poetry, including *American Poetry and Culture, 1945–80* (1985) and *Politics and Poetic Value* (1987). He was also the editor of *Canons* (1984).